'DEAREST BROTHER'

'DEAREST BROTHER'

Lauderdale, Tweeddale and Scottish Politics,
1660–1674

Maurice Lee, Jr

First published in Great Britain in 2010 by
John Donald, an imprint of Birlinn Ltd

West Newington House
10 Newington Road
Edinburgh
EH9 1QS

www.birlinn.co.uk

ISBN: 978 1 906566 16 6

The publishers gratefully acknowledge the support of
Rutgers University Research Fund towards the publication of this book

British Library Cataloguing-in-Publication Data
A catalogue record for this book is available on request
from the British Library

Typeset by IDSUK (DataConnection) Ltd
Printed and bound in Britain by MPG Books, Bodmin, Cornwall

Contents

Preface

Until very recently historians of Scotland paid next to no attention to politics as such in the Restoration era. The basic cause of this neglect was their take on the results of the 'Glorious' Revolution. It had two important consequences for Scotland: the liberation of the Scottish parliament from the control of the crown through the abolition of the Committee of the Articles, and the liberation of the Scottish church from episcopacy. The first change proved ephemeral. Parliament turned out to be so unmanageable that the English government put an end to it by persuading (or coercing, depending on your point of view) the people who counted in Scotland to accept the Act of Union of 1707, a sequence of events on which there is an extensive literature. The second change was permanent: the church of Scotland became, and has remained, Presbyterian in its polity. So there has always been a good deal of writing on religion and politics in the Restoration period. Happily, in the last decade or so, there has been a recrudescence of interest in Scottish politics, partly because, as one of my colleagues remarked to me, we have all, historians of England and Scotland alike, become British historians. We follow along the path marked out some years ago by J.G.A. Pocock and Conrad Russell; the most recent over-all account of the Restoration has three of seven chapters on Scotland and Ireland.[1]

The new century has seen the publication of works on royalist political thought in Scotland, the Scottish parliament in the reign of Charles II, and a new biography of Lauderdale. The only biography of any Restoration political figure (other than the kings) that appeared in the last previous couple of generations was Julia Buckroyd's life of Archbishop Sharp, which she accurately subtitled 'a political biography'.[2] There have also, of course,

---

1 Tim Harris, *Restoration: Charles II and his Kingdoms* (London, 2005).
2 Clare Jackson, *Restoration Scotland, 1660–1690: Royalist Politics, Religion and Ideas* (Woodbridge, 2003). Gillian MacIntosh, *The Scottish Parliament under Charles II 1660–1685* (Edinburgh, 2007). Raymond C. Paterson, *King Lauderdale* (Edinburgh, 2003). Julia Buckroyd, *The Life of James Sharp, Archbishop of St Andrews, 1618–1679* (Edinburgh, 1987).

been brief accounts of Restoration politics in the general histories of Scotland and chapters in works of wider sweep by scholars such as William Ferguson and Allan Macinnes.[3] The recent work is very encouraging. It suggests that the long hiatus caused by the combination of what appeared to be a dead-end subject and a daunting source problem may at last be over.

There are two unpublished doctoral dissertations of great value which should be in print: Roy W. Lennox, *Lauderdale and Scotland: a Study in Restoration Politics and Administration 1660-1682* (Political Science, Columbia University, 1977) and Ronald A. Lee, *Government and Politics in Scotland 1661-1681* (Scottish History, University of Glasgow, 1995). Lennox concentrates on the work of the treasury commission set up in 1667 in the wake of Lauderdale's consolidation of his power. Lee's work is far wider in scope, and is organised topically, focusing primarily on finance, the army and parliament. Both deliberately eschew religion, which is a little like *Hamlet* without the prince. Neither attempts to capture the atmosphere generated by the day-to-day problems facing the Scottish administration, with its absentee leadership and its often harassed and overworked operatives in Edinburgh. This work will attempt to do that, and will make shameless and extensive use, herewith gratefully acknowledged, of the work of Drs Lennox and Lee. They have been indispensable to an author writing on the wrong side of the Atlantic and faced with a very substantial source problem.

Apart from the acts of parliament and the privy council register, very little of the government record for this period is in print. There are the well-known accounts of two prominent contemporaries, Bishop Gilbert Burnet and Sir George Mackenzie of Rosehaugh, the 'bluidy' lord advocate, and the less well known but very interesting work of the Presbyterian minister James Kirkton. There are also a few published diaries, and David Stevenson's recent edition of Sir Robert Moray's letters to the earl of Kincardine, most of which were written before 1660. Not much political correspondence is in print. The three volumes of Lauderdale papers which Osmund Airy edited for the Camden Society (London, 1884–85) were selected to emphasise religious issues and are sloppily done; the texts need to be checked against the original manuscript before a citation can be made with any confidence. So the would-be historian of Scottish Restoration politics faces the considerable task of examining enormous amounts of

---

3 William Ferguson, *Scotland's Relations with England – a Survey to 1707* (Edinburgh, 1977). Allan Macinnes, *Clanship, Commerce and the House of Stuart, 1603–1788* (East Linton, 1996).

unpublished correspondence in addition to the unprinted government record available in the National Archives of Scotland. For the writing of this book two collections in particular have been used: the Lauderdale papers in the British Library (from which Airy made his selections) and the Yester papers in the National Library of Scotland, and, to a lesser extent, the Buccleuch and Hamilton papers in the National Archives. Trolling through them has been an exhilarating, and occasionally exasperating, experience.

The starting point for any consideration of politics in Restoration Scotland is the fact that all of the major decisions and many of the minor ones were made in London, not in Edinburgh. The second fact is that King Charles was only occasionally interested in what went on in Scotland. C.V. Wedgwood once remarked, à propos of the early years of the Restoration, that 'Men who are guided by the desire to avoid something rather than to create something rarely achieve anything notable.'[4] Whatever Charles may have intended respecting his other kingdoms, this comment summarises well his attitude toward Scotland. He was not exactly inattentive; he had to be kept informed; but he left the decision-making to others, as long as those decisions fell within the parameters of his and his government's overall policy. The political history of Scotland in Charles's reign therefore falls into the four time periods that mirror, more or less, what went on in England. From 1660 to 1667 the dominant figure was Lord Chancellor Clarendon, followed by the years of the so-called Cabal, 1667–73, then those of Lord Treasurer Danby from 1674 to 1679. After 1679 the directions are different. The years of the exclusion crisis and the Tory reaction in England saw the future James VII and II installed in Holyrood and pursuing his own agenda in Scotland, at first in person and then through his hand-picked agents after he left for the last time in 1682. There is a decidedly different tone and atmosphere to these years in Scotland. They have been analysed in yet another unpublished dissertation, Kathleen Colquhoun, 'Issue of the Late Civil Wars': James Duke of York and the Government of Scotland 1679–1689 (History, University of Illinois at Urbana-Champaign, 1993), and are not under consideration here.

During three of these four time periods, then, the dominant figure in Scottish politics was not a Scot. Only during the years of the Cabal was a Scot in charge of Scottish policy: one of the members of that disparate

---

4 C.V. Wedgwood, 'Good King Charles's Golden Days', in *The Restoration of the Stuarts, Blessing or Disaster?*, Folger Library Conference (Washington, 1960), p. 11.

group, John Maitland, earl of Lauderdale, the Scottish secretary of state, a denizen of Whitehall and a favourite of the king's. Ronald Hutton in his study of Charles's reign,[5] a 'British' account in that it says much about Scotland – and Ireland – made the case that Arlington was the most important member of the Cabal. He labels the years 1668–72 'the ministry of Arlington'. Arlington was, if anything, less interested in Scotland than Charles, and got along well enough with Lauderdale. So during the Cabal years, for the only time during the three decades of the Restoration, Scottish policy was being made by Scots, with Scottish interests in mind. And, for the only time during those three decades, a genuine effort was made to bring about change in the system. The Clarendon years saw the imposition of the system, turmoil caused by ministerial ineptitude, and the economically ruinous Dutch war, which ended in the year of Clarendon's fall. The Danby years saw almost continual repression, caused in part by the exigencies of English domestic politics, in part by growing discontent with the shortcomings of the Lauderdale regime.

Lauderdale and his colleagues had an agenda after 1667. They wanted to put the finances of the kingdom on a sound footing, not by raising taxes, but by collecting what was due (and overdue: the books had not yet been closed on the tax voted in 1633), cutting expenses and punishing some of those who had had their hands in the till. They wanted to provide tranquillity and prosperity by dealing with religious unrest, maintaining the armed forces as economically as possible, and improving manufacturing and trade. Discussions with England on improving trade led to the most startling and important initiative of the whole of the Restoration period, the proposal for political union with England. In developing and implementing this agenda Lauderdale had one essential principal collaborator in Edinburgh, John Hay, earl of Tweeddale, and, almost as important, the king's close friend and fellow chemist, Sir Robert Moray, Lauderdale's adviser in London, his stand-in as secretary when he went to Scotland, and his agent in carrying out the regime change in 1667 that brought them to power. The three men were cousins. Lauderdale and Tweeddale were grandchildren of James VI's great lord chancellor, Alexander Seton, earl of Dunfermline; Moray's wife Sophia was another grandchild. Lauderdale and Tweeddale became still closer with the marriage of their children,

5 Roland Hutton, *Charles II: King of England, Scotland and Ireland* (Oxford, 1989).

which turned them, for a time, into each other's 'dearest brother'. For four years this triumvirate flourished. At the beginning of 1671 it began to show signs of cracking up. By mid-1673 it was broken; Moray was dead, and Tweeddale and Lauderdale were open enemies. Lauderdale carried on, with other, inferior collaborators; Tweeddale was driven out of politics, not to emerge until after the Glorious Revolution. This book tells the story of that collaboration, its promise, its achievements and its failures. It is only a first step in the sorting out of the workings of Scottish politics and the methods and attitudes of Scottish politicians during the Restoration. It has been written in part in the hope that it will encourage further work in this undeservedly neglected period of Scottish – indeed, of British – history.

Acknowledgements

Putting this book together would not have been possible without the help of many people and institutions. Rutgers University has been enormously helpful with both time and money, and acquired a microfilm of the Lauderdale papers in the British Library for my benefit. I have spent countless hours in that library, and in the Public Record Office, the National Library of Scotland, the National Archives of Scotland, and the Princeton University Library, whose staffs have all been uniformly courteous and helpful. My old friend and former publisher John Tuckwell, Mairi Sutherland, the academic managing editor of John Donald, and Nicola Wood, my gimlet-eyed copy editor, have also been immensely helpful. Kim Macpherson and Philip Hunt of the Scottish National Portrait Gallery made arranging for the illustrations a painless task. Diane Morrison and the splendid staff of D/J Business Services in Princeton transcribed much of my typescript onto the disks that are the *sine qua non* of modern publishing. And, finally, I owe many thanks to my dear friend (and former student) Dr Laurine Purola, who also transcribed much of my typescript, debated terminology and usage with me, and gave me the benefit of her expertise as a scholar and researcher. She, and others, have saved me from many errors; those that remain are mine alone.

Abbreviations

APS	*Acts of the Parliament of Scotland*, ed. T. Thomson and C. Innes, 12 vols (Edinburgh, 1814–75).
BL	British Library, London.
CSPD	*Calendar of State Papers, Domestic Series, 1660–1675*, ed. M.A.E. Green et al. (London, 1860–1904).
HMC	Historical Manuscripts Commission, London.
LP	*The Lauderdale Papers*, ed. O. Airy, 3 vols, Camden Society (London, 1884–85).
NAS	National Archives of Scotland, Edinburgh.
NLS	National Library of Scotland, Edinburgh.
PRO	Public Record Office, London.
RPCS	*Register of the Privy Council of Scotland*, 3rd series, vols I–IV, ed. P. Hume Brown (Edinburgh, 1906–11).
SHR	*Scottish Historical Review*.
SHS	Scottish History Society, Edinburgh.
Argyll Letters	*Letters from Archibald, Earl of Argyll, to John, Duke of Lauderdale 1663–1670*, ed. G. Sinclair and G.K. Sharpe (Edinburgh, 1829).
Burnet, *History*	*Bishop Burnet's History of his Own Time*, ed. M.J. Routh, 6 vols (Oxford, 1823).
Dowden, 'Letters'	'Thirty-Four Letters Written to James Sharp by the Duke and Duchess of Lauderdale . . .', ed. J. Dowden, SHS *Miscellany* I (Edinburgh, 1893), pp. 229–95.
Hamilton Mss	HMC, *Supplementary Report on the Mss of the Duke of Hamilton*, ed. J.H. McMaster and M. Wood (London, 1932).
Kirkton, *History*	James Kirkton, *A History of the Church of Scotland 1660–1679*, ed. R. Stewart (Lewiston, ME, 1992).

Laing Mss	HMC, *Laing Mss*, ed. H.M. Paton, 2 vols (London, 1914–25).
Lamont, *Diary*	*Diary of Mr John Lamont of Newton, 1649–1671*, ed. G.R. Kinloch (Edinburgh, 1830).
Mackenzie, *Memoirs*	Sir George Mackenzie of Rosehaugh, *Memoirs of the Affairs of Scotland from the Restoration of King Charles II*, ed. T. Thomson (Edinburgh, 1821).
Moray Letters	*Letters of Sir Robert Moray to the Earl of Kincardine, 1657–1673*, ed. D. Stevenson (Aldershot, 2007).
Nicoll, *Diary*	John Nicoll, *A Diary of Public Transactions and Other Occurrences*, ed. D. Laing (Edinburgh, 1836).
Paton, 'Gilmour'	'Letters from John, earl of Lauderdale, and others to Sir John Gilmour', ed. H. M. Paton, SHS *Miscellany* V (Edinburgh, 1933), pp. 109–94.
Paton, 'Lauderdale'	'Letters from John, second earl of Lauderdale to John, second earl of Tweeddale, and others', ed H.M. Paton, SHS *Miscellany* VI (Edinburgh, 1939), pp. 111–240.
Tweeddale, 'Autobiography'	John Hay, earl of Tweeddale, 'Autobiography, 1626–1670', ed. M. Lee, Jr, SHS *Miscellany* XII (Edinburgh, 1994), pp. 58–98.
Tweeddale, 'Wrangs'	John Hay, earl of Tweeddale, 'Relation of the Wrangs Done to the Ladie Yester, 1683', ed. M. Lee, Jr, SHS *Miscellany* XIII (Edinburgh, 2004), pp. 266–311.
Wodrow, *History*	R. Wodrow, *The History of the Sufferings of the Church of Scotland from the Restoration to the Revolution*, 2 vols (Edinburgh, 1721–22).

Note

The English pound sterling was worth 12 pounds Scots. Both currencies are used in this book; the context makes clear which is meant when no identification is specified. The spelling and punctuation of most quotations has been modernised.

CHAPTER ONE

Turning Back the Clock, 1660–1662

On 11 December 1666 a wedding took place in London joining two Scottish aristocratic families, a wedding important enough to be graced by the presence of King Charles II and his court. It joined John Hay, Lord Yester, the eldest son and heir of the earl of Tweeddale, also a John Hay, and Mary Maitland, the only surviving child of John Maitland, earl of Lauderdale, secretary of state for Scotland. The bride and groom were second cousins, sharing the same great-grandfather; their fathers, first cousins, would now call each other 'dearest brother'. Also present was their cousin by marriage, Sir Robert Moray, the matchmaker. It was he who played host to the young Yester, aged eighteen, when he came to London for the first time in the spring of 1666, encouraged the courtship, and wrote enthusiastic letters about it to the absent Tweeddale, who had some doubts – he later said – about the suitability of the marriage. Mary was at least ten years older than her suitor, not very attractive, and, perhaps, unable to bear children.[1] But in the end he and Lady Tweeddale left the decision to Yester, and the marriage went forward. A French observer, who complained that he 'was forced to be there', described the bride as 'very homely and like a monkey, clothed with gold and silver'.[2] Despite all this the marriage was very successful, and there was no shortage of children, seven in all, five of whom grew to maturity.

Marriages among the aristocracy in the seventeenth century came about because they furthered the interests of the family. Tweeddale would not have compelled his son to wed Mary Maitland, and no doubt Lauderdale would have behaved similarly, though we have no record of his exchanges with his daughter. But each father had a veto, had he chosen to use it. This marriage had great appeal for both men, for both political and personal reasons – Tweeddale's letters to his son, to Moray, and to Lauderdale in the summer of 1666 display, not hesitation, but eagerness.[3] Both fathers were

---

1 Yester was born in 1648. Mary was mentioned in her grandmother's will, dated 1638. Tweeddale, 'Autobiography', pp. 77–78. NLS Ms. 14547, ff. 11–14. Tweeddale recorded his reservations well after the fact, when he was bitterly at odds with Lauderdale. NLS Ms. 3134, no. 120.
2 Quoted in J.B. Paul, *The Scots Peerage*, 9 vols (Edinburgh, 1904–14), VIII, 458.
3 See NLS Ms. 7001, pp. 110–44. This is a letterbook in which Tweeddale kept copies of his correspondence.

very politically minded. Lauderdale, the king's confidant and agent for the government of Scotland, was working diligently toward obtaining a monopoly of that confidence and agency, which he did not yet possess. If and when he obtained it, he would need a collaborator in Edinburgh who was both able and reliable. The ambitious Tweeddale fit that bill, and the marriage would tie him more tightly to Lauderdale's interest. Tweeddale's calculations were similar. Owing to his checkered political past he could never expect the king's complete confidence. But as the agent of one who had that confidence he could achieve a great deal.

There were personal angles as well. Mary Maitland had considerable expectations: her mother was very wealthy, and the marriage contract provided that the second son of the marriage would succeed to the earldom of Lauderdale. But there was more to it than that. Mary was not the bride Tweeddale originally wanted for his eldest son, but that young woman was now far beyond his reach: Anna, duchess of Monmouth and Buccleuch, his wife's niece, married three years earlier to the king's beloved eldest bastard. Anna was fabulously wealthy. Furthermore, Tweeddale owed the Buccleuch estate a very large sum of money owing to an injudicious financial transaction of his father's. The debt grew annually with the accumulating interest; had Tweeddale been able to marry his son to Anna, it would have disappeared. Now, at the very least, Tweeddale expected that his new 'brother' would help him negotiate a settlement of the debt with Monmouth's and Anna's curators – they were both under age – which, in effect, meant a settlement acceptable to the king. Furthermore, Lauderdale now had good reason to interest himself in the affairs of the Buccleuch estate. Anna's father, Francis Scott, earl of Buccleuch, had entailed the estate to his sister, Lady Tweeddale, his only surviving sibling, if he had no direct descendants. Anna's marriage contract altered the entail, but that alteration might not withstand a legal challenge if circumstances should ever make one possible. Anna was only fifteen and still childless, and the Scotts had a history of dying young. Who knows? Mary Maitland might someday be duchess of Buccleuch, the owner of the largest rent roll in Scotland: no mean inducement for the secretary to welcome Yester as a son-in-law.[4]

The chain of circumstances that led to the marriage began in 1662, with the notorious 'billeting' episode, the attempt by the king's commissioner in

4 For a full account of Tweeddale and the Buccleuch estate see M. Lee, Jr, *The Heiresses of Buccleuch* (East Linton, 1996).

Scotland, John Middleton, earl of Middleton, to drive Lauderdale from office. Middleton was a soldier, not a politician like Lauderdale. He was an ex-Covenanter who became a supporter of the Engagement of 1647 which led to the disastrous Scottish attempt to restore Charles I to his throne in 1648. He did the new king very good service during Charles II's awful year in Scotland in 1650–51. He was a leader of the king's army, which Cromwell routed at Worcester in 1651; he was captured, escaped, went back to Scotland to lead the royalist revolt in the Highlands known as Glencairn's Rising, escaped again, and made his way back to the court-in-exile by 1655. Charles was impressed. 'Middleton,' he said to his principal adviser, Edward Hyde, the future Lord Chancellor Clarendon, 'had the least in him of any infirmities most incident to the nation that he knew, and . . . he would find him a man of great honour and integrity.'[5] Clarendon, who detested and distrusted Lauderdale, a man 'with no impediment of honour to restrain him from doing any thing that might gratify any of his passions,'[6] was delighted that Charles chose Middleton as his principal agent in Scotland in 1660: he could be controlled. Clarendon wanted Lauderdale shut out of the administration altogether, but this he could not accomplish.

Lauderdale was born in 1616, the eldest son of John Maitland, Lord Thirlestane, whom James VI made earl of Lauderdale in 1624. His paternal grandfather had been lord chancellor and King James's principal adviser in the 1580s and 1590s; his mother's father, Alexander Seton, earl of Dunfermline, was lord chancellor from 1604 until his death in 1622. Politics was in his blood. His career began at a young age, when he accompanied the Scottish commissioners negotiating with Charles I from Ripon to London in 1640. His doings in the 1640s are well known and well documented: an enthusiastic and prominent Covenanter and Presbyterian who broke with the extremists and was one of the principal negotiators of the Engagement in 1647. In 1648 he met his future master, Prince Charles, then with the royalist section of the English fleet in the Downs. His mission was to persuade the prince to come to Scotland and participate in the military campaign to restore his father to his thrones. The experienced politician got on very well with the eighteen-year-old prince, who was eager to go to Scotland. In the course of the negotiations Lauderdale made a permanent enemy of the future Lord Clarendon, who did not favour Charles's going.

---

5 Edward, earl of Clarendon, *The History of the Rebellion and Civil Wars in England*, ed. W.D. Macray, 6 vols (Oxford, 1888), V, p. 242.

6 Ibid. IV, pp. 320–21.

The rout of the Engager army at Preston made the issue moot. Charles sent Lauderdale back to Scotland to see how the land lay in the wake of the military disaster. His stay was brief; in January 1649 he returned to what was now the court of a king in exile at The Hague, to report that the anti-Engager extremists were now in control. Nevertheless when the latter sent a delegation to negotiate with Charles in 1650, Lauderdale urged him to accept their terms for his return to Scotland, however onerous they might be: once there, he would easily secure appropriate modifications. Lauderdale completely miscalculated. Charles found circumstances worse than he had anticipated, which caused him to declare, after it was all over, that he would rather be hanged than go back to Scotland – and he never did. Charles held no grudge against Lauderdale for what had happened, and the earl, who was no soldier, in some sense expiated his misjudgments by going on the Worcester campaign. He was captured there, and spent the next nine years in various English prisons, emerging only in March 1660, when the return of the king was imminent.[7]

Charles detested Scotland and most Scotsmen, but he made an exception for those who had accompanied him to Worcester – not only Scots, but also Englishmen like the witty and mercurial duke of Buckingham. Lauderdale had suffered for his king, as had his family. Lady Lauderdale was allowed land worth only £600 sterling a year from the earl's confiscated estate to live on, and this only in 1655.[8] Charles clearly owed him something. Clarendon was aware of this, and wanted him named chancellor, an office that would keep him in Edinburgh and was no longer nearly as important as it had been in the days of James VI. Lauderdale avoided this gilded form of political oblivion and got what he wanted: appointment as secretary of state. The nominal holder of the office, the anti-Engager earl of Lothian, was paid off and backed Lauderdale for the job.[9]

The secretaryship was potentially the path to wealth and power, and Lauderdale knew it. He had learned from his dealings with Charles from 1648 to 1651 that the king disliked paperwork and preferred to make his

---

7 For Lauderdale's early career see W.C. Mackenzie, *The Life and Times of John Maitland, Duke of Lauderdale* (Edinburgh, 1923) chaps 3–11, and R.C. Paterson, *King Lauderdale* (Edinburgh, 2003), chaps 2–6. See also D. Stevenson, *The Scottish Revolution 1637–1644* (Newton Abbot, 1973) and *Revolution and Counter-Revolution in Scotland, 1644–1651* (London, 1977), the excellent standard account. For Charles's year in Scotland see M. Lee, Jr, 'Annus Horribilis': Charles II in Scotland, 1650–1651', in *The 'Inevitable' Union* (East Linton, 2003), pp. 205–22.

8 BL Add. Mss 23113, f. 40.

9 Mackenzie, *Memoirs*, pp. 7–9.

decisions after discussion rather than through memoranda.[10] As secretary Lauderdale would be permanently established in Whitehall, in daily contact with the king. He knew that Scotland was seldom high on the king's agenda, and Lauderdale preferred to keep it that way. So he was extremely patient, always waiting for Charles to indicate that he was willing to talk about Scotland. In February 1668, in handling a question about official salaries, he wrote to Tweeddale that he could get no time with Charles 'without importunity, which you know I never use'.[11] In London he could also be the companion of the king's leisure hours. He was the only Scot whom the king appointed a gentleman of the bedchamber. Charles enjoyed the company of men who shared his amusements; in August 1660 Moray wrote that the secretary had gone off with the king to see a race between two footmen for a purse of £2,000.[12] All matters of patronage would pass through his hands, in that he would be responsible for the paperwork necessary for pensions and appointments. He was not the only channel to the king – not yet, and not on major appointments. But a great many minor matters were left to him from the beginning, for which he could expect a *douceur* from the successful aspirants, enhancing both his power base and his income: sheriff-clerks, for example, and writers to the signet, who paid 500 merks for their commissions. His man of business in Edinburgh, William Sharp, was kept very busy, and so was he: 'The delay of return puts many here to weary of long attendance', Sharp wrote, in some exasperation, in February 1661.[13] Clarendon was aware of the importance of the secretaryship, and wanted it for the earl of Newburgh, a soldier-friend of Middleton's. He failed. But otherwise, with the exception of the treasury, retained by the earl of Crawford-Lindsay, who had also been a prisoner in England, the principal offices went to people who were either Middleton's allies or, in the case of the earl of Rothes, the president of the privy council, another Worcester Scot and a friend of the king's, prepared to support whoever looked to be the winner.

---

10 R.F. Hutton, *Charles II, King of England, Scotland and Ireland* (Oxford, 1989), p. 78.

11 NLS Ms. 7023, f. 129.

12 27 Aug. 1660, Moray to Alexander Bruce, *Moray Letters*, pp. 218–19.

13 21 Feb. 1661, Sharp to Lauderdale, *Laing Mss.* I, pp. 318–19. Sharp expected to clear between £500 and £600 sterling from the sheriff-clerkships. 12 Mar., Sharp to Lauderdale, BL Add. Mss 23115, f. 107. For his efforts he successfully lobbied the secretary to appoint his brother Robert to this office in Banff, which had been their father's office, *gratis*. 19 Jan., Sharp to Lauderdale, BL. Add. Mss 23115, f. 33. For the sheriff-clerkships see R.W. Lennox, *Lauderdale and Scotland: A Study in Scottish Politics and Administration 1660–1682* (PhD diss., Columbia University, 1977), pp. 178–83.

In the first half of 1661 Middleton presided over a long and· extremely successful session of parliament. The king instructed him to see to it that the royal prerogative was restored, all the recent parliamentary limitations on it rescinded, and all the Acts of the convention of estates of 1643 and the parliament of 1649 nullified, since they had not been summoned by royal authority. Charles also authorised the passage of an Act of oblivion, with such exceptions as parliament should think fit to make, but the draft of the Act was to be sent to him for approval before it was adopted. Parliament was to encourage trade and manufacturing, 'and plantations in our dominions in America or elsewhere'. The vexing problem of the collection of debts – many lords and lairds owned substantial sums, and creditors in the burghs wanted the law enforced – was to be addressed and no one whose estate had been confiscated was obligated for the payment of annualrents during the time of confiscation. There were some instructions on specific individuals, including Montrose, the great martyr of the royalist cause, whose estate was to be restored and body given decent burial. Middleton was to give 'our secretary frequent accounts of your proceedings'. On the subject of the church and its future the instructions were conspicuously silent.[14]

Middleton carried out his mandate very efficiently. He had a docile body to work with: only about a third of the members had sat in previous parliaments, and he presided over, and formally approved the membership of, the revived Committee of the Articles. A procedural change accompanied the revival of this committee: it would submit its legislative recommendations to the full parliament on a weekly basis instead of waiting until the end of the session and submitting everything at once. The royal prerogative was reasserted in emphatic language. Parliament voted Charles an annual income of £480,000, to be raised from customs and excise, to pay the costs of government, including an armed force, a large amount but smaller than the exactions of the republican regime. In return Charles promised never again to employ the cess, the monthly assessment levied during the English occupation, which fell heavily upon landowners. A commission on trade, navigation and manufacturing was elected at the same time as the Committee of the Articles, and there was a good deal of economic legislation: a navigation Act similar to that of England, evidently designed to persuade the English not to enforce their own Act against Scottish shipping, the creation of a Scottish fishing company, the

14 The instructions are dated 29 Nov. 1660, BL Add. Mss 23114, f. 88.

prohibition of the export of skins, wool and woolfells, worsted and woollen and linen yarn, and tariff protection for local manufactured goods such as tobacco pipes, all in the interest of encouraging manufactures, as was the offer of tax exemption to foreign artisans. Parliament removed export duties on some manufactured goods such as soap. It issued patents, both definitive (e.g., to Colonel James Weems for light ordnance) and exploratory (e.g., to Colonel Ludovick Leslie and James Scot for, among other things, tanning without bark; if there were no results after three years, the grant would expire). Public companies were to be created to manufacture various textiles and stockings, in order to put 'poor children, idle persons, and vagabonds to work'. There was to be a new book of rates. Nothing, however, was passed respecting plantations, unless the navigation Act can be so construed. Not until the final session of parliament was the question of debt collection addressed. Debtors were granted 'some breathing time and encouragement' – six years' grace – and the interest rate was reduced to 6 per cent; the landed classes had far more influence with Charles's government than the burghs. A so-called 'interval committee', to sit until parliament met again, was to consider the losses and debts of those who had suffered in the king's service.

Picking through the legislation of the civil war period in order to elimi-nate limitations on the prerogative proved difficult. Middleton tried: on 9 February parliament annulled everything done by the parliament of 1649 and all subsequent meetings of parliament or committee of estates, except what was done in meetings 'authorised by his Majesty's presence and . . . not inconsistent with this present act'. Men who sat in such parliaments were not *ipso facto* to be subject to punishment, however, and court judg-ments were not to be nullified merely on the basis of insufficient authority. Later in the month parliament explicitly condemned the Act of January 1647 turning Charles I over to the English: how many more enactments would require such treatment? It is not surprising that Middleton eventu-ally decided to cut the knot by means of an Act which, taken together with legislation previously passed, effectively turned the parliamentary clock back to 1633, even though the king had been personally present at the sessions of 1641 and 1651. Passed on 28 March, this Act Rescissory, as it become known, not only simplified parliament's task very considerably, but also had the added advantage of allowing Charles to adopt whatever form of church government he chose. Episcopacy was the law of the land in 1633; Charles now could reimpose it or allow the existing Presbyterian polity to continue.

The Act Rescissory was in no way called for in Middleton's instructions. In January, according to the future Archbishop Sharp, Middleton had 'dashed the design of the high party, who would have all overturned since [16]38',[15] and he was initially reluctant to endorse the Act. But, according to Mackenzie, he was persuaded to consult London, and Clarendon urged him on.[16] There was a good deal of opposition, and not only from moderate churchmen like Robert Baillie, who bemoaned to Lauderdale 'the return of the Canterburian times . . . If you . . . have swerved towards Chancellor Hyde's principles . . . you have much to answer for.'[17] In parliament the argument was made that the nullification of whole parliaments, even when the king was personally present, was a dreadful precedent; the Act Rescissory drew some forty negative votes. Middleton decided that it was necessary to send the lord chancellor, the earl of Glencairn, and the king's friend Rothes to court to explain matters to Charles. Charles was evidently uneasy; he blocked a proposal that the English parliament follow suit and repeal all the legislation of the Long Parliament.[18] According to Gilbert Burnet, Middleton's purpose was to use Lauderdale's expressed fears about the Act Rescissory to accuse him of the crime of leasing-making because he had misinterpreted parliamentary behaviour, and thus ruin him. Clarendon persuaded Glencairn and Rothes that such tactics would backfire, however, and they desisted. Rothes, who had warned Lauderdale not to believe those who told him that there was a lot of discontent in Scotland, informed the secretary that he had diverted the storm.[19] It seems likely that Lauderdale took this assurance *cum grano*.

The Act Rescissory was the most important, but not the only, legislation not specifically authorised in the king's instructions. Some Acts of the parliaments of the previous twenty years were confirmed, such as that of June 1647 authorising the collection of a debt incurred by those who supplied provisions for the Engagers' army. Many towns were empowered to raise money for specific purposes – Whithorn to repair its harbour, for example, and Wigtown for the upkeep of a bridge. Edinburgh was especially favoured. It

15 10 Jan. 1661, Sharp to James Wood, *LP* I, pp. 292–94. The Act Rescissory should really be 'Acts': the first was so sloppily drawn that a second was necessary, passed the same day, to achieve the desired result. *APS* VII, pp. 86–88. See P.H. Hardacre, 'The Restoration of the Scottish Episcopacy, 1660–1661', *Journal of British Studies* 2 (1962), pp. 33–51, esp. p. 45.

16 Mackenzie, *Memoirs*, pp. 27–29.

17 18 Apr. 1661, Baillie to Lauderdale, *The Letters and Journals of Robert Baillie*, ed. D. Laing, 3 vols, Bannatyne Club (Edinburgh, 1841–42) III, pp. 458–60.

18 R. Lee, 'Retreat from Revolution: the Scottish Parliament and the Restored Monarchy', in J.R. Young, ed., *Celtic Dimensions of the British Civil Wars* (Edinburgh, 1997), p. 191.

19 Baillie, *Letters* III, pp. 463–64. Burnet, *History* I, pp. 199–207. BL Add. Mss 23116, f. 22.

was permitted to collect a special excise on wine and beer for eleven years to help pay its debts, and also to tax its inhabitants to pay its ministers' stipends. Commissions of visitation were to look into the condition of the universities. The franchise for electors in the shires was set at forty shillings of land of Old Extent for holders of land *in capite*, and at a rental of £1,000 or ten chalders of victual after payment of feu duty for heritors, liferenters and wadsetters holding of the king. Noblemen and their vassals could not vote. The commissions of the peace were reestablished, and their duties spelled out. The court of session and the signet office were formally restored[20] and the privileges of the members of the session, notably tax exemption, ratified. Since the courts and the privy council were not yet functioning, a parliamentary committee had to act as a court. At its recommendation parliament issued a decree in a wife-support case, for instance, and ordered Sir Ludovick Stewart of Minto's coal miners to resume working for him. The draconian rules applying to coal miners, who were virtually slaves, were extended to watermen and gatemen as well as those who worked in the pits. Parliament ordered that they work six days a week (except at Christmas), on the ground that they drank too much if given time off.

There was much church legislation, both before and after the Act Rescissory. Parliament prohibited meetings of Anabaptists, Quakers and Fifth Monarchy Men, and the saying of Mass. It banished Jesuits and other priests, and ratified previous Sabbatarian legislation. It reestablished Charles I's commission for planting kirks and valuing teinds, and it allowed the acts of the parliamentary commissions of the 1640s enabling heritors to buy up the teinds on their own lands to stand. The commission on the teinds worked rather haphazardly and often had difficulty raising a quorum. In February 1668 Tweeddale had to ask Charles to appoint replacements for dead members. Complaints that ministers' stipends fell short of the 800-merk minimum were frequent.[21]

Favoured individuals benefited from special Acts of parliament – the earl of Rothes, for example, was granted the right to hold fairs in his town of Leslie. At the request of the earl of Haddington, who said that his tenants were threatening to leave unless something was done, a witchcraft commission was appointed to pass judgment on four women who had confessed and

---

20 In the case of the court of session, parliament officially recorded the names of its members on 5 April; there was no suggestion that parliamentary approval of the king's nominees was necessary. A chalder was c. 96 bushels.

21 *APS* VII, pp. 48–50. 8 Feb. 1668, Tweeddale to Lauderdale, BL Add. Mss 23128, f. 297. W.R. Foster, *Bishop and Presbytery: The Church of Scotland 1661–1688* (London, 1958), pp. 109–10.

accused eleven others, including two men. Two of the accused were in
custody: the commission was to try them. This marked the beginning of a
brief but savage witch hunt which resulted in approximately 300 executions.[22]

Parliament was busy. One thing it did not do, however, was to pass an
Act of indemnity and oblivion, though the king had not only authorised it
but also had issued a proclamation promising one in the previous October.
Middleton thought it best to postpone such action in order to keep dissidents of all sorts in line. Charles acquiesced, but issued a proclamation in
June promising that the next parliament would act. In the meantime no
one was to be pursued for his part in the 'late troubles'.[23] That there would
be no bloodbath was indicated by the fact that parliament tried and
condemned to death as traitors only the marquess of Argyll, whom Charles
detested, the radical minister James Guthrie, and the equally radical lawyer
Archibald Johnston of Wariston, the brains behind the drafting of the
Covenant.[24] Those who disapproved of the parliament's proceedings, especially on religious questions, called it 'the drinking parliament', and singled
out Middleton for censure. Gilbert Burnet wrote that 'the men of affairs
were almost perpetually drunk', which he believed created a prejudice
against episcopacy. James Kirkton thought that the Restoration altered the
national character for the worse. It 'made people not only drunk but
frantic', and sobriety was equated with disloyalty.[25] Perhaps they did drink
a great deal, but they also accomplished a great deal. The Acts of this
parliament fill 362 pages of the printed record – folio pages.[26]

On 12 July 1661 parliament was adjourned rather than dissolved. The Act
of adjournment ended the practice of annual elections of shire and burgh
commissioners, who henceforth sat for the duration of a parliament: the
government was anxious to keep such an amenable body in being.[27] During
and after the session there were spirited discussions in the Scottish council
in London that Clarendon had created in order to help him keep control of
policy there. It had a number of English officials as members – Clarendon

22 C. Larner, *Enemies of God* (Baltimore, 1981), p. 76.
23 Burnet, *History* I, p. 204. NAS GD 90/2/260, pp. 16–17.
24 Argyll and Guthrie were promptly put to death. Johnston was condemned *in absentia*; even-
    tually he was extradited from France, sent to Edinburgh, and executed in 1663.
25 Burnet, *History* I, pp. 194, 207. Kirkton, *History*, pp. 34, 62.
26 The Acts of this parliament are in the *APS* VII, pp. 6–367, A thorough analysis is in J.R. Young,
    The Scottish Parliament 1639–1661 (Edinburgh, 1996), chap. 13. See also R.A. Lee, *Government
    and Politics in Scotland, 1661–1681* (PhD diss., University of Glasgow, 1995), pp. 13–24.
27 *APS* VII, p. 367. C.S. Terry, *The Scottish Parliament: Its Constitution and Procedure 1603–1707*
    (Glasgow, 1905), p. 30. J.R. Young, *Scottish Parliament*, p. 318.

says, appointed at the request of Middleton and his associates in order to counter the influence of Lauderdale,[28] but one might take leave to doubt that. It was intended to overshadow the privy council in Edinburgh, which was not formally reconstituted until after the end of the parliamentary session, fourteen months after the king's return. Throughout the whole of the Restoration period the council in Edinburgh rarely initiated policy; its function was to carry out decisions made elsewhere.

The debates in London focused on two issues. One was the withdrawal of the English garrisons remaining in Scotland, which a group of Scottish nobles, lairds and burgesses summoned to London in 1660 had requested and which Charles had agreed to effect 'in due time'. He meant what he said. England and Scotland had had enough of military rule, that hallmark of the awful republican experiment, which Charles, obviously, also abhorred. Seven years later, in conversation with Lauderdale and Tweeddale, he 'said, next to the people an army was the worst government'.[29] Parliament had also requested their withdrawal, on the ground that they were a badge of slavery and indicated a lack of faith in Scots' loyalty. The Scots found the garrisons expensive: the unpopular cess of the republican era had to be continued in order to pay for them.[30] Lauderdale advocated withdrawal, Charles had promised it, Clarendon dragged his feet but finally agreed. In 1662 the garrisons went, and the fortresses they occupied were demolished. Charles's decision was made easier by the fact that the soldiers could be sent to Portugal to help secure his new bride's homeland's independence from Spain in accordance with the marriage treaty of 1661. Lauderdale's patriotic stance in this matter made him popular in Scotland. Clarendon was not popular there, and Lauderdale 'was said to be colder in pursuing Chancellor Hyde's designs in Scotland than some others'.[31] Lauderdale was also thinking

---

28 Edward, earl of Clarendon, *The Life of Edward, Earl of Clarendon, Continuation*, 2 vols (Oxford, 1760) I, p. 291. One of the members was the English secretary of state, Sir Edward Nicholas. At one point Lauderdale had to ask Charles to instruct Middleton to disregard anything on Scottish business coming from Nicholas; everything concerning Scotland was to come from the Scottish secretary. 20 Mar. 1661, Charles to Middleton, NAS GD 90/2/260, p. 11.

29 BL Add. Mss 23114, ff. 31, 32. 3 Nov. 1667, Tweeddale to Moray, NLS Ms. 7001, p. 160.

30 BL Add. Mss 23116, f. 86. NAS GD 90/2/260, pp. 2–3.

31 July 1661, Baillie to Robert Spang, Baillie, *Letters* III, p. 468. Lauderdale also profited personally. After the removal of the English garrison from Leith Lauderdale acquired the superiority, with the right to erect Leith into a burgh of barony. The Edinburgh city government then purchased the superiority from him for £5,000 sterling, which gave the capital a tight grip on its port. Sir Andrew Ramsay, Edinburgh's provost, brokered the transaction, and won Lauderdale's favour, which helped him to survive the fall of his patron Middleton. Mackenzie, *Memoirs*, pp. 24–25. APS VII, pp. 520–21. Lamont, *Diary*, p. 163.

in terms of patronage. An armed force would continue to exist in Scotland, either standing regiments or a militia or both, but made up of Scots rather than Englishmen. The impoverished and debt-ridden Scottish aristocracy gaped after rewards at the public trough; control of military appointments would be politically and financially rewarding. For the moment, however, the patronage was in Middleton's hands. He commanded his own troop of horse, and on 10 June, toward the end of the parliamentary session, Charles named him commander-in-chief of all armed forces in Scotland.[32]

On the second issue Lauderdale was less successful. The question, following the passage of the Act Rescissory, was the timing of the restoration of bishops in the Scottish church, something Lauderdale would have preferred not to see happen at all. In the discussions in late 1660 on the instructions to be given to Middleton for the holding of the parliament, Lauderdale's eloquence convinced Charles not to include this stipulation: the time was not ripe.[33] It was harder to make that argument a year later. A letter from the future archbishop, James Sharp, who was in London, to Middleton on 21 May 1661, after the passage of the Act Rescissory, made it clear that the only question left now was that of timing. It was also clear enough that the restoration of bishops, the removal of the English garrisons, and the postponement of the Act of indemnity were interconnected. Sharp remarked that Clarendon would never have agreed to the removal of the English garrisons if he were not convinced that Middleton could deal successfully with the church question.

'The great and wise God,' wrote Sharp in this letter, 'hath in a special manner owned your Grace [Middleton]... All opposing designs are dashed, and a foundation laid for a superstructure which will render your name precious to ... succeeding generations.' This is the language of a bootlicker and a careerist, which is how historians have for the most part viewed him. In 1660 James Sharp was forty-two, the eldest son of the sheriff-clerk of Banff, educated in the 1630s at Aberdeen, the Scottish university least unfavourable to episcopacy, in the 1640s a regent at St Andrews, and then minister at Crail, in Fife, the most enthusiastically Presbyterian of shires. Sharp always swam with the tide. By the time of King Charles's unhappy year in Scotland Sharp was prominent in the

---

32 NAS GD 90/2/260, pp. 14, 15, 17. Middleton commanded a supplementary troop of eighty horse; his ally Newburgh commanded the main, 120-man troop. NAS GD 90/2/260, pp. 10, 11.

33 Clarendon, *Continuation*, I, pp. 295–98, pays grudging tribute to Lauderdale's powers of persuasion.

politics of the kirk, as a member of the moderate Resolutioner faction. In 1650 the General Assembly appointed him to the commission to look after the kirk's business until it should meet again, which it never did. Sharp was scooped up and sent to England under arrest after Charles's disaster at Worcester, soon released, and accommodated himself to the republican regime. Over and over again the Resolutioner ministers sent him to London to negotiate on behalf of their perceived interests, where he earned Cromwell's backhanded compliment, 'Sharp of that Ilk'. He was there in 1660, he went to Breda to pay court to the soon-to-be-restored king, he became the king's chaplain in Scotland, he was back again in 1661, this time as Middleton's agent. He accomplished little, but he did lend himself to the king's temporising policy in 1660 while Charles was deciding what to do. Then, with the passage of the Act Rescissory, Sharp did what he had done throughout his career: he fawned on the winners, and received his mess of pottage, the archbishopric of St Andrews, after Robert Douglas, the Resolutioner leader, rejected it, according to his own account, with a curse. The Resolutioner leaders felt betrayed, and small wonder. Sharp compounded his offence by submitting to reordination before consecration as archbishop, thus denying the validity of his own Presbyterian ordination. Julia Buckroyd, his most recent biographer, has done her best to save some shreds of Sharp's reputation by suggesting that he accepted the archbishopric in order to salvage what he could for the moderates from the wreckage of the Presbyterian polity, but her argument is not very convincing.[34] Whatever they thought of Sharp's character, however, those involved in Scottish politics in London and Edinburgh had to take the primate of the church of Scotland into account from now on.

The passage of the Act Rescissory condemned Lauderdale to fighting a rearguard action respecting the revival of episcopacy. He nevertheless tried to limit the inevitable backlash by counselling delay. When Middleton, on arriving in London, pressed for the immediate imposition of episcopacy, Lauderdale proposed that the synods and presbyteries be consulted first, to prepare public opinion for the change. Only the new duke of Hamilton and Sir Robert Moray supported him. Lord Treasurer Crawford's unequivocal support of a Presbyterian polity was not helpful, since it enabled Lauderdale's opponents to tar him with guilt-by-association: he had, after all, been distinguished for his Presbyterian zeal in the 1640s. There were

---

34 J. Buckroyd, *The Life of James Sharp, Archbishop of St Andrews* (Edinburgh, 1987). Sharp's letter to Middleton is in *LP* II, pp. lxxvii–lxxxii.

rumours, which he vehemently denied, that he had had dealings with Cromwell's son-in-law Henry Ireton. 'This is not the first lie that hath been made of me and will not, it seems, be the last.'[35] Middleton and his allies, including the weathercock Rothes, took the line that what the clergy thought was not important and did not reflect the views of their flocks,[36] and that they were in closer touch with Scottish opinion than Lauderdale, who had not been in his native country since 1651. They had Clarendon's backing, and they carried the day with Charles. When the proclamation restoring episcopacy, dated 14 August 1661, was read in the Scottish privy council on 5 September, only Tweeddale and Alexander Bruce, the future earl of Kincardine, suggested that the synods be consulted before it was issued. They got nowhere, and went along with the rest: Lauderdale made it clear that further opposition 'will be construed to have a worse design at bottom.'[37]

Middleton and his allies, flushed with success, set out to consolidate their gains. The first victim was Tweeddale. On 7 September Charles ordered his arrest, pending investigation of reports that his speeches in parliament questioning the imposition of the death penalty on James Guthrie amounted to treason.[38] Middleton loathed Guthrie, before whom he had had to undergo a humiliating penance in 1651 for having supported the Engagement; Burnet, well after the fact, wrote that 'all people were disgusted at the earl of Middleton's eagerness in the prosecution.'[39] In meetings of the Scottish council in London in July and August he accused Tweeddale of, in effect, attacking the king – he was the only member of parliament to oppose Guthrie's execution. Hence the arrest: people were to know that opposition to Middleton had unpleasant consequences.[40] Imprisonment of a prominent privy councillor, who in the absence of Middleton, Glencairn, Crawford and Rothes acted as council president,[41] before any inquiry was held, was certainly overkill. Charles knew it: what,

---

35 26 Aug. 1661, Lauderdale to Sharp, Dowden, 'Letters', pp. 250–51.
36 Rothes had already made this point to Lauderdale in a long letter on 13 Apr. 1661, in which he described his successful effort to prevent the synod of Fife from attacking the Act Rescissory. BL Add. Mss. 23116, f. 22.
37 NLS Ms. 3922, f. 17. There is a good brief account in J. Buckroyd, *Church and State in Scotland 1660–1681* (Edinburgh, 1980), pp. 39–40. See also Burnet, *History* I, pp. 218–25, and Mackenzie, *Memoirs*, pp. 53–56, 59. Burnet says that Charles's consent was given reluctantly.
38 *RPCS* I, pp. 36–37.
39 Buckroyd, *Church and State*, p. 20. Burnet, *History* I, p. 216.
40 On this point see Wodrow, *History* I, p. 90.
41 *RPCS* I, pp. 11–12.

in all likelihood, he was doing was sending Tweeddale a message on an entirely different matter. In the previous June Charles had happily accepted the offer of the hand of the ten-year-old countess of Buccleuch for his bastard son James. The marriage had not yet taken place, could not until 1663, when the children would be of marriageable age. It was well known that Tweeddale had wanted Anna for his own son and that Lady Tweeddale was next in line for the Buccleuch estate. The arrest was a warning: do not interfere with the king's plans for Anna's marriage and the disposition of the Buccleuch estate.[42]

Tweeddale was thunderstruck – his word – protested his innocence, and wrote letters to all and sundry, even to Middleton, asking for help. He pleaded, at the very least, to be released from Edinburgh Castle and placed under house arrest at Yester, since his wife was far gone in pregnancy. His fellow councillors testified on his behalf that he 'did heartily comply with his Majesty's commands' on church government. Tweeddale explained that he had no doubt of Guthrie's guilt. Given the confusion of the times, however, and Charles's merciful character, he did not vote for the death penalty, intending nothing more than to ask the king to mitigate the penalty if he saw fit. Even before Charles received this report he granted Tweeddale's request for confinement to his house, an indication of how seriously he took the charges against the earl.[43] Middleton's case was weakened by the fact that, as Crawford pointed out, he had said nothing at the time Tweeddale made these allegedly treasonous speeches, and that toward the end of the parliamentary session he and the rest of the leadership attended a 'splendid entertainment he [Tweeddale] gave them at Pinkie, and that they parted in great friendship when the Commissioner went to England'. Crawford also raised the issue of free speech in parliament: he had thought that Middleton was going to attack him for his opposition to the Act Rescissory.[44] For Charles the warning to Tweeddale was enough, though the latter would remain under house arrest, sequestered from public business, until the day before parliament reconvened in May 1662.

The first order of business of the new session of parliament was to readmit bishops to its meetings and restore their power over the church. By

42 M. Lee, Jr, 'The Buccleuch Marriage Contract: An Unknown Episode in Scottish Politics', *'Inevitable' Union*, p. 232.

43 *RPCS* I, pp. 41–42, 45, 53–54, 57–58. BL Add. Mss 23116, ff. 121–26. NLS Ms. 7024, ff. 20–23, 14406, f. 26.

44 Tweeddale, 'Autobiography', p. 90. Burnet, *History* I, pp. 218–20. Mackenzie says that Tweeddale also raised the issue of free speech; *Memoirs*, pp. 60–61.

contrast with the restoration of episcopal power under James VI between 1610 and 1612, there was not even a pretence of consulting with the ministry; in December 1661 Charles had, in fact, prohibited meetings of synods, presbyteries and kirk sessions until the bishops were in a position to authorise them.[45] The legislation of 1592 which declared that jurisdiction within the church rested solely with the Presbyterian structure, from General Assembly to kirk session, was repealed. The rights of the patrons of benefices, eliminated in 1649, were restored. Ministers who had acquired their benefices since that date had to obtain not only presentation by the patron but also collation from the bishop in order to stay on. Once again Middleton and his allies had gone beyond the king's instructions, which mentioned only presentation, not collation. This enactment was to cause an infinity of trouble, since it brought together a number of clerical factions which a more incremental approach could have kept separate. Only the Erastians among the moderate Presbyterians, the so-called Resolutioners, were prepared to accept it.[46] To underline the thrust of the Act Rescissory, Charles signed an Act of revocation of any action taken by his father or himself between 1637 and 29 May 1660 that was contrary to the law and the Acts of parliament in force in 1637.[47] Charles thus abrogated his oath to observe the National Covenant and the Solemn League and Covenant. Parliament also denounced these acts and required all public officials, as a condition of holding office, to sign a statement declaring them to have been illegal. Advocates were included in the Act, and resented having to take this oath, since they held no public trust. Middleton had made the mistake of alienating the legal profession. The Act was aimed primarily at Crawford and Lauderdale. The former, a staunch Presbyterian, would not sign, and so Charles ultimately dismissed him as lord treasurer, though Middleton, who wanted the office, did not get it. Lauderdale, however, 'laughed at this contrivance, and told them he would sign a cartful of such oaths before he would lose his place'.[48] So Middleton needed to find another way to get rid of the secretary. The device he adopted brought about, not Lauderdale's ruin, but his own.

45 NAS GD 90/2/260, pp. 19–20. *RPCS* I, pp. 125–26, 130–31. On 22 Jan. 1662 Charles gave Middleton specific instructions as to the church, NLS Ms. 597, f. 71.
46 On this point see Ian B. Cowan, *The Scottish Covenanters 1660–1688* (London, 1976), pp. 50–51.
47 *APS* VII, pp. 370–74, 376, 402–03.
48 Ibid., pp. 377–79, 405–06. Mackenzie, *Memoirs*, pp. 64–65.

Charles had mandated that parliament pass an Act of indemnity at this session.[49] Middleton delayed the Act until September; meantime, he had persuaded Charles that parliament wished to be allowed to ban twelve people of its choice from public office. He subsequently informed parliament that the king wanted such legislation. Lauderdale was caught by surprise when the proposal was made at a meeting of the Scottish council in London; he angrily protested that men were being condemned without trial. Sir George Mackenzie of Tarbat, Middleton's agent, smoothly replied that since life and property were not at stake, no legal trial was necessary, and anyway the king would make the final decision: he could reject parliament's list. By concealing this proposal from Lauderdale in his preliminary discussions with the secretary, Tarbat had provoked him into losing his composure. The tactics worked. The others present, 'weary of Lauderdale's insolence', supported Tarbat; only Crawford backed the secretary.[50] It seems not to have occurred to either Lauderdale or Charles that the proscription would be aimed at men already in public office, but only at those who had blotted their copybooks in the past. They were mistaken.

Middleton's plan was to have the twelve chosen by secret ballot, to prevent embarrassment and reprisals if the king should reject the list, and to lobby vigorously to get his opponents proscribed. His helpers included Chancellor Glencairn and four newly-appointed privy councillors, the king's cousin the duke of Richmond and Lennox, the earl of Newburgh, the earl of Perth and Middleton's indispensable spin doctor, Mackenzie of Tarbat, who hoped for either Lauderdale's or Moray's office. So on 9 September the Act of indemnity was passed, along with a list of wicked people, supporters of Cromwell, etc., who could not receive its benefits without paying a specific fine. The list was very long, covering six and a half pages of the parliamentary record, and some of the fines were very large; as much as £18,000. The total was over a million pounds.[51] Following the passage of the Act the billets were counted, and the list of those proscribed sent secretly to Charles. Tarbat was to carry the list to court, along with Middleton's suggestion that a permanent five-man Scottish council be established in London, to prevent the dangers arising from the king's getting all his information from one man.[52] It seems Middleton was

49 Charles's instructions to Middleton, dated 29 Jan. 1662, are in BL Add. Mss 23117, f. 19.
50 Mackenzie, *Memoirs*, pp. 67–70.
51 *APS* VII, pp. 415–16, 420–29. Wodrow, *History* I, p. 121, App., pp. 57–69.
52 Tarbat's instructions are in Mackenzie, *Memoirs*, pp. 128–30.

hedging his bets with this suggestion: Lauderdale might not lose his position after all.

Middleton had taken every precaution to be sure that Tarbat should be the first to arrive with the news. He had forbidden anyone using post horses to court, and had secured the stages as far south as Durham. Alas for his well-laid plans: Lauderdale already knew all that had happened. His Edinburgh man of business, William Sharp, whose brother James, the new archbishop of St Andrews, was one of the parliamentary tellers and evidently did not vote, had written to Lauderdale with all the details, including the unwelcome news that his name headed the list. His 'colleagues in incapacity' – Moray's phrase – included Moray, Lauderdale's kinsman Lord Duffus,[53] the earls of Cassillis, Lothian and Loudoun, who had all opposed the Engagement, and Alexander Jaffray, the radical former provost of Aberdeen, who had become a Quaker. Crawford missed the list by a few votes: the managers apparently believed that he was done for anyway. Some billets allegedly listed 'any twelve bishops'. Tweeddale was very apprehensive when he first heard of the billeting plan, since his recent record made him an obvious candidate for exclusion. He 'wrought diligently without and within the walls of the house yesterday morning', wrote Sharp, and by 'pure industry has got free'. His successful efforts gave rise to a rumour that he had sold out and voted to billet Lauderdale, Crawford and Moray. He indignantly denied this; Lauderdale knew it was not true, and told him so. Tweeddale was much relieved.[54]

Sharp wrote three letters in all, on 9, 10 and 11 September. As a sort of afterthought he added that if the billeting did not remove Lauderdale his enemies would charge him with treason for his part in turning Charles I over to the English in 1647. He entrusted his letters to a messenger of Duffus's brother-in-law Lord Lorne, who avoided Middleton's roadblocks by sticking to the back roads, and so arrived before Tarbat, who saw no need for haste.[55] Lorne, the son and heir of the executed marquess of

---

53 Alexander Sutherland, Lord Duffus, was married first to Jean Mackenzie, another of Lauderdale's and Tweeddale's many first cousins; she died in 1648. His third wife, Margaret Stewart, was Lady Lauderdale's niece.

54 October 1662, Tweeddale to Lauderdale, 6 Nov., W. Sharp to Lauderdale, BL Add. Mss 23117, ff. 106, 116. Lauderdale was in possession of Lennox's billet, 'written in an English hand who could not spell one of our names right', with Tweeddale's name on it: proof that he had not sold out. BL Add. Mss 23119, ff. 159–60. Wodrow, *History* I, p. 121.

55 Sharp's letters are in *LP* I, pp. 108–19. 27–31 Oct. 1662, Moray to Kincardine, *Moray Letters*, pp. 229–31. Burnet, *History* I, p. 256.

Argyll, was not billeted, even though he was Lauderdale's nephew-by-marriage. Middleton believed that he had dealt with Lorne by a special Act of parliament declaring that the children of those condemned as traitors were disabled from holding public office or petitioning for their parents' estates; he had designs on Lorne's property and on his father's forfeited title. Lorne was, in fact, in prison, parliament having sentenced him to death on a charge of leasing-making, on the strength of a letter he wrote to Duffus which Middleton's agents had intercepted and which was twisted into an attack on king and parliament. Lauderdale was known to favour Lorne's restoration. Clarendon, as usual, ascribed sinister motives to Lauderdale's advocacy. It was 'a design to preserve an interest in the Presbyterian party against the time he should have an occasion to use them'.[56]

When he got Sharp's letters Lauderdale, with Moray, went at once to the king. Charles was outraged, not only at the attempt to deprive him of his officials – Moray was the justice-clerk and a member of the court of session – but also at the fact that Middleton had officially approved parliament's actions without consulting him. On this point Charles was overreacting. The letter he had sent to parliament in July indicated that if parliament followed the guidelines set down for the Act of oblivion, which included the incapacitation of twelve individuals, the text need not be sent to him for prior approval.[57] Charles also found the Act directed against Lorne offensive, since it limited his power to pardon, a point on which he was very sensitive. When Tarbat, accompanied by Lennox and the earl of Dumfries, appeared at court with the billeting list, Charles threw it aside and declared that he could not follow such advice. He sent Tarbat back to Scotland with the order to Middleton that he was not to come to court.[58] Lauderdale was enormously relieved. 'I am not yet uncapable (God bless the King).'[59]

Lord Chancellor Clarendon was furious. He scolded Middleton's agents, and declared that the device was so stupid that Lauderdale must have been responsible for it in order to ruin Middleton.[60] He tried to undo some of the damage by arguing to Charles that ruining Middleton and favouring Lauderdale would damage episcopacy in Scotland – and indeed the bishops had written a letter to Charles full of praise for the commissioner.

56 APS VII, pp. 380–81, 417–18, App., pp. 89–92. Mackenzie, *Memoirs*, pp. 70–72. Clarendon, *Continuation* II, p. 41.
57 NAS GD 90/2/260, pp. 24–25.
58 Paton, 'Gilmour', pp. 141–42.
59 Ibid., pp. 139–40.
60 Mackenzie, *Memoirs*, pp. 76–77.

Archbishop Sharp had to write a weaseling letter to Lauderdale as to his role in the billeting, dissociating himself from Tarbat, and explaining that the bishops' praise was owing, not to the Act of billeting, but to Middleton's work for the church in the recent session of parliament. Clarendon's argument did not convince the king; Lauderdale, however, given his Presbyterian past, could not oppose the bishops' agenda. Burnet opined that Sharp had figured this out, and so became Lauderdale's man.[61]

Middleton was allowed to come to court early in 1663. Charles's annoyance with Middleton had mounted. In December 1662 he wrote a minatory letter to Clerk-Register Archibald Primrose demanding a complete file on the Act of oblivion, the billeting and the fines – he had no list of those fined, or the amounts. When he received the list Charles decided, on 23 January 1663, to suspend the collection of the fines temporarily, until he had time to think about the fairness of the assessments.[62] After his arrival at court Middleton compounded his offences by countermanding Charles's order without authorisation. Kirkton opined that he wanted the fines collected 'to distribute amongst his dependents and retainers for a sort of drink money'. Middleton had complained to Clarendon about the suspension, and accepted the latter's assurance that he would get the king to change his mind. But Charles did not do so. Lauderdale, who had expressed some concern about the financial consequences of not collecting the fines, was astonished that Middleton had acted without a written order from the king. He gleefully wrote to Sir John Gilmour to tell Lord Chancellor Glencairn, who had been very cool of late, to hang onto Middleton's letter in order to protect himself. When Lauderdale told Charles what had happened, the king, who as early as March 1661 had hinted to Middleton that he was aware of the existence of bribery in connection with the fines, was angrier than ever at Middleton, and, this time, at Clarendon as well. He renewed his order on 10 March 1663; Lauderdale needled Glencairn by supposing that Middleton would not attempt to countermand the king's instructions this time.[63] Middleton was

---

61 Burnet, *History* I, pp. 258, 346–47. 24 Oct. 1662, Sharp to Lauderdale, NLS Ms. 2512, f. 13.

62 NAS GD 90/2/260, pp. 26, 27.

63 Kirkton, *History*, p. 84. *RPCS* I, pp. 329–31, 336, 348. 22 Mar. 1661, Charles to Middleton, BL Add. Mss 23115, f. 118. Mackenzie, *Memoirs*, pp. 112–14. 23 Jan., 21 Feb., 10 Mar. 1663, Lauderdale to Gilmour, Paton, 'Gilmour', pp. 146–47, 156–57, 162–63. Burnet, *History* I, pp. 348–49, opines that Charles did agree, orally, to suspend his order respecting the fines, but that he subsequently forgot that he had done so because, at this moment, he was so distracted by his infatuation with the dazzling Frances Stewart, who had recently appeared at court.

doomed. Burnet, looking back many years later, characterised his regime as one 'of much violence and injustice, for he was become very imperious'. But – reflecting his disillusionment with Lauderdale – 'those that came after him grew worse than ever he was like to be'.[64]

In the early months of 1663 Lauderdale, in two great speeches in the Scottish council in London, effectively ended Middleton's political career. His constantly repeated theme was that Middleton had violated the king's instructions. Never before, he said, had any commissioner approved an Act of parliament without consulting the king save on express instructions. Billeting was a practice unknown to monarchies; history afforded nothing like it except ostracism in ancient Athens, 'governed by that cursed Sovereign Lord the People'. There were hints of financial improprieties. There was the business of Lord Lorne and the pardon. And the fines. Middleton put up a defence, but it was not very effective; Lauderdale described it as 'parturiunt montes'.[65] What Lauderdale said, after all, was true.[66] But Lauderdale was careful. He could not afford to involve too many people in Middleton's ruin for fear of backlash. Middleton had had a great many collaborators and allies, including Glencairn and Charles's cousin Lennox: they had to escape. So the only others who suffered were Middleton's smooth-talking agent Tarbat, who had told entirely too many lies, and Newburgh, who had been Middleton's chief parliamentary lobbyist over the billeting lists. Tarbat lost his place on the court of session. Mackenzie opined that he escaped a worse fate by threatening Lauderdale with revelations concerning his role in the delivery of Charles I to the English in 1647. This is unlikely. In January 1663 Treasurer-Depute Bellenden and Primrose had chased down the rumour that there were incriminating papers in the hands of Lauderdale's enemies, who were planning to use them to justify billeting him. But whatever papers there were had evidently been found in a cellar by an Edinburgh shopkeeper who had used them 'as old cast papers for household business'. There was no evidence for Middleton to use – and, indeed, he said nothing about Lauderdale's days as a Covenanter.[67] In May Charles removed Middleton as commissioner, since a new session of parliament was necessary to undo some of what the previous session had done.

64 Burnet, *History* I, p. 350.
65 9 May 1663, Lauderdale to Gilmour, Paton, 'Gilmour', pp. 170–71.
66 Lauderdale's speeches and Middleton's rejoinders are in BL Add. Mss 23118, ff. 15–22, 23119, ff. 9–13, 15–19, 23–25. See also Mackenzie, *Memoirs*, pp. 112–32.
67 Mackenzie, *Memoirs*, p. 131. *LP* I, pp. 125–30.

What the billeting episode meant for Lauderdale was not victory, but escape. Middleton had in effect ruined himself. His fundamental error, in the opinion of that shrewd observer Sir George Mackenzie of Rosehaugh, was that he did not sufficiently cultivate the king. He relied too much on the support of Clarendon, and because he followed Clarendon he allowed himself to drift into hostility to Lauderdale, with whom he had formerly been on very good terms.[68] And, as he himself put it in his defence, 'Want of . . . experience in the matters of state hath made me overreach, and great advantage is taken at my failings.' But he still had a great deal of support in English political circles. According to Burnet, both General Monck and Archbishop Sheldon backed him over billeting.[69] And the implacable Clarendon was still in power. Furthermore, the billeting vote revealed the thinness of Lauderdale's support in Scotland. More members of parliament had voted to billet him than anyone else. Lord Chancellor Glencairn was an irreconcilable enemy. His principal correspondents and informants were his man of business, William Sharp, immensely useful because of his relationship to the archbishop, and two technocrats, Sir John Gilmour, president of the court of session, and William, Lord Bellenden of Broughton, the treasurer-depute, an elderly and difficult man who was also very good at his job. Both were hostile to Middleton. Gilmour thought much of Middleton's behaviour 'rash and illegal', and at Lauderdale's behest complained about it to the king when he was summoned to court in September 1662 to give advice on the Buccleuch marriage contract. Bellenden was angry at Middleton's attempt to prevent the income from the excise going into the exchequer; he was afraid that Crawford, his chief, would be ruined as Louis XIV's finance minister Fouquet recently had been.[70] He and Gilmour were privy councillors, but not in themselves very influential. But there was one of Lauderdale's correspondents who was influential: Lord President Rothes. And it was he, not Lauderdale, whom Charles named as commissioner in place of the fallen Middleton.[71]

John Leslie, seventh earl of Rothes, was an engaging and charming man who was a good friend of the king. He was exactly Charles's age, and so too young to have been involved in the events of the 1640s. He had become

68 Mackenzie, *Memoirs*, p. 7. Sir James Turner, *Memoirs of His Own Life and Times, 1632–1670*, ed. T. Thomson, Bannatyne Club (Edinburgh, 1829), p. 134.
69 Burnet, *History* I, p. 346.
70 Mackenzie, *Memoirs*, p. 114. BL Add. Mss 23117, ff. 37–38.
71 *RPCS* I, pp. 367–68. Burnet, *History* I, p. 350. Rothes's appointment had been rumoured as early as January; 13 Jan. 1663, Bellenden to Lauderdale, BL Add. Mss 23118, f. 3.

friendly with Charles when Charles was in Scotland in 1650–51, bore the sword of state at his coronation, and was captured at Worcester in 1651. He was not held for long; evidently Cromwell's government did not regard him as a threat. He was in touch with Lauderdale in the 1650s,[72] and when Lauderdale emerged from captivity in the spring of 1660 wrote him a series of letters that combined a certain amount of bootlicking with bad-mouthing of a large number of people. Tweeddale was his special target. Tweeddale, he wrote, was spreading the obvious lie that Lauderdale favoured liberty for Johnston of Wariston. Tweeddale did not deserve Lauderdale's friendship: 'really I believe that he will prove to those that trusts [sic] him another Argyll'.[73]

Rothes's enmity to Tweeddale was familial rather than political. Rothes's sister, Margaret Leslie, now married to the earl of Wemyss, had been the wife of Francis, earl of Buccleuch, and was the mother of the two little girls who successively inherited the Buccleuch title and estate. Tweeddale was a threat to Rothes's and Lady Wemyss's control of that estate. Both Rothes and Tweeddale hastened to see the king in 1660, to kiss hands and seek for favour. Rothes went to London in spite of the possibility of a challenge from Charles Howard, whom he had cuckolded. Lauderdale's cousin Lady Balcarres, no mean bad-mouther herself, commented that it was foolish to fight over soiled goods: 'he should have kept his horns in his pocket'.[74] Lady Wemyss wrote to Lauderdale to ask him to protect her little brother from the Howards.[75] She need not have worried. There was no duel. Rothes emerged with the king's favour, appointment as president of the privy council, and, to his sister's considerable annoyance, the wardship and marriage of his two little nieces. Lady Wemyss hastened to London, confronted her brother, and got him to agree that Lord Wemyss be joined in the wardship with him. She also got Charles to 'touch' the young Countess Mary, to cure 'the cruells in her arm'. In vain: Mary died early in 1661 at the age of thirteen. Her sister Anna, aged ten, was now countess of Buccleuch.[76]

After Rothes returned to Scotland in September 1660 he and Lauderdale began to correspond regularly. They even devised a code. Rothes became a

---

72 In May 1657 he wrote to Lauderdale apologising for missing a meeting of Lauderdale's creditors; BL Add. Mss. 23113, f. 57.

73 19 Apr. 1660, Rothes to Lauderdale, ibid., f. 93. See also his letters of 6 and 18 Apr., ibid., ff. 88, 92.

74 11–12 May 1660, Lady Balcarres to Lauderdale, *Laing Mss* I, pp. 358–61. The editor has wrongly dated the letter as having been written in 1666.

75 14 May 1660, Lady Wemyss to Lauderdale, BL Add. Mss 23113, f. 107.

76 Lee, *Heiresses*, pp. 44–48.

conduit for requests for favours addressed to the king for those who were
not in a position to approach Charles directly. If Rothes sent the request in
a holograph letter Lauderdale was to take it seriously; if he used an amanu-
ensis, Lauderdale could disregard it.[77] Lauderdale found this arrangement
very helpful. He had no acquaintance with the technicalities of his job. In
August 1660 he wrote to his friend the duchess of Hamilton asking her to
send him her uncle's register if she could find it – he had been secretary in
the 1640s – 'for I have got the seals from the king but not so much as a style-
book'.[78] Even before his official appointment he was besieged by begging
letters. His impoverished cousin the earl of Kellie declared in May that
'these sad times hath [sic] brought my little fortune to so low an ebb that I
have no other way of subsisting for the future nor hopes of any standing for
my family but by my dependence upon what his Majesty will be pleased to
do for me.' Two months later he sent Lauderdale a petition to be given to
the king, asking for money from the fines which were to be levied on the
disloyal, and saying that he had also asked their cousin Tweeddale for
help.[79] The convention of royal burghs asked Lauderdale to be their
pipeline to the king. The temporary administration in Edinburgh wanted
him to be sure that the English parliament did nothing prejudicial to
Scottish economic interests.[80] Requests like these, asking both for personal
favours and for support on matters of public policy, filled Lauderdale's
correspondence for the next twenty years.

Rothes seemed reliable to Lauderdale. He was helpful in handling
Lauderdale's private business, and he was the son-in-law of Lord Treasurer
Crawford, Lauderdale's stiff-necked political ally. According to Burnet, he
took credit, not entirely deserved, during the parliamentary session of
1661 for preventing Middleton's allies from complaining to Charles
that Lauderdale was misreporting their behaviour. So in the summer of

---

77 13 Nov. 1660, Rothes to Lauderdale, BL Add. Mss 23114, f. 76. There were other channels,
    to be sure. In this same letter Rothes remarked that the provost of Aberdeen was on his
    way to London; 'what his business is I do not know', but he had 20,000 merks with him to
    smooth his way. 'He is to make his request by one Doctor Dun, who I hear is his Majesty's
    physician and skilled in alchemy.' It was already known that scientists could get Charles's
    attention.

78 NAS GD 406/1/8418.

79 14 May, 4 July 1660, Kellie to Lauderdale, BL Add. Mss 23113, f. 105, 23114, ff. 21–22.

80 16 Nov. 1660, the convention of royal burghs to Lauderdale, 17 Nov., the committee of estates
    to Charles and 21 Dec., to Lauderdale, BL Add. Mss 23114, ff. 79, 81, 110. Charles had autho-
    rised the committee of estates named in the last Scottish parliament, in May 1651, to act as a
    temporary government until the privy council could be formally reconstituted.

1661 Lauderdale did Rothes a huge favour: after the death of Countess Mary Lauderdale arranged that Rothes alone should have the wardship and marriage of young Anna, cutting out her stepfather Wemyss.[81] Lady Weymss was mightily upset at this second betrayal on the part of her brother. She and her husband asked General Monck for help, in vain, and when she turned to the king, Charles blandly brushed her off: 'I am confident', he wrote, 'you will not mislike it when you consider it is for the advantage of the family you are come of, and for a person I have so great kindness for.' There was no help for it. Rothes was going to have to be paid off for his consent to Countess Anna's marriage, which Lady Wemyss was in the process of arranging, and paid off he was.[82]

Gratitude was a word frequently in Rothes's mouth but seldom reflected in his behaviour. He was careful to avoid antagonising either Middleton or Lauderdale. He wanted the latter's help in securing appointment as commander-in-chief of the militia, if there was to be such an office: it was a much more appropriate job for him, he thought, than the presidency of the privy council.[83] During the 1661 session of parliament he was civil to Tweeddale, since (he said) Lauderdale wished it, and when Tweeddale was arrested he, along with the rest of the council, petitioned the king to change Tweeddale's imprisonment to house arrest, only, he told Lauderdale, because Lauderdale asked him to do so.[84] These gestures cost Rothes nothing. He did nothing to prevent the dismissal of his father-in-law from the office of lord treasurer, and there was probably nothing he could have done. But he also did nothing to oppose Middleton's billeting plan, and he kept a very low profile throughout. After the end of the parliamentary session of 1662 he attended the synod of Fife and helped Archbishop Sharp keep the fractious ministers in line.[85] They were considerably more successful than Middleton and his cronies on the council, who went to

81 Burnet, *History* I, pp. 206–07. 13 Oct. (1661), Rothes to Lauderdale, BL Add. Mss 23116, f. 142. There is no year date on this letter; its contents indicate that it was written in 1661. Rothes feared that Tweeddale might find a way to block the gift of the wardship; n.d., but written in February 1661, Rothes to Lauderdale, BL Add. Mss 23115, f. 85.

82 23 Apr. 1661, Monck to Wemyss, Sir William Fraser, *Memorials of the Family of Wemyss of Wemyss*, 3 vols (Edinburgh, 1888), III, p. 107. 25 Aug., Charles to Lady Wemyss, Sir William Fraser, *The Scotts of Buccleuch*, 2 vols (Edinburgh, 1878), I, p. 404. Lee, *Heiresses*, pp. 57–60, 67–68. The terms of the payoff to Rothes are in Paton, 'Gilmour', pp. 159–61.

83 n.d., Rothes to Lauderdale, BL Add. Mss 23115, f. 51.

84 BL Add. Mss 23135, f. 85, 23136, ff. 136–37.

85 18 Oct. 1662, W. Sharp to Charles Maitland of Halton, BL Add. Mss 23117, f. 96; 24 Oct., Archbishop Sharp to Lauderdale, NLS Mss 2512, f. 13.

Glasgow and precipitated great confusion by acting very hastily and arbi-trarily.[86] In October 1662 the king summoned Rothes to London to tell what he knew about the goings-on at the parliament.[87] Rothes played his cards with great skill, and emerged, when the dust had cleared, as the winner. He not only replaced Middleton as commissioner to parliament but also succeeded his father-in-law as lord treasurer in June 1663. Lauderdale got some crumbs: his brother, Charles Maitland of Halton, the master of the mint, became a privy councillor, and Lord Lorne was released from Edinburgh Castle, where he had been languishing since his condem-nation for leasing-making in the previous year.[88]

What was now apparent to Lauderdale was that Rothes was not a reliable friend and was now, in fact, a serious rival. He needed political support in Edinburgh and someone to give him reliable advice. There were so many vexing problems, often involving his kinfolk: his wife's nephew Alexander Stewart, earl of Moray, was at odds with the earl of Seaforth, the eventual victor, over the sheriffdom of Ross. Rothes's comment, 'I assure you I think it were better for the king to give it to either of their footmen than either to Moray or Seaforth', because whoever lost out would cause trouble, was amusing but not helpful.[89] The question was where to find such support and advice. One obvious place to look was the list of those billeted, but there was little help to be had there. Only one was potentially useful, Lauderdale's good friend Sir Robert Moray. The difficulty here was Moray himself: he did not want to get involved.

Moray was born in about 1608, the son of a minor Perthshire laird. He became a professional soldier in France in the 1630s, was well and favourably known to Cardinal Richelieu, and was in Scotland in the early phases of the troubles, whether as Richelieu's agent or simply as a recruiter for a new regi-ment for the French army is not clear. The regiment was raised, Moray became its lieutenant-colonel – Argyll's half-brother was its colonel – and saw a good deal of fighting. Late in 1643 Moray was captured and spent some eighteen months as a prisoner in Bavaria before being ransomed in April 1645. Lauderdale was one of the guarantors that the merchant who put up the ransom money would be repaid. Between 1645 and 1650 Moray was heavily involved in the various negotiations for a settlement between Charles I and

---

86 See below, chap. 3, pp. 63–64.
87 2 Oct. 1662, W. Sharp to Lauderdale, BL Add. Mss 23117, f. 86.
88 *RPCS* I, pp. 380–83.
89 15 Feb. 1662, Rothes to Lauderdale, BL Add. Mss 23115, f. 51. *RPCS* I, p. 224.

his enemies. He worked in collaboration with Cardinal Mazarin's agent the sieur de Montereuil; he was also recruiting again for the French army, and got an appointment, which he never took up, as colonel of the Scots Guards. He became an Engager, was with that part of the fleet which had declared for the king in the summer of 1648 and thus, like Lauderdale, came to know the young Prince Charles. He was in Scotland during Charles's year there in 1650–51, and, like Lauderdale, Middleton and the others, did penance for his behaviour in having supported the Engagement. Charles made him a privy councillor, a lord of session and justice clerk. Oddly, since he was a professional soldier, he was not with Charles's doomed army that met its fate at Worcester. His marriage to one of Lauderdale's and Tweeddale's cousins, Lady Sophia Lindsay, the sister of the earl of Balcarres, may have had something to do with this. Tragically, the marriage was very brief: Lady Sophia died in childbirth in 1653. Lauderdale and Tweeddale were both close to Balcarres, who might well have been a major political figure during the Restoration had he not died in 1659. It was on Balcarres's property that Lauderdale buried his charters in three iron chests in the aftermath of the battle of Dunbar in 1650. They suffered serious water damage during their decade below ground; hence Lauderdale's need to get a confirmation of all his holdings in parliament in 1661. The Act of confirmation takes up thirty pages in the printed acts.[90]

In 1653 Balcarres was one of the initiators of the royalist rebellion known as Glencairn's Rising. This was a messy and ill-managed affair from the beginning. Moray and Balcarres opposed the designation of Glencairn as temporary leader pending the arrival of Middleton from Charles's court-in-exile, and expressed a high opinion of one Colonel John Bampfield, of whom Charles was suspicious. And rightly so: he was in the pay of Cromwell's chief of intelligence, John Thurloe. The quarrels became so bitter that at one point Glencairn ordered Moray's arrest on account of a letter he allegedly wrote to his cousin the earl of Dysart indirectly giving evidence of an assassination plot against the king. The letter was soon enough exposed as a forgery concocted by Dysart's discarded mistress. Dysart was the real object of the forgery, being already suspect because his daughter was very friendly with Cromwell. We shall hear of her again.

Moray, once released from arrest, took no part in any further fighting. With the disintegration of the rebellion in 1655 he, like many of its leaders, accepted General Monck's terms and went into exile. His experiences in the

90 *APS* VII, pp. 131–61.

rebellion marked a turning-point in his career. After 1655 he gave up soldiering, not surprising for a man approaching fifty who had led an active and exhausting life. He also wanted no more to do with politics. He spent much of the next five years in the Low Countries, principally at Maastricht, where he set up a chemical laboratory. He needed money – all the exiles did – so in 1659 he went to Paris to try to collect the 130,000 *livres* Cardinal Mazarin owed him for his past services. He was still in Paris when the negotiations for the king's return got under way. Lauderdale asked him and Lady Balcarres, who also was there, to get a number of prominent Huguenot ministers to write to their English counterparts testifying to the staunchness of Charles's Protestantism, which they did, and also in favour of a modified episcopacy (which made Moray uneasy) in the hope that, if Charles adopted it, the English Presbyterians could be persuaded to conform.[91] Moray's religious views were heterodox. 'As the king was pleased to say of Sir Robert Moray and doctor Fraser [the king's physician] I believe he is head of his own church.'[92]

By midsummer 1660 Moray was back in England. The king and Lauderdale both wanted him back. Charles restored his offices, but Moray never took them up: he preferred to remain in London. His reluctance to become politically involved grew with the appointment of the hostile and rather stupid Glencairn as chancellor. Moray had opinions about what should be done in Scotland – he favoured an early meeting of parliament, and of the General Assembly of the church, and the prompt withdrawal of the English garrisons[93] – but the most he would do was to sit with Clarendon's Scottish council in his capacity as a privy councillor, where he followed Lauderdale's line. Hence his being billeted along with his friend. But Moray's great interest after his return was the founding of the Royal Society, in which his role was vital. He obtained the Society's charter and served as its first president, thanks to his friendship with the king rather than his scientific skills. But his scientific interest was genuine, as was that of the king, whose mind, writes a recent biographer, 'seems to have been of a scientific rather than a literary bent',[94] and who had a great curiosity about the natural world. Charles enjoyed Moray's company, provided him with

---

91 See Moray's letter of 7 June 1660 to Lauderdale from Paris, BL Add. Mss 23114, f. 6.
92 See 16 Aug. 1665, Rothes to Lauderdale, BL Add. Mss 23123, f. 157. These paragraphs on Moray's life before 1660 are based on the first six chapters of A. Robertson, *The Life of Sir Robert Moray* (London, 1922) and on David Stevenson's introduction to *Moray Letters*.
93 See his letters to Alexander Bruce in May and June 1660, *Moray Letters*, pp. 210–16.
94 Hutton, *Charles II*, p. 450.

lodgings in Whitehall, and wanted him around the court. Moray clearly was not the answer to Lauderdale's managerial problems in Edinburgh.

What, then, of Tweeddale, who had barely escaped being billeted? He and Lauderdale were neighbours as well as first cousins; Yester House and Lethington (now Lennoxlove) are separated by only about five miles of the East Lothian countryside. Their political relationship went back to at least 1645, when the young Master of Yester, as he then was, was urged by Lauderdale, Crawford, and the earl of Lanark, the secretary of state, to stand for parliament from Peeblesshire.[95] He was then nineteen, the son and heir of the eighth Lord Yester, who was an enthusiastic Covenanter; he had recently married the sister of the earl of Buccleuch, also an enthusiastic Covenanter. He had seen some military service in England, as the commander of his ailing father's regiment, although he did not much like soldiering. He undertook it, he says in his autobiography, to impress his future wife, Lady Jean Scott, and her brother the earl, who ironically, was equally averse to a military life. The only major engagement at which he was present was Philiphaugh. His regiment had fought at Marston Moor, though he was not there; he had gone home to pursue his courtship of Lady Jean, whom he married in October 1644.[96] After Charles I surrendered to the Scots the young Yester went to Newcastle along with his uncle, Charles Seton, earl of Dunfermline, who was a gentleman of the bedchamber. He saw the king frequently; Charles discussed sermons with him, and playfully called him 'Ruling Elder'. Charles wanted to make him an earl, but to keep peace in the family conferred the title on his father, who had 'married a proud wife'.[97] Young Yester became an Engager – his father did not – but missed the campaign that ended in disaster at Preston because his pregnant wife was 'past her reckoning'. When Charles II came to Scotland he made the new king's acquaintance and was present at his coronation, but was not at all conspicuous during Charles's awful year there. His concern for his young family, which, like his brother-in-law Buccleuch, he had sent north, to Dundee and then to Aberdeen, for safety's sake, kept him out of the army. Unlike Lauderdale, Middleton and Rothes, he was not a 'Worcester Scot'.[98]

---

95 Lord Yester had endowed his son with Neidpath Castle, in Peeblesshire, at the time of his marriage in 1644. The Master was elected but did not take up his seat; a delegation of shire representatives dissuaded him on the ground that it was not customary or appropriate for the heirs of noblemen to represent other estates. Tweeddale, 'Autobiography', pp. 74–75.

96 Ibid., pp. 67–68, 71–72, 74.

97 Ibid., pp. 75–76. He was not fond of his stepmother.

98 Ibid., pp. 77–83.

So Tweeddale – he inherited the title in 1654 – had no particular claim on Charles II's gratitude for his behaviour in 1650–51. Worse was to come. He made his peace with the victorious republican regime. More than that: he became a collaborator, and was elected to the Protectorate's parliaments in 1656 and 1659 after the forcible unification of the three kingdoms. In his autobiography he claims that he did so in order to alleviate the draconian conditions under which Scotland was being governed, and that he was successful. 'By the endeavours used by him and the rest of the Scots commissioners their proportion of the burden was brought from £10,000 to £6,000 [sterling] per month and a free trade settled in all the three dominions with one another . . . so that the Scots had the same freedom in England and in their plantations as the English themselves had.'[99] One may take leave to doubt this, as far as the reduction of the monthly assessment was concerned. This action simply recognised the reality that £6,000 sterling a month was as much as the Cromwellian regime could reasonably expect to collect.[100] What is not open to doubt is Tweeddale's enthusiasm for the benefits of union for the Scottish economy. He would hold this view for the rest of his life.

Tweeddale, like many others, hurried to London in the summer of 1660, one of the many place-hunters who flocked there, in the words of the disapproving Presbyterian James Kirkton, 'as the vulture does to the carcase', impoverishing the country, according to the diarist John Nicoll, because they took so much money with them.[101] Charles received the once-more-royalist earl well enough, as he did many other ex-Cromwellians, pardoned him for his conduct in the 1650s,[102] and made him a privy councillor. Tweeddale had, after all, supported the Engagement. But then he had made difficulties over the method of choosing the Committee of the Articles,[103] and had made those unfortunate speeches about Guthrie in parliament – and, of course, he was a potential obstacle to the king's long-range designs on the Buccleuch estate for his son. Hence his arrest and his long detention. Lauderdale did what he could for his cousin. During Lauderdale's own long years in prison Tweeddale had kept in touch with

99 Ibid., pp. 87–88.

100 On this point, see F.D. Dow, *Cromwellian Scotland* (Edinburgh, 1979), pp. 168–76, 213–21.

101 Kirkton, *History*, pp. 34–35. Nicoll, *Diary*, p. 295.

102 20 Aug. 1660, Charles to the committee of estates, NAS GD 90/2/260, p. 1. He also pardoned the earls of Linlithgow and Southesk and Sir John Cochrane. The last, a financial expert, was promptly appointed to the committee to manage the excise. NAS GD 90/2/260, p. 5.

103 Burnet, *History* I, p. 197.

him, and in the confusion of 1659 had delivered Lauderdale's petition for release to his friend General Lambert, who was temporarily very influential. He also spoke to Wariston, Vane and Fleetwood. His efforts failed; Lauderdale was not released until 8 March 1660, after Monck's arrival in London and the return of the members expelled in Pride's Purge.[104] In March 1661 William Sharp informed Lauderdale that Tweeddale and Lauderdale's brother, Charles Maitland of Halton, were doing good work 'in your business' – Lauderdale had named them, along with Rothes, Sir John Gilmour and some others, to handle his affairs while he was not in Scotland.[105] During his long sequestration Tweeddale wrote a rather depressed letter to Lauderdale saying that he would be content to live a retired life hereafter if only he received vindication, but Lauderdale knew better. In this same letter Tweeddale said that because of his perceived lack of favour his creditors were hounding him – an excellent reason for returning to public life.[106] In 1662 Tweeddale did return. He was released from house arrest in May, in time to attend parliament, and in June he resumed attendance at meetings of the privy council. If Lauderdale wanted to make use of Tweeddale as a political ally, however, he had to find a way to convince Charles that Tweeddale's talents could be used to benefit the crown, that he could be another Lord Ashley, that useful little man who had once supported Cromwell and was now Charles's chancellor of the exchequer in England. By an ironic and happy accident the solution, unbeknownst to Lauderdale, was at hand.

104 Paton, 'Lauderdale', pp. 121–25. 20 Mar. 1660, Lauderdale to Richard Baxter, *Bulletin of John Rylands Library* 10 (1925), pp. 528–30.
105 BL Add. Mss 23115, ff. 77, 107. See also their letter of 21 Mar. 1661, also signed by Rothes, giving Lauderdale advice as to how to make good his claim to the lordship of Musselburgh; NLS Ms. 577, f. 19. Lauderdale was successful; 13 Apr., Rothes to Lauderdale, BL Add. Mss 23116, f. 22. Lennox, *Lauderdale and Scotland*, p. 176.
106 18 Nov. 1661, Tweeddale to Lauderdale, BL Add. Mss 23116, f. 157.

CHAPTER TWO

The Triumvirate Forged, 1663

I

One of the major consequences of the billeting episode was the calling of a new session of parliament. The billeting legislation was the law of the land; it had received the approval of Lord Commissioner Middleton, acting – improperly, Lauderdale had argued – in the king's name. What parliament had done parliament had to undo, and also prohibit billeting for the future. Furthermore, the king wanted it publicly demonstrated that he had been misled: there was to be an investigation into all the circumstances surrounding the passage of that unfortunate piece of legislation. Parliament therefore met, after the usual postponements, on 18 June 1663, with the new lord commissioner, Rothes, in the chair.

Rothes was not to manage this session alone, however. Lauderdale was there as well. Whether the initiative for this assignment came originally from him or the king is unknown, but Lauderdale had many reasons for wishing to be present. He had not seen Scotland for twelve years. He wanted to meet people he did not know: members of parliament, lairds and burgesses especially, many of whom must have voted to billet him, some noblemen, minor officials, lawyers, clergy. If he was to become Charles's chief agent for Scottish affairs he needed to build a constituency, to find out who might be useful and who would not. His estates needed looking after. And he did not trust Rothes with the agenda, especially the inquiry into the billeting scandal. On the other hand, there were dangers in leaving the king's side. Middleton and Newburgh were still in London, intriguing to recover favour, and they could count on Clarendon's support. To counter them Lauderdale had to rely on his secretary-depute, Sir Robert Moray, who was absolutely dependable and the king's good friend. How keen Moray was to undertake this job, which was bound to be delicate, difficult and time-consuming, is hard to know. It meant getting more involved in Scottish politics; Moray had given up his positions as justice-clerk and a lord of session, and obviously planned to remain permanently in London. His little house in the privy gardens at Whitehall was close to the rooms where the king established his own laboratory. On the other hand, having been billeted, Moray had a score to settle with Middleton. So he agreed to act as Lauderdale's deputy, a position he would hold until he had a falling-out with Lauderdale in 1672. One of his rewards was £1,000 sterling from the Scottish excise.[1]

In order to forestall any possible trouble Lauderdale and Rothes revived the pre-revolutionary method of selecting the Committee of the Articles, not used since 1633 on account of the absence of the bishops. But they revived it with a wrinkle, to make their grip as secure as possible. As in 1633, the noblemen elected the eight bishops, and the bishops elected the eight noblemen, which, given the character of the episcopate, would create, along with the eight officers of state, a solidly pro-government phalanx. In 1633 the whole body of bishops and nobles then chose the representatives of the other two estates; now, the sixteen already elected to the committee served as electors. Short of direct royal nomination it is hard to imagine a surer way of getting a committee which would obediently follow the government's lead, as Lauderdale pointed out in a letter he drafted and Rothes signed on 31 July. Charles, Moray had written, was well satisfied with the way parliament had begun, and so he should have been.[2]

The king's letter, read at the opening of parliament, praised the loyalty and zeal of the members, but indicated that some of the actions of the previous session were 'very far from our intention', especially billeting. Charles wanted the Act rescinded and billeting prohibited in the future. The matter was referred to the Articles, which appointed a six-man committee headed by Lauderdale. It was empowered to collect facts and documents and put witnesses on oath, report and await the king's orders. The earl of Dumfries, Middleton's principal supporter in the parliament, attempted to block the authorisation of the committee on the floor, but could muster only eleven other votes. Nor could Middleton and Newburgh persuade the king to delay the inquiry.[3] The committee's investigation took time, and was delayed when Lauderdale fell ill in mid-July.[4] It did its work carefully. Tarbat was the chief witness. He admitted to carrying out Middleton's instructions on billeting, but argued that he was only following

1 BL Add. Mss 23119, f. 31. 4 June 1663, *Warrant Book 1660–1670*, NAS GD 90/2/260, no pagination. *Moray Letters*, intro., pp. 25–26.

2 *APS* VII, p. 449. BL Add. Mss 23119, ff. 144–45. 18 June 1663, W. Sharp to Moray, 25 June, Moray to Lauderdale, 25 June, Crawford to Lauderdale, BL Add. Mss 23119, ff. 44, 54–55, 56–57. Crawford, a principled royalist as well as a principled Presbyterian, approved of the change.

3 *APS* VII, pp. 450–51. BL Add. Mss 23119, ff. 29–30. 27 June, 9 July 1663, Lauderdale to Moray, 3 July, Moray to Lauderdale, BL Add. Mss 23119, ff. 59, 67, 78.

4 14 July 1663, Lauderdale to Moray, BL Add. Mss 23119, f. 88.

orders, 'and so dared neither mix my own knowledge nor judgment with his commands'.[5] Lauderdale found this defence scandalous, and wondered why a man who had so abused the king was allowed to remain in parliament; it seems that Tarbat's blindsiding of the secretary in 1662 still rankled. Other witnesses testified that what Middleton's people wanted was that Lauderdale, Moray, Crawford, Cassillis and Duffus be billeted, and that the secret ballot was used in order to avoid naming Lauderdale in public.

At the end of July the committee's report, along with all the depositions it had taken, was sent to Charles. It was accompanied by a series of letters, from Lauderdale and Rothes to Charles, and Rothes to Moray, indicating how they hoped the king would react. Rothes emphasised that Moray, in reporting orally to Charles, should underline the culpability of Middleton and Tarbat. They should lose their positions – Middleton was still commander-in-chief and captain of Edinburgh Castle – and, for good measure, Newburgh should be fired as captain of the guard. Lauderdale agreed. He wrote to Charles that Middleton and Tarbat could be convicted of leasing-making, but losing their positions he thought punishment enough. He urged Charles to give Rothes Newburgh's command. He also stressed the role of Lennox as a promoter of the scheme; as he put it in his summary, Lennox and Newburgh 'are proven by divers witnesses upon oath to have solicited in your majesty's name what your majesty disowns'. Glencairn also was singled out. He had not cooperated with the committee, and if he had opposed the plan in the Articles in 1662, it would never have been adopted. But neither Lennox nor Glencairn should be punished, though the king might wish to ask his cousin Lennox who persuaded him to behave as he did. Parliament unanimously approved the report, with three of Middleton's few supporters, Dumfries, Morton (Middleton's son-in-law) and Aboyne not voting. Rothes in his covering letter urged the king to send his reply promptly, since parliament had been in session for some time, and the harvest was under way. It should end soon: the high cost of living in Edinburgh was burdensome to the members, and until it ended people might feel unsettled, fearing that still more change might be planned.[6]

---

5 NLS Ms. 597, f. 91.

6 For Lauderdale's and Rothes's letters of 31 July 1663 see BL Add. Mss 23119, ff. 140–47. Rothes's letter was drafted by Lauderdale. Lauderdale's letters to Moray are in BL Add. Mss 23119, ff. 72 ff.; see especially that of 21 July, ff. 99–100. For Tarbat's depositions see BL Add. Mss 23119, ff. 111, 122, 125, and Mackenzie, *Memoirs*, pp. 118–21, 124–28. Lauderdale's summary is in BL Add. Mss 23120, ff. 102–06.

Sir William Bruce arrived at court with the reports and the letters on 5 August. Moray did not expect Charles to act in haste: Lauderdale and Rothes had been circumspect in their recommendations, and Charles was still reluctant to be too hard on Middleton. Moray nevertheless pressed for a quick answer, even pursuing the king to Tunbridge Wells; Charles put him off. Clarendon was going on holiday for a month, Moray wrote, and Middleton was going with him, which made Moray nervous. Finally, on 20 August, Charles approved Moray's draft letter. Middleton would be laid aside, but not before the king had given him a hearing, after parliament was over and Lauderdale and Rothes could both be present. The 'lenity and tenderness of his way of proceeding' exasperated Moray, but he assured Lauderdale that Middleton was finished. He urged Lauderdale to dig into Middleton's record as commander of his troop of horse: financial irregularities could persuade Charles to deprive him of that command as well.[7] Bruce was finally dispatched with the king's answers, in which he expressed his satisfaction that the inquiry had ended without any effort to ruin anyone. On 9 September parliament at last voted to repeal the billeting legislation and order it razed from the parliamentary record. The next day Lauderdale wrote the king a cheerful note announcing the result, 'being the day after Saint Billeting's day'. According to the diarists John Lamont and John Nicoll there was much division of opinion. But in his letter to the king Lauderdale said nothing of that.[8]

The billeting inquiry took almost two months to conclude. In the meantime Lauderdale had to deal with the two issues on which he had previously confronted Clarendon, the polity of the church and the nature of the Scottish military establishment. The first was by far the more dangerous. Since Lauderdale had opposed the immediate reestablishment of episcopacy, he was suspect to Clarendon and the resurgent Anglican leadership, and to the Scottish bishops as well. The latter had been urging the authorities to crack down on nonconformists of all sorts, both Presbyterian and Popish. There was resistance, especially in the west. Civil authority apparently collapsed in Kirkcudbright early in 1663, when a rioting mob, mostly female, kept the conforming minister out of his church. On 5 May 1663 the privy council ordered a number of Kirkcudbright men held in the

---

7 Moray's letters to Lauderdale from 4 to 21 Aug. 1663 describe his efforts to get the king to act; BL Add. Mss 23119, ff. 152 ff. The quotation is from the letter of 21 Aug., ff. 173–75.

8 *APS* VII, pp. 471–72. Nicoll, *Diary*, p. 395. Lamont, *Diary*, p. 162. BL Add. Mss 23120, f. 10. 7 Sept. 1663, Moray to Lauderdale, BL Add. Mss 23120, ff. 8–9.

Edinburgh tolbooth until they produced their wives, and sent the earl of Linlithgow, Middleton's second-in-command, to the town with 200 foot and 100 horse, at a cost to the citizenry of £22 10s sterling a day. This was an early instance of what was to become, intermittently, the practice of the next few years: the quartering of troops on religious dissidents in order to enforce conformity. Lauderdale's circle thought that the council had over-reacted. 'There are many ways to break an egg without a hammer,' William Sharp commented to Lauderdale's brother Halton. So, indeed, did Sir James Turner, a captain in the foot guards. 'This inconsiderable and almost ridiculous tumult made a great noise at court, as if the whole Scots army were about to enter England . . . on account of the Covenant.' But the king approved, and wanted the rioters punished.[9] Like the administration in Edinburgh, Charles and the people around him were very nervous about possible uprisings by partisans of the Good Old Cause.

Linlithgow restored order in Kirkcudbright and installed a new set of magistrates, who found caution in the amount of 18,000 merks that they would keep order and protect the bishop of Galloway and the conforming ministers. On 9 June the commission sent to Kirkcudbright reported to the council that it had examined a number of women. Five were to be brought to Edinburgh to prison and fourteen more imprisoned locally until they could find £100 sterling caution for good behaviour. They also arrested Lord Kirkcudbright and the most recent provost, who was ultimately banished. Two men were heavily fined; the five women were ordered to stand for two hours on two different market days 'with a paper on their faces bearing their fault', on pain of whipping and banishment if they refused. Lord Kirkcudbright pleaded bad health and avoided an appearance before the council.[10] Rioting townspeople were not the government's only concern. A determined landowner could be equally difficult. While he was on his pacifying mission to Kirkcudbright, Linlithgow wrote to William Gordon, laird of Earlston, ordering him, as patron of the parish of Dalry, to admit a minister picked by the bishop. Gordon refused, on the ground that such an action would not only violate his rights but also be an affront to God. Furthermore, he had already admitted a minister. His defi-

9 7 May 1663, Sharp to Halton, BL Add. Mss 23119, f. 26. 23 May, Charles to the council, NAS GD 90/2/260, p. 29. The quotation from Turner's memoirs is in R.A. Lee, *Government and Politics in Scotland, 1661–1681* (PhD diss., University of Glasgow, 1995), p. 160.

10 *RPCS* I, pp. 357–59, 365, 372–76, 390, 398–99, 401–02. In October the council had to order Linlithgow to send 160 soldiers back to Kirkcudbright. *RPCS* I, pp. 446–47.

ance continued. Early in 1664 the council banished him for holding conventicles, one of which had met in his mother's house.[11]

The problem, as Lauderdale described it, was that the religious legislation of 1662 was not comprehensive enough. It restored the rights of bishops and patrons, but did not serve to get the recalcitrant to go to church. The west was the problem area. Middleton's trip there after the 1662 parliament 'was only a flaunting and a feasting journey', and simply made matters worse by extruding recalcitrant ministers without providing adequate replacements.[12] Lauderdale hoped that 'penalties will be stronger arguments to move them to outward conformity than any divines could use'. Lauderdale's policy after he achieved virtually unfettered authority in Scotland suggests that he did not believe this: it was an argument designed to appeal to the dominant conservative Anglicans in London. So he saw to it that one of the first actions of the new parliament was to reaffirm the ecclesiastical legislation of 1662 and add a new Act against conventicles that was similar to the bill being considered in the English parliament at the same time. People who did not attend their parish church were considered seditious and could be heavily fined. The Presbyterian historian James Kirkton labelled this Act 'the bishops' dragnet': it cost people more money than 'any Act ever made in Scotland since King Fergus'. There was little opposition; Burnet mentions only Kincardine, 'who was an enemy to all persecution'.[13] Lauderdale, who described the legislation to the king as 'the most effectual Act for the settlement of the church which has yet been made', made a major speech before the vote, endorsing parliament's previous legislation on behalf of the church, including specifically the Act Rescissory, and apologised for his former support of the Covenant, which, he said, was both wrong and unlawful. All the bishops, he added, thanked him for his speech.[14] A week later Moray wrote that Charles was very pleased with the church legislation, and with his speech, as was Archbishop Sheldon. He quoted Charles as saying, 'Sure nobody that repines at church

---

11 Wodrow, *History* I, pp. 181–84, 215.

12 10 July 1663, Lauderdale to Moray, BL Add. Mss 23119, f. 82. This letter was for the king's eyes. On the same day he wrote Moray a shorter note asking for his Hebrew Bible and 'the little glasses of spirit of roses which you will find in the middle drawer of my walnut tree cabinet'. BL Add. Mss 23119, f. 83.

13 *APS* VII, pp. 455–56. Burnet, *History* I, pp. 352–53. Kirkton, *History*, p. 97. 14 July 1663, Lauderdale to Moray, BL Add. Mss 23119, f. 88. This letter was also intended for the king. The English Conventicle Act was not finally enacted until 1664.

14 13 July 1663, Lauderdale to Charles, BL Add. Mss 23119, ff. 86–87.

government will reckon you of his side.'[15] Lauderdale had buried his Covenanting past.

There was further evidence of the secretary's new-found zeal for orthodoxy. He had already seen to it that the two archbishops became privy councillors; they were admitted on 15 June, just before parliament began, along with his brother Halton.[16] On 7 August parliament enacted that all public officials had until 11 November to sign the declaration denouncing the Covenant adopted in the last parliament. Burgesses who refused to sign as a way of avoiding public office would lose their rights as burgesses, a clause included, Lauderdale explained, because some western burghs are 'extremely disaffected'. The earl of Dumfries and some others wanted the oath extended to all heritors. Lauderdale, who regarded the suggestion as an effort to make mischief, an 'ill service for the king and worse for the bishops', publicly wondered why they had not shown equal zeal in 1662 when their friend Middleton was in charge, and killed it on the ground that amendments from the floor were not permitted. The Act was then passed. Charles agreed that Dumfries was acting maliciously and 'raking a dunghill', but thought that the requirement might be extended to those entering the ministry; Moray explained that that was unnecessary. The principal victim of the Act was Crawford, who had already resigned as treasurer. On 4 June 1663 Rothes replaced him. The king admired Crawford's stubborn adherence to principle, a quality Charles conspicuously lacked, and continued to show him favour. Crawford was not a 'Worcester Scot', but Charles treated him like one. As a senior official Crawford had remained behind when Charles led his army to its fate. Monck captured him during the mopping-up after Worcester and sent him to England where, like Lauderdale, he spent the 1650s in prison. Charles did not forget that.[17]

There was further religious legislation. The commission to evaluate teinds which Charles I had established was revived, with the usual provision that heritors could buy up their own obligations within three years of valuation. The Act of 1661 giving the court of session the power to review excommuni-

15 21–23 July 1663, Moray to Lauderdale, BL Add. Mss 23119, f. 101.
16 *RPCS* I, pp. 380–83.
17 *APS* VII, pp. 462–63. 31 July 1663, Rothes to Charles, 8 Aug., Lauderdale to Moray, 23 Aug., Moray to Lauderdale, BL Add. Mss 23119, ff. 147, 159, 182. Two judges of the court of session, Dalrymple of Stair and Dundas of Arniston, also refused to sign the declaration and were dismissed. In April 1664 Stair decided to comply. He was reinstated and in June became a baronet.

cations was repealed, on the ground that it was prejudicial to the authority of the bishops. If a parish had no manse, the heritors had to provide one, and repair those that were dilapidated. The rules for holding a meeting of the General Assembly, now called the National Synod, were established: the archbishop of St Andrews would preside, the royal commissioner would be present, it could consider only those matters the king set before it, and it could adopt nothing contrary to law or the royal prerogative, provisions which, in Burnet's view, made it unlikely that there would ever be any pressure for a meeting, and in fact it never met. On the other hand parliament did levy a tax on the clergy for the next five years to help fund the universities, and the stipends of vacant parishes in the bishoprics of Argyll and the Isles were earmarked for scholarships to train ministers who had the Gaelic. The University of Glasgow, which in January had petitioned the council for help, got £600 sterling from the accumulated stipends of vacant parishes to pay its debts, and, as a sop to Sabbatarians, royal burghs were not to hold markets on Saturday or Monday to avoid Sunday travel.[18] Archbishop Sharp's calculations had proved correct: Lauderdale had become a convert to episcopal polity. What parliament could do, parliament had done. What remained now was the question of enforcement.

Lauderdale's second major project was to make it clear to those in London who disliked the removal of the English garrisons that he was not opposed to the existence of a Scottish armed force. At the same time the cost of maintaining the existing forces had to be reduced. The two troops of horse and six companies of foot cost £32,000 sterling a year, and Middleton got an additional grant of £30,000. These authorisations, 'of which,' wrote Rothes, 'neither I nor his majesty's secretary know anything,' had to be withdrawn, Middleton removed as commander-in-chief, 'a place which never was in Scotland in time of peace', and his troop of horse disbanded. These recommendations were contained in a long set of instructions to Moray dated 31 July: Rothes signed the document as commissioner, but the draft is in Lauderdale's hand.[19]

Lauderdale's solution was to create a 'moderate country militia' once Middleton was removed from his office of captain-general, which gave him authority over the militia as well as the regular troops. (Moray rather irritably informed Lauderdale that he had discovered this fact from reading

18 *APS* VII, pp. 465, 474–76, 478, 481, 491, 498, 502. *RPCS* I, pp. 322, 353–54. Burnet, *History* I, pp. 353–54.
19 BL Add. Mss 23119, ff. 144–45.

Lauderdale's register; the secretary had not mentioned it either to him or to the king.) Parliament had empowered Charles to raise a militia in 1661, but nothing had been done. Once it was in place, Rothes and Lauderdale hoped, the companies of foot could be reduced. The English militia regulations were sent north for Lauderdale to consider in drawing up those for Scotland. On 23 September parliament authorised a militia of 20,000 foot and 2,000 horse, with the numbers to be raised in each shire spelled out, and without cancelling the ancient obligation of all men between sixteen and sixty to turn out if summoned. Traditionally the militia's function was to defend the nation against attack, but now parliament granted the king the right to use it anywhere in his three kingdoms, against either foreign invasion or domestic disturbance. The king, who in the preliminary discussions had laid great weight on this clause, which was bound to be provocative, told Lauderdale and Rothes to include it in a separate statement, which would be printed, if they wished; they decided to put it in the text of the Act. Moray reported that the king 'was pleased with all of his heart' at the result, but this clause was, predictably, alarming to many people in England, who did not relish the prospect of yet another Scottish invasion. Burnet in his *History*, written after his admiration for Lauderdale had turned to bitter hostility, echoed these fears: Lauderdale, he wrote, had shown the king how to set up an arbitrary government in England should he wish to do so. For the moment, however, the Act was not implemented, in spite of the urgings of Treasurer-Depute Bellenden; the coming of the Dutch war necessitated expansion of the army instead.[20]

Lauderdale's agenda did not end there. There were pocketbook issues. Charles did not request a new tax, but he was insistent that arrears of cess be collected. There was the codification of the various statutes that dealt with the collection of the king's rents. The complicated and vexing problem of debt, especially aristocratic debt, gave rise to a commission to consider the claims of the creditors of those landowners whose estates had been confiscated during the troubles. The long list of debtors included most of the great men of the land, Hamilton, Crawford, Lauderdale, even Middleton. The commission could cancel as much as eight years' interest; any cases it could not resolve were to be referred to the privy council. There had been complaints that more was being collected in excise taxes than the

---

20 *APS* VII, pp. 480–81. 31 July 1663, Rothes's instructions to Moray, 21 Aug., 6 Oct., Moray to Lauderdale, 20 Feb. 1664, Bellenden to Lauderdale, BL Add. Mss 23119, ff. 144–45, 173–75, 23120, f. 50, 23121, f. 53. Mackenzie, *Memoirs*, pp. 132–33. Burnet, *History* I, pp. 354–55.

£40,000 sterling per year voted by parliament in 1661, and some shires believed that they were paying more than their fair share. So parliament adopted a revised list of payments for the country as a whole.[21]

The protectionist policies of the English government provoked retaliation. A duty of 80 per cent was levied on English goods. Beyond that, a duty of 20 per cent was placed on a list of foreign manufactures in order to encourage domestic production, provided that domestic producers found surety to produce the goods at prices comparable to the cost of the imports. A swingeing duty of £3 per boll was placed on Irish corn at the behest of the western shire representatives. Parliament encouraged the export of grain, which was to be duty-free unless prices rose to famine levels. Raw materials for Scottish manufactures could be imported duty-free, as could books. Aquavit and beer could not be imported at all, save by Shetlanders, who were allowed to import beer. The export of money was forbidden, save for a £60 allowance for travellers, unless the would-be exporter could demonstrate that his business required it.[22] The king, Moray reported, was not happy about the levy on English goods, 'which startles people here much'. He told some MPs that it was unfair to legislate in favour of a few graziers and saltmakers at the expense of the common welfare. But, Moray thought, he would probably allow the duties to take effect, since another clause in the Act empowered him to remove them if he wished. This clause pleased the king: it was more than the English parliament had granted him. Moray explained to Charles that the issue of Anglo-Scottish trade was an old one, going back to the time of King James, and induced Charles to agree to suspend judgment until after the parliament had ended. So, wrote Moray to the secretary, be prepared to discuss this matter when you return.[23] Perhaps prompted by Moray's comment, Lauderdale and Rothes, in the parliament's final days, had it reaffirm the crown's prerogative respecting foreign trade. The Act, wrote Mackenzie, was passed 'in a trice, without any opposition', and later served as the basis for gifts of monopolies of the importation of such valuable goods as brandy and tobacco. The parliament, Mackenzie concluded in hindsight, had 'burdened the country'.[24] Mackenzie was right

21 *APS* VII, pp. 468–94. 23 Aug. 1663, Moray to Rothes, NLS Ms. 597, f. 98. 18 July, Lauderdale to Moray, BL Add. Mss 23119, f. 93. Lee, *Government and Politics*, p. 110.

22 *APS* VII, pp. 452, 458, 463, 465–66, 469–71, 476. 8 Aug. 1663, Lauderdale to Moray, BL Add. Mss 23119, f. 159. A boll was about six bushels.

23 23 Aug., 7 Sept. 1663, Moray to Lauderdale, BL Add. Mss 23119, f. 182, 23120, ff. 8–9.

24 *APS* VII, pp. 503–04. Mackenzie, *Memoirs*, pp. 133–34.

in one sense: parliament's economic legislation was designed to benefit producers rather than either traders or consumers.

The Act of 1662 limiting the crown's power to pardon the descendants of traitors, which Charles had so much disliked, was repealed and recast: such children were disabled from holding lands and offices unless the king decided otherwise.[25] Another Act of that year, 'that strange act', Lauderdale called it, which gave new and unusual powers to the Lord Lyon, was also repealed. For good measure the incumbent, Sir Alexander Durham of Largo, Middleton's brother-in-law, whose accounts as collector of the excise were the subject of considerable discussion, was replaced by one of Lauderdale's many cousins, Charles Erskine, the younger brother of the impecunious earl of Kellie. This was an indication of how the political winds had shifted, and, indeed, of the great power of the commissioner: Lauderdale commented that the Act in favour of the Lord Lyon had passed unanimously in 1662 and was overturned unanimously in 1663. Of course, he added, Dumfries and three of his allies, 'that considerable cabal', were not there.[26]

The chief beneficiary of the king's restored power to pardon was Lauderdale's nephew Lord Lorne. He was released from Edinburgh Castle in June – he had been there since his conviction for leasing-making in 1662 – and, later in the summer, restored to his lands and title of earl (not marquess) of Argyll. He was awash in debt, not only his own but also those of the Huntly estates which his father had acquired. In addition parliament saddled him with a payment of over £43,000 to the marquess of Montrose. The king allowed him an income of £15,000 a year, and his brother and sister each got something. The rest, not much, said Burnet, was left to his creditors.[27] It is not surprising that Argyll's chief preoccupation over the next decade was the restoration of the depleted Campbell fortune. Lauderdale supported his kinsman in his rapacity, which was noteworthy even by Campbell standards, and in return received the earl's political support, at the cost of having to put up with myriad letters of complaint written in Argyll's round, sprawling, illegible hand.

25 APS VII, pp. 463–64.
26 APS VII, p. 458. 21 July 1663, Lauderdale to Moray, BL Add. Mss 23119, f. 93.
27 APS VII, p. 499. RPCS I, pp. 380–83. 25 June 1664, Argyll to Lauderdale, Argyll Letters, pp. 3–6, Nicoll, Diary, p. 403. A.I. Macinnes, Clanship, Commerce and the House of Stuart, 1603–1788 (East Linton, 1996), pp. 134–36. D. Stevenson, Alasdair MacColla and the Highland Problem in the 17th Century (Edinburgh, 1980), p. 279.

II

The above summary by no means exhausts the recorded activities of parliament, which cover more than seventy pages in the printed *Acts*. Lauderdale's workload was enormous. In addition to managing parliament, including the committee investigating the billeting, he was a member of the privy council, which he attended for the first time on 15 June. The council met with some regularity during the parliamentary session, and was far from idle. Its most important actions concerned refractory clergymen. Ministers who had acquired their parishes after 1649 and had not complied with the law on presentation and collation were in effect holding illegal conventicles. They were ordered to vacate within twenty days and not reside within twenty miles of any cathedral city, including Edinburgh, or within three miles of any royal burgh on pain of being charged with sedition, a requirement more severe than the later English Five Mile Act. Ministers who were in their parishes before 1649 were ordered to attend their diocesan synods, on pain of prosecution for contempt of royal authority. Four ministers in the west who had been holding illegal conventicles were to be pursued at law.[28] Parliamentary enactments would not remain a dead letter.

Lauderdale had another obligation: he had to keep the king informed. It was crucial that he do so – he knew that others would write, and he had to be sure that Charles saw the activities of parliament and council from the proper angle. The letters, some to the king directly but mostly to Moray, had to be very full. 'It is fit,' Moray reminded him, 'that every particular be under your hand, that your letters put together may make up a complete story: remember this.'[29] The king paid attention and read the letters, 'every word, as he useth to do.'[30] And 'He leaves all other things to do it as soon as they are presented to him, except it be at his dinner.'[31] So much for the myth that Charles neglected the business of government. Very early on, he did historians a considerable service. 'The first thing the king said upon his opening your relation of what passed in parliament was ... that if you write not upon better paper and with better pens we will have you billeted again.'[32] The letters were to be printed, so Lauderdale was told to compose them accordingly and try to have them arrive 'on Wednesday before

---

28 *RPCS* I, pp. 396–97, 403–04.
29 BL Add. Mss 23119, f. 182.
30 Ibid., f. 80.
31 Ibid., f. 61.
32 Ibid., f. 54. Moray wrote this on 25 June 1663. Lauderdale complied.

dinner, so the Thursday's journals will always have all that is fit to publish' – it took approximately four and a half days for a dispatch to arrive by ordinary post, one day less by express. For 'any thing he [Charles] needs not know, put it in little billets apart'.[33] Moray's letters were equally numerous. At first he tried using a cipher, but Lauderdale complained that he could not understand 'any of what you have written in this cipher', and in any event it was unnecessary.[34] This cornucopia of communication is, like Lauderdale's upgraded pens and paper, a boon to historians. We have a virtually day-to-day account of the doings of this parliament.

Though he professed not to be, Lauderdale worried that in his absence his enemies might get the king's ear. Shortly after he arrived in Edinburgh Rothes told him that 'great brags' were circulating, having been sent up from London, that 'his Majesty was never kinder to my Lord Middleton'. Lauderdale wanted Moray to tell Charles all this: it was a ploy to make trouble for the new managers of parliament. 'I am sure,' Lauderdale added, 'he [Charles] will not let me be bit to death by a duck.'[35] In July he was vexed that 'it was talked in London that I spoke impertinently of my Lord Duke of Albemarle [Monck] and that we are here endeavouring a charge against my Lord Chancellor of England. These are damned insipid lies. If liars will needs lie, why do they not colour them better?'[36] A week later he was shrugging off the earl of Bristol's silly attack on him in the House of Lords – Bristol might 'remember the House of Peers hath no power to examine in Scotland'.[37] One of his countermeasures was to organise the creation of a commission to investigate possible cases of bribery during Middleton's administration, a move welcomed by the recently resigned Lord Treasurer Crawford. There were the Lord Lyon's questionable accounts, for example, and Sir John Fletcher, the lord advocate, had been accused of asking for a kickback from the master of a seized foreign ship in return for its release. Moray stressed the importance of digging up as much financial dirt as possible. There was plenty to be found: Middleton and his friends, including his brother-in-law the Lord Lyon, had used their positions to pocket large sums of money.[38]

---

33 Ibid. Moray was careful to see that the reports were printed; see, e.g., 31 Aug. 1663, W. Godolphin to Joseph Williamson, *CSPD 1663–64*, p. 260.

34 23 June 1663, Lauderdale to Moray, BL Add. Mss 23119, ff. 51–52.

35 Ibid.

36 14 July 1663, Lauderdale to Moray, BL Add. Mss 23119, f. 88.

37 Ibid., f. 99. Moray told Lauderdale that Charles found Bristol's accusations ridiculous; ibid., f. 91.

38 13 July 1663, Lauderdale to Charles, 31 July, Rothes's instructions, 21 Aug., Moray to Lauderdale, ibid., ff. 86–87, 144–45, 173–75. For Fletcher see 26 Jan. 1663, Lauderdale to Gilmour, Paton, 'Gilmour', pp. 147–48. For Middleton's looting see Lee, *Government and Politics*, pp. 107–09, 157.

Lauderdale felt overburdened. 'No dog leads so busy a life,' he wrote early in July. 'Torment of visitors in crowds, not companies, and incessant meetings. No sleep nor time to write and nothing like recreation makes me a very slave . . . I am perfectly dazed.'[39] Virtually every letter was written late at night, and ended with an expression of exhaustion. 'God send me once to Whitehall again,' he concluded on 7 July – and asked Moray to send him his spectacles.[40] Private matters also took up time, especially completing the sale of the superiority of Leith to the town government of Edinburgh. In mid-July he took to his bed for three days with stomach problems, and had to be let blood.[41] His nominal superior, Lord Commissioner Rothes, sometimes let his mind wander. In mid-August he wrote to Sir William Bruce, then in London, wanting to know if silver lace was in fashion, and asking for information about 'all the fashions of habits that is [*sic*] now most in request at Court'.[42]

Early in July, when parliament had been in session for almost three weeks and Lauderdale was preparing the Act against conventicles which was to pass on 10 July, he received a new requirement from Charles, one which was unexpected, unprecedented and thoroughly unwelcome. 'The first thing his Majesty said to me,' wrote Moray on 2 July, 'was that there was a paper presented to him (which he put into my hand) wherein it was desired that Contract of the D. of Monmouth's marriage might be confirmed by an Act of Parliament in the terms you see in the copy of the paper, the original whereof is to be sent to my Lord Commissioner enclosed in a letter his Majesty commanded me to draw for his hand. He said the thing is perhaps not necessary, yet abundance of law does not break it. You will soon see what is to be done in the case.'[43]

Lauderdale and Rothes were aghast. The proposal was dynamite. They both knew all about that contract. They had been involved in drawing it up in the previous winter, Rothes as one of his niece the duchess's curators, Lauderdale because the king had designated him and Sir John Gilmour, the president of the court of session, to represent Monmouth's interests: the boy had no curators because he had no property. They knew that the

---

39 BL Add. Mss 23119, f. 69.

40 Ibid., f. 72.

41 Ibid., f. 88. For the superiority of Leith see above, chap. 1, fn. 31.

42 Rothes's letters, dated 6 and 13 Aug.1663, are in NAS GD 29/1896/4–5.

43 BL Add. Mss 23119, ff. 65–66. For a detailed treatment of what follows see M. Lee Jr, 'The Buccleuch Marriage Contract: An Unknown Episode in Scottish Politics', in *'Inevitable' Union*, pp. 223–45.

contract violated Scots law because it shattered the entail drawn up by Earl Francis, the duchess's father, which directed that the estate was to pass to his sister, the countess of Tweeddale, Duchess Anna's aunt, should she die childless. The contract stated that in that event Monmouth and his heirs, not Lady Tweeddale, would inherit – all of his heirs, not only his children from a subsequent marriage, but also, if he had none, whoever his heir might be: presumably his father the king. There was a further consideration. The entail specified that should a female heir attempt to alter its terms, she would immediately forfeit the estate. The contract thus jeopardised Duchess Anna's possession of the property once she reached her majority and Lady Tweeddale could take her to court. There was far more at stake here, however, than the rights of Lady Tweeddale. If she could be arbitrarily deprived of her property rights, whose property was safe? Every landholder in Scotland had a stake in the outcome. They might well baulk at voting to ratify the contract, itself an unprecedented proposal: no contract of marriage between subjects had ever been presented to parliament before. Lauderdale knew that, if Charles insisted, he would have to deliver the ratification. All of his good work in the parliamentary session, all of Charles's repeated expressions of pleasure at how well things were going, would come to nothing if Lauderdale failed in this. He knew how the king doted on his beautiful boy.

Rothes and Lauderdale worked very hard to get the king to change his mind. The lawyers were their best hope. On 14 July the unanimous opinion of the judges of the court of session went to Charles. In Lauderdale's paraphrase of the opinion, 'Such an Act could not pass in parliament to make void entails, as to be excepted out of the Act *Salvo juris cuiuslibet* which is the security of subjects in cases of ratifications of private rights.' In other words, parliament had no right to deprive a private individual of his or her legal rights through a private Act of parliament like the proposed ratification. Parliament itself recognised this with the passage of the Act *Salvo*, routinely adopted at the end of every session, giving anyone who believed that a private Act had prejudiced his or her rights the right to sue in court.[44] This proposal was therefore 'most unfit to be pressed by his Majesty'. Lauderdale knew that the originator of the proposal was Anna's mother the countess of Wemyss, who was currently on very chilly terms with her brother Rothes and had little use for Lauderdale – she was the source of the stories that Lauderdale had bad-mouthed Monck and was caballing against

---

44 On this point see R.S. Rait, *The Parliaments of Scotland* (Glasgow, 1924), pp. 449–51.

Clarendon. Lauderdale also knew that Charles did not like her – she was indeed very hard to like. So he hoped that the judges' opinion would 'prevent further importunities upon his Majesty'.[45]

For a few days Charles seemed content to accept the judges' opinion, but he soon brought the matter up again. He may have found Lady Wemyss a tiresome old battleaxe, but in this case they both wanted the same thing. He asked for further explanations, since he knew that the English parliament could break an entail. The Act *Salvo* puzzled him. Parliament had declared in the past that certain of its Acts were excepted from the Act *Salvo*: why could the marriage contract not be excepted? Moray did his best to explain, aided by a stream of letters from Rothes and Lauderdale, but in the end the king insisted. Lauderdale acquiesced, as he had to. On 10 September he wrote to Charles that he and his colleagues could not take action on something 'so positively illegal' without a clear order from him, but now they would proceed.[46] Moray next tried to get the terms of the marriage contract modified, so that if Monmouth as well as Anna should die childless the estate would revert to Lady Tweeddale and her heirs. He failed; the contract was not altered. The only change Moray succeeded in making was in the covering letter containing the king's instructions. It declared that the proposed ratification was not a royal initiative; rather, the king was acting in response to the wishes and advice of persons unspecified. This would save face if parliament declined to ratify the contract – and certainly neither Moray nor Lauderdale nor Rothes thought it impossible that that would happen.[47]

Everything hinged upon Tweeddale. If there was to be opposition to the ratification of the contract, he would have to lead it. If he chose publicly to object to the destruction of his wife's legal rights under her brother's entail, he could make a very strong case. The judges had stood their ground. The marriage contract was legally invalid. Parliamentary ratification could not change that, unless parliament first passed another Act declaring that it had the power to dispose of subjects' property without their consent and contrary to their expressed will. Previous exceptions to the Act *Salvo* involved crown property: that is, the king, in agreeing that a particular

45 7, 14 July 1663, Lauderdale to Moray, 21 July, Moray to Lauderdale, BL Add. Mss 23119, ff. 78, 88, 101–02.
46 BL Add. Mss 23120, f. 12.
47 The course of the discussions in this business can be followed in BL Add. Mss 23119, f. 65 ff., and 23120, f. 12 ff. See also Paton, 'Gilmour', pp. 172 ff.

grant of property could not be challenged under the Act *Salvo*, was acting
to his own prejudice, but he could not prejudice the rights of his subjects
in this way. This opinion, written by Sir John Nisbet, the future lord advocate and Tweeddale's lawyer, and sent to the king, was known to Tweeddale:
there is a copy in his family papers.[48] If Tweeddale made such a case on the
floor of parliament, how likely was it that a body dominated by landowners
would vote to ratify the contract?

Moray was on tenterhooks. The king's instructions provided that if the
contract was not ratified, Rothes was to adjourn parliament rather than
dissolve it, and hasten to court along with Lauderdale, Gilmour, the lord
advocate, and the Buccleuch family lawyers to figure out how to proceed.
If this happened, Moray feared, there would be further hostility aroused
by what would appear to be English dictation. He floated an idea to
Lauderdale: parliament might pass an Act permitting the breaking of an
entail in favour of a royal child who married the heir to an estate with the
consent of the curators. If this were passed before the contract were put to
a vote, there would be no trouble. If the clause restoring Lady Tweeddale
that he had suggested had been inserted, the contract might still have got
through. People could show their loyalty and zeal by voting for it, but 'it
was beyond anyone's thumb to get it done'.[49] Moray's best hope was that
Tweeddale would do nothing. If he could 'find it in his heart' to support the
contract, there was no favour he could not expect from the king. It would
be a greater service to his country and 'a more handsome sacrifice than the
Roman did (I have forgot his name) that saved Rome by leaping into the
Gap'. This wish came at the end of a very long account of the drafting of
the instructions accompanying the Act of ratification. The process took all
day: the king was 'not fully dressed' when they began, and supper was on
the table long before they finished.[50]

What would Tweeddale do? His situation was ticklish. The marriage
between Anna and Monmouth had taken place the previous April; there
was nothing he could do about that. He had gradually been making his way
back into employment. He was a member of the parliamentary committees
to plant kirks, value the teinds and consider the claims of the creditors of
those landowners whose estates had been confiscated during the republican regime; his, of course, had not.[51] In June he was named to a privy

48 It is dated 6 Sept. 1663; NLS Ms. 14543, ff. 218–19.
49 1 Oct. 1663, Moray to Lauderdale, BL Add. Mss 23120, ff. 48–49.
50 28 Sept. 1663, Moray to Lauderdale, ibid., ff. 31–34.
51 *APS* VII, pp. 468–69, 474–76.

council committee to consider the problems of the mint, which was having difficulty gearing up to issue new coins. None had been struck during the republican regime, and at this point in time Lauderdale's brother Halton, who was in charge of the operation of the Edinburgh mint, had been waiting in London for nine months for the new puncheons.[52] By publicly opposing the ratification Tweeddale would wreck his budding political career. On the other hand he had his family to consider. We know what he did, but not why he did it. The records are silent: nothing in his papers, nothing in Lauderdale's, a brief uninformative statement of fact in his *Autobiography*. 'The Act *Salvo* . . . was burthened with an act, and Ratification, past in favours of the Duke and Dutchess of Balcleugh their contract of marriage which was a manifest breach of the entail in favours of the Countess of Tweeddale and her children, which is declared to be no wayes comprehended therin, and then the parliament was dissolved.'[53]

In short, he did nothing. On 5 October parliament ratified the contract, expressly excluded it from the operations of Acts *Salvo* past, present and future, and for good measure prohibited the court of session from hearing any plea against the contract on the ground that it violated the entail,[54] though, presumably, it could hear pleas against it on other grounds: Lauderdale was having a dispute with the Buccleuch estate over the rights to the teinds of the parish of Sheriffhall.[55] The only step Tweeddale took was to absent himself from the formal voting on the final day of the parliament. He had witnesses attest to the fact that he dropped out of the procession and spent the time in the house of a goldsmith named Alexander Reid.[56] He could prove that he had never voted to disinherit his wife and children.

Why did he do what he did? Lauderdale must have worked on him very hard, and perhaps Rothes as well, though Tweeddale was not likely to pay too much attention to Rothes. Moray commented on 21 September that on this issue Lauderdale and Rothes 'I take to be so much one as if [they] were married together.'[57] We do not know what arguments Lauderdale used. The

---

52 *RPCS* I, 384. In December the council had to write to Lauderdale, by then back in Whitehall, to ask that the duplicates of the standard Scottish coins kept at the English mint be sent to them, to get the proportion of precious metal in each right: the specimens in Edinburgh had been lost. *RPCS* I, pp. 465–66. For the coinage of this period see J.D. Bateson, *Coinage in Scotland* (London, 1997), pp. 143–49.

53 Tweeddale, 'Autobiography', p. 91.

54 *APS* VII, pp. 494–95, 526.

55 8 Apr. 1663, Lauderdale to Gilmour, Paton, 'Gilmour', pp. 166–67.

56 NLS Ms. 14543, f. 214.

57 BL Add. Mss 23120, f. 24.

letter he and Rothes wrote to the king announcing their success has
not survived, though we know they wrote one: Rothes prevented Lord
Chancellor Glencairn's express with the announcement of the ratification
from leaving for London until after his had departed.[58] Tweeddale no
doubt made his calculations. Even if he could block the ratification of the
contract, he would ruin himself with Charles. Unless Anna died he had no
hope of any legal redress until she reached her majority, and she was only
twelve. If he acquiesced, Charles would be immensely grateful, and his
political future would be assured. And in fact there was an almost immediate payoff. Four months after the ratification of the contract Charles
adopted the suggestion Moray had made and altered the entail. Should
Anna and Monmouth both die without direct heirs, Lady Tweeddale and
her heirs would inherit the estate as an earldom.[59] Possibly – though this
cannot be proved – Lauderdale held out this hope to Tweeddale.
Contemporaries suspected that promises were made. What they were 'is
not well known nor safe to be inquired into', wrote Gideon Scott of
Haychesters, the author of a remarkable 'Information' on the Buccleuch
family, who detested Tweeddale.[60] Burnet, who admired Tweeddale's intelligence and grasp of public affairs but thought him too cautious and fearful,
wrote that Tweeddale had behaved badly. His 'compliance . . . brought a
great cloud upon him'.[61] But, given what was to happen in the future, it is
difficult to argue that Tweeddale had miscalculated. Anna did not die
young, she did have children, she survived the execution for treason of
her feckless husband, and her descendants are still dukes of Buccleuch.[62]
Tweeddale wanted a political career, and now he had the chance for one.
The king was indeed grateful. Lauderdale's and Rothes's letters, and
Moray's arguments, made him well aware that Tweeddale, by his silence,
had prevented what might have been a nasty political confrontation.
Lauderdale wanted Tweeddale to hurry to London after the parliament,
but he was delayed by a three-cornered family controversy involving the
earl of Callendar and Tweeddale's uncle-cousin Dunfermline, a compulsive
gambler whose financial affairs were in a hopeless tangle. Callendar
had married Dunfermline's widowed mother, who also happened to be

58 *CSPD 1663–64*, p. 291.
59 NLS Ms. 14543, f. 223b. NAS GD 28/1791A. Tweeddale says that the king acted at the suggestion of Gilmour. 'Autobiography', p. 91.
60 NAS GD 157/3079, p. 46. For Haychesters see Lee, *Heiresses*, chs 2–5.
61 Burnet, *History* I, p. 176.
62 For Anna's life after her marriage see Lee, *Heiresses*, chap. 7 and Epilogue.

Tweeddale's father's sister. He and Tweeddale were Dunfermline's creditors and held most of his property in consequence.[63] When Tweeddale finally arrived in London, in January 1664, the king 'gave him as kind a reception as I think he could desire'.[64]

Lauderdale's eagerness to have Tweeddale come to London was understandable. He wanted to cement his and Rothes's unexpectedly easy success with the ratification of the marriage contract. In every way the parliament had been a triumph for both the earls, but especially for Lauderdale. The king's agenda had been passed, the bishops turned into supporters, Middleton dished, the secretary's grip on patronage solidified, and with the development of the militia in prospect, future patronage plums were going to be available. And, by a curious quirk of fate, the marriage contract, which might have been a disaster, became an enormous asset. Rothes and Lauderdale knew that the king was so emotionally involved in this issue that if they had failed to deliver, all their previous good work would have counted for nothing in Charles's eyes. But there had been no difficulty, and everyone knew why: Tweeddale. Lauderdale's smart, ambitious cousin, had, most improbably, become a political asset, his Cromwellian past and his occasional flashes of discontent with the king's policy overlooked in a wave of royal gratitude. The king's effusive reception of Tweeddale was all that Lauderdale, as well as Tweeddale, could wish. Lauderdale had found his Edinburgh agent.

Once the king's final instructions on the contract arrived in Edinburgh, parliamentary action was brisk, but the preliminary discussions had taken time. The session had lasted about a month longer than Rothes and Lauderdale had originally hoped. Members were impatient, and in October petitioned that all legal actions pending against them be suspended, on the ground that they had had no time to look after their own affairs.[65] Rothes and Lauderdale were eager for parliament to end and, as they put it in the July instructions for Moray, that 'this kingdom return to the good old form of government by his Majesty's privy council and all suits at law be decided by the Session'. There had been too many parliaments since the beginning

---

63 10, 26 Nov., 10 Dec. 1663, W. Sharp to Lauderdale, 18 Nov., Dunfermline to Lauderdale (offering to let Lauderdale arbitrate between him and Tweeddale), BL Add. Mss 23120, ff. 68, 81, 91, 123. In January 1663 Rothes had written to Sir William Bruce from Whitehall that Dunfermline was expected at court, 'which made the gamesters here hug themselves for joy, and all ways enquired of me if he was loaded with money'. NAS GD 29/1896/1.
64 7 Jan. 1664, Lauderdale to Gilmour, Paton, 'Gilmour', pp. 178–79.
65 *APS* VII, App., p. 99.

of the troubles in 1637, and three sessions in the last three years. 'The people will never think the king's government peacefully settled nor themselves secured from changes . . . until this Parliament be at an end.' And, if another parliament should be necessary, the king would control it through the Committee of the Articles and his veto: 'the king is absolute master in Parliament both of the negative and affirmative.'[66] Dissolving it, and not calling it again for a while, would make it perfectly clear that, whatever the case in England might be, parliament was not necessary for governing Scotland.

Both Lauderdale and Rothes knew that government by council and session was a myth. The king made decisions, with the advice of whoever he chose. For now that was still Clarendon. Middleton's errors had made it impossible for Clarendon to save his favoured Scottish agent, but Moray's accounts of the discussions of the marriage contract made it clear that Clarendon's intervention had been decisive at several points. Small wonder that Lauderdale was anxious to get back to Whitehall, where he could use his own considerable powers of persuasion on the king. Rothes was a rival: lord commissioner, lord treasurer, commander of a troop of horse, clever and insinuating, the king's good friend, but also a man with serious intellectual limitations and a penchant for the bottle. And there was Archbishop Sharp, a devious and clever toady, who since June was authorised to recommend to all vacant sees. Even those named by his archiepiscopal colleague in Glasgow must have his *imprimatur*.[67] Sharp could be bullied, however, and he was less than popular with his episcopal colleagues. He had heard that they were bad-mouthing him, he complained to Lauderdale, something he professed himself hard put to believe.[68] He was also the man who had the primary responsibility for dealing with the festering problem of nonconformity in the church. By himself he was no danger to Lauderdale, but in combination with Rothes he could prove a serious obstacle to Lauderdale's plans for domination of the Scottish political scene. They could count on the support of Lord Chancellor Glencairn, who got along well enough with Rothes but could not bring himself to come to an accommodation with Lauderdale or think well of Tweeddale: he had married Tweeddale's widowed stepmother, with whom Tweeddale did not get on.[69] Glencairn was stiff-necked, but willing enough to be humble when he

66 BL Add. Mss 23119, ff. 144–45.
67 *Warrant Book 1660–1670*, NAS GD 90/2/260, no pagination.
68 23 Nov. 1663, Sharp to Lauderdale, NLS Ms. 2512, f. 19.
69 On this point see Mackenzie, *Memoirs*, pp. 115–16.

wanted a favour. In December 1663 he wrote to Lauderdale recommending the bearer, who had the 'misfortune' to be his kinsman, hoping 'that he may not find the harder measure for his nearness to me'.[70]

For Lauderdale, then, patience was in order for the present – and however short-tempered he was to become, Lauderdale at this stage of his career was prepared to be patient. He made no effort to purge the council and exchequer of Middleton's friends, as, early in July, Moray had suggested might be done.[71] He was far better off politically than he had been before parliament began. His grip on patronage was tightening: early in October, just before the parliament ended, the council decided a long-running dispute over the right to appoint the sheriff-clerk of Dumfriesshire in his favour, pending ratification by the judges, a foregone conclusion with Lauderdale's ally Gilmour presiding over the court of session. The victory was especially gratifying since his opponent was Middleton's friend Dumfries.[72] When he and Rothes made their personal report to the king, Charles said once again that the parliamentary session had gone even better than he had expected, and he knew very well that Lauderdale deserved most of the credit. Here was a manager who, unlike Middleton, was both able and reliable, and who did not present him with any surprises. Charles did not like surprises. And, as Lauderdale was to Charles, so Tweeddale was to Lauderdale: an able and reliable manager who, thanks to the king's revised opinion of him, was now employable. And Moray had managed very well in Lauderdale's absence, and was evincing a renewed interest in the political game. The triumvirate of cousins was taking shape.

70 BL Add. Mss 23120, f. 130.
71 8 July 1663, Moray to Lauderdale, BL Add. Mss 23119, f. 76.
72 13 Jan., 24 Mar. 1663, W. Sharp to Lauderdale, BL Add. Mss 23118, ff., 4, 40. *RPCS* I, p. 444.

CHAPTER THREE

Balance of Power, 1663–1666

Almost exactly three years elapsed between the end of the parliamentary session in October 1663 and the scuffles in Galloway in November 1666 that culminated in the destruction of the small rebel army at Rullion Green, in the Pentland Hills, southwest of Edinburgh. By coincidence the three cousins were all in London, preparing for the family wedding that would turn Lauderdale and Tweeddale into 'dearest brothers'. So too was Rothes, who had asked for permission to wait on the king to discuss various matters of business and to clear his name of the charge of being an 'infamous drunkard'.[1] The rebellion was a trifling affair; it lasted less than three weeks. But it was embarrassing – the rebels actually captured the unwary (and unwell) Sir James Turner, the commander of the garrison at Dumfries and the man in charge of the soldiery in the southwest. And it touched on the rawest of raw nerves: the restored regime in London's almost paranoid fear of another outbreak in Scotland – everyone remembered what had happened thirty years previously.[2] So this minor affair set in train the series of events and decisions that within eight months brought the cousins to power and gave them their opportunity to bring about serious change.

Two overarching political circumstances prevailed from 1663 to 1666. The first was the even balance of power between Lauderdale and Rothes. Each man manoeuvred carefully to consolidate his position; each was wary of the other; each was prepared to cooperate and collaborate because that was what Charles wanted. In the struggle for influence Lauderdale had two great advantages. He was constantly in the king's presence – Rothes, in asking for permission to come to London in October 1666, said that he had not seen Charles for two years. And Lauderdale could operate at court more freely than before; as Burnet observed, there were 'no more Scottish councils called at Whitehall after Lord Middleton's fall'.[3] Secondly, the ultimate responsibility for what transpired in Scotland did not lie with Lauderdale. Rothes and his associates in Edinburgh had to implement

---

1 4 Oct. 1666, Rothes to Lauderdale, BL Add. Mss 23125, ff. 112–13.
2 The *State Papers, Domestic* for the mid-1660s are full of informants' reports of uprisings which were either in the planning stage or imminent.
3 Burnet, *History* I, p. 369.

whatever policy was decided on. Lauderdale might influence that policy, but he rarely did so. He knew that Clarendon did not trust him, in spite of his public *mea culpa* for his Presbyterian past. So he kept a low profile, especially on religious questions, the issue most likely to cause trouble. He did, however, keep a grip on ecclesiastical patronage. In the spring of 1665 Archbishop Sharp attempted to use his power to nominate to bishoprics; Lauderdale rapped his knuckles sharply. The archbishop might suggest candidates, but he was to accompany his suggestions with blank forms and await Lauderdale's approval before making a formal nomination.[4]

One episcopal appointment turned out unexpectedly badly from Lauderdale's point of view. In November 1663 the archbishopric of Glasgow fell vacant. Sharp came to London and brought with him his candidate for the post, Alexander Burnet, recently returned from over twenty years' absence from Scotland to become bishop of Aberdeen. In December Burnet got the promotion.[5] The combination of rigidity, paranoia and panic that he was to exhibit as archbishop had not been apparent in Aberdeen, the Scottish see most favourably inclined to episcopacy. Burnet's reputation was that of a moderate, as was that of the other candidates for episcopal vacancies under consideration in January 1664, a short list generated by Lauderdale.[6] In February 1664 Burnet ended the first of a long series of complaining letters to Lauderdale about the prevalence of conventicles by asking the secretary to 'present my humble service to . . . my two grand supporters the earls of Argyll and Tweeddale', who certainly would not have been supportive had they known how much trouble Burnet was to cause the Scottish administration.[7] Burnet was a chronic complainer. In March 1664 he deplored the fact that he had to pay annates to the heirs of his deceased predecessor, and asked that the king reissue the order of Charles I abolishing such payments. In May Charles did so, and Burnet was appropriately, if belatedly, grateful.[8] Fortunately for Lauderdale and Tweeddale, the problem of conventicles was Rothes's, not theirs, to solve.

4 NLS Ms. 2512, ff. 72, 74, 76, 78.

5 23 Nov. 1663, Sharp to Lauderdale, ibid., f. 19. NAS GD 406/1/2594.

6 BL Add. Mss 23121, f. 11. 20 Feb. 1664, Sharp to Lauderdale, NLS Ms. 2512, f. 25. See also J. Buckroyd, *Church and State in Scotland 1660–1681* (Edinburgh, 1980), pp. 58–59.

7 23 Feb. 1664, Burnet to Lauderdale, NLS Ms. 2512, f. 27.

8 *Warrant Book 1660–1670*, NAS GD 90/2/260, under date of 18 May 1664, no pagination. 17 Mar., 2 May, 30 Aug. 1664, Burnet to Lauderdale, NLS Ms. 2512, ff. 37, 38, 58. In this last letter Burnet urged Lauderdale to encourage Sharp, who was on his way to London, because he was so prone to anxieties and fears!

The other great fact of Scottish political life in these years, along with the Rothes–Lauderdale bipolarity, was the war against the Dutch, which began in 1664 and later involved the French as well. It was a war fought on behalf of English commercial interests, and was ruinous for Scotland, whose chief overseas trading partners were the Dutch and the French. In February 1664, even before the war began, there had been a quarantine of Dutch ships on account of an outbreak of plague there, first reported in October 1663.[9] The war ended virtually all trade with them. The king's order in September 1664 that Scottish seamen be rounded up and sent south to serve in the navy made all overseas trade almost impossible to pursue.[10] In addition, there was a tariff war with England, caused at bottom by the exclusionary policies of the English Navigation Act, and discriminatory duties laid on such items as salt. The Scottish attempt to retaliate, the 80 per cent duty on English imports, was disastrous; since it was levied, wrote Treasurer-Depute Bellenden to Lauderdale in May 1664, the customs and excise had not yielded as much as £100 sterling. The solution, he felt, was to return to the free trade policies that had existed in the reign of King James. 'Do what you can to prevent a war with Holland,' he concluded, 'for we shall be sunk by it.'[11] Not only did the war destroy Scotland's foreign trade, it also led to a considerable expansion of the armed forces, which of course had to be paid for. The result, therefore, was the imposition of heavy direct taxation in 1665 and 1667. Charles apologised, in a sense, for having to request it. We know, he wrote, that Scotland is poor and suffering, but we want you to have the opportunity to display your affection and zeal.[12]

To ask for direct taxation to help pay for a war was acceptable, in Scotland as in England, because it conformed to the traditional mindset. In peacetime the king was supposed to live on his own income. Customs duties were part of that income in that they fell under his power over external relations. The excise, that other pillar of the crown's ordinary income, was a Dutch novelty first imposed by the parliamentarians in England in the 1640s. Since it was a regressive tax which fell most heavily on the poorer classes, it was acceptable to the political establishment. But in myriad ways the events of the 1640s and 1650s had brought the cake of custom crumbling down. A king had been thrust aside and then executed,

---

9 *RPCS* I, pp. 451–52, 492–93. See also the decree of 8 July 1664, *RPCS* I, pp. 561–63.
10 Ibid., pp. 600–01.
11 BL Add. Mss 23122, f. 27.
12 This letter, dated 25 July 1665, was addressed to the convention of estates summoned to vote the tax. *APS* VII, pp. 528–29.

not merely deposed and murdered in the traditional English way, or the victim of internal or external violence as in Scotland, but after a public trial as a traitor to his people, an unheard-of thing in western civilisation. Kingship itself had been destroyed, and a military dictatorship imposed, however 'civilian' the façade behind which it maintained its grip. The comfortable parameters and conventions that had prevailed in the political and social structure of the three kingdoms in the days of blessed King James, as John Pym once called him, had been shattered. In 1660, after the death of the dictator, the traditional structures in state and church had been put back into place. Once again there were bishops and archbishops, and dukes and earls. But were the forms anything more than forms? Was it truly possible to go back to the way things were, to declare, over and over, that it was unlawful to take up arms against the king until it was no longer necessary to say so, because people truly believed it? There was hope, and on the surface, there was expectation and confidence. But underneath, the men who ruled in church and state were jittery and fearful, and not always able to conceal their nervousness. And, in England, the people who counted expected nothing but trouble to come out of either Scotland or Ireland. Whatever form English paranoia took – murderous popish bog-trotters, glowering supralapsarians (to use Macaulay's phrase), or major generals – these places were the hatching grounds. This was the feverish and suspicious atmosphere within which the politicians of the three king-doms perforce operated. And in this case time, often a calmer of such fears, provided no relief, no healing. The fears and suspicions might shift their emphasis, but they did not disappear. Not until the 1690s was the boil truly and finally lanced and drained.

When Lauderdale returned to court after the dissolution of parliament he and Rothes were made very welcome indeed. His first order of business was to press the king to deal once and for all with Middleton. Charles did so. As he had promised, he held a hearing, at the house of Lord Chancellor Clarendon, who was laid up with the gout, so as to give the latter's protégé a final chance to explain his conduct in the billeting business. Middleton's response, finally delivered on 24 December, was, Lauderdale said, full of fallacies. Rothes thought that he had not dealt fully with the charges against him. The king thought so too, and on the 29th asked Middleton to surrender his commissions as commander of the armed forces and captain of Edinburgh Castle. His career in Scotland was finally over. The king's financial generosity to him irritated Treasurer-Depute Bellenden, who hinted broadly to Lauderdale that Middleton should not be paid at all.[13] The victors shared the spoils. Rothes became, unofficially, commander-in-chief, and Lauderdale keeper of the castle. He promptly took care of his impecunious cousin Kellie by making him captain of the garrison, which Kellie found to have a full complement of men but otherwise to be in poor condition, the great guns unmounted, very little powder and no spare arms. True to form, he concluded one of his reports by asking Lauderdale to get him money from the king to pay his debts.[14] Middleton's troop of horse was disbanded, and later in the year reconstituted under Rothes's command. Rothes kept Middleton's subordinate officers in place after making some of them very nervous about their tenure. The earl of Linlithgow wrote a very defensive letter to Lauderdale explaining that he was only obeying orders as Middleton's lieutenant; he hoped that no one was complaining of him. 'If I go not on smartly at first, I shall never get them to stand in awe of me,' Rothes explained to the secretary.[15]

Middleton's two principal agents suffered along with him. Newburgh lost royal favour, and Tarbat lost his offices. Another of his followers, Sir John Fletcher, the lord advocate, faced a charge of bribery. In January 1664 the king indicated that he should resign if he wanted to avoid an official inquiry. Fletcher failed to take the hint; so on 5 July Charles ordered the inquiry. Only at that point did Fletcher decide to step down; he resigned on 14 September. Rothes felt a twinge of compassion: 'He, poor man, has much to do to endure his wife, so that I must say I think he deserves to be pitied.'[16] His replacement, Sir John Nisbet, was Lauderdale's man and Tweeddale's personal lawyer. He became a privy councillor and a member of the court of session: Lauderdale was building a party within the Scottish bureaucracy.

Middleton's major ally in the higher ranks of Scottish officialdom, Lord Chancellor Glencairn, did not lose his position. Lauderdale made it clear, however, that he expected Glencairn to do as he was told, scolding him for delaying official approval of a couple of grants to the earl of Argyll.[17]

---

13 3 Nov., 5, 26 Dec. 1663, Rothes to Sir William Bruce, NAS GD 29/1896/ 6, 9, 10. 30 Dec., Lauderdale's memorandum, BL Add. Mss 23120, ff. 140–41. Lauderdale's summary is in BL Add. Mss 23120, ff. 102–06, Middleton's in BL Add. Mss 23120, ff. 142–46. 31 Mar. 1664, Bellenden to Lauderdale, BL Add. Mss. 23121, f. 76.

14 RPCS I, pp. 517–18. 24 Mar., 23 June, 16 Aug. 1664, Kellie to Lauderdale, BL Add. Mss 23121, f. 70, 23122, f. 123, Laing Mss I, pp. 341–42.

15 BL Add. Mss 23121, f. 26. The commissions were renewed on 30 Dec. 1663; Warrant Book, 1660–70, NAS GD 90/2/260, pp. 35–36. 14 Jan. 1664, Linlithgow to Lauderdale, BL Add. Mss 23121, f. 15.

16 7 Jan. 1664, Lauderdale to Gilmour, Paton, 'Gilmour', pp. 178–79. BL Add. Mss 23122, ff. 82, 152. 8 Sept., Rothes to Lauderdale, BL Add. Mss 23122, f. 143.

17 See Glencairn's defensive letter of 1 Dec. 1663, BL Add. Mss 23120, f. 110.

Glencairn was nervous and touchy. He professed his friendliness to Lauderdale, was worried by the rumours that Lauderdale planned to have him ousted, and accused Archbishop Burnet of bad-mouthing him – all that Burnet had said, according to his own report, was that the remissness of the great men encouraged schismatics.[18] Relations were still tense when, in late May, Glencairn suddenly died.

On 30 May 1664 William Sharp wrote to the secretary with the news, acting, he said, on Tweeddale's advice. He urged Lauderdale to be sure that the new chancellor was someone he could trust.[19] Lauderdale needed no urging. Tweeddale had just returned to Scotland from a five-month stay in London, his first visit since the summer of 1660. There is almost no evidence as to his activities there; he probably spent his time getting to know the players in the English government. He came back with an appointment as an extraordinary lord of session and instructions to confer with Rothes and Gilmour on the question of the lord advocate.[20] He also was commissioned to help negotiate the proposed marriage (which did not happen) between Lauderdale's daughter and Lady Lauderdale's kinsman Alexander Home, the heir to the earldom of Home. The negotiations ended in the autumn. Lauderdale was prepared to get the prospective groom a viscountcy right away; his exasperated comments to Tweeddale suggest that the boy's mother was responsible for the failure. Lauderdale's cousin Kellie commented, 'I think they are mad who leave a house or a fortune to the governance of a woman.'[21]

Tweeddale was clearly in high favour, and in the secretary's confidence. Lauderdale wrote to Sharp, assuring him that Tweeddale would be 'forward and real for the Church, both for his own sake and mine'. Rumours began to circulate that he would become chancellor, in part, wrote Gilbert Burnet, because Charles was so grateful to him for his acquiescence in the Buccleuch marriage contract. This prospect appalled the two archbishops, especially Burnet, who described 'our great ones' as 'rotten at the heart'.[22] Sharp, who

---

18 12 Jan. 1664, Robert Cunningham to Lauderdale, BL Add. Mss. 23121, f. 8. 23 Feb., 10 Mar., Burnet to Lauderdale, NLS Ms. 2512, ff. 27, 33.

19 BL Add. Mss 23122, f. 39.

20 24, 26 May 1664, Rothes to Lauderdale, ibid., ff. 31, 34. The latter letter was written from Yester; Rothes had hurried down to see him as soon as possible. 19 July, Tweeddale to Lauderdale, Paton, 'Lauderdale', pp. 125–26.

21 15, 25, 29 Oct., 5, 12 Nov. 1664, Lauderdale to Tweeddale, NLS Ms. 7023, ff. 4, 6, 7, 9, 10. 2 Sept., Kellie to Lauderdale, BL Add. Mss 23122, f. 133.

22 Burnet, *History* I, p. 359. 2 May 1664, Burnet to Sheldon, *LP* II, App., pp. iii–v. 26 May, Lauderdale to Sharp, Dowden, 'Letters', pp. 256–59.

badly wanted the job for himself, wrote a bootlicking, indirectly phrased letter to Lauderdale to that end, and he and Burnet bombarded Archbishop Sheldon with alarmist missives to the effect that if 'one of the late professing converts' got the position, the church would be ruined. 'There is an effectual design laid,' wrote Sharp, 'to crush the interest of the clergy and encourage that faction which look for a reviving of the covenant.'[23] Burnet urged Sheldon to lobby for Sharp's appointment. Speculation was rife in Edinburgh that a churchman would get the job. On 22 August Sharp announced rather grandiloquently to Lauderdale that he was coming to court, ostensibly to lay the bishops' situation before the king.[24]

The archbishop's purpose in coming to London was obvious, and fooled no one,[25] but it did pose a delicate problem for Lauderdale. Whatever he may have thought about the advantages of having Tweeddale in the chancellorship, the time was not yet ripe to push him for high office. Shortly after Sharp arrived at court Tweeddale heard that calumnies were being spread about him there. He wrote a worried letter to Lauderdale, who told him to pay no attention: Charles had 'laughed heartily' at the stories.[26] But Tweeddale's favour with the king was too recently acquired, and he was clearly unacceptable to the archbishops. On the other hand, Sharp was unacceptable to Lauderdale. The primate was too slippery and unreliable, and the aristocracy would be deeply resentful; Lauderdale remembered only too well how disastrous the appointment of Archbishop Spottiswoode as chancellor had been for Charles I. Furtherrmore, Sharp had attempted to discredit him. 'My Lord St Andrews makes heavy complaints of mens' slackness, but when the king presses him he will name no man . . . I think I guess . . . who is thrust at by the insinuation.'[27] Lauderdale was not pleased. At the same time he was under pressure to act. Argyll wrote in July that the vacancy in the chancellorship was breeding trouble.[28] Rothes, who had been in possession of the great seal since Glencairn's death, kept pressing for the vacancy to be filled. He had no idea of what he was supposed to do, he said, and had to rely for instruction on Clerk Register Primrose, a pliable,

23 19 June 1664, Sharp to Sheldon, *LP* II, App., pp. v–vii. See also Burnet's letter of the same date, *LP* II. App., pp. vii–viii.

24 20 Aug. 1664, Burnet to Sheldon, ibid., pp. x–xi. 22 Aug., Sharp to Lauderdale, NLS Ms. 2512, f. 54. *Laing Mss* I, p. 342. 14 June, William Sharp to Lauderdale, NLS Acc. 10442, no. 18.

25 On this point, see Burnet, *History* I, pp. 359–61.

26 20 Oct. 1664, Lauderdale to Tweeddale, NLS Ms. 7023, f. 5.

27 8 Sept. 1664, Lauderdale to Tweeddale, ibid., f. 1.

28 BL Add. Mss 23122, ff. 101–03.

efficient intriguer and a Worcester Scot, who had survived the fall of his patron Middleton.[29] As time went by and no acceptable candidate surfaced, Lauderdale and the king decided to leave things as they were. Rothes was summoned to court in September; on 14 October the great seal was officially conferred on him until a chancellor was appointed. He was also given a *douceur* in the form of appointment as commissioner to the projected meeting of the General Assembly of the church scheduled for 1665, which provided him with a handsome *per diem*, and he was authorised to raise and command a troop of horse. His office of president of the council, which as commissioner he could not appropriately fill, went to Sharp as a consolation prize; Burnet became an extraordinary lord of session.[30]

By the end of 1664 the administrative reshuffle precipitated by Middleton's fall and Glencairn's death was complete. Lauderdale's friends and allies, Tweeddale and Nisbet and Sir John Baird, another appointee to the court of session, were in important positions, and his kinsman Argyll was a privy councillor. Charles's favour to Argyll prompted Archbishop Burnet to write to Lauderdale that people in Scotland feared that the secretary intended to monopolise patronage. He urged Lauderdale to dispel this fear by filling the offices of chancellor and lord advocate with men of sound principles, a tactless suggestion at best.[31] Rothes had profited most. His monopoly of offices was unique: commissioner, lord treasurer, keeper of the great seal, commander of the armed forces; and, of course, the king's good friend. His reputation was hardly commensurate with his extraordinary powers. Gilbert Burnet wrote that he abandoned himself to debauchery and allegedly replied, when charged with this, 'that the king's commissioner ought to represent his person'. It seems unlikely that Rothes ever said this; the king would not have been amused. Rothes admitted that the workload was more than he could handle, even before he officially received the great seal, and he continued periodically to complain of overwork.[32] But in fairness he did work hard from time to time, though he was prone to retreat to his house in Fife at awkward junctures. And there was a lot of work to do.

Two highly sensitive issues required attention in the wake of the dissolution of parliament in October 1663: the enforcement of the newly adopted

29 2, 14 July 1664, Rothes to Lauderdale, ibid., ff. 74, 93.

30 *RPCS* I, pp. 608–13. *Warrant Book 1660–1670*, NAS GD90/2/260, under date of 14 Oct. 1664, no pagination. Nicoll, *Diary*, p. 422.

31 16 June 1664, Burnet to Lauderdale, NLS Ms. 2512, f. 42.

32 Burnet, *History* I, pp. 361–62. 13 Sept. 1664, 26 Feb. 1665, 6 Mar. 1666, Rothes to Lauderdale, BL Add. Mss 23122, ff. 147, 282, 23124, f. 176. Lamont, *Diary*, pp. 173–74.

religious legislation, and trade. For the king the first order of business was the enforcement of the requirement that public officials sign the declaration renouncing the Covenants. A trivial rising of Protestant radicals in north England provoked savage reprisals, and Charles was in no mood to be lenient with dissenters.[33] He instructed Lauderdale, Rothes and the two archbishops to prepare a statement on the religious condition of the kingdom, and ordered Glencairn to produce an accounting of all those who had not yet signed the declaration. He would accept no excuses or explanations for failure to sign, wrote Lauderdale to his friend Lady Margaret Kennedy,[34] though, as it turned out, a few privileged recalcitrants who held no office, such as the earls of Cassillis and Lothian, were not disturbed.[35] The council provided a progress report on 23 February 1664, declared that all officials who had not signed by 14 April would be out of their jobs, and for good measure issued a proclamation prohibiting conventicles in Edinburgh.[36] An unforeseen result was that in some south-western towns, such as Ayr and Stranraer, it was difficult to find men to fill the municipal offices. At Irvine the existing magistrates had to be retained because the newly elected ones would not sign the declaration.[37]

On 7 January 1664 Rothes wrote a letter analysing Scotland's discontents for Lauderdale's (and Charles's) benefit. There were two sorts of malcontents: those unhappy about episcopacy, and those who wanted a change of personnel in the government, that is, those who had either prospered under Middleton or hoped for something from him: Middleton had been lavish with promises of reward from collection of the fines the parliament had levied on those who had been on the wrong side in the late troubles.[38] Rothes did not think the first group to be very dangerous 'unless other discontents make people fly to that pretense and concern themselves on that account'. Rothes promised to be watchful. 'It is evident had they any opportunity their evil humours and worse principles would stir again.'[39]

---

33 R.F. Hutton, *Charles II, King of England, Scotland and Ireland* (Oxford, 1989), pp. 210–11.
34 *Warrant Book, 1660–1670*, NAS GD 90/2/260, p. 35. BL Add. Mss 23120, ff. 140–41. *RPCS* I, pp. 475–76. 13 Dec. 1663, Lauderdale to Lady Margaret Kennedy, NAS GD 406/1/2584.
35 15 Jan. 1664, Turner to Lauderdale, BL Add. Mss 23121, f. 15. 11 May, Tweeddale to Lothian, D. Laing, ed., *Correspondence of Robert Kerr, First Earl of Ancram and his Son William, Third Earl of Lothian* (Edinburgh, 1875) II, pp. 470–71.
36 *RPCS* I, pp. 508–09, 511.
37 Ibid., pp. 549, 601, 617–18.
38 See above, chap. 1, pp. 17, 20–21.
39 BL Add. Mss 23121, ff. 6–7. See also 20 Feb. 1664, Bellenden to Lauderdale, BL Add. Mss 23121, f. 53.

The archbishops were convinced that these humours and principles were indeed stirring, and bombarded Archbishop Sheldon, and, to a lesser extent, Lauderdale, with alarmist letters. Sharp emphasised to Lauderdale that the church could do little to enforce the rules without the active help of government officials, and induced him to get royal authorisation for revival of the Court of High Commission to enforce the laws against disobedience to ecclesiastical authority. It was not very effective, in part because questions were raised about the legality of its proceedings. In May 1664 Sharp complained to Lauderdale that only the presence of Rothes and Sir James Renton allowed it to accomplish anything at all; some people, he added, wanted the Commission to fail and make the bishops look bad. Gilbert Burnet in his *History* wrote that he had expostulated with Lauderdale for agreeing to create the Commission, and accused him of imitating the policy of Lord Treasurer Traquair in the 1630s, that is, hoping that the bishops would ruin themselves by giving them enough rope, which Lauderdale in effect admitted.[40] The privy council in December 1663 undertook to appoint commissions in each parish to punish fornication, blasphemy, Sabbath-breaking and vagabondage, and to look after the impotent poor, an odd mixture of secular and religious prescription; and late in the following year it ordered deprived ministers to leave Edinburgh and observe the rules as to where they might legally reside. 'All along we shall find our prelates screw every thing higher than the English laws go,' commented Robert Wodrow.[41]

The state of the church in 1664 can best be described as uneasy. The southwestern shires were the most serious trouble spot. In the autumn of 1662, immediately after the end of the parliamentary session of that year, Middleton and many other privy councillors went to Glasgow, where on 1 October, at the behest of Archbishop Fairfoul, the council decreed that all ministers inducted into parishes since the abolition of patronage in 1649 must vacate unless they had obtained presentation from the patron and collation from the bishop by 20 September, as the parliamentary Act of 11 June stipulated. This was an absurd requirement; Wodrow described the council meeting that adopted it as saturated in drink. On second thought the council extended the time limit to 1 February 1663, but the upshot was

40 21 Apr., 5 May 1664, Sharp to Lauderdale, *LP* I, pp. 194–99, NLS Ms. 2512, f. 40. Buckroyd, *Church and State*, pp. 58–61. Nicoll, *Diary*, pp. 408–11. Burnet, *History* I, p. 356. For Traquair see M. Lee, Jr, *The Road to Revolution: Scotland under Charles I, 1625–1637*, (Urbana, 1985) pp. 155–57, 191–92, 207–08.

41 *RPCS* I, pp. 471–72, 624–25. Wodrow, *History* I, p. 164.

that over two hundred parishes in the south and southwest were vacated.[42] Ian Cowan estimates that at least one third of the ministry was 'prepared to sacrifice their calling and their liveliood for Presbyterian principles'.[43] Disgruntled parishes would not admit the new ministers, allow them lodging, or permit the church bells to be rung.[44] Some ministers stayed on illegally with the support of their parishioners. Others, appointed before 1649, contrived to hold on, although they evaded the requirement that they attend diocesan synods. Such ministers attracted large congregations. Middleton's regime struck back by making it a punishable offence to attend church outside one's own parish.[45] The ousted ministers' replacements came mostly from the north. Gilbert Burnet described them as 'the worst preachers he ever heard . . .' the dreg and refuse of the northern parts.'[46] According to Kirkton one north-country gentleman cursed this chain of events: these newly minted 'curates', as they were called, would otherwise be keeping his cows. 'No man in Scotland,' he wrote, 'was more dissatisfied than [Arch] bishop Sharp, who complained of Fairfoul, and said his folly had ruined them.'[47] The government, faced with the fall-out from this disastrous blunder, chose to do very little; there was the prospect that in 1665 the General Assembly (or more properly, in the phrasing of the time, the National Synod) would finally meet, the first such meeting since the English conquest in 1651.

Plans for the meeting of the National Synod did indeed go forward. In January 1664 Charles instructed Sharp and his colleagues to prepare a list of topics for discussion for Charles's approval by August, including the suppression of Popery and the requirement that bishops reside in their dioceses. At that point the Synod was planned for late November. By October, when Charles appointed Rothes as his commissioner, the meeting had been pushed ahead to May 1665. In January 1665 Tweeddale was expressing doubt that it would ever be held. By March the bishops were saying that there could be no meeting before August: Sharp believed that

42 *APS* VII, p. 376. *RPCS* I, pp. 269–70, 312–15. Kirkton, *History*, p. 86. Wodrow, *History* I, pp. 123–27. Buckroyd, *Church and State*, p. 47. See the figures in W.L. Mathieson, *Politics and Religion: a Study in Scottish History from the Reformation to the Revolution*, 2 vols (Glasgow, 1902), II, p. 193.

43 Cowan, *Covenanters*, pp. 50–58, has an excellent account of the impact of the legislation of 1662 and 1663. The quoted phrase is on p. 53.

44 See, e.g., 8 Sept. 1664, Rothes to Lauderdale, BL Add. Mss 23122, f. 143.

45 *RPCS* I, pp. 312–15, II, 78–79.

46 Mathieson, *Politics and Religion* II, p. 207, quoting Burnet.

47 Kirkton, *History*, pp. 87, 93–94.

the popular temper was such that any decisions the Synod made would get no respect.[48] In summer the difficulties in both church and state created by the Dutch war caused the proposed meeting to be quietly shelved.

The bishops, like everyone else in a position to do so, hoped to be the beneficiaries of gifts from the fines, if not for themselves, at least for their families, even though Sharp told Lauderdale that collecting them was bad policy.[49] It seems likely that he feared that those who had to pay would take out their resentment on the church. Charles had suspended the payment of the fines at the beginning of 1663, but it was common knowledge that the suspension was temporary, since the government badly needed the money. While the collection was suspended Charles authorised the payment of £6,000 sterling from the proceeds to the earl of Atholl, who was much involved in the efforts to keep the peace in the Highlands.[50] So, inevitably, in February 1664 Charles reinstated the fines and ordered the collection of arrears of cess from earlier taxations. Those owing fines must pay half by Martinmas and the remainder by Candlemas 1665. The king also slashed pensions over £60 sterling by half, though he made exceptions for, among others, Sir Robert Moray, Lauderdale's extravagant uncle Dunfermline and his penurious cousin Lady Balcarres, who had written to him in November that she was too poor to pay her servants. Another exception was the king's physician, Sir Alexander Fraser, who, according to Samuel Pepys, was very popular at court for his skill at dealing with venereal diseases and unwanted fetuses.[51] Authorisation did not, however, always mean payment. Lady Balcarres continued to dun Lauderdale, in letters full of sanctimonious religious rhetoric, for the next three years.[52]

Money from the fines was potentially enormously useful to Lauderdale as a means of building political support. He was deluged with begging

48 *Warrant Book, 1660–1670*, NAS GD 90/2/260, under date of 12 Jan. 1664, no pagination; HMC, 4th report, pp. 505–06. 6 Jan. 1665, Tweeddale to Lauderdale, NLS Ms. 7024, f. 4. 11 Mar., Rothes to Lauderdale, BL Add. Mss 23122, ff. 313–14. 13 Mar., Sharp to Lauderdale, 14 Mar., Burnet to Lauderdale, NLS Ms. 2512, ff. 68, 70.

49 17 Sept. 1664, Burnet to Lauderdale, 13 Mar. 1665, Sharp to Lauderdale, NLS Ms. 2512, ff. 60, 68.

50 *Warrant Book 1660–1670*, NAS GD 90/2/260, p. 37. The payment to Atholl was authorised on 18 June 1663; *Warrant Book 1660—1670*, NAS GD 90/2/260, no pagination. RPCS I, pp. 501–02. 4 Feb. 1664, Lauderdale to Hamilton, NAS GD 406/1/2676.

51 19 Sept. 1664, *The Diary of Samuel Pepys*, ed. R. Latham and W. Matthews, V (London, 1971), p. 275.

52 BL Add. Mss 23121, ff. 47–48. NLS Ms. 7033, f. 41. 10 Nov. 1663, Lady Balcarres to Lauderdale, and to Charles, BL Add. Mss 23120, ff. 75, 74. A.W.C.L. Crawford, *A Memoir of Lady Anna Mackenzie, Countess of Balcarrres and afterwards of Argyll, 1621–1706* (Edinburgh, 1868), pp. 27, 48, 64–78.

letters, and with requests to pardon some of those who were liable. These came from some of the greatest in the land; the earl of Moray, for example, asked for a gift because otherwise 'my substance will be hard', and asking that two of his 'vassals' be forgiven their £300 fines; neither was worth nearly that much.[53] Tweeddale himself while in London in April 1664 submitted a short list of those he thought should be forgiven.[54] Where the great were concerned the king had to be consulted. On 20 October Lauderdale had to write to the duchess of Hamilton that Charles could not now pay any part of the debt the crown owed to her as the heiress of her father and uncle; then, Charles ordered Lauderdale to inform her that she and the duke 'do not carry yourself [sic] as you ought' with respect to the church settlement. If they gave no further cause for complaint, then he was prepared to do something for them. 'This letter his Majesty has read.' The duke and duchess hastily wrote to clear themselves of what was, in fact, a baseless allegation. Six weeks later Lauderdale wrote that Charles was pleased with their explanations, and was open to suggestions on the debt.[55]

The hope that the fines would bring about a fiscal improvement was destined slowly to vanish. The times of collection had to be pushed back into 1665 because the collection machinery was not in place – no collector had been appointed even as late as July 1664.[56] By the end of the year Rothes was feeling very gloomy about the fines. Even those who were willing to pay probably would not, because money was so scarce. Unless the king ordered forceful implementation of the Act, 'the ffayns uill not be uirth a grot'. A lot of poor men – beggars, cotters and shepherds – were on the list. In January 1665 Rothes received a delegation from Stirlingshire, seventy strong, headed by two conformist ministers, who argued that they were guilty of nothing and had no money to pay anyway.[57] The king and Lauderdale took note. In October 1665 the council issued the king's order that those who paid the first half of their fines by a specified date, took the

---

53 15 Sept. 1664, the earl of Moray to Lauderdale, NLS Ms. 2955, f. 14.

54 NLS Ms. 7024, f. 7.

55 20 Oct., 13 Dec. 1664, Lauderdale to Lady Hamilton, NAS GD 406/1/8421, 8430. 16 Nov., Hamilton to Lauderdale, Lady Hamilton to Lauderdale, BL Add. Mss 23122, ff. 187, 189.

56 28 July 1664, Rothes to Lauderdale, recommending Sir William Bruce, who got the job. BL Add. Mss 23122, f. 115.

57 31 Dec. 1664, 21 Jan. 1665, Rothes to Lauderdale, BL Add. Mss 23122, ff. 229, 248–49. Rothes's spelling in the first of these letters was worse than usual because 'I am so uerie that I enou not what I am ureating, but I am to sup with my Lord Santandrus and shall drink your helthe.' Happy Hogmanay!

oath of allegiance, and signed the declaration adopted in parliament in 1663 would be excused from paying the remainder.[58]

Money was scarce. One reason, certainly, was the extent to which Middleton and his cronies had feathered their nests; they 'used the military as the pretext for a free-for-all with the King's money'.[59] Perhaps more importantly, Scottish trade was in deplorable shape even before the Dutch war began. Ever since 1558 Scots traders in France had been treated as natives; now, the protectionist government of Louis XIV was taxing them as foreigners. On 30 September 1663 the council appealed to Charles to intercede on their behalf; they dared not retaliate against French goods being brought to Scotland in French ships lest the negotiations be prejudiced. Charles's efforts were without effect, a failure which the Scots ascribed to the growing Anglo-French commercial rivalry.[60]

Scots resentment at English duties on cattle, salt and beer, and the requirement that they be imported only through Berwick and Carlisle, had produced the legislation of 1663 levying the 80 per cent duty on English imports. Legitimate trade slowed to a trickle, though smuggling abounded. Rothes and Bellenden at the treasury were desperately worried by the lack of income from customs and excise. Even the collection of the king's rents, wrote Bellenden, would require the use of 'strong parties . . . which was never the method formerly followed nor as yet conceived fit to be begun', a squeamishness that would soon vanish. By December 1664 a privy council committee of which Bellenden was a member recommended the use of force if necessary to collect the excise in Kincardinehire.[61]

Lauderdale went to work. The key issue was the English Navigation Act. In July 1664 he was able to persuade the English council of trade that it should be modified to include Scottish ships, though the prohibition on trade with the English plantations would continue: a very important exception. The English council had heard from its own constituents: English merchants trading into Scotland were hurting, and had petitioned the king. The commissioners of the Scottish royal burghs, on the other hand, sent

58 *RPCS* II, pp. 92–93, 102–03. This proclamation had been in the works since August; 8 Aug. 1665, Rothes to Lauderdale, BL Add. Mss 23123, f. 141.

59 Lee, *Government and Politics*, p. 107. Lee spells out the details of Middleton's looting on pp. 106–10.

60 *RPCS* I, pp. 433–34, 488. 8 Oct. 1663, Moray to Lauderdale, BL Add. Mss 23120, f. 52. NLS Ms. 597, f. 109. T. Keith, *Commercial Relations of England and Scotland 1603–1707* (Cambridge, 1910), pp. 142–43, 146–47.

61 28 Apr. 1664, Bellenden to Lauderdale, 5 May, Rothes to Lauderdale, BL Add. Mss 23122, ff. 22, 24. *RPCS* I, p. 633.

mixed signals. Appearing before the privy council on 8 July 1664, they petitioned both that the 80 per cent duty be enforced and that English duties
on Scottish goods be reduced. The council of trade's recommendation was
part of a package deal, based on the belief that the balance of trade was
decidedly in England's favour, a view not universally held. The Scots
were to repeal the 80 per cent impost, and there would be a reduction of
English duties on Scottish imports; neither side should charge more than
5 per cent. This was a reasonable trade-off.[62]

There was much detailed discussion, especially about salt. The manufacture of salt and the mining of coal went hand in hand: it took six tons of
coal to make one ton of salt, and coalmasters depended on their sales to
saltmasters for their operating margin of profit. Together they formed a
powerful pressure group, since so many coal owners were major figures,
like the duke of Hamilton and the earls of Wemyss and Kincardine. The last
was also the key figure in the salt business; his interest in the salt tack made
Lauderdale's man of business uneasy.[63] England was the major external
market for Scottish salt; the new English duty of 16s 8d per weigh (forty
bushels) cut Scottish exports by 40 per cent. According to Bellenden,
English merchants were coming to Scotland, buying salt at depressed
prices, and colluding with English tax farmers to pay only 4s per weigh,
so that the Scots suffered doubly. The Scots complained that they could
not bear the English tax; it should be cut to 4s, or at most 6s 8d. The
Tynemouth saltmasters, however, were prepared to contemplate nothing
lower than 8s.[64]

Like their English counterparts, Scottish saltmasters wanted to manipulate the duty on imported salt in order to create a domestic monopoly for
their product. But they had to agree to allow foreign salt to be imported
duty-free for the single purpose of curing oily fish such as herring and
salmon, for which Scottish salt was no use. They frequently complained that
the foreign salt was being improperly diverted to other uses. Bellenden's
analysis of the causes of the decay of Scottish salt manufacture stressed this,
as well as the Navigation Act and the prohibitive English duty on Scottish
salt. The remedy, he said, was for England to treat Scottish ships as they did

62 *CSPD 1663–1664*, p. 651. *RPCS* I, p. 563. For the balance of trade see D. Woodward, 'Anglo-
    Scottish Trade and Commercial Policy during the 1660s', *SHR* LVI (1977), pp. 153–74.
63 18 Aug. 1666, William Sharp to Lauderdale, BL Add. Mss 23125, f. 51.
64 30 June, 28 July 1664, Bellenden to Lauderdale, BL Add. Mss 23122, ff. 68, 110–11. See also
    Moray's letters to Kincardine on 26 July, 18 Aug., 8 Sept. and 24 Sept., *Moray Letters*,
    pp. 242–48.

their own, and to reduce the salt duty to at least the level of their charge on French and Spanish salt. Bellenden's analysis was written in March 1665; by that time the negotiations had effectively ground to a halt.[65]

Salt was the commodity that caused the most discussion in 1664, but it was far from the main issue. The English council of trade's recommendation on the Navigation Act required parliamentary action, and parliament would not budge. Even if it had been willing to do so, Scottish shipping would have been unable to take advantage of the change owing to the insatiable royal demand for seamen for the navy. The press gangs were very busy. Charles was not happy with the government's efforts. In December 1664 he wrote to Rothes saying that the last levy produced only 300 men, not the required 500, and that most were not seamen. He wanted 500 real sailors: Rothes was to see that they were sent, and those responsible for the fiasco punished. The council agreed with the king's assessment; in its circular letters of February 1665 raising more men, it acknowledged the presence of 'robbers and suchlike' in the last batch. A month later Rothes, informing Lauderdale that 250 seamen were being sent south, commented that 'I hope I may say they are pretty men, for I am sure they have pretty bodies, but I cannot judge if they have the spirit of their calling.' He had already pointed out that many if not most experienced sailors were already in royal service.[66]

Another government initiative created a situation that also displeased the king. An order to search shops in Edinburgh for English goods that had not paid duty caused a number of merchants to close their shops to protest both the 80 per cent tax and the searches, which they blamed on the tacksman, Sir Walter Seaton. Soldiers were sent to be sure that the suspect goods remained in the closed shops. The result was a trivial riot. 'Some 20 boys in drink', in the words of an informant of Henry Muddiman's, went to taunt the solders and were dispersed by the provost and the Lord Lyon (the brother of the earl of Kellie, the captain of the castle). The next night a larger crowd invaded Seaton's house. This time the Lord Lyon showed up with musketeers, and one of the rioters was killed. Rothes convened the council the next day, threatened the Edinburgh magistrates 'more . . . than they deserved', wrote Archbishop Burnet, and ordered the shops to be

---

65 BL Add. Mss 23122, ff. 335–36. *RPCS* II, pp. 53–54. For the salt industry see C.A. Whately, *The Scottish Salt Industry 1570–1850* (Aberdeen, 1987), pp. 2, 5, 40–43, 82–83.

66 *Warrant Book 1660–1670*, NAS GD 90/2/260, under date of 22 Dec. 1664, no pagination. *RPCS* II, pp. 16–18. 11 Feb., 23 Mar. 1665, Rothes to Lauderdale, BL Add. Mss 23122, ff. 273, 349. For the press gangs see Nicoll, *Diary*, pp. 429–30.

opened and the streets patrolled; 'no one was heard to move his tongue since'.[67] The king, when he heard about the disturbance, wrote to Rothes praising his handling of the business and ordering a thorough investigation 'lest any other design be promoted under this pretext and lest this may have been a trial how a tumult would take'.[68] A handful of drunken apprentices had made London officialdom intensely nervous. A council committee's report on the investigation soothed the royal nerves. Charles wrote that he was pleased to learn that there was no serious conspiracy, though he was not at all pleased that the town magistrates had to call in the castle garrison to suppress the riot: he thought them neglectful. No one was executed. A few rioters were banished, and two merchants fined 1,000 merks for having instigated the shop closings.[69]

The outbreak of the Dutch war undoubtedly contributed to the king's nervousness over the riot. It also effectively stopped the negotiations over Anglo-Scottish trade. This was not immediately apparent. The council repeatedly petitioned the king to act.[70] Rothes kept repeating like a mantra that without English concessions on trade 'we are all beggared and undone'.[71] When the report circulated in March 1665 that the king was about to ask for a tax, 'there is cruel repining, and saying that this year brings destruction upon us'. Scotland should get trade benefits before being asked to pay.[72] Treasurer-Depute Bellenden went to London to explain to the king just how desperate the financial situation was. Rothes blamed the impasse on trade on the salt question, and argued that it would be better to drop that issue, 'come of the salt what will, than that we should remain in the case that we are in . . . for in no place in the whole world have we any commerce at this time'.[73] Tweeddale wrote on 20 March 1665 that the country was so impoverished by the lack of trade that unless an invasion was imminent no tax should be levied. The war was being fought for English ends, 'and I am sure they intend us no profit, how successful soever the war be'. On the same day Argyll wrote jocularly to Lauderdale, 'Your son [i.e. godson] John, if any ask him if he be an English man, he puts his

67 26 Nov., R. M. to Muddiman, *CSPD 1664–65*, pp. 91, 93. Muddiman was a professional jour-
    nalist who produced a weekly newsletter for his clients. His informant stated that there had
    been two deaths.
68 *Warrant Book 1660–1670*, NAS GD 90/2/260, under date of 30 Nov. 1664, no pagination.
69 *RPCS* II, pp. 6–7, 12–13, 16.
70 See, e.g., the petitions of 3 May and 3 Oct. 1665, ibid., pp. 42, 93–94.
71 7 Mar. 1665, Rothes to Lauderdale, BL Add. Mss 23122, f. 297.
72 14 Mar. 1665, Rothes to Lauderdale, ibid., f. 326.
73 13 May 1665, Rothes to Lauderdale, BL Add. Mss 23123, ff. 42–43.

hand to his backside and says, there.'[74] One might reasonably deduce that the English were not popular. The outbreak of plague in London made matters worse for Scottish merchants. On 12 July the council prohibited all trade to London until November at least.[75] Without action on trade, wrote Lady Wemyss in August, 'we are a broken and ruined people.' John Nicoll the diarist had observed in 1664 that street crime was up in Edinburgh; poverty, he said, was the cause.[76]

There were no English concessions on trade, but, as Rothes and Tweeddale had anticipated, there was a request for money. On 9 March Lauderdale wrote to Tweeddale that the king had discussed the question with him. Charles knew how poor Scotland was, but a Dutch raid was possible, and Scotland was defenceless: it had no militia, as England had. Furthermore, political pressure in England necessitated his getting something from Scotland, no matter how little. The English evidently had a low opinion of Scottish financial management – or so Bellenden told Rothes on his return from London. Rothes was accused of spending all the king's money on himself. He protested that all he took was his maintenance allowance, which in fact came to a tidy sum. He was also accused of drinking too much, a charge he did not exactly deny. But, he said, no one had seen him 'in disorder . . . since I was in this situation', and anyway Newburgh, the captain of the guard, was a much more indiscreet toper than he. He hoped that the king had not heard these stories.[77]

Lauderdale advised the calling of a convention of estates rather than a parliament, since in a convention the agenda could be restricted to the tax question. He also advised the traditional method of a levy on poundland of what was called Old Extent, a valuation that dated back in some cases to the thirteenth century. Unlike a cess, which in any case Charles had promised in 1661 not to levy again, Old Extent would be much less burdensome and would conceal from the English just how little the Scots were actually paying. Lauderdale told Tweeddale to talk to Argyll and report their views to him, whether or not Rothes called them in for consultation. Tweeddale did; Argyll indicated that he preferred Old Extent, rather surprisingly, since the western shires paid a disproportionately high amount under that

74 BL Add. Mss 23122, f. 340. *Argyll Letters*, pp. 17–18.
75 *RPCS* II, pp. 71–74.
76 16 Aug. 1665, Lady Wemyss to Lauderdale, BL Add. Mss 23123, f. 156. Lord Wemyss was a major coal- and saltmaster. Nicoll, *Diary*, p. 408.
77 10 May, 24 June 1665, Rothes to Lauderdale, BL Add. Mss 23123, ff. 40, 88.

system.[78] Lauderdale also wrote to Rothes, who replied on 11 March that, as ordered, he had consulted with a few councillors, though not Tweeddale or Argyll, who were not in Edinburgh. Although the kingdom was so poor, thanks to the late troubles, the lack of trade, and the low price of corn, Rothes was sure that the people would make the necessary sacrifice. This letter, which accompanied a fairly upbeat 'state of the kingdom' report on the condition of the church, the Highlands and military pay, was for the king's eyes. In another letter of the same date, in his own hand, Rothes stated flatly that the kingdom was broke. The late troubles, the £40,000 sterling a year voted in 1661, the arrears of old taxes, including one from the 1630s that Hamilton was still collecting, the lack of trade and low corn prices, the lack of money from the fines, only £8,000 sterling by the beginning of February – all this added up to disaster. He was not at all sure that the political classes would accept an additional burden: the Act of indemnity having been passed, there was no club to hold over their heads. Success would hinge on getting the right people elected to the convention, and that would take time.[79] No money could be expected for the current year's campaigns. There was also the fact that the Old Extent fell very unevenly; Rothes feared that it would provoke opposition.

Charles went ahead nevertheless. Money was desperately needed, to buy arms and ammunition, which were in very short supply, and to pay for the building of a fortification in Shetland. On 6 March 1665 he sent Rothes detailed instructions. Fortifications were to be built in Shetland, and 300 men supplied to garrison them; the guns of a Dutch ship recently wrecked in the islands were to be salvaged for the forts.[80] Rothes believed the policy to be a mistake. It would be difficult and expensive to build fortifications, and there was no point in trying to fortify any given harbour: there were too many of them. Absent a large part of the English fleet, the Dutch could mop up any garrison, especially as the local population was pro-Dutch for economic reasons. But the king insisted, though there was no money to spare, and Rothes had to raise the funds by borrowing on his own credit.[81]

78 NLS Ms. 7023, f. 16. 7 Apr. 1665, Argyll to Lauderdale, *Argyll Letters*, pp. 18–20. See also Argyll's letter of 9 May, BL Add. Mss 23123, f. 38.

79 11 Mar. 1665, Rothes to Lauderdale, 2 letters, BL Add. Mss 23122, ff. 311–12, 317–18. The 'state of the kingdom' report, also dated 11 Mar., is in BL Add. Mss 23122, ff. 313–14. 28 Feb., Sir William Bruce to Lauderdale, BL Add. Mss 23122, f. 288.

80 *Warrant Book 1660–1670*, NAS GD 90/2/260, no pagination.

81 14 Mar. 1665, Rothes to Lauderdale, 2 letters, BL Add. Mss 23122, ff. 324, 326. 1 July, Rothes and Bellenden to Lauderdale, BL Add. Mss 23123, f. 105.

Charles explained that his purpose was to fortify Bressay Sound, off Lerwick, both to deny the harbour to the Dutch and make it a rendezvous for the English fleet. There were the inevitable delays. Charles grew impatient. Finally, by 30 May, Rothes was able to announce that the men would be off in a week.[82] The troops' commander, Colonel Sinclair, was in no hurry, however. He was dragging his feet in June; by August he had got as far as Orkney, where, Rothes wrote in exasperation on 30 August, he had remained until he was sure that there was no enemy in Shetland, or en route, before he ventured out: 'I am afraid we shall have shame of him.' In addition to incompetence Sinclair gave evidence of being sticky-fingered with soldiers' pay and prize goods; Lauderdale suspected him of embezzling.[83] As it turned out, there was no shame, because Shetland never became a theatre of war. The garrison and the fort proved both expensive and unnecessary.

In his letter to Rothes on Bressay Sound Charles explained that his intelligence reports indicated that the Dutch planned to land in Scotland, either in Shetland or in the west country, and build a fortification; and, indeed, such reports were rife. The Dutch were going to land eight, or nine, or sixteen regiments, and, wrote one of Sir Joseph Williamson's correspondents in May, the spirit of rebellion was as vigorous in the south and west as it was when the Scots 'entered into that wicked Covenant, the bane of these three nations'.[84] Hence Bressay Sound. For the west country Charles's plan was to confiscate weapons in private hands, either by using troops to search for them or, if that seemed too drastic, by a general order to lowlanders to surrender their arms because the soldiers needed them to defend the country. In answer to Rothes's question Charles said he meant firearms, not swords.[85] Rothes and his advisers decided that they would be collected only in the western shires, where the real danger lay: Ayr, Renfrew,

---

82 28 Mar. 1665, Charles to Rothes, *Warrant Book, 1660–1670*, NAS GD 90/2/210, no pagination. 20 Apr., 25 May, 30 May, Rothes to Lauderdale, BL Add. Mss 23123, ff. 26, 51, 56. In April there was a report, which turned out to be unfounded, of three Dutch frigates there., BL Add. Mss 23123, f. 24.

83 30 Aug. 1665, Rothes to Lauderdale, BL Add. Mss 23123, f. 173. 1 June, Bellenden to Lauderdale, BL Add. Mss 23123, f. 68. BL Add. Mss. 23128, f. 241. 7 Mar. 1668, Lauderdale to Tweeddale, NLS Ms. 7023, f. 135.

84 *CSPD 1664–1665*, p. 344. See also pp. 235, 271. Williamson was the head of Secretary Arlington's secretarial staff, and would one day succeed him as secretary of state.

85 *Warrant Book 1660–1670*, NAS GD 90/2/260, under dates of 28 Mar. and 11 Apr. 1665, no pagination. 2 Apr., Rothes to Lauderdale, BL Add. Mss 23123, ff. 1–2.

Galloway, Dunbarton, Clydesdale and Kintyre, 'which is a nest of knaves'.[86] As with the Shetland policy, Rothes was unenthusiastic. The collecting would produce little, and make it more difficult for the well-affected to defend themselves. He sent an order to the duke of Hamilton to search all houses in Lanarkshire, even those of public officials and members of parliament; in a separate letter he told the duke that, for those he trusted, he could confiscate the arms for show, and then return them.[87] The order accomplished little enough; it was another illustration of paranoia at court, fed by the steady stream of rumours flowing from the pens of Arlington's, Williamson's and Muddiman's informants.

On 11 April 1665 Charles formally summoned a meeting of the convention of estates to raise money, in spite of his reluctance to tax Scotland, 'being so much ruined by long wars and want of trade'. A month later he stopped payment on all pensions except those of the officers of state and exchequer. Even Lauderdale had his difficulties: in January 1666 Bellenden wrote blaming the shortage of money for Lauderdale's not having received his Martinmas payment.[88] Rothes was sunk in gloom at the prospect of the convention: it would bring together a large number of discontented people who would work on each others' grievances, especially as they would see that they would get nothing out of the tax: the money would go to pay for the military, and all for England's benefit. 'I do assure you there are many whose affection even to the King and kingly government I do very much question.' The best hope for compliance at the convention lay in collecting the fines and distributing nothing until afterwards: 'everyone's expectations may produce a hearty complaisance'.[89] In the discussions in the council leading up to the meeting there was considerable debate. The Old Extent fell disproportionately heavily on the church and the western shires; Bellenden commented that the duke of Hamilton and Archbishop Sharp, who agreed on nothing else, both argued in favour of the cess. Rothes himself favoured cess; he thought it was fairer. At one point the debate

---

86 BL Add. Mss 23123, f. 60. On 9 May 1665 Argyll informed Lauderdale that he had disarmed Kintyre, part of the vast Campbell holdings, but that it was hardly worth the trouble, since he had already done so in 1654! BL Add. Mss 23123, f. 38.

87 16, 22 Apr. 1665, Rothes to Lauderdale, BL Add. Mss 23123, ff. 16–17, 28. 12, 15 Apr. Rothes to Hamilton, *Hamilton Mss*, p. 82.

88 *Warrant Book, 1660–1670*, NAS GD 90/2/260, under dates of 11 Apr., 9 May 1665, no pagination. As before, Charles soon made exceptions for Dunfermline and Lady Balcarres. *Warrant Book, 1660—1670*, NAS GD 90/2/260 under dates of 4 Sept., 9 Sept. 1665, no pagination. 20 Jan. 1666, Bellenden to Lauderdale, BL Add. Mss 23124, f. 22.

89 16 Apr. 1665, Rothes to Lauderdale, BL Add. Mss 23123, ff. 16–17.

produced two very long papers, 'and had they had time I believe they would have been volumes'. In the end, however, the king's decision – really, Lauderdale's decision – prevailed. Old Extent would be used, at the rate of 40s per poundland, higher than the normal rate of 30s.[90] Rothes contrived to defuse opposition by assessing the western shires at 40 merks, which reduced their burden by one third, and ministers' stipends at the valuation of 1633, ignoring subsequent increments. So on 20 July he could cheerfully report that all was settled; there would be no heat or debate at the convention. He believed that the majority would have voted for the cess if they had been left to their own devices, but they would acquiesce in the king's orders.[91] And so indeed it turned out: the convention rubber-stamped the government's proposal for a tax based on Old Extent, to be levied for five years at the rate of 40s per poundland. It all went very briskly, Rothes reported. The convention met on Wednesday (2 August) and voted on Friday. Rothes would have preferred more than five years' worth of taxation – understandable in a lord treasurer with an empty treasury – but accepted five years in order to preserve unanimity. The members of the convention did want to lay the country's grievances before the king; Rothes had to squash a move to have a delegation sent to Charles on the issue of trade.[92] There may have been unanimity at the convention, but it was far from cheerful unanimity.

Lauderdale's success in achieving taxation via Old Extent rather than cess came literally at a price: the tax provided no serious relief for a treasury beset by military expenses and declining customs and excise receipts which led to very heavy defalcations for the tacksman, Sir Walter Seaton. The appointment as collector of the taxation of the duke of Hamilton, who hoped to get some of his debt paid, was unpopular because there had been so much complaint about his efforts to collect arrears of taxation dating back to the 1630s, and resented by those who, like Kellie, felt that the duke had been amply rewarded already. Hamilton had asked for the appointment, however, and Lauderdale at this stage was unwilling to cross him.[93]

90 19 July 1665, Bellenden to Lauderdale, Rothes to Lauderdale, 2 letters, BL Add. Mss 23123, ff. 130–33.
91 20 July 1665, Rothes to Lauderdale, BL Add. Mss 23123, ff. 134–35.
92 *APS* VII, pp. 528–35. 9 Aug. 1665, Rothes to Lauderdale, enclosing his formal report, BL Add. Mss 23123, ff. 150–53. R.W. Lennox, *Lauderdale and Scotland: A Study in Scottish Politics and Administration 1660–1682* (PhD diss., Columbia University, 1977), pp. 49–59, has an excellent analysis of the discussions from March to Aug. 1665 leading up to the convention.
93 13 Mar. 1665, Sharp to Lauderdale, NLS Ms. 2512, f. 68. 5 July, Hamilton to Lauderdale, 18 Sept., Kellie to Lauderdale, BL Add. Mss 23123, ff. 114, 187. Lady Hamilton thanked Lauderdale for getting the appointment for her husband. BL Add. Mss 23123, f. 138.

Ronald Lee's analysis concludes that 'the government had been able to spend only about 44% of the taxation', approximately £6,500 sterling a year, a far cry from the £18,000 to £20,000 Charles had indicated that he wanted; a small enough demand, Rothes thought, but still beyond Scotland's means. Out of these meagre sums the Scots were supposed to pay not only for their own defence but also toward the upkeep of the garrison at Berwick, which drew a vehement protest from Rothes, and the subsidy for the bishop of Münster, Charles's one ally in this war. 'The 1665 taxation,' Lee concludes, 'was actually little more than a shambles.'[94]

The money was to be used for the soldiers: for arms and ammunition, for Shetland and for the armed forces already in existence and those which, in all likelihood, would be raised in future. For the first time in its history the Scottish crown had a standing army at its disposal, two troops of horse and seven companies of foot guards, including the garrisons of Dumbarton, Stirling and Edinburgh castles. They were supposed to be paid and equipped from the excise voted in the parliament of 1661, but pay was frequently in arrears; the soldiers were employed to collect those arrears by being quartered on defaulters. Collecting money by force had become commonplace during the decades of upheaval and interregnum; now it became the policy of the restored regime, an unwelcome continuation of the practices of the monarchy's enemies. The soldiers themselves, however, were far from well off. Shortly after the meeting of the convention of estates Kellie's brother wrote to Lauderdale about the woeful condition of the Edinburgh garrison: 'They have neither washing, bedding, nor dressing of their meat but what they do upon their own expense.' In September the English ordnance commissioners were ordered to ship 4,000 muskets, 2,000 pikes and 300 barrels of powder to Edinburgh Castle.[95]

By the end of the year Rothes was seriously worried about how thinly spread the soldiers were. Some were being sent as far north as Inverness and Sutherland to collect the excise and the king's revenues from his property, and disaffection was growing. The fanatics, he wrote, were becoming much bolder. Where conventicles used to be few, and secretly held, now dissidents went into the fields by the hundreds, and often. The recently reestablished High Commission was ineffective: the lawyers argued that

94 Lee, *Government and Politics*, pp. 115–16. 14 July 1665, Charles to Rothes, *Warrant Book 1660–1670*, NAS GD 90/2/260, no pagination. 19 July, 23 Dec., Rothes to Lauderdale, BL Add. Mss 23123, ff. 131, 267. *Laing Mss* I, p. 347.

95 17 Aug. 1665, Sir Charles Erskine to Lauderdale, BL Add. Mss 23123, f. 162. *CSPD 1664–1665*, p. 547. The order had to be repeated in January 1666, *CSPD 1665–1666*, p. 216.

the Act against conventicles did not specifically declare conventicles seditious, and there were so many 'chatterers' at its meetings that it could no longer strike fear into those summoned before it. The king evidently agreed. He ordered its discontinuation in November 1665 on the ground that it was causing too much trouble.[96]

After Martinmas 1664 the troops had the additional job of collecting fines from those unable or unwilling to pay. The Presbyterian historian James Kirkton charged that the troopers' expenses frequently exceeded the fines of the people on whom they were quartered. He also alleged that the fees of the collector, Sir William Bruce, 'were so great as to enable a broken man to buy land and build palaces'.[97] Whatever the truth of all this, it is certainly true that quartering was unpopular and raised the level of tension in those areas, particularly in the southwest, where the problems seemed greatest to the authorities in Edinburgh. On 17 February 1666 Rothes informed Lauderdale that on account of the 'new difficulties of conventicles' there he was sending Sir James Turner with a considerable number of the 'small handful of horse and foot' at his disposal. One conventicle in Galloway attracted a thousand people, half of them armed. Please keep quiet about this, he added; Whitehall would not be pleased.[98] But Whitehall was informed anyway, thanks to the mounting hysteria of Archbishop Burnet. In April 1665 Burnet described 'our condition' to Archbishop Sheldon as 'very mean and miserable'; in May 'they began to stone ministers even at the gates of Edinburgh, under my lord Commissioner's nose'. In late summer he went to court, where his complaints to Charles in a private audience led to a conference with Clarendon, Arlington and Lauderdale. Charles asked a lot of questions, and issued a handful of instructions on such matters as the education of the young marquess of Huntly and other Catholic noblemen's children, and the punishment of those who refused the oath of allegiance. Lauderdale was annoyed. He 'did not oppose nor question the conveniency of any of these particulars,' wrote Burnet, 'but I hear huffs very much in private.' He suspected that Rothes and Sharp had had a hand in Burnet's tales of woe; Bellenden had written that the three had been conferring before Burnet set out, 'but what he brings the man in the moon knows as much as I'. By

---

96 2, 16 Dec. 1665, Rothes to Lauderdale, BL Add. Mss 23122, ff. 201–02, 23123, ff. 259–60. Burnet, *History* I, p. 368. J. Buckroyd, *The Life of James Sharp, Archbishop of St Andrews* (Edinburgh, 1987), p. 85.

97 Kirkton, *History*, pp. 129–30.

98 BL Add. Mss 23124, f. 59.

December Burnet was complaining to Arlington that nothing was being done, 'even though hundreds and thousands of disaffected persons meet to preach and pray . . . Their impunity will encourage others to worse things.' The king, he wrote Lauderdale, must order a crackdown, or 'we will be disgraced if not destroyed'. 'Disorderly meetings' were growing in number in Galloway, Nithsdale and parts of Ayrshire, and people of influence were speaking favourably of them. If there was a military setback, he feared, the Dutch and French would raise a new rebellion.[99]

Burnet had been expressing this fear for some time. 'The first news of any disaster at sea will dispose us to a new rebellion,' he had written in May 1665. By December he was hopeful that Rothes had come around to this view.[100] Rothes was not eager to crack down, however; doing so would suggest to Whitehall that the Scottish administration had not been managing well. In June 1666 Burnet was condemning 'so much stupidity and security' on the part of 'our great men', and 'so little fear or care of the public peace'.[101]

Given all the dangers, both internal and external, the logical precaution was to increase the size of the army. In the summer of 1666 the king issued his orders. Six more companies of foot guards were raised, as well as an entire new regiment of foot, ten companies strong, and a regiment of horse that by the end of the war consisted of eleven companies.[102] How were they to be paid? Money continued to be appallingly scarce. In January 1666 William Sharp had given Lauderdale a careful accounting of income from the signet office, to which the secretary was entitled. The annual take had declined from its peak of £22,050 sterling in 1662 to £16,833 in 1665; Lauderdale had overdrawn the account by about £5,700. Sharp declared that the shortage of money was to blame.[103] There was only one source of ready cash, the fines that Sir William Bruce had been collecting, and which totalled some £30,000 sterling, not a very large sum, but, Rothes wrote in May, the king should expect no more, 'for they say there will be no more got out of the cat but the skin'.[104] Both the archbishops recommended that

99 *LP* II, App., pp. xviii, xxii, xxiv–xxviii. *CSPD 1665–1666*, p. 84. 29 June 1665, Bellenden to Lauderdale, BL Add. Mss 23123, f. 96. 2 Dec., Burnet to Lauderdale, NLS Ms. 2512, f. 84.
100 *LP* II, App., pp. xxii, xxviii–xxix.
101 8 June 1666, Burnet to Sheldon, *LP* II, App., pp. xxxv–xxxvi. 23 June, Rothes to Lauderdale, BL Add. Mss 23124, f. 178.
102 Lee, *Government and Politics*, p. 153. My account of the military in these years relies on Lee's excellent discussion in chapter 4 of his dissertation.
103 2 Jan. 1666, William Sharp to Lauderdale, BL Add. Mss 23124, f. 5.
104 17 May 1666, Rothes to Lauderdale, BL Add. Mss 23124, f. 143.

the money Bruce had collected be used to pay the enlarged army; in July 1666 the king so ordered.[105]

Rothes received the news with considerable dismay. For the past several months he and Tweeddale had been writing to Lauderdale about the parcelling out of the expected take. In February Lauderdale had begged for Tweeddale's advice, given 'the small sums of the fines, the horrible number of pretenders': Tweeddale would be more likely than Rothes to recommend people who would be politically useful to the secretary. Tweeddale duly produced a list, adding that since £7,000 had already been promised, the remaining cash ought to be distributed right away, to get it into circulation for the sake of the economy. Rothes said much the same thing in May, when he supplied his list, carefully adding that none of those he recommended were his relatives.[106] The flow of begging letters never diminished. Lord Ogilvie pleaded that if he received nothing soon, his mortgages would be irredeemable and his daughters would never be married.[107] Even Lady Lauderdale was not spared: the countess of Atholl asked her to help get her husband a new precept of £6,000 from the fines before the money ran out.[108] When the king's orders made it clear that only the troops would benefit from the fines, Rothes warned about the repercussions: there were so many poor aristocrats who were counting on relief. He mentioned specifically Annandale, who will 'perish . . . at the very next term', and Atholl. The discontent would be enormous, and if they went under, it might 'render others slack in their duty'. The odium would be his: Lauderdale would escape any blame. 'I have carried the whole blame of raising them, for I have done it by quartering . . . Nothing ever I did has procured me the blame of the country before.'[109]

Rothes, royal commissioner, lord treasurer, commander-in-chief of the armed forces, lord keeper of the great seal, and alleged drunkard, was feeling overburdened and overwhelmed. He was 'very weary of my great

---

105　5 Feb. 1666, Burnet to Sheldon, *LP* II, App., pp. xxx–xxxiii. Burnet, *History* I, pp. 368–69. Moray attributed the advice to Sharp; Lauderdale was consulted, 'but no more moved it than you did'. 24 July, Moray to Tweeddale, Paton, 'Lauderdale', pp. 137–38. 31 July, Sir William Bruce to Lauderdale, NLS Acc. 10442, no. 6. Bruce thought that if he were to pay the fines to the troops, he should be named commissary to the forces.

106　20 Feb. 1666, Lauderdale to Tweeddale, NLS Ms. 7023, f. 25. 3 Mar., Tweeddale to Lauderdale, BL Add. Mss 23124, f. 74. 19 May, Rothes to Lauderdale, BL Add. Mss 23124, ff. 149–51.

107　BL Add. Mss 23124, f. 15.

108　BL Add. Mss 23124, f. 63.

109　12 July 1666, Rothes to Lauderdale, BL Add. Mss 23125, ff. 5–6.

titles', he wrote to Sir Robert Moray in June 1666. [110] The office he wished to shed was that of lord keeper: the chancellorship, though very honorific, was now a paper-pushing job carrying very little if any political clout. Rothes had never wanted it. In July 1665, reporting a rumour going around in Edinburgh that Middleton was to become chancellor, he told the secretary that he knew Lauderdale would prevent that from happening. But the king should fill the job, 'to damp all the spirits of that generation of cattle' (i.e., Middleton's friends), adding that Sharp would be the best choice. The close alliance between Sharp and Rothes fuelled the reports that the archbishop would get the job. Sharp's letters to Lauderdale in 1664 and 1665 were full of praise for Rothes. [111] The latter's tone regarding Sharp was cooler, though when he spoke of filling the chancellorship, Sharp's was the only name he mentioned. Bellenden, who found it difficult to work with Rothes at the treasury, dreaded such an appointment, and repeatedly warned Lauderdale that it would be disastrous. Sharp still very much wanted the job, though, as Bellenden wrote in May 1666, he reportedly would push his friend Atholl for it during his impending visit to court, [112] no doubt to mask his own ambitions. In September, however, the archbishop made a serious miscalculation. He recognised Lauderdale as the principal obstacle to his obtaining the chancellorship. The impending marriage between the secretary's daughter and Tweeddale's son, which was now public knowledge, worried him greatly: Tweeddale was no friend to the bishops. Sharp had had a sharp exchange with Tweeddale at a council meeting in August over enforcement of church discipline. [113] So he attempted to revive the political fortunes of his former patron Middleton by persuading Rothes, whose relations with Tweeddale had never been close and were often chilly, to break with the secretary and ally with Middleton. Rothes, who was cooling toward Sharp, was appalled, immediately informed Lauderdale, and protested that he would not touch this

---

110 21 June 1666, Rothes to Moray, BL Add. Mss 23124, f. 176. Moray must have given this letter to Lauderdale, since it is in the Lauderdale papers. It is a reasonable guess that Lauderdale used it when, in 1667, he persuaded the king to ease Rothes out of power.

111 See, e.g., 21 Apr., 5 May 1664, Sharp to Lauderdale, BL Add. Mss 23122, f. 16, NLS Ms. 2512, f. 40.

112 1 July 1665, Rothes to Lauderdale, BL Add. Mss 23123, ff. 100–01. 15 June, 24 Oct. 1665, 31 May, 8 Oct. 1666, Bellenden to Lauderdale, BL Add. Mss 23123, ff. 77, 212–13, 23124, f. 161, 23125, f. 120. Bellenden wrote of his difficult dealings with Rothes in a letter to the earl of Roxburgh in Feb. 1665, Laing Mss I, pp. 343–44.

113 7 Aug. 1666, Tweeddale to Lauderdale, BL Add. Mss 23125, f. 34.

proposal for £100,000 a year.[114] By November Bellenden was assuring Lauderdale that Rothes was firmly attached to his interest and that relieving Rothes of the burden of the chancellorship by conferring the office on Tweeddale would improve relations between the two.[115] That did not happen; the principal result of Sharp's blunder was to leave the archbishops politically isolated when the Pentland Rising burst on them.

Rothes was right to worry about the king's decision on the fines. It did not even stop the begging letters.[116] And the fines did not go very far to pay the new levies, which, Rothes reported on 6 September, were almost all ready.[117] Bellenden was already worrying about how to pay for them once the fines were exhausted; 'both burgh and land' would be most unwilling to have a new tax levied.[118] But there was no other solution. The only question was whether to call a parliament or another convention of estates to vote the tax. The latter could be assembled more quickly, but there was some doubt about whether it could vote anything other than the traditional poundland tax, which clearly would not do. Rothes summoned a group of councillors, most of whom argued that it could vote money any way it chose. So on 8 November the council issued a proclamation summoning a convention of estates for 9 January 1667 to raise money for the kingdom's defence. On the same day it voted that soldiers were to be quartered on taxpayers in arrears in the northern shires and in Argyll.[119] Clearly the new levies were to be used for purposes other than defence against a possible Dutch (or French) invasion. One such purpose was the enforcement of the law requiring people to attend their parish church and prohibiting conventicles. In obedience to a letter from the king the council proclaimed these requirements anew on 11 October. Landlords were to be held responsible for their tenants, who could be evicted for non-compliance. A week earlier Rothes had written to Lauderdale that he was sending troops to the west to ensure obedience to the law.[120]

---

114 23 Sept. 1666, Rothes to Lauderdale, ibid., ff. 88–89. In July he had called Sharp a liar in a letter to Lauderdale, NAS GD 224/173/1.

115 8 Nov. 1666, Bellenden to Lauderdale, BL Add. Mss 23125, f. 138. On 22 Sept. he had written that Tweeddale, when he arrived in London, would fill Lauderdale in on Sharp's designs; BL Add. Mss 23125, f. 84.

116 See, e.g., 16 Aug. 1666, the earl of Moray to Lauderdale, asking for something from the taxation, 'since I hear the fines are to be otherwise disposed of'. BL Add. Mss 23125, f. 47.

117 Ibid., f. 64.

118 1 Sept. 1666, Bellenden to Lauderdale, ibid., f. 62.

119 *RPCS* II, pp. 206–07.

120 BL Add. Mss 23125, f. 114.

Just how dangerous was the situation there? Perceptions varied widely. The law prescribing presentation by the patron and collation by the bishop for all ministers admitted to parishes since 1649 had had the unintended effect of uniting Presbyterian radicals and moderates against the episcopal regime. The consequence was the growth of conventicles, mostly but not exclusively in the southwest. The council periodically sent detachments of troops there, to be quartered on suspected conventiclers, to arrest those ministers suspected of keeping conventicles, and to assure ministers illegally kept out of their churches that letters of horning against ministers illegally in possession of their kirks would be forthcoming.[121] The war heightened the tensions and the nervousness, in Whitehall, in Edinburgh, and in the minds of the archbishops. Burnet, though he wrote circumspectly to Lauderdale at the beginning of 1665, complained to Sheldon that the armed forces were neither numerous enough nor well equipped: he placed his trust only in force, and grumbled that Sharp was not supporting him.[122] Sharp blew hot and cold. In his letters to Sheldon and Lauderdale he sometimes sounded alarmed, but he could see that Burnet's constant complaining annoyed Lauderdale, and since neither Lauderdale nor Rothes was willing to push extreme measures, neither was he. Rothes's official 'state of the kingdom' report in March 1665 was quite cheerful about the prospects for religious quiet. This was to be expected: the king must not be allowed to imagine that his Scottish administrators were not doing their job. In a private letter to Lauderdale he was equally upbeat. People were gradually reconciling themselves to the episcopal structure; 'a very little time will render both opposers and withdrawers very insignificant'.[123] In August he sent a troop of ten horsemen to disperse a large gathering at Ormiston where there was 'a world of deposed ministers'.[124] Burnet fumed at officialdom's unconcern. Rothes would not act 'lest the court should apprehend (which we industriously avoid) that there were some cause of fear'.[125] 'Between June 1664 and December 1665,' writes Julia Buckroyd, 'there was virtually no action taken against what appears to have been continuing nonconformity'.[126]

---

121 24 Nov. 1663, the council to Sir James Turner, *RPCS* I, pp. 461–62. Turner's instructions are in NLS Ms. 597, f. 129. He found problems in only four Galloway parishes; 17 Nov. 1663, Peter Wedderburn to Lauderdale, BL Add. Mss 23120, f. 77.

122 21 Jan. 1665, Burnet to Lauderdale, NLS Ms. 2512, f. 66. 2 Feb., Burnet to Sheldon, *LP* II, App., pp. xvi–xvii.

123 BL Add. Mss 23122, ff. 313–14, 23123, ff. 16–17.

124 30 Aug. 1665, Rothes to Lauderdale, BL Add. Mss 23123, f. 173.

125 23 Nov. 1664, Burnet to Sheldon, *LP* II, App., pp. xii–xiii.

126 Buckroyd, *Church and State*, p. 64.

By the end of 1665, however, Rothes found it necessary to bestir himself. In November he visited the west country, and sent a long report to Lauderdale in his inimitable orthography. Conventicles were frequent, and their elaborate precautions made it difficult to make arrests. The chief troublemakers were 'outed' (i.e., ousted) ministers, who preached 'in greay clos and long pediuicks', and sometimes in masks, and 'thes roges stirs [*sic*] up the uimin so as they are uors than deivils'. If it were not for the women, he went on, there would be little trouble with conventicles, but 'ther ar such a ffulith jenerasione of pipill in this cuntrie uho ar so influensied uith ther fanatick uayffs as I thinck uill bring reuin upon them'. He also remarked that the situation in Jedburgh and Teviotdale was very unsettled.[127]

The persistent complaints of the archbishops – Sharp now, as well as Burnet – the continuing meetings of conventicles, and the impotence of the recently dissolved ecclesiastical commission made a show of activity imperative. So the council in December 1665 issued yet another proclamation against conventicles, which 'threaten no less than the confusion and ruin of church and kingdom'.[128] They were growing larger and more frequent, wrote Burnet in February 1666, and the attendees were armed. So, as has been said, Rothes ordered Sir James Turner to the west, to repress 'these insolencies which of late have been too frequent there'.[129] The soldiers were not happy about this assignment, and the popular perceptions accompanying it. Some called them the bishops' guard, wrote Sir William Drummond, some called them favourers of the service book, that ill-fated attempt to force a new liturgy on the Scots thirty years before, some, bringers-in of the Mass. Drummond favoured forcible obedience to the laws.[130] His comments may have been provoked by the fact that changes in the liturgy had been under discussion for some time, with, Burnet confided to Sheldon, the expectation of greater conformity with the church of England, if the war was a success.[131] Turner, the commander on the spot, felt, in June, that matters were going well, however, and Rothes professed to be unworried unless there was a foreign invasion, though he feared that the great fire in London might prompt the French to try one – in the south.[132] He was prepared to behave

---

127   24 Nov. 1665, Rothes to Lauderdale, BL Add. Mss 23123, ff. 236–37.
128   *RPCS* II, pp. 108–09.
129   5 Feb., 12 Mar. 1666, Burnet to Sheldon, LP *II*, App., pp. xxx–xxxv.
130   6 Sept. 1666, Drummond to Lauderdale, BL Add. Mss 23125, ff. 66–67.
131   8 Mar. 1666, Burnet to Sheldon, *LP* II, App., pp. xxxiii–xxxiv. BL Add. Mss 23122, f. 315.
132   8 June 1666, Turner to Lauderdale, *Laing Mss* I, pp. 351–52. 11 Sept., Rothes to Lauderdale, 2 letters, BL Add. Mss 23125, ff. 74, 76.

arbitrarily if necessary where the church was concerned: 'the formalities of law I think in some cases may be dispensed with.'[133] On the whole he was optimistic. 'I will positively say,' he wrote on 20 March 1666, 'there is no hazard nor scarcely a possibility of any stirring in this country to oppose the established laws and government of church and state.' By contrast, Tweeddale a week earlier had observed to Moray that all was not well in Scotland, 'but I am so apprehensive of worse that I desire no change.'[134] The Pentland Rising caught Rothes and most of Edinburgh officialdom completely by surprise.

Historians have often described the actions of the administration in Edinburgh that prompted the western rebellion as a deliberate policy of repression.[135] If policy there was, it was driven by the nervousness of the king[136] and the almost hysterical Jeremiads of Archbishop Burnet. Archbishop Sharp, a former Presbyterian, came around to the policy of repression by 1666, partly because of the king's attitude, partly because of his uneasy relations with Rothes and his fear of the growing closeness between Lauderdale and Tweeddale, the man who was an MP during the Protectorate. Rothes had shown no zeal for the persecution of dissenters, though he had expressed alarm at the growth of conventicles. The possibility of a Dutch invasion did worry him: hence the increase in the armed forces in 1666. On 4 October of that year, in his letter to Lauderdale requesting royal permission to come to London, he declared that the threat of a foreign invasion had ended for the year. So he would use the newly raised army in the west 'to draw that stubborn people to give obedience to the laws and to force them to know their duties.'[137] He certainly did not view the situation with alarm, or he would not have planned to go to London. His chivvying of dissenters in 1666 was sporadic and in response to pressure: hardly a sustained effort which justifies the term 'policy' to describe it. Still, it was the case that the first skirmishes came about because soldiers were collecting fines for non-attendance at church, and at church doors on those who were not members of the parish. The soldiers were also instructed to collect excise taxes in the southwest, which they did with vigour because their pay depended upon successful collection. John Nicoll

---

133   22 Aug. 1666, Rothes to Lauderdale, BL Add. Mss 23125, ff. 58–59.
134   BL Add. Mss 23124, f. 101. NLS Ms. 7024, f. 10b.
135   See, e.g. Buckroyd, *Church and State*, pp. 64–65; Hutton, *Charles II*, pp. 244–45.
136   See e.g., Argyll's letter to Lauderdale in Aug. 1666 in which he refers to the king's questioning him about disorders in Scotland during his recent visit to London, *Laing Mss* I, pp. 352–54.
137   BL Add. Mss 23125, ff. 112–13.

the diarist commented that Turner was oppressing 'simple people' for going to parish kirks other than their own.[138]

Wherever responsibility for provoking the uprising lay, it was not with Lauderdale. The secretary was playing a careful waiting game in a situation dominated by the problems of the war and their implications for the future of Lord Chancellor Clarendon. Lauderdale knew that the authority he aimed at in Scotland was not attainable as long as Clarendon retained the king's confidence. By the latter half of 1666 there were indications that Clarendon was losing that confidence. The English parliamentary session did not go well. It culminated in the passage early in 1667 of an Act prohibiting the importation of Irish cattle into England, which Clarendon's enemies, led by the mercurial duke of Buckingham and Charles's chancellor of the exchequer, Lord Ashley, all supported, and about which Lauderdale and all the Scottish cattle interests were very enthusiastic for obvious reasons.[139]

Lauderdale was building his own political party. In September 1665 Archbishop Burnet described it as consisting of Sir Robert Moray in London, and 'in Scotland . . . Argyll, Tweeddale, Kincardine, Crawford, etc.'; if they could enmesh Rothes by means of the proposed marriage between Rothes's niece and the earl of Loudoun, Argyll's kinsman, they would be all-powerful.[140] None of the four earls Burnet mentioned was a friend of the bishops. Crawford was a stiff-necked Presbyterian whose religious views made him officially unemployable, but he was a man of considerable government experience, a long-time friend of Lauderdale, and Rothes's father-in-law. Kincardine was an old friend and correspondent of Moray's. He and Tweeddale had been the only privy councillors who had advocated consulting the synods before the reimposition of episcopacy.[141] At the beginning of the war he, Tweeddale and Argyll had protested against what they regarded as the illegal imprisonment of twenty west-country gentlemen at Archbishop Burnet's urging.[142] Later in 1665 he got into trouble because Charles had been told that he had attended an allegedly

---

138 Buckroyd, *Church and State*, p. 65. Lee, *Government and Politics*, p. 159. Wodrow, *History* I, p. 186. Nicoll, *Diary*, p. 451. Kirkton's description of the behaviour of Turner's soldiers is lurid; see *History*, pp. 128–29.

139 14 Feb. 1666, Argyll to Lauderdale, BL Add. Mss 23124, ff. 57–58. P. Seaward, *The Cavalier Parliament and the Restoration of the Old Regime 1661–1667* (Cambridge, 1989), pp. 268–69.

140 4 Sept. 1665, Burnet to Sheldon, *LP* II, App., pp. xxv–xxviii. The marriage did indeed take place.

141 See above, chap. 1, p.14.

142 Burnet, *History* I, pp. 363–64.

illegal communion service. Kincardine blamed Sharp for spreading this report, and wrote him a stinging letter denying that the service was irregular and stressing that he had always been loyal to the monarchy while 'others [i.e., Sharp] did take engagements to the usurpers, were courting and cajoling Oliver Cromwell'. Sharp snapped back, denying his responsibility, but eventually he had to climb down: Kincardine was too well connected. In April 1666 Sharp asked that Kincardine be rewarded from the fines, as a way of making amends. By May Burnet was trying to saddle Bishop Leighton of Dunblane with responsibility for reporting the story. In July Moray informed Kincardine that he was once again in good odour at court.[143]

Argyll was Lauderdale's kinsman. Once he was restored, he was concerned to revive the Campbells' power and authority in the Highlands, and to add to it if possible. The Highlands were relatively quiet in these years, save for the seemingly endless dispute between the Camerons and the MacDonalds for control of Lochaber. Rothes paid as little attention to the area as he decently could, and blew hot and cold. In June 1664 the Highlands had never been so peaceable. Seven months later, after he had spent considerable time trying to achieve a 'right understanding' among all the nobility with interests there, he declared that they were so broken that he did not know what to do. One month later still, he was hopeful that they would be peaceable; otherwise he had wasted a lot of effort.[144] Argyll was careful at first. In September 1665 he declined to get involved in Lochaber without instructions from Rothes. A year later he was telling Lauderdale that it was a mistake to use 'mean persons such as have no interest in the country' to settle the Highlands; it could be done efficiently only by people with local knowledge and influence, who knew where stolen cows were to be found, for example. None of his people lived by theft, he said, but his neighbours leased lands to common thieves who stole from his tenants. He spluttered indignantly at the report that Montrose had been authorised to raise a thirty-man watch to pacify the Highlands, especially as the watch was to operate in his jurisdiction. If he thinks he can do better than

143 The exchange of letters between Kincardine and Sharp in November 1665 is in *LP* I, pp. 229–33. Kincardine supplied copies to Lauderdale. See also 15 Aug. 1665, 20 Apr., 3 July 1666, Moray to Kincardine, *Moray Letters*, pp. 252–53, 255–56. 8 May 1666, Burnet to Lauderdale, NLS Ms. 2512, f. 87. There is a much longer letter from Sharp to Kincardine printed in T. Stephen, *The Life and Times of Archbishop Sharp* (London, 1839), pp. 307–18.
144 4 June, 31 Dec. 1664, 21 Jan., 11 Feb. 1665, Rothes to Lauderdale, BL Add. Mss 23122, ff. 45, 229, 248–49, 273.

I, Argyll wrote, 'he shall have leave to try it'. At the same time, as tacksman of the excise herring on the west coast he got letters of horning for non-payment issued against, among others, Maclean of Duart, who, Argyll complained, committed violence against the local exciseman on Mull. The campaign that would lead to the expropriation of the Macleans in Mull and Tiree for Argyll's benefit was under way.[145]

As for Tweeddale, his relations with Lauderdale were becoming ever closer. A regular correspondence began in the latter part of 1664, after Tweeddale's return from London. Tweeddale was a privy councillor, and much involved in public affairs. Lauderdale consulted him about the fines, Rothes about the issue of a new book of rates.[146] He was a member of council committees to deal with the suppressing of Quaker meetings, keeping order on the borders, and doing something about the plantation of kirks, and it was he who persuaded the council to make landlords responsible for keeping their tenants away from conventicles.[147] But most of his dealings with Lauderdale in these years involved private and family business. He was one of the managers of Lauderdale's Scottish properties, looking into the question of digging for coal on Lauderdale's lands, and, with Lauderdale's brother Halton, vetting a proposed park at Lethington.[148] He and Lauderdale were both curators for the duke of Monmouth and Buccleuch during his minority; in May 1665 Lauderdale told Tweeddale that the king was very pleased with his work on Monmouth's affairs.[149] These were complicated. Both Monmouth and Duchess Anna, Lady Tweeddale's niece, were extravagant; their debts by July 1666 amounted to £25,000 sterling,[150] about twice the annual income of the Buccleuch estate. Beyond that, there were the claims on the estate resulting from Charles's having granted the wardship of the (then) Countess Anna to her uncle Rothes. His fee for his consent to Anna's marriage was £12,000 sterling, now being paid at the rate of £1,000 a year. Then there was the question of

145 21 Sept. 1665, Oct. 1666 (2 letters), Argyll to Lauderdale, *Argyll Letters*, pp. 22–24, BL Add. Mss 23125, ff. 101–05, 132. *RPCS* II, p. 181. A.I. Macinnes, *Clanship, Commerce and the House of Stuart, 1603–1788* (East Linton, 1996), pp. 134–37.

146 30 Jan. 1664, Rothes to Lauderdale, BL Add. Mss 23121, f. 37. Rothes added that he had been at 'surche' that day, where the 'earth bishop' of St Andrews preached suitably: it was the anniversary of the death of Charles the Martyr.

147 *RPCS* I, pp. 490–91, II, pp. 36, 43–46. Aug. 1666, Argyll to Lauderdale, *Laing Mss* I, pp. 352–54.

148 2 Dec. 1665, William Sharp to Lauderdale, BL Add. Mss 23123, f. 240. 25 May, 1 June 1666, Tweeddale to Lauderdale, NLS Ms. 7024, ff. 16–18.

149 NLS Ms. 7023, f. 18.

150 NLS Ms. 7024, ff. 31–32.

the executry, as it was called: the amounts Rothes and Anna's stepfather the earl of Wemyss would be allowed to collect as executors of the will of Anna's deceased older sister Mary, the previous countess of Buccleuch. The curators had raised questions about some aspects of Mary's will in 1664. Doubts had also been raised about the legality of the wardship. In 1666 both these matters were under advisement – Rothes and Wemyss had, indeed, submitted all their claims to Charles's judgment. Rothes was understandably nervous. His financial future hinged to a considerable extent on the king's favourable judgment, a judgment which Lauderdale and Tweeddale, as Monmouth's curators, were in a position to influence. He was not likely to do anything to alienate either man; hence his vehement rejection of Sharp's effort to persuade him to associate with Middleton.[151]

Tweeddale had his own concerns with the Buccleuch estate. His debt stood at about £64,000 in 1664; now that he was in good odour at court, he began to think about ways of reducing or even eliminating it. He had a claim to the lands of Easter Hassenden, currently held by the estate. Tweeddale's father had got a favourable ruling from the court of session in 1633, but for one reason or another the claim had not been pursued. In April 1665 Tweeddale asked Lauderdale if he should pursue it. Lauderdale replied that the king was willing to hear about it; Tweeddale should make his statement 'as short as you can, and written in a fair hand'.[152] Furthermore Lady Tweeddale had a claim as the heiress of her deceased brother David, who had died intestate. She was his nearest of kin, and since he had died after her marriage to Tweeddale, it could be argued that her renunciation of her claims on the Buccleuch estate in her marriage contract did not cover David's share of that estate. Tweeddale raised the claim in June 1666 as a consequence of Charles's letter to Monmouth's curators on 26 April declaring that he would soon make a decision on Rothes's and Wemyss's claims as executors of Mary's will. Tweeddale forestalled the obvious question of why he had not acted sooner by saying that he had only recently looked into the details of Lady Tweeddale's claim.[153] If the Tweeddales had got all that they argued was rightfully theirs from these

---

151 For further discussion of these questions see Lee, *Heiresses*, chaps. 4, 5.

152 4 May 1665, Lauderdale to Tweeddale, NLS Ms. 7023, f. 18. Tweeddale recapitulated the history of the claim in a long letter to Moray and Bellenden in April 1666, NLS Ms. 14542, ff. 22–23.

153 Charles's letter is in NLS Ms. 12544, f. 1. 15 June 1666, Tweeddale to Lauderdale, NLS Ms. 7024, ff. 19–20.

two claims, they would have more than wiped out the debt: the Buccleuch estate would have owed them more than £ 70,000. All these claims – the Tweeddales', the executors' and Rothes's wardship – were under discussion in the summer of 1666. In June Lauderdale wrote that Tweeddale should cooperate with Rothes, or else 'you will both be irrevocably mumped'. He also urged Tweeddale to come to London: 'without your own presence it will run great risk to miscarry, and your friends cannot help you in your absence as they can in your presence'.[154] Tweeddale replied that he was not inclined to come to London until all the encumbrances on the Buccleuch estate had been laid before Charles. He suggested that his lawyers and Monmouth's might confer and make a proposal to the king, if Charles wished.[155] But soon Tweeddale had another very good reason for coming to London: his son was courting Lauderdale's daughter.

In the summer of 1665 Tweeddale wrote to Moray and Lauderdale about sending his firstborn, Lord Yester, now seventeen, to France to complete his education. Both discouraged him: France was quarantining English ships because of the plague, and a French declaration of war on account of their alliance with the Dutch was likely. Lauderdale added that 'I think few are the better and most the worse of going to France'.[156] Yester postponed his journey on account of the plague in England, and, wrote his father, was melancholy about not going to France.[157] In April 1666 he set out for London and the court, his first time away from home. His father sent a spate of letters with him, asking the recipients to show favour to him; Moray agreed to look after him.[158] He was made welcome at Lauderdale's house in Highgate, where he and Mary Maitland came to know each other. By June rumours had reached Tweeddale in Edinburgh. Yester was to let him know, 'if you fancy that lady', before tipping his hand to anyone. Yester replied that none of her relatives thought he had intentions toward her; 'as I am more ambitious than amorous', he would follow his father's advice. Tweeddale was cautious. As he explained to both Yester and Moray, he hardly knew Mary, having seen her rarely and never talked to her. He relied

154 23 June 1666, Lauderdale to Tweeddale, Paton, 'Lauderdale', pp. 130–34. Tweeddale's claims on the Buccleuch estate featured extensively in his correspondence with Lauderdale in 1665 and 1666. For a brief summary see M. Lee, Jr, 'The Troubles of a Family Man: the Earl of Tweeddale and his Kin', in *'Inevitable' Union* pp. 252–53.

155 n.d. (late June 1666), Tweeddale to Lauderdale, NLS Ms. 7024, ff. 28–29.

156 30 Sept. 1665, Moray to Tweeddale, 3 Oct., Lauderdale to Tweeddale, Paton, 'Lauderdale', pp. 126–29.

157 20 Mar. 1666, Tweeddale to Moray, NLS Ms. 7024, ff. 10b–11.

158 Ibid., ff. 12–13.

heavily on Moray's advice as to the pair's compatibility. Moray, who had suggested the match some time previously, replied most enthusiastically, and Tweeddale replied that his doubts were resolved. He asked Moray to approach Lauderdale, who received the proposal very warmly. Yester waited on his future father-in-law constantly at night, and was shown great favour at Highgate, wrote Tweeddale's London kinsman Andrew Hay. On 18 August Tweeddale wrote to Lauderdale expressing his delight that Lauderdale favoured the marriage; he looked forward to a happy future for the two families.[159] Though Mary was a bit coy at first,[160] the wooing and winning took little more than two months. By early September the match was public knowledge. Tweeddale informed Rothes, who sent congratulations.[161] Good wishes flowed in from friends, relatives, officials and favour-seekers alike. A plaintive note sounded from Tweeddale's and Lauderdale's cousin Kellie, wishing the happy couple 'greater contentment and felicity in their married condition than he doth who subscribeth himself . . .'[162]

So Tweeddale went to London, to make the final arrangements for the marriage, to discuss plans for the summons of a convention of estates to vote money for the war, and to work on reducing or eliminating his debt to the Buccleuch estate, with the help of the father of the bride and their mutual friend and kinsman Moray. There, in late November, they received the news of the rising in the southwest, that 'horrid insurrection', as one of Tweeddale's correspondents called it,[163] which was to put an end to the power-sharing of the past three years and give the cousins their chance at power.

159 The progress of the courtship can be followed in Tweeddale's letterbooks, NLS Ms. 7001, pp. 127–42, Ms. 7024, ff. 14–30. See also NLS Ms. 7003, ff. 22, 29, 7023, f. 27 and Paton, 'Lauderdale', pp. 135–40.
160 28 Aug. 1666, Yester to Tweeddale, NLS Ms. 7023, f. 28.
161 10 Sept. 1666, Tweeddale to Lauderdale, NLS Ms. 7023, f. 28. Rothes already knew that the match was being made; 6 Aug., Rothes to Lauderdale, BL Add. Mss 23125, f. 32.
162 24 Dec. 1666, Kellie to Lauderdale, BL Add. Mss 23125, f. 265. Kellie had recently remarried. Lauderdale vehemently disapproved of the match, in part because of the shoddy condition of Kellie's estate, and Tweeddale was initially unhappy about it. Perhaps they were right. See 5 Nov. 1664, Lauderdale to Tweeddale, NLS Ms. 7023, f. 9; 4 July, 30 Aug. 1666, Kellie to Lauderdale, BL Add. Mss 23123, ff. 112–13, 169.
163 20 Nov. 1666, Lord Newbyth to Tweeddale, NLS Ms. 7003, f. 41.

CHAPTER FOUR

Lauderdale Triumphant, 1666–1667

As rebellions go, the Pentland Rising was small potatoes. It began with a scuffle in the town of Dalry on 13 November 1666; the decisive rout of the rebels at Rullion Green, in the Pentland Hills, took place on the 28th. Their so-called army, which never numbered more than eleven hundred, and was certainly smaller than that on the 28th, was poorly armed and badly fed, though it fought bravely enough; General Dalyell's force was much larger.[1] Some fifty rebels were killed and eighty captured. Reprisals began rapidly. The first trials were held on 5 December, after two prisoners had been tortured in the boots; ten were convicted, and hanged two days later. In all there were thirty-six executions. Many more of the captured were sentenced to transportation to Barbados, whose governor in July 1667 wrote a grateful letter to Lauderdale, expressing his pleasure at the number of Scots in Barbados and wanting more of them so that he could 'grapple with Monsieur' in case of a French attack. He much preferred Scots to Irish because Scots 'I am certain will fight without a crucifix about the neck'.[2]

How spontaneous was this rebellion? There is no doubt that the initial fracases, at Dalry and then at nearby Balmaclellan, were unpremeditated. But the fact that a sizeable group of horse and foot could collect, and fifty horse sweep into Dumfries, more than sixty miles from Dalry, early in the morning of 15 November and seize Sir James Turner, suggests that some sort of preparation for an uprising, perhaps in the wake of a hoped-for Dutch landing, was under way, and that the revolt broke out prematurely. Officialdom thought so. The privy council, when it learned of Turner's capture, sent General Dalyell to Glasgow to suppress the rebellion, ordered the fencible men of various shires to turn out on specified dates, made preparations for the defence of Edinburgh and Stirling, and shut down all ferry traffic across the Forth save that originating in Leith.[3] Clearly the

---

1 The standard account is C.S. Terry, *The Pentland Rising and Rullion Green* (Glasgow, 1905). There is an excellent brief summary in Ian B. Cowan, *The Scottish Covenanters 1660–1688* (London, 1976), chap. 4.

2 26 July 1667, Sir William Willoughby to Lauderdale, BL Add. Mss 23127, f. 158.

3 *RPCS* II, pp. 211 ff. The operative dates are 17–27 Nov. 1666. On the 29th they notified Charles of the victory of the previous day and dismissed the fencibles of Fife, Angus, Perth and the Mearns. *RPCS* II, pp. 228–29.

council expected widespread trouble. In the immediate aftermath, on 17 December, Rothes wrote of the 'damned fools who . . . anticipat(ed) their time of rising', and others who were more cautious but 'we may be sure if we have alarms on our coasts of foreigners they will rise behind us, for I doubt not but they will be content to join with Turks'. Twelve days later he reported that some of those hanged had confessed that the rising had been planned for March or April of the following year.[4]

General Dalyell likewise opined that the rebellion 'if it had not been mistimed had been much more terrible'. Dalyell blamed the women, who 'upbraided their husbands and children for not dying' and becoming martyrs.[5] General Drummond felt the same way, though he blamed the preachers rather than the women.[6] Archbishop Burnet wrote to Sheldon that 'many things in the rising look like a design', but he was not worried 'if it be not done by correspondence with England and Ireland'. Three weeks later he was becoming panicky: whatever might be said at court, 'our fears and apprehensions of danger are greater than when the rebels were marching in a body'. In late January Argyll reported that Burnet, basing his opinion on the confessions of some of the 'rogues' who were hanged, 'thought the design of the late rebellion more general than I [Argyll] imagined'.[7] Half a year later Lauderdale's two principal collaborators differed in their assessments. Moray's inquiries led him to conclude that it was spontaneous, and might have been put down more easily than it was. Tweeddale thought that the soldiers provoked it, but that 'there was somewhat of design there on foot'.[8] Modern historians have echoed Tweeddale's view.[9] Probably there was much more accident than planning involved; some contingency plans may have been made, but by whom is far from clear. The rebels' ultimate purposes are equally murky. They declared that they were for king and Covenant, and that their only 'quarrel was at the bishops newly set up in the land'.[10] The exact truth is unknown and probably unknowable.

4 17, 29 Dec. 1666, Rothes to Lauderdale, BL Add. Mss 23125, ff. 251–52, 269.
5 27 Dec. 1666, Dalyell to Lauderdale, ibid., f. 267.
6 14 Dec. 1666, Drummond to Lauderdale, ibid., f. 246.
7 27 Nov., 17 Dec. 1666, Burnet to Sheldon, *LP* II, App., pp. xl–xli, xlii–xliv. 31 Jan. 1667, Argyll to Lauderdale, *Argyll Letters*, pp. 60–61.
8 1–2 July 1667, Moray to Lauderdale, 20 Aug., Tweeddale to Lauderdale, BL Add. Mss 23127, ff. 88–90, 215. At the end of the year Moray reiterated his view that there was no conspiracy, BL Add. Mss, 23128, ff. 235–36.
9 See, e.g., Cowan, *Covenanters*, p. 64, J. Buckroyd, *Church and State in Scotland 1660–1681* (Edinburgh, 1980), p. 66.
10 Quoted in Cowan, *Covenanters*, p. 66.

In the absence of Rothes the privy council, with Sharp presiding, 'managed the little war, and gave all the orders and directions in it'. Sharp did not impress Gilbert Burnet, who described him as extremely defeatist and cowardly.[11] At the council meeting on 17 November, which ordered Dalyell to Glasgow to pursue the rebels and notified Rothes of what it had done, Bellenden asserted that Sharp wanted to hush the whole business up, lest the administration look bad. The earl of Dumfries retorted that that made as much sense as trying to keep the billeting secret, when the account of what had happened reached the court before the official letter. Sharp showed confusion, and everyone laughed at him.[12] When word of the uprising reached London, Charles ordered Rothes home post-haste, with the formal title of commander-in-chief, which he had not had before, and orders to do 'speedy and exemplary justice' on the rebels, and adding Generals Dalyell and Drummond to the council.[13] Rothes was no more than halfway home on the day of Rullion Green. He wrote that day to Lauderdale from Boroughbridge, explaining that he had had a fall and injured his arm and leg: he would have to travel by coach, but would make what haste he could. Shortly after he arrived he set out on a tour of the disaffected areas, and concluded that only force would serve. 'They are all incorrigible and never to be trusted,' he wrote from Glasgow on 10 December. Four days later he was fuming about 'damned incorrigible fanatics' who would rebel again if they had the opportunity. He was full of praise of the generals, who echoed his sentiments. Dalyell wrote that the rebels were 'more numerous than any can apprehend'; the country could only be settled if the inhabitants were removed or destroyed.[14] Rothes felt that the council was being too soft and cautious, not being willing to hang enough people until they received the king's instructions; and, indeed, Rothes himself, before he set out for the west, wanted to know about the 120 prisoners currently in Edinburgh, 'mean and beggarly fellows', who were 'declaring their willingness to die for the Covenant, which renders them in my opinion uncapable of mercy'. But since there were so many, the council wanted to know if the king wanted them hanged or sent to Barbados.[15] In his letters from the west Rothes left no doubt that he

11 Burnet, *History* I, pp. 406–08.
12 *RPCS* II, pp. 211–12. 17 Nov. 1666, Bellenden to Lauderdale, BL Add. Mss 23125, f. 147. Bellenden wrote 'read and burn' at the top of this letter.
13 BL Add. Mss 23125, f. 157. *RPCS* II, pp. 234–35, 241–42.
14 BL Add. Mss. 23125, ff. 159, 189, 194, 196–97, 242.
15 6 Dec. 1666, Rothes to Lauderdale, 2 letters, ibid., ff. 184–85.

preferred the noose. After two days in Ayr he concluded that except for the earl of Eglinton and Lord Cochrane and their families 'there is scarcely one gentleman in this whole country to be trusted'. He was thinking of ordering a general confiscation of arms, and of all horses worth £5.[16] The generals, meanwhile, were complaining that litigious members of the council and cautious judges were delaying the necessary business of getting on with the hangings and the accompanying confiscations, from which they hoped to fill their pockets. Dalyell did his best to keep the pressure on Rothes. 'Without extirpation the most part of this country will second this rebellion with a greater,' he wrote at the end of the year.[17]

The rebellion caused understandable nervousness at court. There were wild rumours: one report had the rebels 4,000 strong, one 7,000, one, from Norwich, 40,000![18] Fortunately Sir Joseph Williamson's principal correspondent in Edinburgh was quite accurate as to the rebels' numbers, leadership and equipment.[19] Lauderdale's brother, who was with Dalyell's army, sent a long account of the battle which, apart from his exaggeration of the enemy's numbers, was also accurate.[20] And the rising had been easily put down. Nevertheless the king was not inclined to be merciful. The council, in announcing the victory, declared that there was so much disaffection that 'a more rigorous application of your Majesty's authority' would be necessary to secure the peace, a view which Rothes, after his return from the west, made it clear that he shared.[21] Archbishop Burnet stressed to Sheldon 'how little I have failed in my unhappy prediction'. What the rebels wanted, in their enthusiasm for king and Covenant, was to revive the bargain made with Charles I, to preserve royal authority and destroy episcopacy. Without the standing army 'the Covenant had been as universally received as ever'.[22] Rothes, the archbishops and the generals were in agreement: military repression was to be the order of the day.

16 17, 20 Dec. 1666, Rothes to Lauderdale, ibid., ff. 251–52, 255–56.
17 20 Dec. 1666, Dalyell to Lauderdale, 22 Dec., Drummond to Lauderdale, ibid., ff. 259, 261–62. Typically, Kellie also hoped to profit from the confiscations. 24 Dec., Kellie to Lauderdale, ibid., f. 265. 29 Dec., Dalyell to Rothes, LP II, App., p. lxxv.
18 CSPD 1666–1667, pp. 290, 295, 296.
19 See the letters of Robert Mein, starting on 17 Nov. 1666, ibid., pp. 268 ff.
20 BL Add. Mss. 23124, f. 171.
21 29 Nov. 1666, the council to Lauderdale, 6, 10 Dec., Rothes to Lauderdale, ibid., ff. 161, 185, 196–97.
22 8 Dec. 1666, Burnet to Sheldon, LP II, App., pp. xli–xliii. His language to Lauderdale was less vehement; he recommended promising the lesser prisoners their lives in return for confessions. NLS Ms. 2512, f. 91.

Yet in the end there was no bloodbath. Lauderdale did not want one, as his policy after he achieved power makes clear. To this end Charles had to be persuaded that severity would do no good, that such a policy would, in fact, be counterproductive. This took some doing. Charles expected the further rebellion in the west that Dalyell had predicted, especially if there was a foreign invasion. Such a prospect made him nervous. He did put an end to the hanging of the less important people: 'the rest of the rabble you shall send to Barbados', he wrote in January. By mid-March he was beginning to recover his balance: there had been no rebellion. On 12 March, in a letter which the Presbyterian Kirkton characterised as 'one of the best ever Lauderdale subscribed', the king ordered the disaffected areas disarmed, a plan for a militia drawn up, and the prosecution of only those rebels who were heritors, ministers or officers. The order was in some respects ambiguous. The council, wrote Drummond, 'after some jangling' decided to apply it to the nine western shires only, and to ask Charles if the order to collect horses from the disaffected applied everywhere. Regarding the militia it suggested that only half the number parliament had authorised be got ready, in view of the shortage of money and arms. Rothes worried about filling the commands: those appointed would be annoyed at not getting more lucrative positions in the standing army. The behaviour of that army occasionally angered the king. After a report from Newburgh he wrote a stiff letter about the conduct of some troopers, which Lauderdale deftly arranged for Archbishop Burnet, one of the army's principal advocates, to carry back to Rothes in Edinburgh. Burnet had come to London to complain, among other things, that many councillors had spoken in support of leniency for the rebels at a recent meeting, but was unwilling to name names; Charles ordered the council to do so.[23] But by this time, early May, his vindictive mood had vanished.

Lauderdale's success in bringing the king around to a more moderate view of the rebellion was the first step in the regime change which he, his newly minted 'dearest brother', and the indispensable Moray planned to bring about. There was a necessary precondition to this: Clarendon had to lose the king's support. The English parliament's passage of the Irish cattle

23 *Warrant Book 1660–1670*, NAS GD 90/2/260, under date of 5 Jan. 1667, no pagination. *RPCS* II, pp. 267–69, 284–86. Kirkton, *History*, p 152. 20 Mar., Drummond to Lauderdale, 11 Apr., Rothes to Lauderdale, 2 May, Dalyell to Lauderdale, BL Add. Mss 23126, ff. 139, 155–56, 205. 4, 16 May, Lauderdale to Tweeddale, NLS Ms. 7023, ff. 33, 38. Newburgh's own troop was disorderly, perhaps because he was ill and reportedly near death. Lauderdale was not so sure: 'it may be he hath only taken a surfeit of drink'. 11 Apr., Lauderdale to Tweeddale, NLS Ms. 7023, f. 31.

bill in January 1667 over Clarendon's opposition was an indication that his influence was waning.[24] By that time the cousins' strategy was being developed. Tweeddale was still in London; he had remained there after his son's wedding in order to work out a settlement of his debt to the Buccleuch estate, which he was able to reduce substantially.[25] Rothes was the cousins' principal target, of course, but the groundwork for an attack on him had to be carefully prepared. Charles might be weary of Clarendon, but Rothes was his friend. The latter's successful handling of the January convention of estates did not make the cousins' campaign any easier. Rothes and Argyll, whose letters became very frequent in these months, kept Lauderdale supplied with an almost day-to-day account of what went on. The letters in fact began the day before the estates assembled, when Rothes, at the end of a letter of (for him) moderate length, said that he had to stop and prepare his speech as royal commissioner for the coming session: 'I must say somewhat, though never so great nonsense.'[26]

The estates met on 9 January and heard a letter from the king that acknowledged Scotland's poverty. But money was needed for the army, one year's supply, and Charles stressed that the old method of taxing employed in 1665 was too slow. So the estates authorised Rothes to appoint a committee to consider ways and means. The committee met on 10 January and, by prearrangement, Argyll moved that the estates raise £72,000 a month for a year, over and above the existing taxes. The money was to be used to pay the army, which was being increased in size, and the militia; Rothes explained that current military expenses ran at about £60,000 a month. The committee accepted Argyll's motion without opposition, to Rothes's delight, and a few days later voted to collect the money by means of a cess, with only four negative votes. Since the cess was a land tax, the committee recommended a poll tax on non-landholders. Only colleges, hospitals and stipendiary clergy were exempt; at Charles's request, the members of the court of session waived their exemption without prejudice.[27] The committee also recommended the suspension of repayment of principal on debts for two years for heritors, except for those owed to the

24 The Scottish privy council followed suit on 1 Feb. 1667 by prohibiting the importation of Irish cattle and beef, and salt and corn as well, after 1 Mar. *RPCS* II, pp. 253–54.

25 For this agreement, and its subsequent fate, see below, chap. 10, pp. 293–94, 311–12, 318.

26 8 Jan. 1667, Rothes to Lauderdale, BL. Add. Mss 23126, f. 16.

27 Ibid., f. 14. £72,000 (£6,000 sterling) per month became the standard rate for all future levyings of cess.

crown, so that they could afford to pay the tax, but they did have to pay annualrent (interest). Rothes viewed the suspension as essential. Without it creditors would have descended on the nobility like locusts after Whitsun, the next due date, prisons would have been filled, and 'the whole kingdom would have been by the ears'.[28]

The estates received the committee report on 15 January. They accepted the cess after a long debate, with only a handful voting for raising the money by Old Extent, as in 1665. Since there was no time to reevaluate the cess, the valuations of Cromwell's government would be used. The estates also accepted the recommendation that stipendiary ministers be exempted; only the earl of Kinghorn argued for taxing them, and he was shouted down. Two days later, again after considerable debate, the convention authorised the poll tax. The families of gentlemen paid £6 per month, tenants £4, tradesmen and others £1; burghs could levy on their residents at the same rate. Two days later still the recommended suspension of debt payments was accepted. Rumours that there would be a tax on annualrents proved to be just rumours; such a proposal, in combination with the suspension of payments on principal, might well have produced a creditors' revolt. Finally the convention, following what had become the settled practice of Restoration regimes, authorised the quartering of soldiers on those in arrears, at the rate of 15d for a trooper and 4d for a foot soldier. The convention did its work expeditiously. It convened on 9 January and finished up two weeks later, on the 23rd. Rothes, who had moved things along as swiftly as possible, to avoid the growth of 'evil humours', was very pleased at his success, and so was King Charles. After the event Argyll, who had backed Rothes in arguing against reevaluation even though he believed that the rates were unfair both to Scotland as a whole and to his lands in particular, urged Lauderdale to create a committee of reevaluation in case the cess was levied again.[29]

Whatever satisfaction the proceedings of the estates generated in Edinburgh and Whitehall faded rapidly in the face of the government's

---

28 19 Jan. 1667, Rothes to Lauderdale, ibid., ff. 51–52.

29 The official record of the convention is in *APS* VII, pp. 538–47. See also 10, 15, 17, 19 Jan., 12 Feb. 1667, Rothes to Lauderdale, BL Add. Mss 23126, ff. 24–25, 41–42, 46–48, 51–52, 82. In a note appended to his letter of 15 Jan. Rothes explained that it was not holograph because he had spilled ink on his handwritten report and had to send a copy; one wonders if he had been drinking. BL Add. Mss 23126, f. 43. 10, 11, 15, 22 Jan., 28 Mar., Argyll to Lauderdale, BL Add. Mss 23126, ff. 27–28, *Laing Mss* I, pp. 355–56, *Argyll Letters*, pp. 49, 52–53, 77–78. 22 Jan., Charles to Rothes, *Warrant Book 1660–1670*, NAS GD 90/2/260, no pagination.

necessities and reputation and the poverty of the country. Money could be borrowed only on private security, not on public credit. Rothes, Dalyell and Sir William Bruce, the collector-general of the new tax, had to find money for the army out of their own pockets. People would not lend on the strength of the new tax: the 'public trust . . . has so much formerly been abused in this kingdom'. Thus General Drummond, who went on to comment that Hamilton, who borrowed in the expectation of being repaid out of the tax, had to pay very high interest.[30] Rothes's essential fecklessness was also on display. He acknowledged that money was desperately needed to buy arms, but still hoped that something could be allowed out of the taxation to reward deserving nobles.[31] Rothes and the generals, the advocates of repressive measures in the west, were now hand-in-glove. General Drummond was to marry Rothes's niece, the earl of Eglinton's daughter, and become Viscount Inchaffray: Sharp was willing to yield Inchaffray abbey's lands to him because of his meritorious services.[32]

Since Rothes had been so successful in handling the convention, Lauderdale decided to focus first on Archbishop Sharp, the weakest link in Rothes's cabal. Lauderdale had no love for him: he had attempted to undermine Lauderdale's position with the king. His advocacy of repression was less vehement and more recent than that of Burnet, but he was dangerous and slippery. Furthermore Charles did not like him. But Lauderdale had to move carefully. As long as Clarendon was in power he dared not work for Sharp's dismissal: his Presbyterian past would be resurrected and thrown in his face. Furthermore the archbishop's brother William was Lauderdale's indispensable informant and man of business, whom he could not afford to alienate. He correctly read Sharp as a bootlicker; what he had to do was to contrive that his were the boots Sharp would lick in the future. To this end Bellenden's letters were very helpful. Bellenden was full of contempt and scorn for Sharp, whom he accused of great cowardice as the rebels approached Edinburgh. More importantly, he insinuated that Sharp, who

---

30 20 Mar., 2 Apr. 1667, Drummond to Lauderdale, BL Add. Mss 23126, ff. 139, 145. Bruce, Kincardine's kinsman, best known as an architect, was a rising man; he was also the collector of fines.

31 21 Mar. 1667, Rothes to Lauderdale, ibid., ff. 134–35.

32 20 Jan. 1667, Sharp to Lauderdale, NLS Ms. 2512, f. 98. 12 Mar., Bellenden to Lauderdale, BL Add. Mss 23126, f. 122. The wedding did not happen, although Drummond did get the temporalities of Inchaffray. Lauderdale regarded him as dangerously violent and kept him at arms' length. He eventually married the daughter of Johnston of Wariston (of all people); his peerage had to wait until the reign of James VII.

wanted Dalyell to seize the rebels' estates, was conniving with the generals to feather their nests, 'to wash the Generals' mouth with church holy water', as he put it, hence to exaggerate the peril in order to give the generals a freer hand. Confiscation of estates and grants of property were the business of the exchequer, Bellenden insisted. When Sharp continued to grumble, Bellenden snapped that the council ought to investigate his financial practices as archbishop.[33] Sharp's motive in baying for blood could be painted as suspect.

Lauderdale's campaign began in January 1667. There was a rumour that the king had named the duke of Hamilton to preside over the council instead of Sharp, a story which caused a good deal of comment and conjecture and, predictably, delighted Bellenden. Reports circulated that Charles was dissatisfied with the bishops as a group, rumours sufficiently alarming to impel the bishops at the convention of estates to urge Burnet – not Sharp – to go to court to see the king. The stories of Sharp's intrigue with Middleton resurfaced, prompting an unconvincing denial from Sharp which his brother sent to Lauderdale. The archbishop was showing signs of jangled nerves. He made some unflattering comments about Lauderdale, which he attributed to the earl of Dumfries, who denied them. Rothes, who reported this, was irritated at what looked like an obvious attempt by Sharp to sow discord between him and Lauderdale; Sharp was 'strangely cast down, yea, lower than the dust', at Rothes's reaction. Sharp made a condescending remark to Argyll, calling him a good man, for a Presbyterian; Argyll, not surprisingly, bridled at it.[34] Sharp's last appearance at the council board came on 1 February. He retired to his diocese and became seriously ill; in May Tweeddale thought he might die. Burnet told Sharp that at one point Charles had considered removing him and replacing him with the bishop of Edinburgh, or with a commission, but had finally decided to do nothing.[35] When Sharp finally reemerged, in July, he was a changed, and broken, man.

For by July the regime change that Lauderdale had so carefully nurtured was under way. Rothes was no longer lord treasurer. Instead, there was a treasury commission, which he did not control. Both Tweeddale and

33 11 Dec. 1666, Bellenden to Lauderdale, BL Add. Mss 23125, ff. 201–02. See also his letters of 17 and 29 Nov., BL Add. Mss 23125, ff. 147, 165–67.

34 8, 19 Jan. 1667, Rothes to Lauderdale, 8 Jan., Bellenden to Lauderdale, 26 Jan., William Sharp to Lauderdale, BL Add. Mss 23126, ff. 16, 51–52, 22, 60–61, 12 Jan., Burnet to Sheldon, *LP* II, App., pp. xliv–xlv. 1–2 Feb., Argyll to Lauderdale, *Argyll Letters*, pp. 61–64.

35 23 May, 6 July 1667, Tweeddale to Lauderdale, BL Add. Mss 23126, f. 220, 23127, f. 105.

Moray opined that Sharp was now sufficiently chastened to become Lauderdale's tool. The tip-off was that Sharp, when he emerged from his semi-enforced retirement, publicly supported the policies of the cousins, especially with respect to the army. It should not be maintained merely in order to support the bishops, Sharp said, nor would he support Rothes in his rear-guard action to retain some of his authority. 'He will never more be for Commissioners nor armies,' Moray wrote on 1 July.[36] On the 13th Lauderdale wrote to Tweeddale that the story that he had questioned the archbishop's privileges was false. Burnet had raised the issue of those privileges; Lauderdale asked what they were and spoke to the king, who confirmed them. Furthermore he had never been present at any discussion of Sharp's removal from office. Tweeddale was to use this letter and report the reaction.[37] With tears in his eyes Sharp expressed his gratitude, confessed to Tweeddale that he had asked Sheldon to block Tweeddale's appointment as chancellor, and declared that 'you and your friends would do more for the settlement of the Church than those they had trusted more'. Gone was any thought of trying to impose the English liturgy in Scotland and maintaining the army to that end: a bad idea, he said. Nor was there any need for a large army to prevent further trouble: the 'people in the west . . . were now quite broken'. Sharp was persuaded that Lauderdale had always dealt 'generously and nobly' with him; he would follow Lauderdale's lead unquestioningly from now on.[38]

On 27 July Sharp wrote his own bootlicking letter to Lauderdale, expressing his delight that his enemies had not persuaded the secretary to ruin him, admitting having said some offensive things about Lauderdale through 'mistake, misinformation, and passion', and denying that he had ever conspired with Dumfries against him. He also expressed his pleasure at Lauderdale's favour to his brother, whom the new treasury commission had recently appointed as cashkeeper; Sharp may well have calculated that his own new posture of humility and his brother's new eminence were not unrelated.[39] Lauderdale was not mollified. Sharp was still trying to justify himself, he wrote: the letter 'sticks in his stomach'. Tweeddale advised him to reply. Moray also encouraged the secretary not to be too

---

36 BL Add. Mss 23127, ff. 88–90. 28 June, 6 July 1667, Tweeddale to Lauderdale, BL Add. Mss 23127, ff. 82–83, 105.
37 NLS Ms. 7023, f. 61.
38 23 July 1667, Tweeddale to Lauderdale, BL Add. Mss 23127, ff. 141–42.
39 Ibid., f. 166.

hard on Sharp: he 'may certainly be made very good use of'. So on 2 September Lauderdale wrote to Sharp, once again sending the letter to Tweeddale with instructions to deliver it and report the archbishop's reactions. If he showed any further reluctance to humble himself, 'I know what to do next'. He would not go into the baselessness of Sharp's innuendos, but was prepared to let bygones be bygones. The tone was menacing. The result was a letter sufficiently abject for Lauderdale, praising Tweeddale (who was carrying the letter to London) to the skies, no longer doubting Tweeddale's 'affection to the settled government' of the church, praising his 'pious carriage and sobriety', and pledging to follow 'your lordships' (plural) policies of moderation and indulgence 'to gain such as are gainable'.[40] It must have galled the archbishop to write these things about a man he so deeply mistrusted, but if he was to keep his job he felt that he had no choice. The archbishop, and through him the religious establishment, over which he 'hath the absolute rule',[41] would follow the cousins' line.

Rothes was no longer lord treasurer because Lauderdale had convinced the king that the treasury had to be better managed, and that Rothes was inadequate for the job. But there would be no new lord treasurer, who would automatically become a potential rival for Lauderdale. Instead there would be a five-man commission. Rothes's pain would be eased by making him its president, but he would have no more authority than his colleagues. Bellenden, the treasurer-depute, would of course be a member. The others were Tweeddale, Moray and William Cochrane, Lord Cochrane. He was one of the most active of Monmouth's curators, and was largely responsible for the initiative that led to parliament's granting the king the permanent tax of £40,000 sterling in 1661. The king thought well of him; Rothes called him 'an infamous knave'. Completely omitted from the commission was the duke of Hamilton, to whom the crown owed a great deal of money and who badly wanted an appointment. He is 'lost to you', wrote Tweeddale, 'for not making him a commissioner of the treasury'.[42] The key man was

40 3, 10, 17 Aug., 3, 17 Sept. 1667, Lauderdale to Tweeddale, NLS Ms. 7023, ff. 69, 75, 78, 86, 89. 8 Aug., Moray to Lauderdale, 9 Aug., Tweeddale to Lauderdale, 2 Sept., Lauderdale to Sharp, BL Add. Mss 23127, ff. 187–88, 191, 23128, f. 1. 15 Oct., Sharp to Lauderdale, NLS Ms. 2512, f. 104. A second grovelling letter followed on 23 Oct., NLS Ms. 2512, f. 106.

41 The phrase is Tweeddale's, in his letter of 28 June 1667 to Lauderdale, BL Add. Mss 23127, ff. 82–83.

42 14 June 1664, Rothes to Lauderdale, BL Add. Mss 23122, f. 53. 19 July 1667, Tweeddale to Lauderdale, BL Add. Mss 23127, f. 131. For Cochrane and the tax of 1661 see Mackenzie, *Memoirs*, p. 18.

Tweeddale, who, with Moray and Cochrane, would have the votes to deter-mine policy.

The king's decision on the treasury commission was made by mid-April, quite possibly before Tweeddale, having reached his settlement with the Buccleuch estate, left London at the end of March.[43] There were to be commissions in both kingdoms. Because Charles regarded Scotland as an excellent testing ground for changes he contemplated for England – as Moray wrote, 'his pleasure is readily complied with in Scotland'[44] – Charles had intended to make the change in Scotland first. But as it happened Lord Treasurer Southampton died suddenly in May; so the English commission was appointed first. Moray was to carry Charles's decision about Scotland northward in person. Unlike Tweeddale he got on well with Rothes, and was both persuasive and charming: he could ease the blow. His instructions are dated 16 April. On that same day the 'infamous knave' Cochrane joined the council. Charles had appointed him on 5 March, an indication, perhaps, that he had made his decision about the commission by then. On 20 April Lauderdale wrote to Tweeddale that Moray would leave in the following week. That did not happen. On 7 May Lauderdale wrote that he was being 'stayed for money, which troubles me but no remedy'; he was still waiting ten days later.[45]

It seems possible that a better reason for the delay was that in April the discussions between Rothes and Monmouth's curators over the amount of his pay-off for Duchess Anna's wardship were reaching a crisis. The legality of the wardship hinged on the status of one piece of land, Blackgraine, which had been in the family's possession since the previous century. It had originally been held *cum maritagio*, but a regrant of 1604 made no mention of its being held that way. Was the language of the regrant a clerical error, or a deliberate expression of James VI's intentions? The lawyers argued. Rothes became more and more nervous: if his own lawyers could be shown

---

43 Lauderdale's first letter to Tweeddale after his departure is dated 2 April 1667. It reported the king's rage at the elopement of Frances Stewart, 'la belle Stuart', whom he had been trying to seduce for at least four years. NLS Ms. 7023, f. 30.

44 14 June, 4 July 1667, Moray to Lauderdale, BL Add. Mss 23127, ff. 38–41, 102.

45 NLS Ms. 7102, no. 6, 7023, ff. 33, 35, 39. A draft of the commission's membership and instruc-tions is in NLS Ms. 597, ff. 147–48. Because Moray and Tweeddale were the only two members not currently on the list of pensioners, they were to divide the amount a lord treasurer would have collected, which came to £707 3s 4d apiece. *Miscellany of the Maitland Club* III (Edinburgh, 1843), pp. 149–55 RPCS II, pp. 278–79. Kincardine, who was at court in April, knew of the king's decision, probably from his good friend Moray, and informed Gilbert Burnet. Burnet, *History* I, p. 418.

to have obfuscated, he might not only get nothing more but also be penalised for taking advantage of his niece.[46] He alternated between confidence and despair, and finally authorised Lauderdale to make a settlement with Monmouth's commissioners and/or the king, for as little as half of what he was owed.[47] On 21 May Lauderdale reported this to Tweeddale, along with the 'great news' that following Southampton's death on 16 May, Charles had appointed a five-man treasury commission for England 'with never a great officer on it, all of his own election, and all unpleasant to somebody', i.e. Clarendon. 'The king,' Lauderdale went on, 'says he will be Lord Treasurer himself and sit weekly with them.' On the 28th Tweeddale replied, rejoicing that 'the keys will hang at the right belt, and will doubtless alarm somebody'. He urged Lauderdale to send Moray to Scotland right away; he had been eager for Moray's dispatch for some time. On the same day Lauderdale wrote that Moray was about to leave; he departed on 3 June.[48] The slow process of easing Rothes out of power could now begin.

In the weeks after his return from London Tweeddale was very busy. The bishops' spokesman, Archbishop Burnet, had gone to court to lay their complaints before the king, and got an audience which included Clarendon, Charles's brother and Archbishop Sheldon. Lauderdale described Burnet as vague and incoherent, but he did impel the king to order the privy council to take steps to protect those clergymen who were being harassed. The council appointed a committee that included Tweeddale to consider the matter.[49] On 13 June the council proclaimed that if a minister was harassed, and the perpetrators not caught, the whole parish would be fined.[50] 'We have daily incredible proof of the cruelty of the fanatics' against the ministers in the west, wrote Rothes. Soldiers were sent to pacify the area and put a stop to the harassments. They were hated there, as Rothes admitted. The hostile population would give them no information and in turn complained about their behaviour.[51] Rothes and his troops also had to deal with the

---

46 NLS Ms. 14944, ff. 8, 10.

47 14 May 1667, Rothes to Lauderdale, BL Add. Mss 23126, f. 210. This letter is not holograph; two days later he repeated his concession in his own hand. BL Add. Mss 23126, f. 216.

48 NLS Ms. 7023, ff. 41, 42, 44. BL Add. Mss 23126, ff. 195, 232.

49 *RPCS* II, pp. 284–86. 16 May 1667, Lauderdale to Tweeddale, NLS Ms. 7023, ff. 33–34.

50 *RPCS* II, pp. 290–92.

51 25 May, 6 June 1667, Rothes to Lauderdale, BL Add. Mss 23126, ff. 224–25, 23127, ff. 10–12. A paper detailing the grievances of the Stewartry of Kirkcudbright against the occupying soldiery, dated 18 May, is in BL Add. Mss 23126, ff. 218–19.

threat of a Dutch invasion. At the end of April fifteen Dutch warships showed up in the Forth, went as far up as Burntisland, and, wrote Rothes, fired at least 500 shot 'without so much as killing either cat or dog'; they only knocked down a few chimneys. Rothes ordered up the troops, but fortunately they were never tested, thanks to the wind, which favoured the defenders. English informants in Edinburgh reported that the attack on Burntisland 'caused uproar' in Edinburgh, that the inhabitants behaved resolutely, and that the death toll amounted to a dead hen and a dead rat that lived in a chimney. But there was genuine fear of invasion.[52]

Tweeddale feared what might happen if an invasion occurred: the soldiery was in very bad shape.[53] His letters to Lauderdale in these months are full of criticism of the condition and behaviour of the soldiers, who, though well paid, behaved as if they were penniless: 'though the soldiers have English pay, they take German quarter'. They moved around a lot to avoid paying for billets, which they were not required to do if they were in transient quarters. Rothes's own troop of horse was as extortionate as any: Perthshire paid it £4,000 to persuade it to move on. Tweeddale asked Lauderdale to get the king to say publicly that the soldiers must pay for what they receive, or else the country would be ruined. Ordinary people, he added, despaired of having their complaints redressed, since privy councillors commanded thirteen of the fourteen troops in question. Lauderdale replied that Charles had written 'sharply' about the quarterings, and gave Tweeddale leave to say that he feels kindly toward 'poor Scotland'. He added, 'we have a great alarm, as if the Dutch had a design upon Scotland'.[54] Rothes worried about an attack on Shetland. No one had any confidence in the garrison's ability to fend off an invasion; even Rothes's allies the generals complained that he had been lax in supplying it with arms.[55] The commander-in-chief's military reputation was in serious jeopardy.

On 4 June Lauderdale wrote to Tweeddale that Moray was en route at last. 'What he carries you will know time enough from himself, for I take no

---

52 30 Apr. 1667, Rothes to Lauderdale, BL Add. Mss 23126, f. 182. *CSPD 1667*, pp. 62–63, 71, 75.

53 9 May 1667, Tweeddale to Lauderdale, BL Add. Mss 23126, f. 195.

54 9, 23, 27 May 1667, Tweeddale to Lauderdale, ibid., ff. 195, 220, 226. The quotation comes from the letter of 23 May. 1 June, Lauderdale to Tweeddale, NLS Ms. 14406, f. 34. As it turned out, the Dutch design was upon England; in mid-June their fleet was in the Thames, burning English warships.

55 6 June 1667, Rothes to Lauderdale, BL Add. Mss 23127, ff. 10–12. 8 June, Drummond to Lauderdale, BL Add. Mss 23127, f. 18. Drummond enclosed a list of popular complaints against the army, such as the use of free quarters. BL Add. Mss 23127, ff. 20–21.

great pleasure to tell it.'⁵⁶ Rothes would indeed cease to be lord treasurer, but Charles decided to save his old friend's face by kicking him upstairs into the office of lord chancellor. Rothes had been reluctantly performing the duties of this office for some time, and fervently wished to be rid of it. Lauderdale had lobbied for the appointment of someone else (not named in his letters); the king was favourable at first, but then some negative stories about Lauderdale's candidate surfaced. The king chose Rothes, and Lauderdale could not budge him: 'You know how positive he is in Scots resolutions which once he takes.' He wanted Moray to stress to Rothes that 'I am not the designer of this matter and that I endeavoured otherwise.'⁵⁷ It is quite possible that Lauderdale's lobbying was not as vigorous as he implied. He knew that Tweeddale, at least, and probably Moray as well, wanted Rothes's power reduced as much as possible. Moray arrived in Edinburgh on 14 June. Tweeddale met him and they went in a coach straight to Holyroodhouse. Rothes was there; after dinner, he and Moray had their fateful interview. The rest, Tweeddale wrote, Moray will tell you himself.⁵⁸

His appointment as chancellor caught Rothes, and all of official Edinburgh, completely by surprise. Not even Tweeddale was in on the secret, though of course he knew about the treasury commission. Rothes was appalled. On 15 June he wrote to the king and to Lauderdale, protesting that he did not know how to do the job, that he had no knowledge of Latin or the laws (true enough), that he would simply expose his ignorance, that he was too young, that he had the wrong sort of temperament, that he could not be both chancellor and commissioner – any argument he could think of to get the king to change his mind. He positively would not accept until he had pleaded his case with Charles, preferably in person; he explained to Lauderdale that he could make a quick trip to court and not stay more than a week. The tone of his letters became increasingly desperate: Lauderdale must help him, 'or you are not so much my friend as I believe'. On 20 June Moray officially notified the council of the changes, which Rothes wanted him to delay, 'but my desires prevails [*sic*] but little'. Rothes unwisely made his unhappiness clear at the council meeting, because he, and everyone else, knew that in the end he had to do as the king wished. Rothes was indeed beset: the Dutch might land at any time, and his discussions with Monmouth's commissioners and curators over

56 NLS Ms. 7023, f. 44.
57 22, 25 June 1667, Lauderdale to Moray, ibid., ff. 49, 52.
58 14 June 1667, Tweeddale to Lauderdale, BL Add. Mss 23127, f. 32.

Duchess Anna's wardship were not going well. They were allegedly going to offer no more than £3,000 sterling, very little 'considering my just pretensions'; he wanted at least £6,000. His desperation is understandable.[59]

Moray went patiently to work. He explained to the horrified Rothes that he had to notify the council, and that Rothes must comply with the king's wishes. Charles was showing his confidence in Rothes by giving him the most eminent job in the kingdom. He had taken no soundings ahead of time because he knew that Rothes would take it on. Furthermore he was relieving Rothes of an immense burden by putting the treasury in commission. The king would not be pleased if Rothes were to 'stick' at accepting the appointment, an argument Moray repeated on the day he made the official announcement of the king's decisions to the council. What Rothes must do, Moray said, is acquiesce. If Charles later decided that Rothes's deprecatory excuses were justified, he could then make a change. Rothes's argument that he could not serve as both chancellor and commissioner, Moray suggested, might lead the king to think that Rothes wanted to hang on permanently as commissioner, an office which was, in theory, both *ad hoc* and temporary in nature. Besides, the two offices could be combined, as they were in the days of Lauderdale's grandfather, Lord Chancellor Dunfermline. On 22 June Charles, having digested Rothes's reaction, wrote a soothing and sugary letter to his new lord chancellor, rejecting his plea that he was unfit for the job and pointing out that he had plenty of relevant experience as a member of the court of session, president of the council, and keeper of the great seal for the past three years. He intended to have treasury commissions in both kingdoms, and the only way he could properly reward his faithful servant and old friend, and not demote him, was by making him chancellor. Lauderdale wrote to Moray three days later to the effect that Charles would neither change his mind nor allow Rothes to come to London now. Rothes allowed himself to be persuaded; he had no choice. On 27 June he accepted the office, saying a week later that he did so 'with a sad heart', since neither his humour nor his qualifications matched the job.[60]

59 4, 15, 18, 20 June 1667, Rothes to Lauderdale, ibid., ff. 8, 34, 42, 52.
60 15, 17, 20, 27 June 1667, Moray to Lauderdale, 27 June, 4 July, Rothes to Lauderdale, ibid., ff. 36, 38–40, 56, 71, 72, 98. 22 June, Charles to Rothes, 27 June, Lauderdale to Moray, NLS Ms. 7023, ff. 50, 52. 20 June, the day Moray informed the council of the king's decisions, marked his first appearance as a councillor. *RPCS* II, p. 294. Rothes subsequently admitted that he had been a negligent lord treasurer. 7 May 1668, Tweeddale to Lauderdale, BL Add. Mss 23129, f. 94.

On that same day, 27 June, Archbishop Burnet wrote to Sheldon that the governmental reshuffle 'is variously construed here'. Moray and Tweeddale wrote that everyone was pleased except Rothes 'and one other', possibly Hamilton or Sharp, who wanted Hamilton appointed to the treasury commission.[61] Tweeddale seems to have studiously avoided involvement in Moray's combination of arm-twisting and sales pitch with Rothes, save to suggest that Rothes might argue that he had been appointed lord treasurer for life, an argument rendered irrelevant by his promotion to chancellor and his chairmanship of the treasury commission. Rothes might also try to claim a veto over the decisions of the commission by virtue of his position as chairman. Tweeddale wanted Lauderdale to be sure that that did not happen, and in fact it did not: the appointment of William Sharp to the new office of cashkeeper went through on a 3–2 vote, with Rothes and Bellenden, who wanted the job, in the minority. To fuel the ex-treasurer's chagrin the decisive vote was that of the 'infamous knave' Cochrane.[62] The purpose of the new office was to centralise the collection of revenue in the interest of more efficient accounting and payout procedures. Moray proposed Sharp's appointment within a month of the establishment of the commission, which meant that it had been decided upon by Moray and Lauderdale before Moray left London. Charles promptly approved it. Ever since the beginning of the Dutch war Lauderdale had had difficulty in collecting his pension. Bellenden's letters on the subject were full of apologies and excuses; Sharp was sure that Bellenden was managing the matter badly, and Lauderdale thought so too. Having his own dependable man of business in the post would, no doubt, put an end to the delays – and so it did. Once Sharp became cashkeeper these problems ceased to exist.[63]

Tweeddale's letters in June, while Rothes's mini-drama was being played out, dealt extensively with the problems of the armed forces: complaints against the soldiers, and their impotence owing to lack of equipment. A wild rumour circulated in June that the Danes, allies of the French, were going to send 20,000 men to attack Scotland. No one believed this, but if

---

61 *LP* II, App., p. xlv. 25 June 1667, Moray to Lauderdale, 27, 28 June, 2 July, Tweeddale to Lauderdale, BL Add. Mss 23127, ff. 69, 78, 82–83, 92.

62 20, 27, 28 June, 18 July 1667, Tweeddale to Lauderdale, BL Add. Mss 23127, ff. 54, 76, 82–83, 132–33.

63 For Sharp's appointment see R.W. Lennox, *Lauderdale and Scotland: A Study in Scottish Politics and Administration 1660–1682* (PhD diss., Columbia University, 1977), pp. 121–24, 171–74. Lauderdale expressed his surprise that Bellenden opposed the appointment; 25 July 1667, Lauderdale to Tweeddale, NLS Ms. 7023, f. 66. He had evidently expected Rothes's opposition.

they did come, wrote Tweeddale, 'we must bang them with hands and feet', since arms were so scarce.[64] He had considerable distaste for the generals. During a discussion in the council of war Dalyell argued that the war council had the right to judge the rebels and added, 'There was no more to be done but take them out and hang them.' He was informed that that was not proper procedure. He is, Tweeddale commented, 'better acquainted with Muscovy than Scotland'. Drummond was reportedly going to London. If he was going in order to defend the conduct of the soldiers, his hearers should be aware that people dared not complain. If the council were authorised to receive the country's complaints, 'its sad condition will soon appear'. On the other hand, Drummond's purpose might be to ask the king to make him chancellor, since Rothes was so unhappy about his appointment, but Tweeddale was sure that Charles would not listen. What the generals wanted was 'an unlimited power backed by the sword over a poor nation that I dare say would fain live in quiet . . . free . . . of arbitrariness and oppression and if a remedy be not found will be rendered miserable.'[65]

The necessary precondition for any sort of progress was an end to the war, which everyone wanted and which had been under discussion at Breda since March. Lauderdale feared, unnecessarily as it turned out, that the Dutch success in the Thames in June might derail the peace process, since it 'will raise the enemies' pride past sufferance'.[66] What Tweeddale wanted when peace came he summarised in his long letter of 22 June to Lauderdale: 'endeavour . . . to put us in the condition the parliament left us in when you went last out of Scotland', i.e., without a swollen military. The remedy was to be found in 'a well-ordered militia, for better the country be all in arms than ruined by a few that are not sufficient to defend it if invaded'.[67] Tweeddale and everyone else knew that only with peace could the swollen and inefficient armed forces be reduced – even Archbishop Burnet severely criticised them – and a militia, to which even Rothes paid lip service, be constituted.[68] Implicit in Tweeddale's language was not only

---

64 27 June 1667, Tweeddale to Lauderdale, BL Add. Mss 23127, f. 76. Moray and Rothes reported the rumours at about the same time; BL Add. Mss 23127, ff. 69, 72.

65 22, 27 June 1667, Tweeddale to Lauderdale., ibid., ff. 64–66, 78. His 'Muscovy' comment was written on 10 October; BL Add. Mss 23128, f. 87. Dalyell had spent some years in the Russian army.

66 15 June 1667, Lauderdale to Tweeddale, NLS Ms. 7023, f. 46.

67 BL Add. Mss. 23127, ff. 64–66.

68 20 June 1667, Rothes to Lauderdale, ibid., f. 50. 29 June, Burnet to Williamson, *CSPD 1667*, pp. 242–43.

the reduction of the army to the levels of 1663 but also the end of Rothes's special position as commissioner and commander-in-chief, a view he made explicit five days later. The king should be made aware of the danger implicit in that unique concentration of power; it was doubtful if any court was competent to overrule Rothes's decisions.[69] On 28 June, in another long letter, he returned to the theme of leaving so much authority in Rothes's hands. If the nobility believed that Rothes, because he was commissioner and commander-in-chief, still controlled virtually all patronage, 'I fear few or none will acknowledge you to have any share', an argument bound to have an impact on Lauderdale. If Rothes remained as commissioner until he went to court, 'little discovery will be made of the evils the country groans under . . . whereas a truer prospect will be had of the condition of affairs in one month after this curtain is drawn, than a whole year's sufferings will make appear'.[70] Tweeddale's message was clear: Rothes's power must be broken, and as soon as possible.

On 1 July Moray, in an equally long letter, confirmed much of what Tweeddale had said. His attitude to the military commanders was, if anything, even more hostile. They wanted Rothes, their friend and supporter, to remain as commissioner. Their aim was to have a military government, and they were using the security argument with Charles. 'They talk of nothing more than imminent and unavoidable insurrections in the west. To this they add assurances of an universal disposition in the whole kingdom to shake off Episcopal government.' The recent changes, they alleged, were all 'Presbyterian designs'. Fortunately the two archbishops held aloof: Burnet would not meddle, and Sharp was now thoroughly cowed. The military pillagers and Rothes's 'compagnons de la bouteille' were the only people dissatisfied with the changes. Moray added that Rothes himself was more upset at the secrecy, and the surprise, 'as importing . . . a distrust in the king and unkindness in Lauderdale', than in the substance of the change. Rothes's drinking was becoming a problem. Sharp commented to Gilbert Burnet that the commissioner was always drunk.[71] A few days later Moray emphatically endorsed Tweeddale's argument that Rothes must go. The first few meetings of the treasury commission hinted at unimaginable corruption. 'I am deadly afraid we shall discover more horrid things in the management of the king's rents than

69 BL Add. Mss 23127, f. 78.
70 Ibid., ff. 82–83.
71 Ibid., ff. 88–90. Burnet, *History* I, p. 470.

would ever have entered in your heart to think of. But of these and all other grievances by the misgovernment of civil and military affairs we shall not know the bottom till the great Buckler, the Commission, be taken away . . . Hasten the downlaying of the Commission. The Generalship may stand a while.'[72] Lauderdale shared his allies' view that Rothes was likely to be an obstacle to the changes they all wished to see. When he broached the subject to Charles, the king replied that he kept Rothes as commissioner because the council had been so lax in punishing offenders. Lauderdale bit his tongue; he could have told Charles, he wrote, that the only time Rothes had gone beyond what the council recommended was in 'putting the preaching fellow in the thieves' hole, which had been better not done' and was reversed. The king did agree, however, that he would put an end to Rothes's commission after peace was made.[73]

Lauderdale knew that Charles, at this delicate juncture in the affairs of the tripartite monarchy as a whole, and of English domestic politics in particular, could not be hurried. The disaster of the Dutch naval raid up the Thames had unleashed a political storm in England and enormously damaged Charles's reputation. Pepys reported that Charles and his mistress, Lady Castlemaine, were chasing a moth around their supper table in Whitehall while the Dutch were carrying off his flagship; he subsequently remarked that it was generally agreed that Charles was governed by wine, women and rogues.[74] Damage control was the first order of business for Charles. What he urgently needed was peace and a scapegoat for the unsuccessful war, both of which – provided the scapegoat was Clarendon – Lauderdale and his allies urgently needed also. Among the many causes for Charles's dissatisfaction with Clarendon, and one which has escaped historians' notice, was the latter's 'insufferable passion' when Scotland was mentioned after Middleton's fall and his refusal to listen to anyone about Scotland 'unless he were his creature'. But Charles would do nothing until the end of the war, which, Lauderdale wrote on 11 July, had finally been agreed upon. The peace treaty was signed on the 21st, and ratified and proclaimed on 24 August.[75] On the next day Charles asked Clarendon to resign. When he dragged his feet Charles dismissed him and sent Secretary of State Morice for the great seal.

72 13 July 1667, Moray to Lauderdale, BL Add. Mss 23127, ff. 113–14.
73 9 July 1667, Lauderdale to Moray, NLS Ms. 7023, f. 58.
74 Cited in John Miller, *Charles II* (London, 1991), pp. 130, 133.
75 NLS Ms. 7023, f. 59. R.F. Hutton, *Charles II, King of England, Scotland and Ireland* (Oxford, 1989), p. 249. For Charles's assessment of Clarendon's attitude to Scotland see 30 June 1668, Lauderdale to Tweeddale, NLS Ms. 7023, f. 175.

Morice 'brought it through all the Court openly under his arm like a bagpipe', wrote the exultant Lauderdale. Clarendon 'will do no more hurt'. Lauderdale added that Middleton, who had now lost his patron, came to see him after Clarendon's fall, and they agreed to let bygones by bygones. The ex-commissioner also could now do no more hurt.[76] Nor, for the moment, would Archbishop Sheldon, the recipient of Burnet's endless complaints. He had supported Clarendon to the end, which, Lauderdale observed, 'will not prove advantageous to him'.[77] Charles now, Lauderdale went on, 'carried himself like a right Protestant king' in council meetings. A week later the secretary expressed even greater delight at 'the new world we have here and how bravely all the king's business goes on . . . now the king is the king himself'.[78]

On 27 August, in anticipation of the proclamation of peace, Tweeddale summed up his agenda: 'the army disbanded, the country settled, the peace secured, the customs and excise well farmed', and 'the government in the old channel', i.e., without a commissioner.[79] The first three items were all connected: there had to be peace and security to justify disbanding the army. 'For God's sake,' Lauderdale wrote to Tweeddale that same day, 'do what you can to quiet that woeful West'.[80] Tweeddale and Moray had been working on proposals for disbandment and the raising of a militia since June. In mid-July they sent their recommendations to Lauderdale. The pre-war level of forces would be sufficient, they thought. The Shetland garrison should go. And there should be no delay in setting up the militia. Tweeddale enclosed estimates of how much money could be saved. There will be pressure to keep a larger establishment, they warned, not only from the generals but also from Rothes and Hamilton, who will want to keep the troops of horse they had been authorised to raise, at a cost to the crown of £200 sterling a day.[81] Moray, having been in Scotland for two weeks, echoed

---

76 31 Aug. 1667, Lauderdale to Tweeddale, NLS Ms. 7023, f. 85.

77 7 Sept. 1667, Lauderdale to Tweeddale, ibid., f. 88. It took almost two years for Sheldon to recover; John Miller, *After the Civil Wars: English Politics and Government in the Reign of Charles II* (Harlow, 2000), pp. 203, 206.

78 7, 14 Sept. 1667, Lauderdale to Tweeddale, NLS Ms. 7023, f. 88. Paton, 'Lauderdale', pp. 140–41. In October, as Clarendon's impeachment got under way, Moray commented that his fate was 'a mighty instance of God's wisdom in governing the world'. BL Add. Mss 23128, ff. 148–49.

79 BL Add. Mss 23127, ff. 234–35. Peace was officially proclaimed in Edinburgh on 28 August; *RPCS* II, pp. 336–39. 'Bells and bonfires were not ordered', and so there were none. 29 Aug. 1667, Tweeddale to Lauderdale, BL Add. Mss 23127, f. 242.

80 27 Aug. 1667, Lauderdale to Tweeddale, NLS Ms. 14406, f. 37.

81 16 July 1667, Moray to Lauderdale, 18, 19 July, Tweeddale to Lauderdale, BL Add. Mss 23127, ff. 128, 132–33, 134.

what Tweeddale had been saying for a long time: the generals had 'a design
. . . to establish a military extraordinary power' and keep their ally Rothes
in office.[82] There was a disturbance in Galloway; two local lords, Herries
and Annandale, said that it did not amount to much, and the local heritors
offered to catch the troublemakers themselves. But Rothes sent troops
anyway, who, according to Moray, proceeded to harass innocent and guilty
alike, and to try to collect fines for not going to church – precisely the sort
of behaviour that touched off the rising of 1666.[83]

It was not until the end of August that Lauderdale could get the king to
focus on the details of the recommendations for disbanding. Throughout
the month Moray and Tweeddale kept up a steady stream of observations
and comments. By mid-month Tweeddale concluded that cutting back to
pre-war levels, two troops of horse and seven companies of foot, would not
be wise, given the ticklish situation in the west. The government should
keep three and ten, respectively. He advocated a first-in first-out system of
demobilisation, which would have the desirable result of getting Rothes
and Newburgh out of their commands – Tweeddale argued that they were
neglectful, and the level of fraud in Newburgh's musters had come even to
the king's notice – and leaving Halton in his. Plans for the militia should go
forward, to appease the nobility, who could have commands in it. He also
put forward the startling proposition that Moray should be the general of
the militia, 'unless you think fit he be a reserve in case the chancellor
should weary of his employ'. Moray 'is displeased with this raillery, but I am
in good earnest'.[84]

Later in August Tweeddale sent Lauderdale a set of recommendations on
pacification of the west. The thrust of the paper was reliance on local nota-
bles, amnesty for those willing to behave in future, and the use of persuasion rather than force to get people to go to church.[85] Some privy councillors
were nervous, and wanted to retain Hamilton's recently raised troop to keep
the peace in his troubled area. Tweeddale thought this was a dreadful idea.
Hamilton was not competent, his men misbehaved, and anyway soldiers
should be commanded by 'meaner men', i.e. professionals, and by people
better able to 'attend' than the likes of Rothes and Newburgh. The militia

---

82 1 July 1667, Moray to Lauderdale, ibid., ff. 88–90.
83 11 July 1667, Rothes to Lauderdale, 23, 25 July, Tweeddale to Lauderdale, 24 July, Herries to
     Tweeddale, 16–17 Sept., Moray to Lauderdale, ibid., ff. 115–16, 141–42, 146, 152, 23128. ff. 36–42.
84 15, 16, 20 Aug. 1667, Tweeddale to Lauderdale, BL Add. Mss 23127, ff. 203–06, 215. 17 Sept.,
     Lauderdale to Rothes, NLS Ms. 7003, f. 56.
85 BL Add. Mss 23127, f. 226.

was the place for privy councillors and noblemen to hold commands, 'lest the country verge to military'. If the retained troops were paid Scottish, not English, wages the resulting savings would pay for the third troop Tweeddale recommended. Since soldiers spend what they get, paying them too much 'doth but debauch them'. Moray, who had gone to Lanarkshire to look at Hamilton's country – Hamilton had complained that both the area and he personally were insecure – reported that there was no such danger there as had been talked of. He told the duke that if he stopped mistreating his tenants he would be safe enough. According to Kirkton, Tweeddale suggested that if Hamilton was really worried that 'his enemies . . . might kill him at his sport', a squadron of guards might be quartered at Hamilton, at the duke's expense, of course. Hamilton and Rothes, a couple of 'unvirtuous men', were now hand-in-glove. Their plan was that Rothes should go to court and work on Charles and Lauderdale to keep himself, and therefore Hamilton, in power. Thanks to Rothes Hamilton was now drinking a lot. Moray was trying to get him to stop. He warned Hamilton that the king would be angry if Hamilton persisted in arguing in council for keeping more troops than Charles wanted. The duke promised to stop.[86]

Finally, at the end of August, Lauderdale had his conversation with the king and received his instructions on the future of the army. The troops to be disbanded were those recently raised: Charles 'stumbled' at Tweeddale's proposal of first-in-first-out. So Rothes and Newburgh would retain their troops of horse and Dalyell his regiment of foot, and so, ultimately, would Linlithgow, with Kellie as his lieutenant-colonel. There was to be no muster-master general: the office facilitated corruption and was expensive and unnecessary. There would be no third troop of horse; ironically, Charles adopted the recommendations Tweeddale sent in July before he received the modifications of mid-August. Lauderdale scolded Tweeddale for making 'impracticable' suggestions about changing the officers of the guards and giving Halton a command.[87] What emerged was an establishment much reduced from the wartime levels but about 30 per cent larger than that of 1666. It totalled about 1,200 men. There were no instructions

---

86 19 July, 15, 23, 27 Aug. 1667, Tweeddale to Lauderdale, ibid., ff. 134, 203–04, 224–25, 234–35. 25, 28–30 Aug., 2 Sept., 20 Oct., Moray to Lauderdale, ibid., ff. 230, 236–39, 23128, ff. 6–7, 148–49. Kirkton, *History*, p. 153. Moray compared Hamilton and Rothes to Simeon and Levi, Jacob's deceitful and murderous sons. *Genesis* xxxiv.

87 27 July, 13, 22, 31 Aug., 3 Sept. 1667, Lauderdale to Tweeddale, 6 Aug., Lauderdale to [Moray?], NLS Ms. 7023, ff. 67, 71, 76, 81, 85, 86. The king's orders are in *Warrant Book 1660–1670* under dates of 2 Sept. and 1 and 29 Oct., NAS GD 90/2/260, no pagination.

as yet regarding the militia; Lauderdale had warned Tweeddale that Charles believed that a militia should not be established until it could be properly armed.[88]

The end of the war had repercussions far beyond the reduction of the size of the standing army. With the end of the threat of a Dutch invasion a policy of leniency toward the prisoners still languishing in the wake of the western rising became much less dangerous. Now also, for the first time since the Restoration, the government undertook an active policy of pacification in the Highlands. On 3 August the council, after considerable debate, authorised the earl of Atholl to raise a force to keep the peace there. His commission ran for a year and a half; he was given broad powers and a grant of £200 sterling to raise his force. His commission covered the entire area from Dumbarton to Inverness, Seaforth had responsibility for Ross, Sutherland and Caithness, and Argyll for the area within his justiciary. There was no commission for the Gordons: young Huntly was a Catholic whose guardians had resisted official attempts to effect his conversion. Thus was inaugurated a policy of pacification by independent commission in the Highlands, 'a practice which was to be continued throughout the Restoration era'.[89]

Once peace was officially proclaimed in August Tweeddale and Moray waited anxiously for the all-important news that Charles had ended Rothes's tenure as commissioner. Lauderdale wrote on 31 August that Charles was planning to wait and deal with it himself when Rothes came to court, that the commission would end only after the disbanding was complete, and that Lauderdale had no problem with all this.[90] Tweeddale and Moray were horrified. Tweeddale's reply, written on 7 September, was almost hysterical. The commission 'has stood in the way of all attempts whatsoever at recovery and at this hour does [so] more than ever'. Proposals for reform would go nowhere, 'for he will suffer nothing to be done before he goes in hope to return as he went'. Our reputations will be ruined, the hope of giving 'a check to those violent proceedings [that have] occasioned the late rebellion' will be dashed, and the disbanded soldiers will add to the discontent. 'Let not all our hopes be shipwrecked in the

---

88 R.A. Lee, *Government and Politics in Scotland, 1661–1681* (PhD diss., University of Glasgow, 1995), pp. 153, 187. 15 June 1667, Lauderdale to Tweeddale, NLS Ms. 7023, f. 46.

89 A.I. Macinnes, *Clanship, Commerce and the House of Stuart, 1603–1788* (East Linton, 1996), p. 131. *RPCS* II, pp. 324–29. 3 Aug. 1667, Moray to Lauderdale, BL Add. Mss 23127, f. 178. Lauderdale endorsed the policy. 10 Aug., Lauderdale to Moray, NLS Ms. 7023, f. 75.

90 NLS Ms. 7023, f. 85.

harbour . . . We cannot answer for the peace . . . after my lord commissioner is gone in that capacity to England.'[91] Tweeddale was clearly
overwrought.

Moray's letter of the same date was a good deal calmer, but said much the
same thing. He was sure that when Lauderdale thought about it, he would
realise that the king would find it much easier to dismiss Rothes by letter
than in person: 'You know it is not easy for the King to say black things.'
Rothes wants to hang onto the commission and will say anything he can
think of to do so, to you as well as Charles, and if he says things that 'be not
as he says, none there can contradict . . . and what his submissions and
insinuations may do, and his airs in conversing with the King and others
may produce, you can easily judge.' Delaying his dismissal will gravely
disappoint all those who hope for change and 'will strike people's minds
with apprehensions that must needs be of bad consequences'. The adoption
of Moray's proposals for the settlement of the west, which he drew up
following his visit there, would be jeopardised: Rothes would draw up
counter-proposals and expect to get his way if he were still commissioner
when he spoke with the king.[92]

Moray's proposals for the west, which he regarded as 'the sure way to
settle and secure episcopacy,' were the first step in a change of policy toward
the religiously disaffected. Force had been tried, and had provoked rebellion. Now that peace had come it was time, so the cousins believed, to see
what might be done through conciliation. There would be a general pardon
for all rebels except those already forfeited and those accused of violence
toward clergymen. Landlords, especially in the southwest, were to provide
guarantees for themselves and their tenants to keep the peace, in the form
of bands and sureties. The king was to be asked if those who bound themselves over 'need to be pressed with taking the declaration' abjuring the
Covenants – Moray clearly hoped that Charles would find this unnecessary.
The debate in the council was rancorous. There was some quibbling over
phraseology, and some very close votes, especially on the issue of taking the
declaration. Tweeddale and Moray both felt that it should not be forced on
those who were willing to give surety for keeping the peace, though
Tweeddale, the ex-Cromwellian, strongly supported requiring church attendance. This, according to Moray, surprised and pleased Sharp, 'and
produced altum silentium'. Neither Rothes nor Hamilton, who wanted

91 BL Add. Mss 23128, ff. 16–17.
92 Ibid., ff. 18–20.

troops to be sent to the disaffected areas with Rothes in charge, would sign off on the proposals, nor would any of 'the graces here save one', probably Sharp. Dealing with Hamilton was particularly awkward. He and the generals had been indiscriminately harassing western landowners, and he was reprimanded in the council for failing to produce the list of those who had not yet been summoned to give surety for keeping the peace. Predictably, Archbishop Burnet was full of praise for him. He and Rothes and the others argued that many landed rebels had not been pursued at law; their valuable estates had been promised to deserving officers. Tweeddale and Moray replied that in fact many had been prosecuted; a new proscription list would run counter to the king's policy of clemency and would make the Edinburgh administration look bad, if these 'ringleaders' had thus far escaped their notice. The trouble was, Tweeddale explained, that Rothes had given the generals permission to meddle with rebels' estates; the treasury commission had had to stop them. These confrontations, Tweeddale observed, were the sort of thing he hoped to avoid in the future.[93]

Fortunately for Moray and Tweeddale the advocates of force could be charged, with some justice, with 'snooping after forfeitures'. General Dalyell was in fact going to court to ask the king for grants of forfeitures with the paperwork all in hand. General Drummond, in a letter to Lauderdale about the proposed indemnity, opined that it should not be hastily extended to landed men. Let them be investigated – no one, he went on, wanted to prosecute the poor. Tweeddale and Moray were eager to get them both out of their commands.[94] Archbishop Burnet was another of those who hoped to profit from forfeitures. He continued to complain to Archbishop Sheldon that the king's instructions were being ignored. 'I find it is resolved that nothing which I propose shall be pursued; by this connivance and impunity these rogues are now come to that height of impudence to brag that they shall not have a curate who owns a bishop in all that country.'[95] When Sheldon confronted Lauderdale with what he

---

93 12, 14, 17 Sept. 1667, Tweeddale to Lauderdale, 7, 14, 16–17 Sept., Moray to Lauderdale, ibid., ff. 18–20, 23–24, 27–28, 30–31, 36–42, 46–48. The proposals are in ibid., ff. 25–26. The bishops, perhaps to appease Lauderdale, wrote him a fawning letter on the 16th, stressing their belief that peace in church and state were inseparable. Ibid., f. 32. 24 Oct, Burnet to Sheldon, *LP* II, App., pp. lii–liii.

94 13, 23 Aug. 1667, Tweeddale to Lauderdale, n.d. (Aug.), 7 Sept., Moray to Lauderdale, BL Add. Mss 23127, ff. 199, 224–25, 23128, ff. 18–20, 44–45. 19 Sept., Drummond to Lauderdale, BL Add. Mss 23127, f. 49.

95 7 Sept. 1667, Moray to Lauderdale, ibid., ff. 18–20. 9 Aug., Burnet to Sheldon, *LP* II, App., pp. xlvi–xlvii.

described as the chaos in Scotland, Lauderdale – after Clarendon's fall – felt strong enough flatly to deny the archbishop's charges and to reprove the primate for bad-mouthing him to the king. With the disbanding of the troops and the end of Rothes's authority it was up to the new regime to keep the country quiet. 'If the devil should again possess our foolish fanatics,' he wrote Moray, 'there will be no way but the extremity of cruelty.' They are, he added, 'more fanatic than Quakers'.[96]

Lauderdale concluded that Tweeddale and Moray were right in wanting Rothes dismissed at once. On 14 September he wrote to Tweeddale that he had read his and Moray's letters to Charles, and that the king had accepted their arguments. Three days later he wrote to Rothes that Charles would remove him as commissioner and go back to 'the old channel without the place of commissioner', but that the king intended that he should still have 'the eminentest place of Government there', viz., the chancellorship. Charles's letter was tactful: he withdrew the commission on the ground that the proposed national synod of the church was not going to be held, at least not now.[97] Tweeddale was predictably delighted, and speculated rather maliciously on 'what satisfaction he [Rothes] would express at being relieved of the burden of £300 sterling a month'.[98] Rothes, knowing from his experience when he lost the treasury that it would do no good to argue, put a good face on his acquiescence, asked permission to go to court, which he got, and went off to visit his mistress. Moray for his part applauded Lauderdale's tactics in stripping Rothes of his offices one at a time: it was far less humiliating that way. Tweeddale wrote Lauderdale a cheerful letter for the first time since Rothes was removed as treasurer. There was even a certain levity in it. Dalyell had left for London; Tweeddale suggested that Lauderdale should greet him with 'Tam, how have you guided Scotland?' This letter was written on 26 September; on the same day Lauderdale wrote that he had seen the king that morning and briefed him on the substance of all of Tweeddale's letters. 'He is fully satisfied with your whole carriage.' A few days later Charles gave his formal approval to Moray's new religious policy, and the council duly issued the necessary administrative

96 2 Sept. 1667, Lauderdale to Sheldon, NLS Ms. 14406, f. 38. 7 Sept., Lauderdale to Tweeddale, 24 Sept., Lauderdale to Moray, NLS Ms. 7023, ff. 88, 95.

97 NLS Ms. 7003, f. 56, 7023, f. 89, Paton, 'Lauderdale', pp. 140–41. *Warrant Book 1660–1670* under date of 20 Sept., NAS GD 90/2/260, no pagination. Lauderdale sent Tweeddale a copy of Charles's letter, NLS Ms. 7023, f. 94.

98 23 Sept. 1667, Tweeddale to Lauderdale, BL Add. Mss 23128, f. 58.

orders.[99] Scotland is on the old footing now, wrote Lauderdale to Tweeddale on 3 October. 'God forgive you all if it not be kept peaceable.'[100] He also wrote a rather stilted letter to Sharp, expressing his pleasure that Sharp would conduct himself obediently in future, and his wish that the bishops 'moderate severities as much as may consist with the peace and order of the Church' in order to win back peaceful dissenters: the carrot, not the stick.[101]

Rothes did not give up easily. By late October he was on his way to court, to see what he could salvage from the wreckage of his political fortunes. Before he left he buttered up Tweeddale, who told him rather bluntly that he was glad Rothes was no longer commissioner: it was bad for the country if anyone stayed too long in that office. Tweeddale wrote that they parted in friendly fashion, but Rothes could have been none too pleased. Still, he talked confidently of his ability to get what he wanted from the king. He was still allied with Hamilton, whom Moray called a publican. The duke was unhappy that the crown's debt to his family, £14,000 sterling, was still unpaid and resentful that, as a western landowner, he had to vouch for the good behaviour of his tenants in the aftermath of the recent rebellion. He continued 'jangling' at having to sign the necessary band until it was drawn in such a way that he as landlord could seize the possessions of any tenant found liable for a breach of its terms.[102] He and Rothes cheered each other up: 'he is linked with his drinking master, to stand and fall with him', wrote Moray, who thought Hamilton a fool. Hamilton and Archbishop Burnet apparently took at face value Rothes's boast that he had so much influence with the king that he could get almost anything he wanted. As for Rothes, Moray wished him well, 'yet I cannot see how he can be a good friend and fit servant or a virtuous man'. Moray wanted Lauderdale to be nice to Rothes, now that he had fallen. He thought that Charles might usefully speak to him, and Hamilton too, about their drinking, and predicted that no matter what happened, Rothes 'will seem to be the best pleased man in the world whenever he comes home, as if everything had succeeded to his wishes'.[103] Before Rothes departed Tweeddale speculated that if he indeed

---

99 24 Sept., 8 Oct. 1667, Rothes to Lauderdale, 24, 26 Sept., Moray to Lauderdale, 26 Sept., Tweeddale to Lauderdale, ibid., ff. 63, 67–69, 73, 103. 26 Sept., Lauderdale to Tweeddale, NLS Ms. 7023, f. 92. *RPCS* II, pp. 343–44, 347–53.

100 NLS Ms. 7003, f. 56.

101 2 Oct. 1667, Lauderdale to Sharp, Dowden, 'Letters', pp. 261–63.

102 8, 10 Oct. 1667, Tweeddale to Lauderdale, BL Add. Mss 23128, ff. 105–06, 117–19.

103 1, 31 Oct., 16–17 Dec., n.d. 1667, Moray to Lauderdale, ibid., ff. 89–90, 156–57, 225–26, 239–40.

did go to London he might resign as chancellor and suggest his new drinking companion as his successor while he stayed on as commander-in-chief with a pension. This was obviously a non-starter. Tweeddale mentioned a lot of people as possible replacements: various lawyers, Kincardine, Montrose and, of course, Moray 'who you know would make a non-such chancellor for this country at this time'[104] – not least because Moray would then have to remain in Scotland, as Tweeddale devoutly wished.

Rothes when he arrived in London was perhaps disconcerted to discover that Tweeddale had arrived at court before him. Tweeddale had hastened to London to be present at the birth of his first grandchild, who was due at Michaelmas but thoughtfully awaited Grandfather's arrival before coming into the world.[105] The king was friendly but unyielding to both Rothes and Hamilton, who also turned up in London, without Charles's permission and to Lauderdale's considerable annoyance. Hamilton kept nagging the king about his money – he wanted an assignment on the cess for it, said Moray – and got nowhere. Predictably he was in a bad mood. He pestered Lauderdale when the secretary was sick, and drank away his days. He was 'beastly drunk with E. Denbigh last week', wrote Lauderdale on 19 November, and since then with 'his own cabal; sure I am he hath a jolly red nose'.[106] Hamilton sulked throughout the winter, but when he left London for home, early in March 1668, he assured Lauderdale that he would follow Tweeddale's and Moray's lead: 'in a word he promised to be very good'.[107] And so he was, for a while. The increase in conventicles in the west alarmed him, and he realised that he had to cooperate with the new regime; he would get nowhere otherwise. By June Tweeddale could report that he and Hamilton were dining together regularly and discussing the problems of the militia in the west; Lauderdale in reply rejoiced that 'our Duke grows good'.[108]

104 1 Oct. 1667, Tweeddale to Lauderdale, ibid., f. 87. Montrose, the son and heir of the 'martyred' royalist hero, was in Lauderdale's good graces because he had proved reasonable in settling his claims against Lauderdale's nephew Argyll.

105 23 July 1667, Lauderdale to Tweeddale, NLS Ms. 7023, f. 65. Tweeddale arrived in London on 22 October; his grandson was born on the 25th. NLS Ms. 7001, pp. 152, 155–56.

106 20 Oct. 1667, Moray to Lauderdale, BL Add. Mss 23128, ff. 148–49. 15 Nov., Lauderdale to Moray, NLS Ms. 7003, f. 61.

107 3 Mar. 1668, Lauderdale to Moray, Paton, 'Lauderdale', pp. 157–58. For Hamilton's sulking see Lauderdale's letters in Jan. 1668, Paton, 'Lauderdale', pp. 145ff.

108 7, 12 May, 16, 18 June 1668, Tweeddale to Lauderdale, BL Add. Mss 23129, ff. 92–93, 102–03, 160, 166–67. 23 June, Lauderdale to Tweeddale, NLS Ms. 7023, f. 172.

As for Rothes, Charles was clear that the treasury would remain in commission, 'In a word, all is here as to our affairs as you could wish.'[109] Rothes also lost his position as commander-in-chief. On the last day of 1667 Charles, citing the reduced size of the army, vacated the commissions of all general officers, including of course, Dalyell and Drummond. Rothes 'took it cheerfully', wrote Lauderdale, 'much like a wise man',[110] And otherwise the king let him down gracefully. He was promised an exoneration for his official conduct as both treasurer and commissioner – Tweeddale was none too pleased – and a generous settlement of the Buccleuch wardship. He got £8,000 sterling instead of £12,000, which was very favourable considering the dubiousness of his claim, and more than the £6,000 for which he had been prepared to settle. He was 'highly pleased', wrote Lauderdale, 'and whispered that he would give it out for reputation' that the king was rewarding him for his good service. 'This I wondered to hear.'[111] His mood as he returned home, however, was not very cheerful. He knew that he faced a wigging from his battleaxe of a sister: he and her daughter the duchess of Monmouth had launched a 'great assault' upon the king, wanting him to help Lady Wemyss 'out of the common condition', presumably debt; the king merely 'laughed at it'.[112] But, like the astute time-server that he was, Rothes knew that, like Hamilton, he must follow the cousins' lead for now.

The cousins had good reason to rejoice. Rothes's great power in the state was permanently broken. All he had left was his unwanted chancellorship and his command of his own troop of horse – Tweeddale's suggestion that Argyll should replace him as its commander went nowhere.[113] Rothes was far from a cipher, but he was no longer a major player. The unreliable and solipsistic Hamilton never had been one, but because of his great position as Scotland's only resident duke, and an immense landowner, he could not be ignored. But the cousins were in control. The constructive years of the Restoration in Scotland were about to begin.

109 7 Nov. 1667, Lauderdale to Moray, Paton, 'Lauderdale', pp. 144–45.

110 *RPCS* II, pp. 389–90. 2 Jan. 1668, Lauderdale to Moray, Paton, 'Lauderdale', pp. 145–46.

111 28 Nov. 1667, Tweeddale to Moray, NLS Ms. 7024, ff. 74–75. 9 Jan. 1668, Lauderdale to Tweeddale, NLS Ms. 7023, f. 116, Burnet, *History* I, pp. 422–23. The terms of the wardship settlement are in NLS Ms. 14544, f. 45.

112 24 Feb. 1668, Lauderdale to Tweeddale, NLS Ms. 7023, f. 130.

113 17 Sept. 1667, Tweeddale to Lauderdale, BL Add. Mss 23128, ff. 46–48.

CHAPTER FIVE

The New Brooms, 1667–1668

I

On 14 June 1667 Sir Robert Moray arrived in Edinburgh; a year later, almost to the day, he left for London. He would never see Scotland again for the five years of life that remained to him, although no one knew that at the time; Tweeddale in particular clamoured for his return. Tweeddale found the work load overwhelming, and it was indeed enormous, even with Moray there to share it. There were several major problems, all of which had to be dealt with at once: reducing the army and creating the militia; financial difficulties; negotiations with England over trade; the aftermath of the western rebellion; and a reconsideration of religious policy in order to prevent another rebellion. There were also many minor issues such as, for example, the disposition of the wardship of the heir of a major landowner, the earl of Cassilis, who died in April 1668. And there were private matters – Tweeddale was much involved in the management of Lauderdale's Scottish properties. In the voluminous correspondence between Lauderdale and his two collaborators all these topics were jumbled together.

There were three posts a week, leaving on Tuesday, Thursday and Saturday. Virtually every one contained a letter in each direction, sometimes more than one, and Lauderdale sometimes sent newsbooks as well. Some letters are missing – how many we don't know. It is nevertheless almost possible to construct a day-to-day account of the doings of the Edinburgh administration. Such a chronicle, while it would underline the daily pressures, confusion and difficulties Moray and Tweeddale and their colleagues faced, would shirk the historian's duty to set out, clarify and explain. At a distance of more than 300 years we simplify, and we must. The most recent study of the political developments of these years, Ronald Lee's *Government and Politics in Scotland 1661–1681*,[1] consists of a series of topical chapters. The following account will also, to some extent, be topical. But it is worth remembering that the men who made the decisions hopped about from one topic to another. Some of the inconsistencies, mistakes and

---

1 See ref. above, chap 1, fn. 26.

failures of the years of the cousins' administration are certainly attributable to their inability to focus on and keep track of one problem at a time. In February 1668 Lauderdale asked Tweeddale and Moray, when they replied to his letters, to remind him of what he had said: he often forgot, because he wrote so often, and kept no copies.[2] Under the circumstances it is surprising that the cousins' administration functioned as well as it did.

Almost all of the issues the new regime faced had to do with money. The treasury commission therefore became the most important body in Edinburgh. It eclipsed the privy council, which had never recovered the influence it had had in the later years of King James VI and I. It had been of only second-rate importance since the Restoration – witness the fact that it was not even reconstituted until July 1661, more than a year after the king's return. From Lauderdale's point of view the treasury commission, which his friends dominated, was easier to deal with than the council, which had a much larger membership that included awkward but inevitable grandees like the duke of Hamilton. Even on those issues within the council's remit, such as religious policy and the appointment of regular army and militia officers, the treasury commissioners, who were all councillors, exercised a determining influence. Charles made the relationship of the two bodies clear from the beginning. In August 1667 he ordered the council to follow the instructions of the treasury commission in raising money to pay off the soldiers who were to be disbanded, and in November he informed it that, on the treasury commission's advice, he was disbanding the Shetland garrison. The commission met four days a week, and was small and efficient. Attendance was frequently thin. Rothes was neglectful and Bellenden in chronic bad health, so that in November 1668, when Cochrane was very ill, Tweeddale suggested that there should be provision for proxies, which would make him sometimes 'sole treasurer and for most part half a one'. As this remark indicates, Tweeddale dominated the commission. He could count on the support of Moray and Cochrane, who got an earldom in 1669. Patronage was increasingly in Tweeddale's hands, in that his recommendations carried most weight with Lauderdale; Rothes found it more and more difficult to get anything for his clients.[3]

The appointment of William Sharp as cashkeeper tightened the grip of the commission's ruling triumvirate. The creation of this office was

2 11 Feb. 1668, Lauderdale to Tweeddale, NLS Ms. 7023, f. 125.

3 *RPCS* II, pp. 334–36, 367–69. 3 Dec. 1667, Cochrane to Tweeddale, NLS Ms. 7003, f. 62. 27 July, 20 Oct., 5 Nov. 1668, Tweeddale to Lauderdale, BL Add. Mss 23129, f. 257, 23130, ff. 76, 99. On the patronage issue see 6 July 1669, Rothes to Lauderdale, BL Add. Mss 23132, f. 7.

enormously important. All the crown's revenues, from whatever source, including the cess, were to be paid to the cashkeeper, and all expenditures paid by him. What this meant was centralisation of control of the crown's finances, and the ability to determine, at any given moment, what the crown's balance sheet looked like. R. W. Lennox's analysis of the government's income and expenditure in the years after 1667 concludes that 'Expenditure was, in most instances, tightly controlled by the treasury commission . . . It never exceeded income to any significant degree.' In other words, a more or less balanced budget. What the commission created was 'a firm fiscal and administrative base for royal power in Scotland'.[4] The haphazard administrative practices of Rothes – and his predecessors – permanently vanished.

Another key player besides Sharp was Sir Thomas Moncrieffe, the collector of the brewing excise, a protégé of Crawford when the latter was lord treasurer. He became the principal clerk of the commission, responsible for correspondence, record-keeping and turning out reports. Tweeddale was not convinced of his honesty, but admitted that he was useful and diligent.[5] 'It is said,' wrote Tweeddale to Lauderdale after the appointment of Sharp, 'that now you are both secretary and treasurer' – Lauderdale was, of course, also a member of the commission, though he could attend meetings only when he was in Edinburgh. But Tweeddale was the one who bore the principal burden of the Edinburgh administration. Please send him home, Sharp begged Lauderdale in December 1667, when Tweeddale had been in London for a month: nothing gets done without him.[6]

Throughout the Restoration period the most serious problem facing Charles's financial officers, whether a lord treasurer or a commission, was finding the money to pay the army. The less it cost, the healthier the crown's finances would be, as Tweeddale and his colleagues knew full well. Their first task in 1667, therefore, was to arrange to pay the disbanded soldiers of the swollen military establishment when, on 13 August 1667 Charles finally gave the official order for disbandment. They also had to fight off the last-minute attempts by Hamilton and Archbishop Burnet,

4 R.W. Lennox, *Lauderdale and Scotland: A Study in Scottish Politics and Administration 1660–1682* (PhD diss., Columbia University, 1977), pp. 352, 385. For his analysis of income and expenditure see pp. 290–353, 398–408, for the office of cashkeeper, pp. 171–202.
5 Ibid., pp. 103–04, 120–21.
6 BL Add. Mss 23127, ff. 132–33, 134. NLS Ms. 14406, f. 41. Cochrane also wanted him home: 3 Dec. 1667, Cochrane to Tweeddale, NLS Ms. 7003, f. 62. For the commission's jurisdiction see Lennox, *Lauderdale and Scotland*, pp. 125–64.

among others, to keep a larger force than the cousins thought necessary. On this score Archbishop Sharp was helpful, writing to Sheldon that the disbanding of the army was the right thing to do – it was both expensive and unnecessary – and being very critical of his fellow archbishop.[7] Overriding Hamilton's objections, the commissioners decided that the best way to raise the necessary money was to ask the shires and burghs south of and including Aberdeen to pay four of the six remaining months of the cess immediately; the commissioners themselves, with the notable exception of Rothes, stood surety for their own shires, as did other supporters of the government such as Argyll. The king ordered that interest be guaranteed to those paying in advance. Tweeddale wrote that he would stand surety for Peeblesshire and Haddingtonshire, and had guaranteed Roxburghshire in Monmouth's name as one of his curators, and Berwickshire in Lauderdale's. Rothes, he added, had his money tied up in building projects – a neat dig at the ex-treasurer. In addition the king ordered that the proceeds of the second year of the taxation of 1665, of which Hamilton was the collector, be used to provide a supply of arms and ammunition for storage in Edinburgh Castle, along with the arms collected from the disbanded soldiers. At the same time he ordered that money be obtained from Hamilton to pay off the disbanded troops; the duke would be repaid from the proceeds of the cess.[8]

On the whole the disbandment went smoothly enough. On 23 August Tweeddale had been 'on the rack' for two days over money, but in September he wrote cheerily to Lauderdale about the prospect of money from the shires, patting the treasury commission (and thus himself) on the back for doing so well for the soldiers. He opined that there would be enough to buy arms after the men were paid off. Should the government buy the troopers' pistols if the latter wanted to sell them? he asked.[9] In November one more disbandment, delayed by Monck's opposition, took place: the king put an end to what was left of the useless Shetland garrison, whose fortification was made of peat, flammable in dry weather, as Moray

7 8 Aug. 1667, Moray to Lauderdale, BL Add. Mss 23127, ff. 187–88. 2 Nov., Sharp to Sheldon, *LP* II, App., pp. liii–lvii.

8 13, 27 Aug., 2 Sept. 1667, Charles to the council and treasury commission, *Warrant Book 1660–1670*, NAS GD 90/2/260, no pagination. *RPCS* II, pp. 334–36. 22 Aug., Rothes to Lauderdale, 22, 23 Aug., Tweeddale to Lauderdale, BL Add. Mss 23127, ff. 217–18, 219–20, 224–25. NLS Ms. 597, f. 11.

9 23 Aug., 2, 12, 17 Sept.1667, Tweeddale to Lauderdale, BL Add. Mss 23127, ff. 224–25, 23128, ff. 3, 23–24, 46–48.

pointed out. Charles also ordered that the council examine the behaviour of Sir James Turner at Dumfries, where he had been surprised by the rebels. Turner and another officer, Sir William Bellenden, a captain in Dalyell's regiment, were notorious for the brutality of their exactions. There had to be exemplary punishment if the disaffected areas of the west and south-west were to be reconciled to the cousins' regime, so that the reduced armed force would suffice. This was especially true since the government did not intend to change the policy of using the army to collect arrears of taxation.[10]

Turner and Bellenden were guilty of gross abuses. The total of their exactions from the Stewartry of Kirkcudbright amounted to over £66,000, while the Stewartry and Wigtownshire together were supposed to pay £38,000 in cess – so that Kirkcudbright alone paid almost twice as much as a much larger area. According to Moray Turner collected over £150,000. His technique was to send out horsemen in pairs to quarter on those owing fines for not attending church, and charge them for ten troopers, threatening to summon the other eight if the money was not forthcoming. One minister complained to Moray that his parishioners were so beggared that they could no longer afford to pay his stipend, 'though he be well loved in his parish'.[11]

Long before Charles ordered the hearing on Turner the rumour was flying that he would be fired and his command given to Kellie. The post was worth £1,000 sterling a year, and Kellie was in his usual begging mode. In August Lauderdale had observed to Tweeddale that there was nothing to be done for Kellie unless some serving officer was cashiered, and it seems likely that Kellie's necessities and Turner's trial were not unconnected.[12] Turner tried to stave off the impending inquiry by offering his command to Kellie if he could remain as Kellie's subordinate officer, but in vain. According to Turner, Kellie was prepared to accept this, but the king, at

10 21 Nov. 1667, Charles to the treasury commission, *Warrant Book 1660–1670*, NAS GD 90/2/260, no pagination. 21 Nov., Lauderdale to Moray, NLS Ms. 7023, f. 109. 6 Aug., Moray to Lauderdale, BL Add. Mss 23127, ff. 182–83. For an example of their brutalities see Adam Blackadder, 'A True Narration', D.G. Mullen, ed., *Protestant Piety in Early-Modern Scotland*, SHS (Edinburgh, 2005), pp. 197–200.

11 R.A. Lee, *Government and Politics in Scotland, 1661–1681* (PhD diss., University of Glasgow, 1995), pp. 165–66. 20 Oct., 7 Nov. 1667, Moray to Lauderdale, BL Add. Mss 23128, ff. 148–49, 167–68. The letter dated 7 Nov. may have been written on 7 Dec.; see 14 Dec., Lauderdale to Moray, where he says Moray misdated the letter.

12 22 Aug. 1667, Lauderdale to Tweeddale, NLS Ms. 7023, f. 81. 3 Oct., Tweeddale to Lauderdale, BL Add. Mss 23128, f. 93.

Tweeddale's urging and with Rothes's acquiescence, ordered the trial: Tweeddale wanted to be rid of an officer he regarded as troublesome and provocative.[13] On receipt of Charles's order the council appointed an investigating committee, of which Moray was a member – Tweeddale was very anxious that he should be – and also a local committee of important people headed by the earl of Nithsdale to convene at Dumfries and gather evidence.[14] The committee report, which emerged in February 1668, was devastating. Turner pleaded that he was only following Rothes's orders, and gave a disingenuous explanation for his having been surprised and captured by the rebels. On 20 February the council voted unanimously to accept the report, though Turner had some defenders there, old soldiers like himself such as Dalyell and Drummond, 'in remembrance of old doings in Yorkshire and Lancashire' – all three were Worcester Scots. Tweeddale warned that a trial for his malfeasance would take a long time, given the nature of the evidence, but he had already confessed enough to justify firing him. On 3 March Charles did so, and ordered him to account for his takings from the church fines. The council duly held a hearing, after Turner laid down his commissions, and let him off lightly. He was held to have owed £38,000; he countered that the correct figure was £30,000, of which he could account for £28,000, 12 shillings. On 6 May the council accepted this, and Turner vanished from public life.[15] He might have been punished much more severely, but what the cousins wanted was to be rid of him, not only for the public relations value of such a public firing, but also to get Kellie off their backs for a time – Kellie got Turner's company.[16] The council then turned its attention to Bellenden, who was accused, among other things, of trying to stir up another anti-episcopal rebellion in Galloway, no doubt in order to profit from cracking down on the rebels. He also had his defenders in the council, who succeeded in postponing but not

---

13 8, 14 Oct. 1667, Tweeddale to Lauderdale, BL Add. Mss 23128, ff. 105–06, 127. 21 Nov., Tweeddale to Moray, NLS Ms. 7001, pp. 167–68. 21 Nov., Lauderdale to Moray, NLS Ms. 7023, f. 109. Sir James Turner, *Memoirs of his Own Life and Times, 1632-1670*, ed. T. Thomson, Bannatyne Club (Edinburgh, 1829), pp. 200–01.

14 *RPCS* II, pp. 367–69, 369–70. 21 Nov. 1667, Tweeddale to Moray, NLS Ms. 7001, pp. 167–68. 26 Nov., Bellenden to Lauderdale, BL Add. Mss 23128, f. 197.

15 *RPCS* II, pp. 407–10, 426, 442–43. 18, 20 Feb., 10 Mar. 1668, Tweeddale to Lauderdale, BL Add. Mss 23128, ff. 313–14, 326–27, 23129, f. 17. 3 Mar., Lauderdale to Tweeddale, NLS Ms. 7023, f. 133. Turner, *Memoirs*, pp. 201–27, contains a full account of his hearings, which does not markedly diverge from the council's reports.

16 27 Feb. 1668, Lauderdale to Moray, Paton, 'Lauderdale' pp. 155–57.

avoiding condemnation. In August the council fined him £200 sterling and banished him.[17]

In mid-January 1668 Tweeddale returned to Edinburgh after a two-month absence in London to see his first grandchild. The snow made it a wretched trip; he was glad to be home and back at work. He found things quiet. Moray was pleased with the current state of affairs, but the numbers for the military establishment worried Tweeddale. It would cost more than £50,000 sterling a year, which was the limit the government could afford. He was well aware of the connection between the reduction of military expenses and financial recovery for the government. His estimate of the cost was a huge exaggeration: the total expenditure for the next few years came to less than half of Tweeddale's figure.[18] It was all the more urgent to establish the militia, in order to make possible future reductions in the size of the regular army. But the situation in the west was worrisome. Tweeddale wanted troops stationed in the area until the administration could restore some stability there. He clearly was torn between concern for the balance-sheet and military security. Moray, on the other hand, believed that militia units would be both cheaper and more effective: they could act more promptly in case of trouble, without waiting for instructions from the council. Action on the militia had to be delayed, however. In September 1667 Lauderdale had promised that if Tweeddale and Moray supplied him with the necessary information he would have the king's orders for the militia drawn up for the scheduled meeting of the council on 8 October. But before Moray's draft letter could reach Lauderdale the king backed off. Charles had to cope with a session of the English parliament that threatened to be very tricky, in the wake of an expensive and unsuccessful war and the fall of Clarendon. Issuing orders for a Scottish militia now might cause English MPs to think that he was raising an army there.[19]

So the establishment of the militia hung fire until the prorogation of the English parliament in May 1668. In November 1667 the king made it clear that he wanted the necessary weapons and military supplies, cheaper and more plentiful since the end of the war, available in Edinburgh Castle

---

17 *RPCS* II, pp. 510–11. 29 Feb., 3 Mar., 11 Apr., 9, 21 July 1668, Tweeddale to Lauderdale, BL Add. Mss 23128, ff. 338–39, 23129, ff. 3–4, 65–66, 209, 243–44. 10 Apr., Wedderburn to Lauderdale, BL. Add. Mss 23129, f. 61. Tweeddale wanted him fined £500 sterling and imprisoned.

18 14 Jan. 1668, Tweeddale to Lauderdale, BL Add. Mss 23128, ff. 260–61. For the costs see Lennox, *Lauderdale and Scotland*, pp. 334–35, 401.

19 24 Sept., 12 Oct. 1667, Lauderdale to Moray, 24 Sept., 1 Oct., Lauderdale to Tweeddale, NLS Ms. 7023, ff. 95, 96, 98, 102. 5, 17 Oct., Moray to Lauderdale, BL Add. Mss 23128, ff. 101, 143–45.

before the militia was constituted, a point he reiterated in the instructions he gave to Tweeddale on the latter's return to Edinburgh. In early April Tweeddale could report that there were 8,000 muskets and 4,000 pikes in the castle; this, he thought, would satisfy the king.[20] On 29 April the king finally sent his orders. The council registered them on 6 May and followed on two days later with a spate of instructions that had clearly been drawn up in anticipation of those orders. The legal basis for action was the parliamentary Act of 1663, which authorised a force of 20,000 foot and 2,000 horse, though it was never intended that the militia should be of that size.[21] The militia commission in each shire would be made up of that shire's militia officers, JPs and excise commissioners. Militias would be constituted only in reliable districts, not in the west, southwest, or Highlands, except for Argyll, where Tweeddale, in response to a query from Lauderdale, opined that a militia there, 'how little soever', would be useful. The earl was pleased, though he remarked to Tweeddale that it would take some drilling to teach Highlanders to use pikes and muskets. The colonels of foot were to be great nobles, including absentees such as Lauderdale and Monmouth: lists were supplied. Clearly their underlings would do the real work. Lauderdale wanted Tweeddale to suggest a lieutenant-colonel for his regiment, and was miffed when Tweeddale failed to reply.[22]

The shire's heritors would bear the cost of equipping its militia; the government would pay its daily allowances, 6s for foot, 18s for horse. A six-man council committee, which included Tweeddale and Moray, would supervise the operation. In its covering letter to the king the council recommended that, in addition to the shires for which the militia had been authorised, it also be established in Dumfriesshire and Dunbartonshire, and horse troops raised in Lanarkshire, Ayrshire and Renfrewshire as well.[23] Hamilton had made a fuss about these omissions in the council, but inadvertently demonstrated why they had been made by his 'dreadful representation' of the

---

20 3 Nov. 1667, Tweeddale to Moray, NLS Ms. 7024, ff. 54–55. 11 Apr. 1668, Tweeddale to Lauderdale, BL Add. Mss 23129, ff. 65–66. The king's instructions are in NLS Ms. 597, f. 46. In July 1668 the council exempted arms and ammunition imported for the militia from customs and excise duties. RPCS II, pp. 505–06.

21 APS VII, pp. 480–81. Lee, Government and Politics, p. 172, estimates that in the 1670s as many as 12,000 foot may have been mustered at different times, and that there may have been more than 2,000 horse.

22 24 Mar., 16, 28 Apr. 1668, Lauderdale to Tweeddale, NLS Ms. 7023, ff. 139, 148, 150. 30 Mar., Tweeddale to Lauderdale, BL Add. Mss 32129, ff. 41–42. May, Argyll to Tweeddale, NLS Ms. 7003, ff. 94–95.

23 RPCS II, pp. 438–42, 447–51, 454.

proliferation of conventicles in Clydesdale. Force must be used against them, Tweeddale opined; 'I am afraid they spoil with forbearance too long.' He was uneasy about raising militia in the southwest, given the unsettled conditions and the necessity of employing unreliable grandees such as the earl of Dumfries. He kept changing his mind about the need for a regular guard there, to Lauderdale's exasperation. For now the king preferred to use regular army horse in the west, which might be partially paid for by the heritors, who were being spared the expense of raising a militia.[24]

During the summer of 1668 the process of establishing the militia got under way, but went very slowly. Tweeddale was expeditious with his own regiment in Haddingtonshire. In June he presented a list of its officers to the council: the first shire to report. Not all great lords were willing to cooperate. In the Merse, for instance, the earl of Haddington declined the command. More embarrassingly, so did Lady Lauderdale's kinsman the earl of Home, who wrote that he believed that there should be a militia, but that 'this charge is now clogged with such subjection to the justices of peace and commissioners of excise I humbly conceive it dishonourable.' Lauderdale described the letter as 'ugly', and told Tweeddale to find a replacement. Home, after considerable pressure and considerable grumbling, finally took the job.[25] Little enough had in fact been accomplished by the time Moray returned to London; in August the council had to prod the shire commissioners to get their militias settled. On 23 July Tweeddale wrote Moray a mournful letter about the insolence and incorrigibility of the fanatics and the disarray of the militia, which was in disorder in all but two or three shires: 'We hold the wolf by the ears.' The government needed two more troops of musketeers, who could be paid by cutting pensions and the pay of the present guards, also in disarray. Lauderdale and the king should be told how unsettled the situation was, 'and lastly remember how insupportable a burden you have left me under' – he hadn't eaten since morning, and it was now 8 p.m.[26] No doubt hunger deepened Tweeddale's gloom.

---

24 7, 21, 28, 30 May 1668, Tweeddale to Lauderdale, BL Add. Mss 23129, ff. 92–93, 112, 124–25, 128–29. 19 May, 6 June, Lauderdale to Tweeddale, 23 May, Lauderdale to Moray, NLS Ms. 7023, ff. 157, 159, 166.

25 *RPCS* II, pp. 462–63. 7 May, 11 Dec. 1668, Tweeddale to Lauderdale, BL Add. Mss 23129, f. 94, 23131, ff. 26–27. 16 May, Home to (Lauderdale), NLS Ms. 14406, f. 53. 26 May, Lauderdale to Tweeddale, NLS Ms. 7023, f. 163. 25 June, Home to (Lauderdale?), NLS Ms. 10442, no. 12.

26 NLS Ms. 7024, f. 103. *RPCS* II, p. 506. For an overview of the role of the militia see B. Lenman, 'Militia, Fencible Men and Home Defence, 1660–1797', in N. MacDougall, ed., *Scotland and War, AD 79–1918* (Edinburgh, 1991), pp. 170–92.

One of the causes of the insolence of the fanatics, Tweeddale wrote, was the leniency shown to those involved in the recent rebellion. Some of these were prisoners. In the previous July Tweeddale had identified a total of fifty-seven: twenty-two captured in arms and thirty-five arrested on suspicion of aiding and abetting. The council's view was that those captured in arms who were willing to take the oath of allegiance and subscribe to the declaration renouncing the Covenants should be pardoned; the obdurate should be sent to Barbados or Virginia, which was done quietly so as to avoid any demonstrations on their behalf. Of those arrested on suspicion the obdurate should face trial, and the willing released on caution.[27] Moray's proposal for a general pardon, save for those who had been forfeited or were 'under the process of forfeiture' was rather more sweeping and made Tweeddale nervous. Moray's frequent visits to the area persuaded him that further uprisings on the part of the disaffected were just that, rumours, and that the size of the rebellion had been exaggerated. Tweeddale, though he had advocated the amnesty in the previous August, had then been gloomy about the 'unhappy and obstinate people' whom 'neither severity doth secure nor lenity reclaim'. Pardoning rebels for treason might have unintended consequences – could they then be prosecuted for having robbed ministers' houses? Under such circumstances 'peccadillos are not to be stuck at, as old Klenurqhy [Glenorchy] said when he caused cast into a remission of his incest and witchcraft'.[28] Tweeddale was still gloomy in December – 'I am sorry that the rod must be taken up again' – but by mid-February 1668 there were some signs of progress: more heritors were pledging to keep the peace.[29] Getting Moray's amnesty proposal through the council had been difficult, but once it was accepted only Archbishop Burnet continued to rail at it, and at the cousins' regime. 'If those noble persons now at court [Tweeddale and Rothes] and their friends be not engaged to . . . secure our peace,' he wrote to Archbishop Sheldon in November, 'I shall not expect much tranquillity in my time.'[30]

---

27 9 July 1667, Tweeddale to Lauderdale, BL Add. Mss 23127, f. 111. *RPCS* II, pp. 307–08. See also 4 June 1668, Tweeddale to Lauderdale, *Laing Mss* I, 367–69.

28 15 Aug., 21 Sept. 1667, Tweeddale to Lauderdale, BL Add. Mss 23127, ff. 203–04, 23128, f. 56. His memorandum on the pacification of the west, enclosed in a letter of 23 Aug., is in BL Add. Mss 23127, f. 226.

29 26 Dec. 1667, Tweeddale to Moray, NLS Ms. 7024, f. 87. 18 Feb. 1668, Tweeddale to Lauderdale, BL Add. Mss 23128, ff. 313–14. See also Linlithgow's report of 27 Feb., BL Add. Mss 23128, f. 334.

30 *LP* II, App., pp. lvii–lix. Sharp, by contrast supported the amnesty. 2 Nov. 1667, Sharp to Sheldon, *LP* II. App., p. liv.

Dealing with the prisoners was only one aspect of the much larger problem of what to do with what Lauderdale called the 'woeful West'. The major issues were security and conventicles, both of which might best be addressed in the long run by an alteration in religious policy. Making such an alteration would be very tricky. Lauderdale could not afford to give the impression that, with Clarendon's restraining hand removed, he was giving way to his ancient Presbyterian proclivities.[31] In the wake of Rothes's removal rumours were flying that Crawford, Cassilis and Lothian, ardent Presbyterians all, would be added to the council and the archbishops removed. Such stories were false – 'impudent lies', Tweeddale called them. Lauderdale wrote that 'the king will never fly in the face of an Act of parliament' and give 'fools occasion to talk as if the king would alter the government'. Lauderdale would have liked to shake up the council, he wrote Moray in September, but tactically this was not the time to try it, unless there was some obvious and public reason to do so. Tweeddale nevertheless hoped for changes. From London he asked Moray for a memorandum on alterations to its membership, which, the clerk register had said, took place every seven years.[32] But it was not to be. Another damaging rumour that surfaced in early 1668, when Lauderdale was expected to visit Scotland for the first time in five years, was that one of his purposes was to get rid of the bishops.[33] If Lauderdale had to walk warily, so too did Tweeddale: he could not afford to remind the king that he had sat in the parliaments of the Protectorate.

Security in the west, therefore, become the first order of business, along with the amnesty that had been proclaimed in September 1667. Troops were to be employed, regular troops, until the militia was up and running, and probably even after, though fewer and at less cost. A total of 150 horse and 400 foot were to be quartered in Dumfries, Glasgow and Lanark, with 300 foot and Rothes's troop of horse in Edinburgh as a reserve. The council issued these orders on 9 October 1667, in connection with the proclamation of the amnesty voted in September. The council also declared that the order issued in March to surrender arms and horses would be rescinded for all those who gave surety to keep the peace, took the oath of allegiance and signed the declaration against the Covenant. Those who gave surety and

---

31 On this point see Burnet, *History* I, p. 414.
32 24 Sept., 12 Oct. 1667, Lauderdale to Moray, NLS Ms. 7023, ff. 95, 102. 22, 31 Oct., Tweeddale to Moray, NLS Ms. 7024, ff. 44, 52.
33 NAS GD 16/34/201.

took the oath would not be pressured to sign the declaration, but only those who signed were permitted to bear arms.[34] This was a vital step, in Moray's view. It was also vital that the soldiers be paid on time and by the treasury, so that they would not behave as Turner's troopers had. They had to be held responsible for their behaviour, which had been such that even Middleton commented to Tweeddale that 'he was sure Scotland would hate the name of a soldier for what they had done'. In February 1668 the king thoughtlessly acquiesced in Newburgh's proposal that soldiers not be compelled to pay their debts. Tweeddale was horrified, and wrote to Lauderdale that this must be rescinded; the treasury commission, he added, would write formally to Charles if necessary.[35] Since no more was heard about the matter, Charles evidently complied.

With the disbanding of the wartime army and the use of many of the remaining troops in the west there was some concern about whether quartering on tax delinquents was still feasible. Kincardine at one point proposed privatisation: hiring professional quarterers at 8d to 10d per day, a suggestion that went nowhere. But there was to be strict regulation of both the circumstances under which soldiers were to be used for this purpose and the numbers to be so employed – no more than twelve per shire, the council decreed in February 1668 at the behest of the treasury commission, after the council had sent a troop of twenty-five to Caithness to collect arrears of customs and excise in January.[36] It was a policy designed to minimise friction while keeping in place the safeguards that Tweeddale believed to be necessary. He continued to fret about conditions in the west. Reports had reached Carlisle in October of the holding of large conventicles in Galloway. 'We do look on this obstinacy as the symptom of some wicked design,' he wrote on 26 December 1667. Moray was far less worried. On Christmas Day of 1667, writing from Hamilton, he observed to Lauderdale that the more he learned about the late rebellion the less he feared a recurrence. The disaffected had no weapons, and the king no enemies abroad who could supply them. 'The party is broken,' he wrote two days later: those who refused the necessary subscriptions would not speak to the conformists.[37]

34 *RPCS* II, pp. 347–54. The March proclamation is in *RPCS* II, pp. 272–76.
35 24 Dec. 1667, Tweeddale to Moray, NLS Ms. 7024, ff. 85–86. 15 Feb. 1668, Tweeddale to Lauderdale, BL Add. Mss 23128, ff. 307–08. Lee, *Government and Politics*, p. 169.
36 16–17 Sept. 1667, Moray to Lauderdale, 28 Jan. 1668, Tweeddale to Lauderdale, BL Add. Mss 23128, ff. 36–42, 280–81. *RPCS* II, pp. 361–64, 396–97, 406.
37 NLS Ms. 7001, pp. 175–76. BL Add. Mss 23128, ff. 231–32, 233–34. For the Carlisle reports see *CSPD 1667*, p. 555.

On 27 February 1668, the council sent a report to Lauderdale on the workings of the new policy. In Lanarkshire 147 heritors had accepted the terms of pardon and signed the band; 100 had not. In Ayrshire the comparable figures were fifty-seven and seventy-two. In Kirkcudbright and Dumfriesshire only fourteen had signed; 158 had not. These were far from satisfactory results. In November Charles had expressed surprise at how slowly signatures were coming in; now that the cousins were in charge in Scotland Lauderdale wanted to be sure that the king believed that matters were going well there. The council put the best possible face on the figures, observing that the non-signers were mostly 'very mean' persons. It recommended granting more time for delinquents to sign and pursuing the recalcitrant as rebels. The figures alarmed Tweeddale, who, shortly after his return from London, began to worry about conventicles. A list of outed ministers alleged to be illegally in towns was to be drawn up, and the burgh magistrates instructed to seize them, a policy which Lauderdale endorsed. Catching them 'will preserve the poor silly sheep', he commented.[38] Moray travelled to the west country once more, and returned agreeing with Tweeddale that troops must be sent there, even though this would delay reducing the size of the permanent establishment. Lauderdale agreed. The troops should come from 'well-affected' shires, he wrote; as strangers they would be less prone to wink at the doings of the ringleaders. Regulars would cost more than militia, so the shires to which the troops were sent would pay what arming the militia would cost, and the king would make up the difference, using the income from the estates of the forfeited rebels for that purpose.[39] The earl of Linlithgow, the *de facto* commander of the regular forces, took the troops to Glasgow and distributed them. Things were quiet, he reported. He had heard nothing new about conventicles since his arrival, though he suspected that if there were trouble it would erupt in Clydesdale, where the radicals were as recalcitrant as ever and believed in suffering for their principles.[40] Tweeddale was less sanguine. The disaffected were not taking advantage of the king's offer of pardon, he wrote on 21 May. Two days later he passed on a report about a conventicle in the west which met on nine successive nights, on some of

38 RPCS II, pp. 412–15. 24 Nov., 12 Dec. 1667, Tweeddale to Moray, NLS Ms. 7001, pp. 168, 172. 28 Jan. 1668, Tweeddale to Lauderdale, BL Add. Mss 23128, ff. 280–81. 28 Jan., Lauderdale to Tweeddale and Moray, Paton, 'Lauderdale', pp. 150–52.
39 23 May 1668, Lauderdale to Moray, NLS Ms. 7023, f. 159, and to Tweeddale, f. 160.
40 25 May 1668, Linlithgow to Lauderdale, ibid., f. 162. 26 May, Linlithgow to Tweeddale, NLS Ms. 7003, f. 88.

which it snowed. The attenders 'have catched violent colds, in so much as they may be tried and found out by coughing'.[41]

As the cousins saw it, one of the major obstacles to a settlement in the west was Archbishop Burnet. The disaffected must be kept in hand and those who went to conventicles punished: on this they agreed. But, as Tweeddale had written in August 1667 in his memorandum on pacification in the west, persuasion should be used to get people to go to church; Burnet believed in nothing but force. Worse still, he kept saying so with great vehemence, moved in part by his fear that the new regime intended to suppress episcopacy.[42] His public opposition to any concessions at all, his repeated Jeremiads to Archbishop Sheldon, his attempts to turn the clergy of his archdiocese into a pressure group, his public hand-wringing and direct attacks on the administration, especially Tweeddale, were becoming intolerable. For example, on 6 November 1667 Burnet recounted to Sheldon the sad tale of the minister of Borgue, a small town near Kirkcudbright. The treasury commission had fined the parish £110 to repair the damage the rebels had done to his house, but 'the parishioners told him if he returned back they could not secure his life, and since that time he durst never return . . . as the earl of Tweeddale knows very well; and this is the severity they so much brag of'.[43] According to Gilbert Burnet the archbishop accused some councillors of pleading for traitors in the course of a debate over whether to hang a rebel who was clearly crazy. Such language might well sustain a charge of leasing-making, the offence of which Argyll had been convicted in Middleton's time; Lauderdale was reportedly gathering such evidence.[44] But the secretary chose not to go that route, which might give rise to renewed doubts about his support of episcopacy as such. Lauderdale had no difficulty accepting bishops, as long as they behaved as Sharp was now behaving. On the day of Burnet's letter to Sheldon, Sharp wrote to Lauderdale that the church is 'now put into your hands, to sink or swim as you shall be disposed towards the bishops of it'. He also congratulated Lauderdale on the birth of his grandson, who, he hoped, would inherit the 'eminentest virtues' of both his grandfathers.[45]

---

41 BL Add. Mss 23129, ff. 112, 114.
42 7 Sept. 1667, William Sharp to Lauderdale, BL Add. Mss 23128, f. 22.
43 *LP* II, App., pp. lvii–lxix.
44 Burnet, *History* I, pp. 417–18. 17 Sept. 1667, Tweeddale to Lauderdale, BL Add. Mss 23128, ff. 46–48.
45 NLS Ms. 2512, f. 108.

Two more different attitudes would be hard to imagine. Archbishop Burnet's real fault was not the substance of his complaint but the fact that he complained at all, writing his 'dismal' letters to Archbishop Sheldon, wanting to make formal addresses to the king, smearing the pretty canvas the cousins' government was trying to paint for Charles's benefit.[46] What every Restoration regime, the cousins as well as Middleton and Rothes before them, expected was that the bishops should, as Tweeddale and Moray put it in a letter to Lauderdale, 'presume that your Lordship's ends and ours are the same, and if there happen any difference about the means conducing thereunto, we shall not stick to our opinion, but in submission and paying all becoming deference to your Lordship's great judgment and experience'. Moray and Tweeddale could hardly conceal their contempt. 'These people,' Moray wrote of the bishops, are 'unfit, or indeed unable, to manage matters aright.' Moray, who was visiting Yester, and Tweeddale 'laughed until we were weary' at the letter of this 'silly company of people'. They were equally contemptuous of Sharp's toadying. In November the archbishop wrote to Sheldon praising all the leaders of the Scottish administration. 'I am so proud of my own place,' Tweeddale wrote to Moray from London, 'that I envy not yours in his good graces.'[47] In Julia Buckroyd's view the successive administrations' publicly contemptuous attitude, which with some justice she calls 'anti-clericalism', caused 'a general disbelief among the political nation and in the country at large that there was any fixed resolution to maintain an episcopal system'.[48] This was certainly not the cousins' intention. Bishops were useful if, like Sharp, they deferred to secular authority. Still, it is noteworthy that Tweeddale, the only one of the three who lived to see the revolution of 1688–89, had no difficulty accommodating himself to the new Presbyterian regime, and wound up as King William's lord chancellor.

In September 1667 Tweeddale's patience with Burnet snapped. He wrote a long letter to Lauderdale about the archbishop's false charges against him, his attacks on the government, and his allegation that there was a design afoot to subvert episcopacy itself, his neglect of his diocese in order to sit with the court of session – he was an extraordinary lord – to pursue his

46 1 Oct. 1667, Lauderdale to Tweeddale, NLS Ms. 7023, f. 98.
47 The bishops' letter is dated 16 Sept. 1667; BL Add. Mss 23128, f. 32. 20 Sept., Moray to Lauderdale, BL Add. Mss 23128, ff. 54–55. 16 Nov., Tweeddale to Moray, NLS Ms. 7024, f. 64.
48 J. Buckroyd, 'Anti-Clericalism in Scotland during the Restoration', in N. MacDougall, ed., *Church, Politics and Society: Scotland 1408–1929* (Edinburgh, 1983), pp. 167–85. The quotation is on p. 174.

own causes there. The chief purpose of this letter was to give Lauderdale an account of the debate in the council on the proposed settlement in the west, which (of course) Burnet opposed. He regretted that Dalyell's policy of extermination was not being followed, and commented to Sheldon that the policy of lenity was what had ruined Charles I. Moray, too, was irritated; the archbishop should be 'mortified', he wrote, 'come from whom it will'.[49] Tweeddale discovered, when he arrived in London that autumn, that Lauderdale had decided to proceed gradually. Getting rid of an archbishop was a serious business, and Charles had to be persuaded. The first step was to get him off the court of session, and possibly the council. Tweeddale urged Moray to take advantage of Archbishop Sheldon. 'Your moral friend,' he wrote, 'upon every occasion drinks your health'; a word from Moray would probably dish Burnet. He asked Moray to get the name of another bishop from Sharp, if there had to be two on the council. Lauderdale was not sure that Sheldon could help: 'Your moral friend declines daily and I cannot help it.' Sharp had assured both Tweeddale and Moray that 'the mortification of Long Face (Burnet) would not displease nor stumble him'.[50] The king also was becoming weary of Burnet's complaints, and, indeed, according to Sir Andrew Ramsay, the provost of Edinburgh, Burnet was 'full of jealousies and fears and discontented to that height as made him express a willingness to part with his employment'.[51]

Burnet's complaints became so vehement that in January 1668 the council thought it wise to write to the king denying that rebels 'are countenanced and pleaded for at your Council board'. Lauderdale urged Moray and Tweeddale to write blaming Burnet for starting that rumour. Charles, he said, was pleased with the council's letter. His reply, he later added, would 'misifie L.F.'[52] Tweeddale, meantime, had sent Lauderdale a draft of a letter to Burnet firing him from the court of session, along with a covering letter citing Charles I's habit of removing extraordinary lords of

49 17 Sept. 1667, Tweeddale to Lauderdale, BL Add. Mss 23128, ff. 46–48. 9 Aug., 23 Sept., Burnet to Sheldon, *LP* II, App., pp. xlviii–li. 1 Oct., Moray to Lauderdale, BL Add. Mss 23128, ff. 89–90.

50 16, 28 Nov., 19 Dec. 1667, Tweeddale to Moray, NLS Ms. 7024, ff. 64, 74–75, 81–82. 14 Dec., Moray to Lauderdale, BL Add. Mss 23128, ff. 223–24. 14 Dec., Lauderdale to Moray, NLS Ms. 7023, f. 111. The quotation is in Tweeddale's letter of 16 Nov. At this point the cousins began to refer to Burnet as 'Long Face', often abbreviated to 'L.F.' It is not clear why, perhaps because of his appearance – there is no known portrait – perhaps because he stuck his nose into matters they thought none of his business.

51 12 Dec. 1667, Ramsay to Lauderdale, *Argyll Letters*, pp. 122–24.

52 *RPCS* II, pp. 386–87. 18 Jan. 1668, Lauderdale to Moray and Tweeddale, Paton, 'Lauderdale', pp. 147–48. 1 Feb., Lauderdale to Tweeddale, NLS Ms. 7023, f. 123.

session. Charles, wrote Lauderdale, was 'startled' at first, but was ultimately persuaded; 'I shall not let it cool.'[53] A month later Charles removed Burnet from the court of session, though not from the council. This was a useful first step, but hardly adequate. Lauderdale told Moray and Tweeddale that he needed more information to get Charles to proceed further.[54] The king might describe Burnet as 'a great calf with a white face', and be tired of his complaints, but he was still in charge of his archdiocese, where, Tweeddale lamented in May, 'the condition . . . is not good . . . the want of ministers or such as can say any thing . . . and there is no better will ever be planted by L.F.'[55]

On 19 May Sharp, most unusually, wrote a long letter to Tweeddale. It was a gloomy one, straightforward and without the usual bootlicking. Burnet had informed him that conventicles were getting more frequent and numerous in the west. This was nothing new, coming from Burnet, but Sharp was sure that 'seditious eruptions' would follow if nothing was done. What was worse was that conventicles were spreading eastward. In the past week there had been a large gathering at Anstruther, attended by 'some women of quality'. Sharp was sure that if 'persons of power and interest', both in the west and in Fife, would act, things would be quiet. But people were evidently either unwilling or afraid to move against the disaffected, who acted as if they knew that nothing would be done. Ordinary people were bewildered, and the conformist clergy were despondent because of the contempt in which they were held. Something had to be done. Sharp concluded by saying that he was complaining only to Tweeddale; in public he continued to profess optimism.[56]

Tweeddale took this letter seriously. He sent it to Lauderdale, who was also jolted by the intelligence Tweeddale sent on 26 May. 'The whole outed ministers,' he wrote, 'have a design to set up and preach again in private houses . . . in the time of divine worship when there is none in the parish, and after sermons where churches are planted.' They do this 'from a despair they have even the soberest of them ever to be admitted to churches . . .

53 18 Jan. 1668, Tweeddale to Lauderdale, BL Add. Mss 23128, ff. 270–71. 25 Jan., Lauderdale to Moray, NLS Ms. 7023, f. 121.

54 11, 27 Feb. 1668, Lauderdale to Moray, Paton, 'Lauderdale', pp. 153–54, 155–57. 5 Mar., Lauderdale to Tweeddale, NLS Ms. 7023, f. 135.

55 21 Nov. 1667, Tweeddale to Moray, NLS Ms. 7024, ff. 67–68. 6 Feb. 1668, Lauderdale to Tweeddale, NLS Ms. 14406, f. 46. 7 May, Tweeddale to Lauderdale, BL Add. Mss 23129, ff. 92–93.

56 NLS Ms. 2512, f. 116.

They think it well enough if they gather not people to the fields as the mad fellows do.' The problem, he observed, began with 'the Act of Glasgow in E. Mid [dleton's] time' – Lauderdale hardly needed to be told that. What was especially disturbing was that Robert Douglas, the most prominent and among the most moderate of the outed ministers, had preached in a private home. 'Be thinking of it,' Tweeddale urged his colleague, 'and consider how we are to provide from danger.'[57]

Up to this point the cousins' administration had really had no church policy, except to try to keep things quiet so that the king would not be upset. Hence the carrot-and-stick tactics used in the western shires, and the existence of 'tolerated' ministers, including one at Anstruther, where the large conventicle Sharp mentioned had taken place.[58] Hence, too, the privy council's sporadic attempts to ride herd on Quakers and Papists, which usually involved the appointment of a committee on which, inevitably, Tweeddale and Moray sat.[59] Lauderdale dismissed Sharp's letter; the archbishop's 'whining is no news to me', he commented. But the news that outed ministers were holding services in private houses was alarming. So Lauderdale picked up on an idea he had first discussed with Sharp when he was in Scotland in 1663. He had then spoken to Douglas and 'some of the soberest of those ministers' about accepting a vacant parish from the king. Douglas was willing. He would not attend presbyteries and synods, but agreed to be punished if he meddled in politics. Charles had no objection, and Sharp appeared to be contented, 'but I do not remember how it came not to be practiced'. Now, Charles wanted it done: Lauderdale had read him Tweeddale's letter about preaching in private houses, and Charles was very worried. So, Douglas and other moderates were to be provided with churches 'in convenient places where they may be connived at' for non-attendance at presbyteries and synods. Tweeddale hardly needed to be told that Charles wanted the line drawn at former Remonstrants and 'phanatick young fellows' who kept conventicles. And Tweeddale and Sharp were to move speedily. 'The king did read and approve this, every word.'[60]

Here, at last, by June 1668, was a policy, which seems to have been stumbled upon almost accidentally. As many moderates as possible from among

57 BL Add. Mss 23129, ff. 116–17.
58 A 'tolerated' minister usually was one appointed before 1649, so that he did not require presentation from the patron and collation from the bishop. If he kept a low profile otherwise, his absence from the meetings of presbyteries and synods might well be overlooked.
59 See, e.g. RPCS II, p. 306.
60 30 May, 4 June 1668, Lauderdale to Tweeddale, NLS Ms. 7023, ff. 164–65.

the outed ministers were to be co-opted, in an effort to isolate the radicals. Lauderdale's letter suggests that the initiative came from Charles rather than himself, which was clearly intentional: this was the king's policy, not that of an ex-Covenanter. Sharp approached Robert Douglas first, offering him, wrote Tweeddale, the church at Auchterarder, in Perthshire, with a manse and a good stipend.[61] There was no suggestion that he should go west. Burnet would certainly object, and in any case the crucial first step was to shore up the church in the east. Lauderdale received conflicting views: Halton's were alarmist, Provost Ramsay's much less so.[62] Eventually the policy would be extended to Burnet's archdiocese, either with his acquiescence or without it: that remained to be seen. But in June 1668, when Moray left Scotland, all that was in the future. Lauderdale's letter to Tweeddale conveying Charles's approval of 'the beginning of your negotiation with the secluded ministers' was written as he and the king awaited Moray in London.[63]

II

In a letter to Lauderdale two weeks after the creation of the treasury commission Tweeddale remarked that the regime changes were popular. People were pleased that the government now stood 'upon old foundations of law and administration'.[64] With Moray acting as secretary the commissioners set to work with a will. The financial situation of the government, none too robust from the beginning, had deteriorated alarmingly owing to the Dutch war. Shortly after William Sharp's appointment as cashkeeper they ordered the receivers of royal rents to send the cash in their possession to him, and instructed Sir Walter Seaton, the erstwhile tacksman and current collector of the customs and foreign excise, to do the same, save for £200 sterling earmarked for the earl of Atholl for policing the Highlands. The management of the king's rents and Sir William Bruce's accounts as

61 13 June 1668, Tweeddale to Lauderdale, BL Add. Mss 23129, f. 150. Auchterarder had a minister, so why Tweeddale wrote this is unclear. Douglas eventually accepted the church at Pencaitland.

62 14 May 1668, Ramsay to Lauderdale, ibid., f. 104. 23 May, Halton to Lauderdale, NLS Ms. 7023, f. 161. See also 20 May, Halton to Rothes, NLS Ms. 7003, f. 87.

63 18 June 1668, Lauderdale to Tweeddale, NLS Ms. 7023, f. 170. Lauderdale remarked that the weather must be unusually cold in Scotland: Tweeddale had dated his last letter 11 Dec. 1668. Tweeddale was frequently careless about dating his letters.

64 27 June 1667, Tweeddale to Lauderdale, BL Add. Mss 23127, f. 78.

collector of the 1667 cess and paymaster of the forces would be checked. There was to be a survey of forfeited estates; in September Moray adjured Lauderdale to prevent Charles from giving any of them away until the survey was complete – he had in mind General Dalyell, who was on his way to London.[65] A discussion began as to whether to collect customs and foreign excise by farming or by direct collection, perhaps placed in the hands of the burghs, an issue which was to be fateful for Tweeddale's political future.

Tweeddale and Moray also set to work on a scrutiny of the list of fees and pensions, which were supposed to be paid from traditional sources of revenue and which now came to over £23,000 sterling a year. There were two pension lists. The first, which also included fees, was in effect official salaries. The second, far more likely to be scrutinised and cut, consisted of grants to important people, retired officials, needy aristocrats and people the king wished to favour, such as the countess of Balcarres. A revised list was ready for Tweeddale to take to London when he went south in October. Charles signed off on the revisions in December, before Tweeddale's return. He was, according to Tweeddale, more generous to the Scots than to the English: he cut Scottish pensions in half, but in England he stopped paying entirely. According to Sharp's accounts pensions and fees fell in a year to no more than £11,400 sterling, a huge saving. Whether it would endure was doubtful, given the political influence of some of the pensioners, people like Lauderdale's and Tweeddale's feckless uncle Dunfermline. Ending Rothes's fee as royal commissioner was a major saving: he was entitled to £10 sterling a day – £3,650 sterling a year. Tweeddale and Moray, with Cochrane's not-very-active support, carried the workload themselves. Sometimes they irritated Lauderdale – in August 1667 he wrote a stinging letter to Moray when he was importuned to provide Kincardine with a grant of £1,500 sterling.[66] Of the other two members, Rothes sulked and caballed with his new-found drinking companion, the duke of Hamilton, and Bellenden was suspicious and

65 6 July 1667, Tweeddale to Lauderdale, 9 July, Bellenden to Lauderdale, 13 July, 2 Sept., Moray to Lauderdale, BL Add. Mss 23127, ff. 105, 107, 113–14, 23138, ff. 6–7. Lennox, *Lauderdale and Scotland*, pp. 191–92. For an excellent summary of the government's finances 1661–67 see Lee, *Government and Politics*, pp. 105–19.

66 6 July, 17 Sept. 1667, Tweeddale to Lauderdale, 6, 8, Aug., Moray to Lauderdale, BL Add. Mss 23127, ff. 105, 182–83, 187–88; 23128, ff. 46–48. 3 Nov., Tweeddale to Moray, NLS Ms. 7024, ff. 54–55. 3 Aug., 10 Dec., Lauderdale to Moray, NLS Ms. 7023, ff. 70, 110. Lennox, *Lauderdale and Scotland*, pp. 397, 402.

unhelpful. He feared, rightly, that the new brooms would regard him as responsible for what Moray described as 'villainies we have already discovered in the management of the treasury'.[67] In August he gave out that he was ill; he suffered from the stone (gallstones or kidney stones). Moray, who suspected that he was not as ill as he said he was, thought that he might resign if he could be appropriately rewarded for his departure.[68]

On 27 August Charles wrote to the commissioners, endorsing their decision that the customs and excise be farmed, and that Newburgh's separate tack of the border customs should end, so that the entire package could be auctioned at once. Now that peace had come, wrote Charles, the result should be good.[69] It exceeded his expectations. In September Moray and Tweeddale were preoccupied with ending Rothes's position as royal commissioner, so that it took the treasury commission a little time to organise the auction, which attracted considerable interest. Talks with England about removing obstacles to Anglo-Scottish trade were under discussion, which, if successful would substantially increase the profitability of the farm. The duke of Hamilton, always in search of ways to extract his money from the crown, was interested in getting involved, a prospect that appalled Lauderdale. 'First it is to make him pay himself his £14,000 [sterling, which the crown owed him] whether the King will or not. Secondly, what an infamous thing is it for a Duke of Hamilton to become a publican. He is I doubt too much a sinner already . . . Stop it or I shall curse you all.' Charles also, Lauderdale added two days later, 'does not like D. Ham. for a publican'.[70] The duke was kept out. Sir Walter Seaton was a more serious problem. He offered £31,000 sterling for the tack, for which he had paid £19,000 in 1664 and 1665. The commissioners, who knew very well that he was dishonest and were about to launch an investigation of the abatements he had received during Rothes's administration of the treasury, did not want him. Tweeddale, Moray and Halton organised 'our cabal', which outbid Seaton by £300. The inclusion of the tack of the border customs, worth £3,000 sterling a year, certainly increased the size of the bids. Newburgh wanted an annuity of £1,000 sterling for his lost tack.

---

67 BL Add. Mss 23128, ff. 44–45.
68 14 June 1667, Tweeddale to Lauderdale, 16 Aug., Moray to Lauderdale, BL Add. Mss 23127, ff. 32, 207. See also NLS Ms. 7003, f. 56. For a discussion of the pensions see Lennox, *Lauderdale and Scotland*, pp. 339–50.
69 *Warrant Book 1660–1670* under date of 27 Aug. 1667, NAS GD 90/2/260, no pagination. See also 17 Aug., Lauderdale to Tweeddale, NLS Ms. 7023, f. 78.
70 24 Sept. 1667, Lauderdale to Moray, 26 Sept., Lauderdale to Tweeddale, NLS Ms. 7023, ff. 92, 95.

Lauderdale was prepared to give him a pension for that amount: pensions could always be cut or even ended. At all events 'His fat Lordship will not last, for he takes often apoplectic fits.'[71]

The auction, a genuine one, was held on 10 October. The bidding began at £25,000 sterling. The commissioners would have been happy with £26,000, and hoped for £29,000 or £30,000. Charles and Lauderdale were delighted at getting £31,300, larger than Lauderdale's outside guess by £5,000. The secretary warned that it might not be paid, and urged Moray to get good security from the consortium.[72] He was right to worry. Within a few months the farmers were regretting their bargain and petitioning to end the farm. The commissioners contemplated going back to direct collection. Tweeddale consulted Kincardine, who warned him that such an abrupt ending to the farm would lead people to suspect that direct collection had been the objective from the beginning. There was no agreement, however, as to who should be made collectors. Tweeddale firmly rejected Kincardine's proposal of the merchant Alexander Milne, an entrepreneur from Linlithgow who was interested in beginning a tobacco monopoly, and said that he wanted no merchants involved.[73] So the tack was left in place. When it was finally wound up, late in 1668, Tweeddale guessed that the farmers would have collected £26,000 – the final figure was £28,000 – and expressed the hope that Charles would not 'suffer the gentlemen to be losers when cheats have gained so much by embezzling and bringing his revenues to as good as nothing'.[74]

The 'cheat' Tweeddale was referring to was Sir Walter Seaton – hence the plausibility of Kincardine's suspicion that Tweeddale was not sorry to see the farm fail; that the purpose of the auction was to remove Seaton from his position as collector and then pursue him for fraud. The fact that Tweeddale became the most eager advocate of collection rather than farming as a way of collecting customs and excise suggests that perhaps Kincardine was right. Be that as it may, as soon as the customs tack was settled, and Seaton shut out of it, Moray began to press for an investigation of the huge abatements Seaton had received as tacksman in 1664 and 1665, a total of almost £17,000

71 23 May 1668, Lauderdale to Tweeddale, ibid., f. 160. Lennox, *Lauderdale and Scotland*, p. 230, fn. 118.

72 17 Oct. 1667, Lauderdale to Moray, NLS Ms. 7023, f. 104. See Moray's letters of 10 and 11 Oct. and Tweeddale's of 10 Oct. describing the auction, BL Add. Mss 23128, ff. 117–19, 121–23, 125.

73 12, 16 Jan. 1668, Tweeddale to Moray, NLS Ms. 7024, ff. 90, 92. NLS Ms. 597, f. 161b.

74 21 Aug., 3 Sept. 1668, Tweeddale to Moray, NLS Ms. 7024, ff. 112, 114. Lennox, *Lauderdale and Scotland*, pp. 229–30.

sterling out of a total of £38,000. Moray wanted a special warrant for this purpose when the exchequer undertook the auditing of the previous lord treasurers' accounts.[75] Investigating Seaton would be difficult and delicate. Rothes and Bellenden, as lord treasurer and treasurer-depute, had authorised Seaton's defalcations. If Seaton was guilty of fraud, how guilty were they? Furthermore Seaton was not sole tacksman but the head of a consortium; two of its members were Thomas Moncrieffe, the clerk of the treasury, and the cashkeeper William Sharp, who wrote to Lauderdale that he could not believe that Lauderdale would ruin Seaton and 'in some part poor W.S', – i.e., himself.[76] Moncrieffe was useful, but to Lauderdale Sharp was indispensable. Lauderdale could not afford to see him ruined.

There was the further complication of the salt tack, which had been in Seaton's hands since June 1665, when the council authorised a duty of £12 Scots per boll of imported salt (not English or Irish) save for that certified as intended for the curing of fish, for which Scottish salt was unsuitable.[77] The beneficiaries of the levy were the Scottish saltmasters, who were also the producers of coal: the use of coal in saltmaking was what made coal mines profitable. They were a very influential group; among them was Kincardine, who would replace Moray on the treasury commission after the latter returned to England in 1668. Consumers generally detested the salt duty, as did the merchant and the fishing interest, which found the requirement to register imported salt vexatious. In December 1667, with the investigation of Seaton impending, the burghs prepared a petition of protest, which prompted a letter from the saltmakers urging retention of the tax: it was good for the kingdom, and for their industry, which would collapse without it.[78] There was a great deal of discussion of the tack in the cousins' correspondence in the latter half of 1667. They did not want the tax removed, though Moray at one point suggested this as a way of breaking Seaton's tack, but it did create inequities, and they wanted Seaton removed as tacksman.[79]

75 17, 31 Oct. 1667, Moray to Lauderdale, BL Add. Mss 23128, ff. 143–45, 156–57. The exchequer was a court and was responsible for auditing treasury accounts, but in practice it was subordinate to the treasury, whether a lord treasurer or a treasury commission, and did what it was told. See Lennox, *Lauderdale and Scotland*, pp. 130–34.
76 Lennox, *Lauderdale and Scotland*, p. 223.
77 *RPCS* II, pp. 53–54. Lennox, *Lauderdale and Scotland*, pp. 205–06.
78 12 Dec. 1667. Provost Ramsay to Lauderdale, *Argyll Letters*, pp. 122–24. 3 Jan. 1668, the coal and salt proprietors to Lauderdale, BL Add. Mss 23128, f. 242. C.A. Whately, *The Scottish Salt Industry 1570–1850* (Aberdeen, 1987), p. 83.
79 19 Nov. 1667, Moray to Lauderdale, BL Add. Mss 23128, ff. 181–84. 19 Dec., Tweeddale to Moray, NLS Ms. 7024, ff. 81–82.

It took some time for the investigation of Seaton to get formally under way. A great deal of preliminary work had to be done, but once the process began it moved with great speed. On 30 March 1668, the king authorised the exchequer commission, along with one or more members of the treasury board, to look into Seaton's defalcations. Five exchequer commissioners – Kincardine was one – sat with Tweeddale, Moray and Cochrane. Rothes and Bellenden 'were conveniently omitted'.[80] It met on 29 April, and in spite of having great difficulty prying Seaton's records out of him, had its report ready by 7 May. Before the investigators submitted their report to the full exchequer commission Tweeddale showed it to Rothes, who was happy that he and Bellenden had not been directly accused of malfeasance. He admitted to sins of omission and neglect, but he did not wrong the king 'wittingly or willingly'. He asked Tweeddale to show the report to Bellenden, who thanked Tweeddale for his courtesy but declined to read it: he did not wish to have to respond, at least not unless and until he had to. He justified his refusal by saying that if he read it, and could not sign it because it reflected on him, Charles would be angry, whereas a failure to sign because he had not read it would be understandable. Tweeddale did not press him. In reporting this Tweeddale added that Seaton was beginning to show signs of nervousness; if he said anything worth passing along, Lauderdale would know.[81]

The committee presented its report to the exchequer on 12 June 1668, just before Moray's departure for England. Rothes and Bellenden were not there, and for good reason. The report focused on Seaton's unjustified claims, but it was plain enough that the real culprits were those who so readily granted them: Rothes and Bellenden.[82] Seaton's claim was based on his profits for 1663, £10,000 on his tack of £19,000, a figure which seems to have been artificially inflated. He argued that he should have the same profit for 1664 and 1665, but did not; he asked that defalcation be granted in the amounts that would cover the difference between the profits he actually made during those years, £2,007 and £400, respectively, and £10,000. He justified his request by citing his losses from the 80% duty on imports from England which

---

80 Lennox, *Lauderdale and Scotland*, p. 208. I have relied heavily on Lennox's excellent account of the Seaton affair, *Lauderdale and Scotland*, pp. 202–26. Charles's authorisation is in *Warrant Book 1660–1670*, NAS GD 90/2/260, no pagination.

81 11, 30 Apr., 2, 7, May 1668, Tweeddale to Lauderdale, 6 June, Bellenden to Lauderdale, BL Add. Mss 23129, ff. 65–66, 84, 86–87, 94, 142.

82 There is an excellent detailed analysis of the report, which is in ibid., ff. 150–51, in Lennox, *Lauderdale and Scotland*, pp. 211–18.

parliament had imposed in 1663. This claim did not stand up to investigation: the committee established that Seaton had made no effort to collect it. What was worse, Rothes had approved the request for 1664 even before the end of the fiscal year – i. e., before he, or anyone, could know what Seaton's profit, if any, for the year would actually amount to. In 1665 Seaton never even made a formal request for an abatement; Rothes granted it anyway.

What Tweeddale and Moray chose to focus on, however, was not the scandalous behaviour of Rothes and Bellenden, but rather Seaton's exorbitant profits. After all, he had not lost money, even without the abatements. Furthermore, they never forgot that Rothes was the king's friend. There was certainly a legal case to be made, but Seaton could not be held criminally responsible for making an unjustifiable request unless there were kickbacks involved, which the report did not allege. One reason for this may have been that the committee could not pry Seaton's accounts out of him until the day the report was signed; it had proceeded without them. Rothes and Bellenden, on the other hand, could certainly be charged with malfeasance. There would be political repercussions from such a court case, however, and the king might well be unhappy. Bellenden was already complaining that the investigating committee had treated Seaton highhandedly: Tweeddale and Moray had refused to see him, and had not allowed him to speak in his own defence. If there was a legal hearing, Bellenden went on, it 'may produce another determination than what is expected by Sir Robert [Moray]'.[83] On the whole it seemed best to Tweeddale, who was left to deal with the situation after Moray's departure, to leave Rothes and Bellenden alone and focus on extracting some of Seaton's ill-gotten gains from him.

On 18 June Tweeddale met with Seaton, who wanted the report delayed. Tweeddale refused, saying that any shortcomings in the report were Seaton's own fault for failing to submit his entry books until the day it was due to be signed. If the king summoned them to court, then the report might be reconsidered. Seaton admitted to making a profit – he said £7,000 a year, not £10,000 – with a big profit the first year; and to applying for defalcations large enough to match that profit. Tweeddale said that the defalcations were not justified; Seaton should think about how much he was willing to give back and make an offer. If he were perceived to be recalcitrant, Charles would be angry. If Charles accepted an appropriate

83 30 Apr., 2 May, 19 June 1668, Tweeddale to Lauderdale, BL Add. Mss 23129, ff. 84, 86–87, 173–74.
18 June, Bellenden to Lauderdale, BL Add. Mss 23129, f. 164.

offer, Seaton would fare much better than if he provoked the king. Seaton wanted to think it over; he asked that in the meantime the report not be shown to Charles. Tweeddale was willing to accept this; he knew, he wrote to Lauderdale, that the secretary would want to digest it, and probably talk it over with Moray, before taking it to the king. After discussing various other matters in this letter – the new cooperativeness of the duke of Hamilton, the possibility of the crown's acquisition of the Bass Rock – he patted himself vigorously on the back: 'I serve neither for profit nor thanks, but in pure zeal to his majesty's service and love to his person.'[84] What Lauderdale thought of this bit of blather is not recorded.

So the negotiations began. Tweeddale's position was simple: he wanted to get as much as possible out of Seaton, who at first was disposed to defend himself against the charges. Lauderdale was unhappy. He wrote to William Sharp that Seaton and his friends (meaning Sharp, among others) were to be 'put . . . to the squeak'. He thought half the defalcation, i.e. £8,500, would be fair, but 'I will meddle no more in it.' He told Sharp that if Seaton wanted a trial, which would happen if the king saw the report, there was no more to be said. What he preferred was that Tweeddale, Cochrane and Seaton meet to thrash out a composition acceptable to the king; then the whole matter could be hushed up. Sharp preferred this too; he knew that Seaton would have trouble convincing a court of the merits of his case.[85] The meeting was duly held; Tweeddale reported that Cochrane had thoughtlessly set the payback too low. Tweeddale wanted £4,000 in cash and the surrender of the salt tack, which he thought was worth £2,000 to £3,000 sterling a year, and which had three years to run.[86] The importance of the meeting was that Seaton, perhaps under pressure from Sharp and his other partners, and hoping that Halton might intervene on his behalf, was now willing to bargain. Lauderdale, taking note, spoke to Charles, who, he said, was prepared to accept £4,000. Charles wanted such a deal rather than 'to ravel further into that matter, for he desires not that others be reflected on', meaning Rothes.[87] Seaton's first offer was £3,000; Lord Advocate Nisbet,

---

84 19 June 1668, Tweeddale to Lauderdale, ibid., ff. 173–74.

85 30 June 1668, Tweeddale to Lauderdale, ibid., f. 197, and to Moray, NLS Ms. 7024, f. 94. 11 July, Lauderdale to Tweeddale, NLS Ms. 7023, f. 180, and to Sharp, NLS Ms. 7023, f. 295. 16 July, Sharp to Lauderdale, BL Add. Mss 23129, f. 233.

86 18 July 1668, Tweeddale to Lauderdale, BL Add. Mss 23129, ff. 241–42, and to Moray, NLS Ms. 7024, f. 101. Tweeddale's estimate of the salt tack is in NLS Ms. 7024, f. 40.

87 28 July 1668, Lauderdale to Tweeddale, NLS Ms. 7023, f. 185. For Seaton's approach to Halton see 16 July, Tweeddale to Moray, NLS Ms. 7024, f. 100.

John Maitland, 2nd earl and 1st duke of Lauderdale.

By Sir Peter Lely. Scottish National Portrait Gallery.

John Hay, 2nd earl and 1st marquess of Tweeddale.

By Sir Peter Lely. Scottish National Portrait Gallery.

John Hay, Lord Yester, later 2nd marquess of Tweeddale.

By Jacob Ferdinand Voet. Scottish National Portrait Gallery.

John Leslie, 7th earl and 1st duke of Rothes.

By L. Schuneman. Scottish National Portrait Gallery.

James Sharp, archbishop of St Andrews.

Unknown; after Sir Peter Lely. Scottish National Portrait Gallery.

William Douglas, 3rd duke of Hamilton.

By Sir Godfrey Kneller. Collection of Lennoxlove House.

Archibald Campbell, 9th earl of Argyll.

By L. Schuneman. Scottish National Portrait Gallery.

Alexander Bruce, 2nd earl of Kincardine.

By Adrian Hanneman. Collection unknown; image recorded in
Scottish National portrait Gallery reference section.

whom Tweeddale consulted, thought that Seaton might be able to pay £5,000. Tweeddale, meanwhile, had raised his sights: he wanted £6,000 and the salt tack, as an initial bargaining position at least, but as he remarked to Moray, 'we must do as we can and not as we would in an evil time.'[88] A few weeks later Tweeddale had another discussion with Sharp and thought that Seaton would now be prepared to pay £4,000 and surrender the tack, but then, Tweeddale wrote, Seaton had heard from London that £4,000 would be enough. From whom did he hear this? Lauderdale was vexed; he said that he had discussed the matter only with Moray. On 19 August Seaton was hoping that the embattled customs farmers might quit, so that he might try to get control again and 'return to the old channel of confusion.' Meantime he had actually reduced his offer, to £2,000, but he now knew, said Tweeddale, that he must find £5,000, or less if he surrendered the salt tack. Breaking that tack, Tweeddale wrote, 'will be the greatest task I have yet taken in hand.'[89]

Early in September Seaton appealed directly to Lauderdale. He had been told that he must pay £4,000 and surrender the salt tack, a new demand, he said. He would do what Lauderdale wanted, but he begged for mitigation of these draconian terms. This produced results. On 15 September Lauderdale wrote a rather irritable letter, evidently influenced by Sharp's insinuations that Tweeddale was being unduly inflexible. 'I tell you,' wrote Lauderdale, 'the King will be content with £3,000 sterling in money and quitting the tack. This sum will buy the Bass . . . This I have advised Sir Walter to offer, and I advise you to take, which I assure you the King will accept. [Moray] did hear, said little, but was ill-pleased afterwards. If you mislike it too, then learn not to trust my good nature nor consent to refer such a matter to me again.' Tweeddale did indeed mislike it. He pointed out that Lauderdale had originally suggested £4,000, which would more than buy the Bass Rock and leave perhaps £1,500, which could be used to satisfy Moray's debts. But of course, he went on, if Lauderdale had already accepted Seaton's offer, that was that.[90] Lauderdale backed off.

For a while negotiations stopped. Cochrane had the gout, Bellenden also was ill, Rothes and Kincardine, newly appointed to the treasury

---

88 25, 30 July 1668, Tweeddale to Moray, NLS Ms. 7024, ff. 104, 105.

89 5, 8 Aug. 1668, Tweeddale to Lauderdale, BL Add. Mss 23129, ff. 266, 268. 15 Aug., Lauderdale to Tweeddale, NLS Ms. 7023, f. 192. 19 Aug., 3 Sept., Tweeddale to Moray, NLS Ms. 7024, ff. 110–11, 114.

90 4 Sept. 1668, Seaton to Lauderdale, BL Add. Mss 23130, f. 7. 15 Sept., Lauderdale to Tweeddale, Paton, 'Lauderdale', pp. 161–62. 22 Sept., Tweeddale to Lauderdale, BL Add. Mss 23130, f. 38.

commission, were absent.[91] And there was much else on Tweeddale's plate. In November Bellenden had the gall to suggest that Tweeddale was deliberately stalling on Seaton's accounts so that Bellenden would be blamed. Tweeddale erupted: he was present at the meetings of the treasury commission more frequently than anyone else. Bellenden snapped back: Tweeddale was always absent on Saturdays. The earl rejoined that he owed Bellenden no account; the latter 'mumbled according to his custom that he heard I was to be treasurer'. Lauderdale was annoyed at the 'impertinencies' of the 'old fretful man', and encouraged Tweeddale to put pressure on Sir Walter.[92] After a new outburst from Bellenden on an unrelated matter, Tweeddale asked for the appointment of a new exchequer commission, which was necessary with the addition of Kincardine, with himself as presiding officer in the absence of Rothes. Bellenden as treasurer-depute was entitled to preside in Rothes's absence, but 'the king's service is not to be done at this rate'. It would be best if Bellenden were removed from office, so that business would no longer be 'clogged by one man's folly'.[93] Lauderdale would not go that far; he was prepared to 'mortify' Bellenden but not to fire him. Tweeddale's reports of Bellenden's ill health caused Lauderdale to get Charles to promise that Halton would get the place when it became vacant: 'I may be allowed to provide for my brother,' with whom Tweeddale was on rather cool terms. 'Be kind and frank to him,' Lauderdale went on, 'and I hope he will mend his faults.' The king's promise to Halton caused heart-burning later, but for now Tweeddale got what he wanted. In the new commission Tweeddale was named as president of both treasury and exchequer absent the chancellor, and Bellenden was the recipient of a 'mortifying letter' which, said Tweeddale, caused him to behave much better.[94]

Tweeddale's persistence in Seaton's business finally paid off. Sir Walter continued to stall, and hold up what he owed on the salt farm, until, on 6 February 1669, the king took a direct hand. He wrote to the treasury commission, ordering that Seaton either pay £5,000 sterling and surrender the last two years of the salt tack or take his chances in court; this was what

91 7 Nov. 1668, Tweeddale to Moray, NLS Ms. 7024, f. 130.
92 26 Nov. 1668, Tweeddale to Lauderdale, BL Add. Mss 23130, f. 137. 1, 3 Dec., Lauderdale to Tweeddale, Paton, 'Lauderdale' pp. 171–74.
93 12 Dec. 1668, Tweeddale to Lauderdale, BL Add. Mss 23131, ff. 30–31.
94 17 Nov., 5, 26 Dec. 1668, Lauderdale to Tweeddale, Paton, 'Lauderdale', pp. 168–69, 175–76, 181–83. 5 Jan. 1669, Tweeddale to Moray, NLS Ms. 7024, f. 141. The commission, dated 21 Dec. 1668, is in *Warrant Book 1660–1670*, NAS GD 90/2/260, no pagination.

Tweeddale now wanted.[95] Lauderdale, in sending this directive to Tweeddale, advised him to talk first to William Sharp, so that he could prepare Seaton 'before you send for him and shoot him with 5000 lib. Weight'. Moray 'did like a Turk press for £6,000'. Lauderdale would have settled for the old offer of £4,000, 'but his Majesty would hear of no less than £5,000'.[96] Seaton complained that he had been cruelly treated and never allowed a hearing, blaming Tweeddale for all his misfortunes. The latter rejoined that now he could be heard – in court – but doubted that he would go that route. Rothes shrugged off the king's decision when he heard it; he thought the matter had already been settled – this from the presiding officer of the treasury commission! Rothes was more concerned about Moncrieffe, the commission's clerk, who had been, to say the least, neglectful in Seaton's business and had also been involved, along with Seaton, in concealing money owed to the government from prize ships taken in Shetland during the war. He admitted his errors, Crawford and Rothes spoke for him, and so Tweeddale, who probably would not have been sorry to see him go, relented. Moncrieffe was able, and might be 'honester under more diligent masters'. Moncrieffe was a survivor. He remained in office through all the changes of the next four decades, until the abolition of the treasury in 1708.[97]

Seaton finally capitulated. On 16 March 1669 Moray wrote a cheerful letter to that effect to Kincardine and emphasised that Seaton would never again be employed.[98] On 22 March, after Charles's return from Newmarket and Lauderdale's from Hampton Court, where he had been on a 'very merry diverting journey' with Uncle Dunfermline and 'nostre fils' Lord Yester, the king signed three copies of the papers and 'laughed at my diligence. I told him I would take triple pains rather than he should forfeit £5,000'.[99] One wonders whether the secretary's good humour was due to a

95 2 Feb. 1669, Lauderdale to Tweeddale, Paton, 'Lauderdale', pp. 198–99. NLS Ms. 3136, f. 158. As an indication of Charles's preferred methods of work, he made it clear that he had not read the commission's reports: they were read to him.

96 5 Jan. 1669, Tweeddale to Moray, NLS Ms. 7024, f. 141. 6 Feb., Lauderdale to Tweeddale, Paton, 'Lauderdale', p. 200. Lauderdale's formal instructions, addressed to Tweeddale, Kincardine and Cochrane, were sent at the same time. Paton, 'Lauderdale', p. 201.

97 23, 26 Jan., 2, 9, 16 Feb. 1669, Tweeddale to Moray, NLS Ms. 7024, ff. 143–46, 149. 15 Feb., Tweeddale to Lauderdale, BL Add. Mss 23131, f. 85. 30 Jan., Lauderdale to Tweeddale, Paton, 'Lauderdale', pp. 197–98. For Moncrieffe, see A. Murray, 'The Scottish Treasury 1667–1708', *SHR* XLV (1966), pp. 94–95.

98 *Moray Letters*, pp. 261–62.

99 20, 23 Mar. 1669, Lauderdale to Tweeddale, Paton, 'Lauderdale', pp. 209–11.

visit to Ham House, where since mid-January he had been calling regularly, often staying the night, to console his beautiful and recently widowed friend, Elizabeth Murray, countess of Dysart.

Catching up with and punishing a corrupt official was rare in Restoration Britain. In Scotland the most conspicuous such case was that of Halton, then treasurer-depute, who after Lauderdale's loss of power and subsequent death in 1682 was without a protector. Seaton had protectors: business partners such as Sharp, and the negligent officials who had granted his requests. And Lauderdale himself had never shown any great interest in the rooting out of corruption The looting practised by Middleton and his cronies had gone unpunished; all that Lauderdale cared about was their fall from power, which, of course, had the incidental benefit of stopping their looting. Tweeddale's and Moray's zeal in going after Seaton was unusual. Tweeddale in particular, once he had made up his mind, showed a stubborn, single-minded determination, verging on inflexibility, which was often to characterise his behaviour during his years of power. It seems likely also, that the extent of Seaton's corruption as tax farmer, and the difficulty of bringing him to book, led Tweeddale to conclude that direct collection of taxes was vastly preferable to farming. At least from this point on, and ultimately to his cost, he became an enthusiastic advocate of direct collection. His manner alienated Bellenden, who admittedly was 'an old fretful man'. There had been friction between the two ever since the appointment of the commission. Bellenden's trip to London in October 1667 Tweeddale regarded as 'unsufferable' since he had so much accounting to do, and he urged Lauderdale to send him back 'with a flea in his ear'.[100] And he had been on chilly terms with Rothes for years. But they were still his colleagues on the commission. Bellenden, in particular, would make Tweeddale's life difficult until he was pushed into retirement in 1671.

There was much to occupy the days, and sometimes the nights, of the treasury commissioners during the first half of 1668 besides the pursuit of Sir Walter Seaton. Some were trade-related. The commission recommended banning the importation of brandy; it cut into the profits, not only of the customs farmers (on French and Spanish wines) but also of the manufacturers of 'aquavite and other strong waters'. Lauderdale observed that brandy could be added to the wine farm, but endorsed the ban, as did

100 BL Add. Mss 23128, ff. 105–06.

Charles. Brandy made people drunk; furthermore, Sir Alexander Fraser, the king's physician, said that 'aquavitae is much wholesomer'. The council imposed the ban on 13 February.[101] At the behest of the western heritors the council on 3 March wrote to Lauderdale seeking the prohibition of importing horses from Ireland. Charles duly authorised this; the necessary proclamation, adding horses to the already-prohibited Irish cattle, salt beef and grain, was issued on 9 April.[102]

Another matter, of less concern to the commissioners than to the royal burghs, was the Scottish staple at Veere. This trade had been seriously damaged thanks to the two Dutch wars, and was becoming less relevant. The list of staple goods was short – skins, hides, woollen textiles, salmon, tallow and beef – whereas coal, the principal Scottish export to the Netherlands, went to Rotterdam. The issue in 1668 was the conservator of the staple, Sir William Davidson, a neglectful absentee whom the convention of royal burghs regarded as unfit. He came to Edinburgh to lobby the royal burghs; Provost Ramsay of Edinburgh commented that he did himself no good, but that – in mitigation – he meant well. The difficulty was that the crown rather than the convention was now responsible for the appointment. He was Lauderdale's man, and Lauderdale wanted him kept. He stayed, but he remained so deeply unpopular that Lauderdale, when he got to Scotland in the autumn of 1669, found it politically impossible to order the treasury commission to authorise a pension, which the king wanted him to have. Only Lauderdale's protection stood between him and a burgh-inspired lawsuit.[103]

The burghs had reason to regret their inability to replace Davidson. They were not satisfied with Veere as a staple port and wanted to discuss moving the staple, preferably to Rotterdam, the logical place given the importance of the coal trade. Lauderdale at first professed indifference, but by September 1668, much to the burghs' chagrin, the word came from London that the staple was to be moved to Dort, which they regarded as less desirable even than Veere.[104] The coal masters ignored the requirement

101 1, 8 Feb. 1668, Lauderdale to Tweeddale, NLS Ms. 7023, f. 123, Ms. 14406, f. 48. *RPCS* II, pp. 397–98, 402–03.

102 *RPCS* II, pp. 421–23, 428, 432. The prohibition was renewed in August; the wording suggests that much smuggling went on. *RPCS* II, pp. 511–12.

103 See Ramsay's letters to Lauderdale starting in March 1668, BL Add. Mss 23129, ff. 5, 23, 120, 152. 23 June, Tweeddale to Lauderdale, BL Add. Mss 23129, f. 182. 2 Dec. 1669, Lauderdale to Moray, BL Add. Mss 23132, f. 182.

104 9 Apr., 2 July 1668, Lauderdale to Tweeddale, NLS Ms. 7023, ff. 145, 176. 19 Sept., Ramsay to Lauderdale, BL Add. Mss 23130, f. 36.

that they, too, should use the staple port. Lauderdale, annoyed, ordered the council to issue a proclamation to that effect, with appropriate penalties for non-compliance. The coalmasters indicated their willingness to negotiate, and Lauderdale instructed Davidson to get the officials at Dort to offer good terms. Rotterdam, he informed Tweeddale, had offered nothing. Kincardine undertook to deal with the coalmasters; the plan was to negotiate a package for both coal and salt. Some of the coalmasters were recalcitrant, notably the earl of Wemyss, whose nose was out of joint because Lauderdale had blocked his plan to turn his private harbour at Methil into a free port, which, said the secretary, would ruin all the saltmasters in Scotland. 'It is to take us all for fools,' wrote Lauderdale, 'for the harbour is for his private advantage . . . Stop it, therefore, stop it, stop it,' and stopped it was. By mid-December the coalmasters agreed to give Dort preference if no better offer materialised elsewhere. Nothing came of the negotiations. Their principal use, as Kincardine observed in November 1669, was to alarm the English and make them more receptive to trade concessions on their own part. The staple continued to languish.[105]

Another concern of the treasury commission was to expand the king's income from crown lands. It pursued Middleton's former ally, the earl of Morton, wadsetter [mortgagee] of Orkney and Shetland, for his failure to surrender to the crown the treasure contained in a Dutch East Indiaman wrecked in Shetland in 1664. Lauderdale thought that as much as 22,000 gold ducats might be involved. This inquiry was the thin end of the wedge: the commission's purpose was to force Morton to surrender his wadset, which Charles I had granted to Morton's grandfather in 1643 as security for the loans he had made to the crown, reckoned at £30,000 sterling. The crown lands in the earldom were worth about £2,400 to £2,500 sterling a year, which, Tweeddale estimated, was half Morton's income. In February 1668 the exchequer levied a whopping fine, over £11,000 sterling, on Morton for his behaviour over the East Indiaman. Bargaining began, and in due course Morton surrendered his wadset. When the matter was settled, in August 1668, Tweeddale sourly commented that Morton had got

105 10 Nov., 3, 5 Dec. 1668, Lauderdale to Tweeddale, Paton, 'Lauderdale' pp. 165–67, 174–76. RPCS II, p. 558. 10 Nov., 19 Dec., Tweeddale to Lauderdale, 4 Dec., Lauderdale to Davidson, 13, 17 Dec., Kincardine to Lauderdale, BL Add. Mss 23130, ff. 118, 141, 23131, ff. 5, 28–29, 36, 42–43. 3 Nov. 1669, Kincardine to Tweeddale, NLS Ms. 7003, f. 172. Lennox, *Lauderdale and Scotland*, pp. 247–48, 250–51. T.C. Smout, *Scottish Trade on the Eve of Union* (London, 1963), pp. 185–88. Lauderdale's quoted comment is in his letter of 5 Dec.

a better bargain than he deserved.[106] The financial picture, after a year of peace and retrenchment, still looked bleak to him. Cash flow had been a major problem all year. In July 1668 he urged Moray to be sure that Lauderdale refused Earl Marischal's request for payment of his pension; you know, he wrote, 'how far the revenue is like to fall short'.[107] But at least the crown had recovered its income from Orkney.

The exchequer's decree against Morton whetted the king's appetite. Tweeddale had once talked of reducing Maclean's feu of Mull and Seaforth's of Lewis, technically escheated for non-payment of feu duties; Lauderdale (and Charles) now wanted to hear more. Tweeddale hoped it might be possible to triple the revenue from crown lands, 'which he [Charles] says will make him king indeed'. This did not happen, but royal rents rose from £3,600 sterling in 1668 to almost £4,000 in 1671, and in the 1670s Orkney and Shetland brought in £2,500 a year.[108] Another, more problematical property that Charles wanted for the crown was the Bass Rock, off the North Berwickshire coast opposite the great Douglas fortress of Tantallon. It was currently in the hands of Provost Ramsay of Edinburgh, Lauderdale's close ally, who wanted £5,000 sterling for it. Tweeddale thought that was absurd: it was fit only to be a prison. It was worth no more than £250 a year; a fair price would be perhaps £2,800.[109] The haggling began; it would last for three years.

III

In Sir Walter Seaton's argument for defalcations the Scottish duty of 80 per cent on English imports figured prominently, even though he had failed to collect it. It was also a factor in bringing about formal Anglo-Scottish negotiations on trade, which opened in January 1668. The Dutch war had had a disastrous impact on Scottish foreign trade. With the end of

106 16 July 1667, Lauderdale to Moray, NLS Ms. 7023, f. 63. 8, 20 Feb., 5 Aug. 1668, Tweeddale to Lauderdale, BL Add. Mss 23128, ff. 297, 326–27, 23129, f. 266. 3 July, Tweeddale to Moray, BL Add. Mss 23128, f. 96. F.J. Shaw, *The Northern and Western Islands of Scotland* (Edinburgh, 1980), pp. 21–22, 57. P.L. Thompson, *History of Orkney* (Edinburgh, 1987), pp. 183–85.

107 6 Feb., 7 May 1668, Tweeddale to Lauderdale, BL Add. Mss 23128, f. 293, 23129, ff. 102–03. 3 July, Tweeddale to Moray, BL Add. Mss 23128, f. 96. Lauderdale did see to it that Marischal was not pursued for his debts. NLS Ms. 14406, f. 62.

108 22 Feb. 1668, Tweeddale to Lauderdale, BL Add. Mss 23128, ff. 330–31. 3 Mar., Lauderdale to Tweeddale, NLS Ms. 7023, f. 133. Lennox, *Lauderdale and Scotland*, pp. 398–400.

109 Feb., 19 June 1668, Tweeddale to Lauderdale, BL Add. Mss 23128, f. 301, 23129, ff. 173–74. 15 Feb., Lauderdale to Tweeddale, NLS Ms. 7023, f. 127.

the war and the fall of Clarendon, whom the Scots regarded as a major obstacle to any acceptable trade agreement with England,[110] there was hope for accommodation. In mid-August 1667, even before Clarendon's dismissal, Lauderdale reminded the duke of York's secretary, Sir William Coventry, that if England was not prepared to be helpful the Scots could now trade with the Dutch. Two weeks later Lauderdale got a ruling that Scots, like other aliens, could bring timber to London in spite of the Navigation Act, to further the rebuilding of the city after the great fire.[111] On 13 September 1667, after Clarendon's dismissal, the new Lord Keeper, Sir Orlando Bridgeman, brought a petition from a group of English merchants to the English privy council asking for a settlement of Anglo-Scottish trade and a removal of barriers, especially the 80 per cent impost. Expanding the volume of trade was important to both sides, given the importance of customs revenue to both countries' budgets. After the Restoration each had adopted protectionist measures, ending abruptly the free trade that had existed during the Cromwellian union. The current balance of trade heavily favoured England, which exported to Scotland goods at least three times as valuable as her imports. The figures Lauderdale gave in a letter to Moray in October 1667 were £318,000 and £100,000 sterling respectively.[112] A high-powered English conciliar committee was appointed to make recommendations; it quickly decided that it could not advise the king to suspend any of the English levies, whatever his prerogative powers might be, since parliament was about to meet and the levies were 'so tied by the late Acts'. Anticipating negotiations, Lauderdale urged Tweeddale and Moray to develop an agenda for them.[113]

Lauderdale was very hopeful. But at first things moved slowly: the king was hunting at Bagshot, others were out of town as well, and Bridgeman was ill. For Lauderdale Bridgeman was the key: 'he is our plight anchor next the king', he wrote to Tweeddale on 3 October.[114] A week later Bridgeman's speech at the opening of parliament stressed the government's wish that the Scots be satisfied in the matter of trade, lest they take their

---

110 See e.g., 7 Sept. 1667, Tweeddale to Lauderdale, 19 Sept., Rothes to Lauderdale, BL Add. Mss 23128, ff. 16–17, 52.

111 NLS Ms. 7023, ff. 76, 83.

112 NLS Ms. 7024, ff. 47–48. Robert Mein, in a letter of Oct. 1668, estimated the imbalance at only £50,000–£60,000 a year. *CSPD 1668–69*, p. 40.

113 14 Sept. 1667, Lauderdale to Tweeddale, 17 Sept., Lauderdale to Moray, NLS Ms. 7023, ff. 90–91.

114 NLS Ms. 7003, f. 56..

business elsewhere. His speech was well received, more, perhaps, because Charles had fired Clarendon than because he wanted to please the Scots, never a priority of any kind with English MPs. Lauderdale was gratified that Bridgeman had given the Scottish question so much emphasis, and also at Tweeddale's imminent arrival, so that they could work on the trade question together. Moray duly prepared the requested agenda, and urged Lauderdale to 'squeeze' Tweeddale quickly and send him home: he was needed in Edinburgh.[115]

Tweeddale spent little enough time on trade during his two months in London because the English parliament was in session. The king wanted the Houses to authorise the appointment of a commission to discuss the issue. A great deal of time was spent on whether or not such a commission, and the king, could alter existing regulations, the Navigation Act and the 80 per cent tariff, for example, without parliamentary approval, since they were the result of parliamentary legislation. The English parliament consulted Lennox and Middleton on this point with respect to Scotland; their answers were unhelpful. Eventually parliament voted to approve the appointment of a commission, but there was opposition, especially in the Lords, and there was delay, because there were matters of greater concern, such as the impeachment of Clarendon. Lauderdale was not sure that anything much would come of the proposed discussions, but he did know, he said, that Charles had worked very hard to bring them about, 'and no Scotsman looked after it (except to obstruct it) but only Tweeddale and I'. Tweeddale was, of course, appointed as a member of the Scottish delegation, along with, among others, Rothes, Hamilton, Moray and Kincardine. But Lauderdale thought that Tweeddale would be more useful in Edinburgh, gathering information, which Tweeddale much preferred: he wanted to go home. When the commission met, though other Scotsmen might have been there, the only one who mattered was Lauderdale. Moray, whom Lauderdale consulted about the makeup of the commission, replied that the secretary could do all the negotiating himself, and urged him to get the job done quickly.[116]

115 10, 15, 17 Oct. 1667, Lauderdale to Moray, NLS Ms. 7023, ff. 101, 103, 104. 14, 19 Oct., Moray to Lauderdale, BL Add. Mss 23128, ff. 136–37, 146. Lauderdale's letter of 15 Oct. described the scene in the Banqueting Hall at which both Houses thanked Charles for dismissing Clarendon, and Charles gave an assurance that the fallen chancellor would never again be employed.
116 9 Nov., 21, 24 Dec. 1667, Tweeddale to Moray, NLS Ms. 7024, ff. 61, 83–86. 19 Dec., Lauderdale to Moray, NLS Ms. 7023, f. 112. 27, 30 Dec., Moray to Lauderdale, BL Add. Mss 23128, ff. 233–36.

The commission held its first meeting on 13 January 1668. Everyone turned up except Uncle Dunfermline, 'who would not leave play at Hampton Court for so small a matter'. The circumstances were less than ideal. There were no chairs and no fire – in January! – so the commissioners all stood around and read their commissions. When the English commissioners asked where to begin, Lauderdale was ready: with the Navigation Act, which, he said with considerable exaggeration, had ended fifty-six years of free trade. The duke of Buckingham, whose qualifications as a commissioner were no more readily apparent than those of Dunfermline, and who, three days later, was to wound fatally his mistress's husband in a duel, wanted to deal with other matters first, but the Scots stood firm and carried their point.[117]

There is little point in following the negotiations in detail; in the end they came to nothing.[118] There were faults on both sides. The English commissioners were for the most part an able and hard-nosed group. They were suspicious that if they made any concessions on the Navigation Act the Scots would find ways of cheating, as they had in the 1650s. The key man was Sir George Downing, the secretary of the English treasury commission, which, like its counterpart in Edinburgh, had to sort out the financial mess left by the recent war. Downing's financial ingenuity had helped the government scrape through during the war; he knew far more about commercial and fiscal matters than anyone else on either side. He opposed any weakening of the Navigation Act, in part because of his hatred of the Dutch, at whom the Act had principally been aimed. Although he did not say so, he could not have been pleased that the Scots were so delighted at the signing of the Triple Alliance with the Dutch and the Swedes in January 1668. One clause of the treaty which particularly pleased Lauderdale obligated the Dutch to expel 'those libel-writing rogues' who had taken refuge there after they had been formally condemned in Scotland.[119] Tweeddale thought that the English might now make concessions on the Navigation Act, to avoid the diversion of Scots trade to

---

117 14 Jan. 1668, Lauderdale to Tweeddale, NLS Ms. 7023, f. 117.
118 The record of the commissioners' proceedings is in NLS Ms. 14492, pp. 26–113. See also Edward Hughes, 'The Negotiations for a Commercial Union between England and Scotland in 1668', *SHR* XXIV (1926–27), pp. 30–47, and Lennox, *Lauderdale and Scotland*, pp. 254–64, and pp. 65–66, fn. 45.
119 7 Jan. 1668, Lauderdale to Moray, Paton, 'Lauderdale', pp. 146–47. When the treaty was presented to the English privy council it proved to be an embarrassment. 'The treaties being in Latin were put into my hand and I did read them into English,' wrote Lauderdale – no comment was necessary. 21 Jan., Lauderdale to Tweeddale, NLS Ms. 7023, f. 118.

Holland. Downing, however, was unmoved. In an informal discussion of the trade of the plantations in the king's presence in March he made a 'bitter, tedious speech', and he and Lauderdale engaged in an acrimonious slanging match. He will ruin the treaty if he can, Lauderdale opined. Tweeddale suggested trying bribery. 'Sir George Downing barks for a bone', he wrote. 'He has been accustomed to get money from Scots men.' Lauderdale replied that Charles thought that might be worth trying; the difficulty was that if it failed there would be serious trouble.[120] There is no evidence that it was tried, and in the end Downing had his way. The exchange does say something about the nature of Restoration politics: the king contemplating the offer of a bribe to one of his own officials.

In spite of Downing the English commissioners were prepared to discuss some partial and temporary modifications of the Navigation Act, though they rejected out of hand the Scots' argument that the common citizenship they had enjoyed since Calvin's case made the Act inapplicable to Scots. But first the English wanted a complete list of Scottish ships, including those acquired as prizes during the recent war. The Scots were slow to provide this. Lauderdale asked that it be sent quickly; Tweeddale replied that it would take time. A month later Lauderdale complained that the first list did not indicate which ships were prizes, and therefore foreign-built. Tweeddale replied that the Scots had kept very few prizes – they had sold most prizes to the English – and had no more than 272 ships in all, where the port of Kirkcaldy alone used to have eighty: 'We are in nothing so thriving a condition that way as they suppose.' Lauderdale rejoined that he still wanted the list sent, 'though I confess every day I have less hope of our trade'. Tweeddale sent the list on 11 April, complete except for Inverness and Orkney: a total of 305 ships, of 22, 613 tons. A few days later he commented that Lauderdale's accounts made the negotiations sound hopeless. One major problem, as he saw it, was the cattle trade. England was virtually the only market for Scottish cattle; if this issue could be resolved, the Scots would be better off with respect to the rest of their trade by dealing with the Dutch. If the Dutch became Scotland's chief trading partners, he added, the tack of the border customs which Newburgh had surrendered would be worthless, and that even now it was not worth half the money promised to Newburgh: his pension 'sticks in my crop'.[121]

---

120   31 Mar., 6 Apr. 1668, Lauderdale to Tweeddale, NLS Ms. 7023, ff. 142, 144. 30 Jan., 30 Mar., Tweeddale to Lauderdale, BL Add. Mss 23128, f. 282, 23129, ff. 41–42.

121   18 Feb., 24 Mar., 6 Apr. 1668, Lauderdale to Tweeddale, NLS Ms. 7023, ff. 128, 139, 144. 27 Feb., 30 Mar., 11, 14 Apr., Tweeddale to Lauderdale, BL Add. Mss 23128, f. 336, 23129, ff. 41–42, 65–66, 71–72. The treasury commission authorised Newburgh's pension on 4 Sept. NAS E6/1/116.

In the end Lauderdale, apparently acting on Tweeddale's advice, never did give in the list of ships. He had come up with an alternative plan. 'We have resolved,' Lauderdale wrote on 23 April, 'not to pursue the treaty any further unless they do it (which I do not expect), but that the King shall do it himself in Council. For by the law his Majesty may dispense with the Act of Navigation, and hath done it all this war to all nations.' Tweeddale was to tell no one save Moray. Tweeddale was delighted with the ploy, if it could be made permanent. He added that Lauderdale need not worry about secrecy: no one asked about the negotiations any more, they were so out of hope.[122] It is not clear whether Lauderdale ever asked Charles to suspend the Navigation Act. At all events Charles did not, knowing what an uproar that action would cause. He used his prerogative on behalf of Scottish trade on only one issue, the importation of Scottish cattle. In July 1668, thanks to a petition from the Scottish privy council, the English customs farmers were ordered to appear before the English treasury commission to explain why they were charging 18d a head on imported cattle. After a long struggle, an English Order in Council ended the duty, on Charles's orders, in April 1669. Lauderdale was cock-a-hoop: the king, he wrote, was very favourable to the 'Land of Cakes'.[123]

The fiercest English opposition to concessions to the Scots came, not from the merchants over the Navigation Act, but from manufacturing interests alarmed by the prospect of free trade. Leading the way were the producers of coal and salt, perhaps the two most important Scottish exports. They immediately put pressure on the English commissioners to maintain the protection these commodities currently enjoyed, especially salt. The English position was that the Scottish salt was more cheaply manufactured and of inferior quality, an argument made about English salt by English merchants in the Scottish salt trade, who naturally had an interest in reducing the duty on Scottish salt. Furthermore, said the English manufacturers, during the Cromwellian union, when trade was free, one third of the Newcastle salt pans shut down. And after the Restoration the

---

122 23, 30 Apr. 1668, Lauderdale to Tweeddale, Paton, 'Lauderdale', pp. 158–60. 30 Apr., Tweeddale to Lauderdale, BL Add. Mss 23129, f. 84. The provost of Edinburgh reflected the general discouragement; see his letter of 21 Apr. to Lauderdale, BL Add. Mss 23129, f. 75.

123 18 July 1668, Lauderdale to Tweeddale, NLS Ms. 7023, f. 183. 24 Apr. 1669, Lauderdale to Kincardine, BL Harleian Mss 4631, I, p. 107. During the trade negotiations the English commissioners proposed raising the duty to 2s 6d per head. NLS Ms. 14492, pp. 93–98. M. Lee, Jr, The Cabal (Urbana, 1965), pp. 48–49. On the same day the English privy council exempted Scottish corn from the general ban on importing corn. RPCS III, pp. 16–17.

Scots had started the trade war by slapping a heavy tax on English salt in 1661; the English tax was levied in retaliation in 1662. In Hughes's view it was the opposition of these vested interests, as well as that of the English customs farmers, who wanted both high tariffs and the Navigation Act, which minimised their administrative costs, to remain intact. The only exception among the English tax collectors was Sir Thomas Strickland, the farmer of the salt duties, who wanted some reduction in order to increase his profits. Hughes felt that Lauderdale's threat to short-circuit the commissioners by persuading the king to act by prerogative undermined the negotiations. This is hardly fair; Lauderdale made this threat only after the negotiations had been stalled for four months.[124]

The meetings of the commissioners were far from continuous. There are gaps in the minute-book from mid-February to mid-March, from 1 April to mid-May, from mid-June to 29–30 July, then again to mid-September. Position papers had to be prepared, and responses to those of the other side drafted. Lauderdale had insisted before the first meeting of the commission that everything be put in writing, to avoid 'misreporting', and his 'good friend' Bridgeman had agreed. The last item in the minute-book, dated 27 October, was a letter from the English commissioners to their Scottish counterparts, requesting an answer to their memorandum of 29 July listing their demands, a formidable list indeed, giving evidence of an unyielding mind-set. Lauderdale's declared intention, in a meeting of the English council, to put the controverted issues before the king for judgment alarmed the English commissioners but made them no less intransigent.[125] They followed the July memorandum with another in September which focused largely on salt. It firmly backed the position of the English salt manufacturers, and begged Charles not to ruin 'many thousand families' by removing the English duty on Scottish salt. Robert Mein, the Edinburgh postmaster and a correspondent of Sir Joseph Williamson, commented late in October, with considerable exaggeration, that 'the taxes on both sides are so heavy that they are obliged to trade with other countries rather than with each other'.[126] The joint commission never issued a report or formally adjourned. It simply became irrelevant with the

---

124 The argument about salt can be followed in the minute-book of the commissioners' meetings; see fn. 118 above. Hughes, 'Negotiations', pp. 43–47.

125 9 Jan., 21 May 1668, Lauderdale to Tweeddale, NLS Ms. 7023, ff. 116, 158.

126 NLS Ms. 14492, pp. 93–98, 108–13. 29 Oct. 1669, Mein to Williamson, *CSPD 1668–1669*, p. 40.

onset of the union negotiations, which had been mooted as early as October 1667.[127]

On 22 February 1668, a month or so after the trade negotiations began, Lauderdale wrote to Moray that he was planning to come to Scotland soon. He had not been back for five years, nor had there been a session of parliament in that time; one might be necessary, especially if the trade negotiations went well. Charles would certainly name him royal commissioner to the parliament; Lauderdale fancied the perks. He was also anxious to see the refurbishing of the Maitlands' ancestral home at Lethington, which Tweeddale and Moray were monitoring for him, and which, Moray had written, would make it the best house in Scotland.[128] Tweeddale and Moray had hoped that he might come in the previous summer, but that was impossible for Lauderdale for a number of political reasons, as well as Mary Yester's pregnancy: Tweeddale should come to London instead – which he did.[129] But now Lauderdale was eager for the journey. Moray must prepare 'to come hither. You must be here 3 weeks or a month before I part. Think therefore with SS [Tweeddale] when you may be spared, that I may get you a call': formal permission from the king. 'SS' was not happy that Moray might be leaving, given the press of business. 'I will not think of it but when I resolve to flee out of Scotland,' he wrote, 'for alone I will not stay in it.'[130] But Moray's presence was essential in London to act as secretary in Lauderdale's absence. He was Charles's good friend, and had done an excellent job in that capacity in 1663. Lauderdale regarded Moray's absence from Scotland as temporary, so he passed over Tweeddale's comment in silence. 'I have bespoke my coach for my journey,' he informed Tweeddale on 6 April; Provost Ramsay was preparing his seat in St Giles.[131] Eight days later Lauderdale demanded to know whether Moray was coming or not. 'Resolve whether you think him more necessary here or there,' he wrote to Tweeddale, 'taking it for granted if he be not here nothing can be done in my absence.' Two weeks later: 'You need not doubt his return . . . I expect clear answer.' He set his departure date for the second week of June, and on 19 May he was still pressing Tweeddale: 'Torment me not with

---

127 For the start of the union negotiations see below, chapter 6, pp. 190 ff.
128 Paton, 'Lauderdale', pp. 154–55. 22 Aug. 1667, Moray to Lauderdale, 1 June 1668, Tweeddale to Lauderdale, BL Add. Mss 23127, f. 221, 23129, f. 130. In August 1669 Tweeddale boasted that the park at Lethington now had the best wall in Britain, BL Add. Mss 23132, f. 71.
129 23 July 1667, Lauderdale to Tweeddale, 10 Aug., Lauderdale to Moray, NLS Ms. 7023, ff. 65, 75.
130 27 Feb. 1668, Tweeddale to Lauderdale, BL Add. Mss 23128, f. 336.
131 NLS Ms. 7023, f. 144. 13 June 1668, Ramsay to Lauderdale, BL Add. Mss 23129, f. 152.

uncertainties.' Moray could have £500 sterling for his journey, he added four days later.[132] At last, very reluctantly, Tweeddale gave way. 'I am definite, and so I think is RM [Moray] that if you come he must go,' he wrote on 26 May, and he must get to London before Lauderdale departed. 'So set you the day.'[133]

Then Charles hesitated. On 4 June Lauderdale wrote that the king wanted a full report from Moray in person on Scottish issues before he decided whether or not Lauderdale should go. If he did not, Charles 'bade me give assurance he [Moray] should be returned speedily . . . [Charles] did read and approve this, every word.'[134] Moray left Scotland on 16 June. When he arrived, Charles was delighted to see him, 'crushing and shaking his hand', listening to Moray's long report and saying that he was 'very well satisfied with you that are now trusted by him'.[135] Within a week the king decided that Lauderdale would not go until the following spring, but Moray made no speedy return. In fact, he made no return at all. He had suddenly developed a middle-aged passion for his niece, Lady Sophia Lindsay, who had accompanied him from Scotland and was reportedly in poor health. So she may have been, but Moray's concern for her was clearly more than avuncular. 'He is so constantly with Lady Sophia that I seldom see him,' wrote Lauderdale on 9 July. By 14 July Tweeddale was grumbling that Moray was paying more attention to Sophia than to the nation's business; two days later Lauderdale wrote that he had not seen Moray. 'What you have done with him in Scotland I know not, but truly he is much changed.'[136]

On 30 September Tweeddale received the crushing news that Charles would not allow Moray to return this year. He wrote Lauderdale a 'wild epistle' with a long list of what needed to be done during the winter, more, he said, than could be handled even if Moray were there. The last four months had been awful; his own affairs were going badly; 'Mortal man must have some ease and relief.' Moray had said that France was more easily governed than Scotland, and had not wanted to leave. But Lauderdale had been so sure that he would be coming to Scotland, and that Moray would return after Lauderdale's visit, that Tweeddale, supposing that Moray's absence would be only temporary, had not tried to prevent his

132 NLS Ms. 7023, ff. 147, 150, 151, 157, 160.
133 BL Add. Mss 23129, ff. 116–17.
134 NLS Ms. 7023, f. 165.
135 30 June 1668, Lauderdale to Tweeddale, ibid., f. 175.
136 NLS Ms. 7024, f. 99, 7023, ff. 179, 181. A. Robertson, *The Life of Sir Robert Moray* (London, 1922), pp. 140, 178.

departure. He asked Lauderdale to beg Charles to reconsider, but Charles enjoyed Sir Robert's company too much to let him go.

Lauderdale tried to calm his 'dearest brother'. He too wanted Moray to return, he said, and he spoke to the king about it, but in vain. The king did not want him to go, and Moray showed no signs of wanting to go. Tweeddale's attitude annoyed him: 'The king hath now twice declared his pleasure, and yet S.S. gives not over grumbling,' he observed to Kincardine in November. There was the lure of the science and a new laboratory, as well as Lady Sophia. 'He minds nothing but his niece and his alchemy,' Lauderdale wrote on 29 September. A month later: 'The bewitching chemistry (on which our dearest Master spends at least 2 or 3 hours every day) are [sic] like to be too hard for you and me both'; And, three weeks later still: Moray's 'delight, his heart is here' – Lady Sophia, doubtless. And 'He spends at least 9 hours each day in the Laboratorie.' Tweeddale sourly regarded this enthusiasm as an unwelcome distraction from business, for Charles as well as for Moray. Among Tweeddale's other worries, his wife was having a difficult pregnancy; she was safely delivered on 3 November. Lauderdale should tell Moray that he should not play nursemaid to his niece: 'I protest MR's stay will ruin all.'[137]

For Tweeddale, now bereft of his partner, the burden of responsibility was crushing. 'You may apprehend me near dotage,' he wrote to Lauderdale a week after Moray left, admitting that he had once again misdated a letter, 'For I am sure I shall not hold long out at this rate of business.'[138] In a bleak Jeremiad of 27 July he recounted the problems he currently faced, and predicted that 'all our endeavours . . . without more hands and more force will be disproportioned to the difficulties we meet with and which I do foresee will occur.'[139] His continual complaining vexed Lauderdale. 'You do well to say no more of MR,' he wrote in November. 'He will do you no good this year, and himself neither hurt nor good here.'[140] His own workload was as great as Tweeddale's; perhaps even greater. In addition to his Scottish responsibilities he had to cultivate the king, fulfil his duties as a gentleman

137 7 Sept. 1668, Tweeddale to Moray, NLS Ms. 7024, f. 115. 24 Sept., 1, 6 Oct., 3 Nov., Tweeddale to Lauderdale, BL Add. Mss 23120, ff. 42, 56, 95–96, NLS Ms. 7024, f. 121. 29 Sept., 17, 22, 24 Oct., 12 Nov., Lauderdale to Tweeddale, NLS Ms. 7023, ff. 205, 208, 210, 211, Paton, 'Lauderdale', pp. 167–68. *Moray Letters* pp. 259–60.
138 BL Add. Mss 23129, f. 175.
139 Ibid., f. 257. At the end of the letter he wrote, 'Burn this.' Fortunately for the historian, Lauderdale paid no heed.
140 Paton, 'Lauderdale', pp. 169–70.

of the bedchamber, and monitor the English political scene for its effect on Scotland (and vice versa.) 'There is nothing but toil and little pleasure for me in this world,' he wrote on 4 July, when he announced, rather theatrically, that 'I received my doom, that I must not this year enjoy the satisfaction of seeing fair Scotland and my friends in it which I have so longed for.'[141] His irritation at Tweeddale's complaints is understandable. For the latter there was to be no relief. His hope that Scotland 'may be formed into a citadel for his Majesty's service in time,'[142] if it was to be realised, would be for him to achieve. He had to soldier on alone.

---

141 NLS Ms. 7023, f. 177.
142 3 Apr. 1668, Tweeddale to Lauderdale, BL Add. Mss 23129, ff. 48–49.

CHAPTER SIX

Tweeddale at Work, 1668–1669

I

By the time of Moray's departure in the summer of 1668 all the initiatives that were to characterise the cousins' regime were either under way or under discussion, accompanied by a far more vigorous and efficient administration of the country's finances thanks to the treasury commission.[1] They were the new religious policy of indulgence for a number of the outed ministers, the possible adoption of direct collection of the customs and excise instead of farming, trade negotiations with England which were to lead to the proposal of an Anglo-Scottish union, and the creation of a militia as a replacement for a much reduced military establishment. All save the last were to end in failure for reasons that had little or nothing to do with the merits of the proposals themselves, and the one administration in the thirty-year history of Restoration Scotland that could be called a reforming one collapsed also. The central figure after Moray's return to London was Tweeddale; the rise and fall of this regime was to a very large extent the story of his rise and fall. He had his shortcomings as a politician, but in his case the cliché applies: he was more sinned against than sinning.

It was difficult for Tweeddale to get things done. He had to stay on good terms with a chief whose principal concern was to carry out the king's wishes rather than to improve the condition of Scotland and who, as the Seaton affair showed, was quite prepared to wink at administrative corruption. And, indeed, to practise it. On 27 June 1668 the exchequer commission fined the sheriff-clerk of Forfar £1,000 sterling for misbehaviour. Two days before, Lauderdale had written Tweeddale that the king had promised him the fine if it was big enough to be worth having, as this certainly was. Lauderdale told Tweeddale to have the fine paid to Cashkeeper Sharp 'without account, which is the way here to do such things privately'.[2]

---

1 To give one example: on 2 Feb. 1669 Earl Marischal, who was sheriff of Aberdeen, accounted before the commission for the proceeds of the sheriffdom from July 1661 to July 1668, and for what he owed for his lordships of Altrie and Deir from the year 1624! NAS E6/1, p. 146.

2 27 June 1668, Bellenden to Lauderdale, BL Add. Mss 23129, f. 193. 25 June, Lauderdale to Tweeddale, NLS Ms. 7023, f. 173.

The most immediate issue Tweeddale faced was religious: the discussions with Archbishop Sharp, and with Robert Douglas and George Hutcheson, another prominent moderate nonconformist minister, on the terms of their admission to vacant parishes. These proceeded apace in June. Sharp was hesitant, and wanted to go to court to discuss the matter. Douglas was also being cautious; Lauderdale was annoyed that he 'should make that nice now which he was so desirous of four years ago'.³ As for Hutcheson, he refused to submit to presentation and collation, but gave the necessary assurances about peaceableness and good behaviour and – reluctantly – preaching only to his own congregation, a necessary condition for all outed ministers, in Tweeddale's view.⁴ By 9 July Lauderdale was asking Tweeddale about the terms of the warrants for Douglas and Hutcheson, which included exempting them from attending presbyteries and synods. He added that Sharp had the king's permission to come to court if he wished, but that he should not expect to achieve anything: Sheldon, after all, was out of favour. Lauderdale had written in June that Charles had taken away Sheldon's authority to make recommendations on church appointments and given it to a three-man committee, Arlington, Bridgeman and Herbert Croft, bishop of Hereford, which 'makes great noise here' and will 'mortify L.F.'⁵ Then, very abruptly, the whole process came to a dead stop.

On the afternoon of 11 July Sharp and Bishop Andrew Honeyman of Orkney were getting into a coach in Edinburgh's High Street when someone in the crowd fired a shot at the archbishop. He missed, hit Honeyman in the arm, and fled before anyone could react rapidly enough to catch him. 'The cry arose, a man was killed,' wrote Kirkton. 'The people's answer was, It's but a bishop; and so there was no more noise.' The council immediately offered a reward for the capture of the would-be assassin: 5,000 merks, or 2,000 and a pardon for a turncoat accomplice. All those involved in the recent rebellion who were in Edinburgh were to be rounded up and asked to account for themselves.⁶ Sharp was panicky. He 'whines still and speaks still of overturning and revolutions', wrote Tweeddale. The archbishop blamed the late rebels, and asserted that the murder was planned at a recent

---

3 30 June 1668, Tweeddale to Lauderdale, BL Add. Mss 23129, f. 197. 25 June, Lauderdale to Tweeddale, NLS Ms. 7023, f. 173.

4 3, 11 July 1668, Tweeddale to Lauderdale, BL Add. Mss 23129, ff. 203, 213–14.

5 NLS. Ms. 7023, ff. 166, 179.

6 J. Buckroyd, *The Life of James Sharp, Archbishop of St Andrews* (Edinburgh, 1987), pp. 90–91. *RPCS* II, pp. 486–89. Kirkton, *History*, p. 160.

conventicle. He, like the king, recently the object of what Sharp called a 'hellish design' to assassinate him, was the target of the murderous rage of the enemies of religion.[7] Charles wanted exemplary punishment for the assassin when he was caught, and vowed that the office of archbishop would not die even if Sharp did – cold comfort for the terrified incumbent.[8] But the king's resolve respecting the outed ministers did not change. He instructed Tweeddale to discuss details with Sharp: who should be appointed, and where. If Tweeddale preferred, this discussion with Sharp could take place if and when the latter came to court, with Tweeddale sending his suggestions along ahead of time. Lauderdale hoped that the journey might settle Sharp's nerves and make him more amenable to the admission of the outed ministers. When Sharp arrived Charles would order him not to drag his feet on the issue; so Lauderdale wanted to know, did Tweeddale prefer to get Douglas and Hutcheson installed before Sharp left, or to have the matter formally settled while Sharp was at court? In a mean gesture Lauderdale told Tweeddale not to tell Sharp that Charles had approved his journey, so that the crown would not have to pay Sharp's expenses, which it would have done had Charles issued a formal summons.[9]

The attempt on Sharp's life shocked and alarmed Tweeddale. Three days after the event he wrote to Lauderdale that all the bishops were so upset that the plans for change would have to be put on hold for some time.[10] He himself was very uncertain about what to do next. The fanatics were grown insolent, he wrote to Moray on 23 July. Both archbishops were under a cloud – the attempt on Sharp generated no sympathy for him. The pardons to the rebels, the punishment of Turner for his exactions, the rumours about the restoration of the outed ministers: all gave great encouragement to the discontented. The bishops were very discouraged, and Burnet was writing alarmist letters. The administration's only security was that the nonconformists were divided. More force was needed: two more troops of musketeers, since the militia was still in such disarray. They could be paid for by cutting pensions and the pay of the present troop of guards, also in disarray: 'we hold the wolf by the ears'. Four days later Tweeddale wanted two troops

7 23 July 1668, Sharp to Lauderdale, NLS Ms. 2512, f. 118. The quoted phrase is from Tweeddale's letter of 21 July to Lauderdale, BL Add. Mss 23129, ff. 243–44.
8 18 July 1668, Lauderdale to Tweeddale, NLS Ms. 7023, f. 182.
9 23 July, 1 Aug. 1668, Lauderdale to Tweeddale, ibid., ff. 183, 187. The king's instructions are in ibid., f. 184. 30 July, Tweeddale to Lauderdale, BL Add. Mss 23129, ff. 260–61.
10 BL Add. Mss 23129, f. 227.

of horse, fifty or sixty each, again paid for by cutting the pay of the standing forces, to be kept until the militia could be settled, which would not be finished until the spring of 1669.[11] It was impossible to readmit the outed ministers now: it would look as though the government, and the bishops, were acting out of fear.[12] The bishops were hopeless: of the ten or twelve who had been in Edinburgh in June and July, not one had preached. The fanatics were incorrigible, the moderates did nothing to quiet them, conventicles flourished, malcontents were fishing in drumlie waters, and the indifferent looked on and laughed. Once again Tweeddale pleaded with Lauderdale to send Moray back: 'in compassion to me haste him home, for I expect you will not delay an hour after what you have heard'.[13]

Lauderdale tried to calm his 'dearest brother', even holding out hope that Moray might at some point return. But he did not agree that the plan to settle the outed ministers be delayed; he favoured going ahead in order to split the nonconformists 'till the cursed remonstrators be crushed'. Still, he acknowledged, Tweeddale was in the best position to judge when this might come about.[14] Tweeddale decided to await the outcome of Sharp's journey to court. Before the end of July his would-be assassin had been identified as one James Mitchell, alias Small, one of those forfeited for his part in the Pentland Rising; now he had to be found.[15] Archbishop Burnet, his paranoia increased by the attempt on Sharp, continued to complain: outed ministers were to be intruded without consent of the bishops, and a commission was 'to visit my diocese of purpose to affront me'.[16] None of this had yet happened, and no one paid him heed.

In mid-August Tweeddale played host to Sharp at Yester as the archbishop started his journey south. He learned that Sharp still had 'no stomach' to admit outed ministers, and sent him on his way with a formal note of praise which was designed for his eyes rather than Lauderdale's.[17] While he waited he sent Lauderdale a long analysis of the state of the church as he saw it. The bishops had no friends and no influence. There had to be

11 NLS Ms. 7024, f. 103. 23, 27 July 1668, Tweeddale to Lauderdale, BL Add. Mss 23129, ff. 249, 257.
12 6 Aug. 1668, Tweeddale to Moray, NLS Ms. 7024, f. 107.
13 23, 27 July 1668, Tweeddale to Lauderdale, BL Add. Mss 23129, ff. 249, 257. The quoted sentence is in the letter of the 23rd.
14 30 July, 6 Aug. 1668, Lauderdale to Tweeddale, NLS Ms. 7023, ff. 186, 189.
15 30 July 1668, Tweeddale to Lauderdale, BL Add. Mss. 23129, ff. 260–61. Buckroyd, *Sharp*, p. 91. He eluded capture until 1674; for the ugly story of his subsequent treatment see Buckroyd, *Sharp*, pp. 100–03.
16 11 Aug. 1668, Burnet to Sheldon, *LP* II, App., pp. lxii–lxiv.
17 17, 18 Aug. 1668, Tweeddale to Lauderdale, BL Add. Mss 23129, ff. 290, 292.

change, for which parliamentary legislation would be necessary; without
change the country could not be quiet, or serviceable to the king. The status
quo was in accord with neither 'the genius of the nation nor the interest of
the magistrate'. The bishops needed to be taught how to govern the church,
and to stay out of politics. Sharp's meddling must be stopped – and yet the
king had to treat him well, so that the other bishops and the fanatics would
understand that he was not under a cloud. It was a difficult tightrope for the
government. As for the outed ministers, the soberest could be permitted
unofficially to preach in vacant churches, as long as they behaved well. If
they did not, the local magistrates could oust them. Since this procedure
was unofficial, there need be no formal presentation, and the issue of episcopal authority would be moot – an ingenious idea, but hardly a solution to
the problem.[18] This was a perceptive letter, but a rash one, stating in almost
so many words that the episcopal system, not the shortcomings of the
bishops, was to blame for the difficulties the regime was facing. A few days
later Tweeddale explained himself more fully and more guardedly to Moray.
The scheme for indulging the outed ministers had to be put on hold, lest the
legitimate incumbents be discouraged and the laity hold in contempt the
order established by law. Any Act of indulgence should be enacted in parliament; the present system had been thus established and should not be
subverted by 'the sole act of the king'. A clandestine presbytery, of which
Sharp knew nothing, was operating in Edinburgh, ordaining young men
illegally. Tweeddale expected a scolding from London, but now Moray and
Lauderdale had the facts, and Sharp was there: so, decide something and
don't lay all the responsibility on him. He worried that his usefulness as a
negotiator with the nonconformists might be compromised by the recent
crackdown in the west, for which the fanatics there held him responsible.
He advised Lauderdale to ask Sharp what the church was doing for itself if
he started to whine. The answer was, nothing: hence the conventicles.
Tweeddale wanted, and got, £500 sterling per year to pay informers for intelligence about them. In his letter of 15 September asking for the money he
remarked that he was glad Lauderdale liked his proposals, 'whatever they
were, for I do not remember them, and would therefore gladly see my own
letter' – an indication of the strain he was under.[19]

---

18 15 Aug. 1668, Tweeddale to Lauderdale, ibid., ff. 288–89.
19 19, 25 Aug. 1668, Tweeddale to Moray, NLS Ms. 7024, ff. 110–11, 113. 10, 15 Sept., Tweeddale
    to Lauderdale, BL Add. Mss 23130, ff. 18–19, 26. 22 Sept., Lauderdale to Tweeddale, NLS Ms.
    7023, f. 204.

Sharp stayed in London for somewhat more than two months and accomplished nothing. This was not altogether his fault, since the king and Lauderdale were frequently out of town, at Newmarket and elsewhere. He plunged into a prolonged melancholy fit after a dinner at Highgate, and wrote to Lauderdale at Newmarket about the 'calumny and persecution' he would face when he returned home. The question of the outed ministers, supposedly the purpose of his journey, was not settled. His only achievement was the renewal of an annual £200 sterling subvention for the university of St Andrews, on which the penny-pinching Tweeddale was not keen: the university's own revenues should be restored 'before the king's revenue be burdened'.[20] During the archbishop's absence Tweeddale and Provost Ramsay floated a plan to revise Edinburgh's parish structure. Currently there were six parishes, each served by two ministers. They proposed that there should be eight, with one minister apiece. There would be no additional expense, and the six 'secondaries', who were both discontented and not much good, could be transferred out. Ramsay strongly advocated doing this, since good preaching was the best way to keep Edinburgh clear of conventicles. He promised that if Sharp accepted the plan, no appointments would be made in Edinburgh without his advice. Nothing happened.[21]

Tweeddale wanted Sharp back home. No church business could be done without him, and meanwhile Archbishop Burnet 'is as busy as ever, suspending for not coming to synods men otherwise quiet and peaceable, and deposing the formerly suspended'.[22] Late in October Burnet held a synod at Peebles which drew up a complaint about the increase of Popery, Quakerism and conventicles, and lax law enforcement. Burnet proposed to send it directly to Charles, bypassing the privy council. Tweeddale commented that some bishops had not yet reported on Papists, and that conventicles were now few, with none in Edinburgh. Furthermore 'the law and authority have much recovered their vigour and lustre'; what Burnet seemed to want was a return to the days of Sir James Turner.[23] Tweeddale facetiously suggested that Burnet be translated to Ireland, which amused

20 30–31 Oct. 1668, Lauderdale to Tweeddale, Paton, 'Lauderdale', pp. 162–65. 8 Oct., Sharp to Lauderdale, NLS Ms. 2512, f. 122. 5 Nov., Tweeddale to Lauderdale, BL Add. Mss 23130, f. 99.
21 22 Sept., 21 Oct. 1668, Tweeddale to Moray, NLS Ms. 7024, ff. 118, 126. 24 Sept., Tweeddale to Lauderdale, BL Add. Mss 23130, f. 42. 24 Sept., Ramsay to Lauderdale, *Laing Mss* I, pp. 370–71.
22 10 Sept. 1668, Tweeddale to Moray, NLS Ms. 7024, f. 116.
23 29 Oct. 1668, Tweeddale to Lauderdale, BL Add. Mss 23130, f. 88.

Archbishop Sheldon. By autumn Burnet had apparently concluded that Sheldon either could not or would not be helpful, and had started to write to Bishop George Morley of Winchester, an opponent of both comprehension and indulgence, who had been a companion of the king's exile and was, after Sheldon, politically the most influential of the English episcopate.[24] Lauderdale commented that 'L.F. is as yet incorrigible', and hoped that Sharp, when he returned, would quash the Peebles petition. Since nothing more was heard of it, Sharp evidently did so.[25]

Sharp returned in November a 'well-pleased man'. He had behaved very well, Lauderdale thought; at his final audience he had good words for Tweeddale, and so did Charles – Lauderdale wanted to bolster his 'dearest brother's' morale. When Sharp got back he gave Tweeddale a long account which 'fills my mind with various reflections', a Delphic phrase.[26] Tweeddale complained again about 'L.F.'s enraged, wicked practices', and waspishly commented to Moray that he wished the clergy would preach the gospel and 'forbear meddling in government'.[27] In December, after a five-month hiatus following the attempt on Sharp's life, serious discussions with the outed ministers resumed, on the basis of dispensing with the requirement for attending synods and presbyteries. Tweeddale had a long session with Sharp and urged him to be flexible: it was crucial to split the dissenters and co-opt those who were more hostile to schism than to bishops. Robert Douglas was most forthcoming; he said only that he did not wish to be put into a parish from which some other minister had been removed.[28] The discussions went slowly, however, and inevitably provoked Archbishop Burnet. Tweeddale told Sharp that he had to take Burnet in hand, and get more involved himself in removing inefficient and scandalous ministers; Burnet favoured only the most violent and headstrong. Burnet 'seemed to be mightily humbled' when he saw Tweeddale, and promised to follow his advice.[29] But he proved to be incapable of change.

24 30–31 Oct. 1668, Lauderdale to Tweeddale, Paton, 'Lauderdale', pp. 162–65.
25 5 Nov. 1668, Lauderdale to Tweeddale, NLS Ms. 7023, f. 298. Buckroyd, *Sharp*, p. 92.
26 29 Oct. 1668, Lauderdale to Tweeddale, NLS Ms. 7023, f. 213. This letter sounds as if Lauderdale expected Sharp to read it. 12 Nov., Tweeddale to Lauderdale, BL Add. Mss 23130, f. 108.
27 5 Nov. 1668, Tweeddale to Lauderdale, BL Add. Mss 23130, f. 99. 12 Nov. Tweeddale to Moray, NLS Ms. 7024, f. 131.
28 11 Dec. 1668, Tweeddale to Lauderdale, BL Add. Mss 23131, ff. 26–27.
29 9 Feb. 1669, Tweeddale to Lauderdale, NLS Ms. 7024, ff. 147–48.

Religious disquiet in the west continued to give disquiet to the government. Churches in Ayrshire were being abandoned and children left unbaptised, which prompted a privy council order that children must be baptised only by their parish ministers. The commissioners of militia were to impose large fines for violation of this order and for holding conventicles, which were beginning to proliferate once more, even in Edinburgh, where one was held on 28 February 1669. The council ordered Linlithgow to send troops to the west to enforce the law, and appointed a committee to look into the problem of conventicles.[30] Rumours of governmental leniency to conventicles in England and Ireland were sweeping Scotland and encouraging the disaffected. Tweeddale commented that Charles could afford to be lenient with English Presbyterians, who 'scruple not at bishops nor the government', but Scottish dissidents would not acknowledge bishops at all. Lauderdale agreed: 'the beasts we have to deal with are furious unnatural irrational brutes, and so the king understands them right'. The cousins' policy was accurately summarised in Kincardine's remark that 'I am . . . in favour of a qualified toleration, but I would have it given and not taken.'[31]

Something had to be done in the west, however, and quickly: the 'people grow mad through discontent,' wrote Tweeddale on 27 March 1669. The minister of Dunfermline spent some time in Paisley. He explained to Tweeddale that he had gradually won over the congregation by dealing with its members one-on-one and refusing to take umbrage at affronts. So most of the parishioners came to church. When he refused to delate the non-attenders, Archbishop Burnet savaged him, and he left, lest he be officially suspended. As long as Burnet was in charge nothing useful could be done.[32] The council treated the ministers Burnet delated very gently. They were not guilty of anything much, wrote Kincardine; they were not rebels and had not baptised improperly. All they had done was allow a few irregular meetings, technically conventicles, in private houses, believing the reports from England that the crown had adopted a policy of toleration.[33]

30 20 Feb. 1669, Tweeddale to Moray, ibid., f. 150. *RPCS* II, pp. 614–16, 618–21.

31 23, 25 Feb. 1669, Tweeddale to Moray, NLS Ms. 7024, ff. 151–52, 153. 6 Mar., Lauderdale to Tweeddale, Paton, 'Lauderdale', pp. 206–08. 2 Mar., Kincardine to Lauderdale, BL Add. Mss 23131, f. 103.

32 27 Mar. 1669, Tweeddale to Moray, NLS Ms. 7024, ff. 161–62.

33 6 Apr. 1669, Kincardine to Lauderdale, BL Add. Mss 23131, ff. 123–24. *RPCS* III, pp. 3–4, 3 May, Cochrane to Tweeddale, NLS Ms. 14406, ff. 82–83.

Such rumours were not true, Lauderdale wrote on 25 March. The king was inclined to be lenient, but he would not tolerate unlicensed preaching – 'thus their insolence obstructs the favour intended,' – and wanted Tweeddale to come to London to discuss the religious issue.[34]

Charles had never been a persecutor of religious nonconformity, and had issued a general indulgence in England in 1662, only to withdraw it in the face of fierce parliamentary resistance. Piecemeal indulgence, if it worked in Scotland, might work in England as well, now that Clarendon was gone, Sheldon out of favour, and no devoted Anglican in Charles's inner circle, his Cabal. Hence his summons to Tweeddale, who at this critical juncture became ill and had to delay his departure. He recovered slowly, and was not able to leave until the beginning of May. He had sent Gilbert Burnet, a young clergyman recently in disgrace for his public hostility to the behaviour of the bishops, on a fact-finding trip to the west. Burnet's report was scathing: people there regarded the ministers as simoniacally appointed, and looked on them 'as their persecutors and not as their pastors'. The archbishop's behaviour was extremely arbitrary: he would hold synods, refuse to allow votes on controversial issues, and simply declare his own opinion to be that of the synod. Burnet suggested that the crown bring about an exchange of dioceses between the bishops of Galloway and Dunblane, and force the appointment of the latter, Robert Leighton, already known for his distaste for the behaviour of his episcopal colleagues and his open-mindedness about admitting outed ministers, as head of a commission of inspection of the Glasgow archdiocese, so that he would be able, in effect, to run the western church. Tweeddale took this report with him to London.[35] Before he left he consulted with Sharp, as Charles had instructed him to do. Sharp urged caution. Too many appointments of outed ministers, free from their bishops' jurisdiction, would promote schism in the church. Those appointed in the west should be few and peaceable.[36]

Tweeddale's stay in London lasted about two months; he was back home by 6 July. During his absence there were rumours once more about frequent

34 25 Mar. 1669, Lauderdale to Tweeddale, Paton, 'Lauderdale', pp. 211–12.
35 30 Apr.–3 May 1669, Gilbert Burnet to Tweeddale, NLS Ms. 7121, f. 1. Burnet's report is in ibid., ff. 18–19. J. Buckroyd, Church and State in Scotland 1660–1681 (Edinburgh, 1980), pp. 76–79. NLS Ms. 7024, f. 43. The nature of Tweeddale's illness is not clear. Whatever it was caused his face to swell and delayed him en route to London. 8 May Moray to Kincardine, Moray Letters, p. 263.
36 10 May 1669, Sharp to Lauderdale, NLS Ms. 2512, f. 126.

conventicles, but, he reported on his return, things were quiet. While he was in London the king formally approved the admission of outed ministers – Resolutioners, not Remonstrants – to vacant parishes. There were to be no more than fifty nationwide, no more than three in any presbytery, and none in the four university cities. And there would also be a parliament in October, the first for six years.[37] During his stay Tweeddale received a signal mark of the king's favour: on 9 June Charles appointed him to the English privy council. He also evidently saw a good deal of 'our friend at Ham', whose health and well-being seemed to concern Lauderdale rather more than that of his wife, who had been seriously ill. Lauderdale had hoped to return to Scotland with Tweeddale. He had announced in January that he planned 'to come home bag and baggage' early in the summer, but now he had to await the preparations for the meeting of parliament.[38]

'Our friend at Ham', the recently widowed Elizabeth Murray, countess of Dysart in her own right, had known Lauderdale for a long time. Though a royalist during the late troubles, and a member of a secret royalist organisation, the Sealed Knot, she was also close to Cromwell, and may well have helped to save Lauderdale from being put on trial for his life after his capture in 1651. Lauderdale's most recent biographer doubts that he was in serious danger, but Lauderdale apparently believed that he was – at least in 1671 he bequeathed her £1,500 sterling in token of his gratitude.[39] On hearing of her husband's death in January 1669 Lauderdale immediately went to call on her, and found her 'very sick'. On his next call, two weeks later, he spent two nights. The calls became more and more frequent, and not in the least clandestine. He frequently took Uncle Dunfermline and 'nostre fils' with him; your health was drunk at every meal, he informed Tweeddale, after one jolly weekend there in March.[40] His chief's uncharacteristic behaviour puzzled Tweeddale, who drafted a letter in March about his 'choosing another place and company for diversion than was your custom', as reported to him by Yester and Moray: this was 'all riddles to me'.[41] There is no evidence that he sent it. If riddles there were, Tweeddale's visit cleared them up. Elizabeth Murray was a factor to be reckoned with.

---

37 The king's instructions, dated 7 and 15 June 1669, are in NLS Ms. 14488, f. 67.
38 NLS Ms. 7024, ff. 165, 166, Ms. 14488, f. 15. 20 Jan., 25 Mar., 5 Aug. 1669, Lauderdale to Tweeddale, Paton, 'Lauderdale'. pp. 196–97, 211–12, NLS Ms. 7023, f. 218.
39 R.C. Paterson, *King Lauderdale* (Edinburgh, 2003), pp. 114–16.
40 16, 30 Jan., 2 Feb., 16 Mar. 1669, Lauderdale to Tweeddale, Paton, 'Lauderdale', pp. 192–93, 197–99, NLS Ms. 14406, f. 71.
41 NLS Ms. 7024, f. 160.

Tweeddale carried Charles's letters on the parliament and the indulgence back home with him. He also carried orders for a commission headed by Bishop Leighton to conduct a visitation of the western countries and for Archbishop Burnet to come to court to discuss conditions in his diocese.[42] Tweeddale held up the delivery of the latter two instructions until he could consult with Sharp, who quibbled about the makeup of the proposed commission. Meanwhile Lauderdale was having second thoughts. He felt that the timing was bad: 'it should be let sleep until after the Parl't.' The commission could not finish its work before parliament met; 'it would make great noise and do little good'. Better to wait until the following spring. By then there would be evidence about the behaviour of the newly-appointed nonconformist ministers, and the investigation would not appear one-sided. The king, Lauderdale went on, agreed with this analysis, but had issued no orders: Tweeddale was to do what he thought best.[43] Tweeddale took this not-very-subtle hint; the letters were held in abeyance.

The success of the indulgence hinged to a considerable extent on the acquiescence of Archbishop Sharp. He was in a difficult situation, caught between the demands of Tweeddale and the irritation – indeed, the outrage – of Archbishop Burnet and many of his colleagues. He made a speech in the council on 20 July that quibbled about much of the phrasing of the declaration and sent it to Lauderdale, saying that he relied on his and Tweeddale's promise that the church would not suffer, and that he had urged his clerical colleagues to do their duty 'without desponding'. This speech irritated Tweeddale enormously, as did Sharp's assertion in committee two days later that the king had to have the concurrence of the clergy for any action in church questions: he is, wrote Tweeddale, 'as far out of tune as ever'. Tweeddale charged him with reneging on his promise to submit to the king's pleasure. Sharp pleaded the pressure he was getting from Burnet, but in the end he caved in and caused no trouble in the meeting of the full council, which on 27 July approved the first ten appointments of outed ministers.[44] Tweeddale gave Burnet a tongue-lashing of such violence that 'his eyes stood back water, as we say'; he promised

42 RPCS III, pp. 35, 38–40. 6 July 1669, Tweeddale to Lauderdale, NLS Ms. 7024, f. 166. The king's orders as to the Glasgow archdiocese are in NLS Ms. 7103, ff. 14, 16.

43 3 Aug. 1669, Tweeddale to Lauderdale, BL Add. Mss 23132, ff. 47–48. 10 Aug., Lauderdale to Tweeddale, NLS Ms. 7023, f. 219.

44 20 July 1669, Sharp to Lauderdale, NLS Ms. 2512, f. 130. 22, 27 July, Tweeddale to Lauderdale, Laing Mss I, pp. 372–74, BL Add. Mss 23132, ff. 32–33. The quoted phrase is in the first of these letters. RPCS III, p. 47.

'absolute submission'.[45] It soon became apparent that his view of absolute submission differed considerably from Tweeddale's. He baulked at absolving those ministers who had been censured for not attending presbyteries without a meeting of his synod. Tweeddale cracked the whip again and he climbed down temporarily, but a week later reiterated his refusal. Lauderdale commented that he must be subjected 'to some way of mortification . . . for otherwise it seems he is soon again apt to misken himself'.[46] Tweeddale threatened him with the creation of the authorised royal commission; the only way to avoid it was to purge the inadequate ministers himself.[47]

Once again Burnet made promises; once again he failed to keep them. Instead he convened a meeting of his synod in mid-September and accepted a paper, probably the work of the dean of his cathedral, which argued that the policy of indulgence, by allowing outed and censured ministers to preach, was promoting schism in the church, that the charges against the conformist clergy were malicious and untrue, and that conventicles were being tacitly condoned.[48] Tweeddale erupted. In his opinion the admission of outed ministers was going very well, and the council had issued a proclamation against conventicles at the beginning of August, to coincide with the admission process.[49] Furthermore many members of the Glasgow synod, those who met separately at Peebles, its ablest members in Tweeddale's view, did not agree with what amounted to public defiance of the king's policy, and urged Burnet, who had not been present, to get rid of unsatisfactory clerics and be less hasty in censuring ministers who did not attend presbyteries. Tweeddale wanted 'to mortify Long F',[50] but he did not want a public airing of the divisions in the church at this juncture. He showed the synod's petition to Rothes, who was indignant that Burnet had not kept him informed, and Kincardine, and then confronted the archbishop. If the petition was suppressed and removed from the record, no

45 29 July 1669, Tweeddale to Lauderdale, BL Add. Mss 23132, f. 36.
46 29 July, 30 Aug., 8 Sept. 1669, Tweeddale to Lauderdale, ibid., ff. 36, 47–48, 87. 16 Sept., Lauderdale to Tweeddale, NLS Ms. 14406, f. 113.
47 5 Aug. 1669, Tweeddale to Lauderdale, BL Add. Mss 23132, f. 56.
48 *LP* II, pp. lxiv–lxvii. See the summary in Buckroyd, *Church and State*, p. 84.
49 *RPCS* III, pp. 61–62. 3 Aug. 1669, Kincardine to Lauderdale, 10 Aug., Tweeddale to Lauderdale, BL Add. Mss 23132, ff. 46, 61–63. Kincardine was much less optimistic than Tweeddale about the experiment, 'but now *jacta est alea*'. BL Add. Mss 23132, f. 65.
50 28 Sept., 12 Oct. 1669, Tweeddale to Moray, NLS Ms. 7024, ff. 179, 181. The Glasgow synod, which was very large, was divided for administrative purposes, meeting in both Glasgow and Peebles.

more would be said, to avoid 'raising too much dust about the Bishop's ears'. Burnet refused: he could not act without consulting his synod. Tweeddale believed that Burnet was planning to stir up further trouble by going from synod to synod with his petition. So the archbishop was summoned to appear before the council on 14 October, along with the clerk of the synod and its records, by which time Lauderdale would have arrived in Edinburgh to conduct the meeting of the parliament.[51]

Moray, when he received Tweeddale's account of this confrontation, showed Burnet's paper 'that looks so like the spirit of Rebellion' to Charles. The king was angry. He approved the council's summons to Burnet, and said he would think about sending special instructions. Moray thought that Burnet and the leaders of his synod should be deposed: 'I take this to be the greatest ignomity that ever Episcopal government fell under since the Reformation.' Charles was still fuming when Moray next saw him, and gave Lauderdale carte blanche to handle Burnet as he saw fit, even as far as having the 'malicious libel' publicly burnt. The king thought the 'course with L.F. . . . will make a noise', but he was not worried. 'He thinks the peace secure' because of the government's military strength. 'This damned paper,' Charles observed, 'shows Bishops and Episcopal people are as bad on this chapter as the most arrant Presbyterian or Remonstrator.'[52] Defiance of the king's orders was utterly unacceptable, no matter whence it came: Charles – and therefore his officials – must be obeyed.

Thus matters stood as the king's new-minted commissioner prepared to meet parliament. Moray directed this letter to Yester House, where, he assumed, it would find Lauderdale. The first reports on the new policy were encouraging. Lady Margaret Kennedy wrote to Tweeddale on 26 September that the newly installed ministers were behaving well, and that there had been no conventicles since they had returned to preach.[53] The policy of indulgence was at this point more Tweeddale's than Lauderdale's; the latter was now uneasy. Putting in some of the outed ministers 'would not quiet but render them more insolent', he opined in March. He thought that negotiations on comprehension might succeed if the Resolutioners believed that acceptance would lead to their admission to the vacant parishes. He worried about an indulgence's repercussions in England, where it might be

51 RPCS III, pp. 77–78. 30 Sept. 1668, Tweeddale to Moray, NLS Ms. 7024, f. 180.
52 6–7 Oct. 1669, Moray to Lauderdale, BL Add. Mss 23132, ff. 111–12.
53 NLS Ms. 7003, ff. 166–67. Lady Margaret's testimony must be taken *cum grano*; she was sympathetic to the Presbyterians and was subsequently to marry Gilbert Burnet.

thought to be the first step in the elimination of episcopacy. Even Tweeddale's wife was sceptical. The duchess of Hamilton, on the other hand, thought the plan would work, as did his western fact-finder, Gilbert Burnet.[54] But the only apparent alternative, which Bishop Leighton had suggested in 1667, of a conference to discuss comprehension, i.e., the concessions which the crown would have to make to bring in the moderate nonconformists, would be so time-consuming that by the time of Tweeddale's visit to London in 1669 Leighton was prepared to support Tweeddale's policy.[55] Lauderdale, whose idea this had been six years previously, was willing to try, since Charles liked the idea and spoke forcefully in the English council against the persecution of peaceable dissenters. Tweeddale's first, upbeat reports encouraged him.[56] But the troublesome Burnet had not been silenced. What made matters worse was that his protests were not unjustified; the government's policy violated the legislation of 1662 restoring the authority of the bishops, notably their power to grant (or withhold) licences to preach. But what parliament could do parliament could change, and such change looked to be increasingly likely.

II

The potentially rebellious southwest was the government's most serious security problem but not its only one. The Highlands had always been a concern to any Scottish government, but by the Restoration the nature of the problem there had changed. Major clan warfare and rampant lawlessness were no longer the issues. The various Edinburgh regimes wanted from the Highlands what Charles and his London officials wanted from both Scotland and Ireland: a minimum of trouble and as much income as possible. What this meant for the Highlands was, first, a reversion to the policy of James VI: all landlords (including Lowland landlords) and clan chiefs must be responsible for those who lived on their lands. The chiefs were required to appear annually before the privy council to give an

54 11 Mar. 1669, Lauderdale to Tweeddale, Paton, 'Lauderdale', pp. 208–09, Burnet, *History* I, pp. 478–81, 487–88. For Lady Tweeddale's opinion see NLS Ms. 14402, f. 27. Some years later Sir George Mackenzie wrote to Tweeddale asking him for various documents for his history, including an account of 'the rise of the indulgence', since 'it is charged only upon you'. NLS Ms. 3134, f. 129.

55 Buckroyd, *Church and State*, pp. 71, 78.

56 4, 10 Aug. 1669, Tweeddale to Lauderdale, BL Add. Mss 23132, ff. 52–55, 61–63. 19 Aug., Lauderdale to Tweeddale, NLS Ms. 7023, f. 232.

account of the behaviour of those for whom they stood surety, an awkward obligation for those – virtually all of them – who feared arrest for debt while they were in the capital. The other thing the government wanted was the money owed to the crown in feu duties and taxes. In the interest of better communication on both these matters it set up a foot post from Edinburgh, once a week to Inverness, twice weekly to Aberdeen, in January 1669. At the same time the council renewed a commission for the Borders originally set up in 1665 to consider crime there, but the 'middle shires' were no longer a major concern.[57]

In the 1660s lawlessness in the Highlands took two major forms. In Lochaber, an area where responsibility was diffused among three shires – Inverness, Argyll and Perth – the principal troublemaker was Euan Cameron of Lochiel. He had been a favourite of General Monck, and was determined to maintain and expand his grip in the area; the Camerons' occupation of land legally owned by others caused constant turmoil.[58] Second, there were the caterans, robber bands of men mostly from broken clans, often patronised by leading Lowland families on the periphery of the Highlands, such as the Gordons.[59] They preyed especially on the cattle business, which was flourishing and flourished still more with the end of the English duty on Scottish cattle in April 1669. Another factor in the Highland mix was the earl of Argyll, who, now that his uncle Lauderdale was supreme in Scottish affairs, could resume the traditional expansionist policies of Clan Campbell, and attempt thereby to reduce his mountainous debt. His weapon was his justiciarship in Argyll and the Western Isles, to which he had been restored in 1663.

Argyll was none too pleased at the grant in August 1667 of the commission to keep the peace in the Highlands to the earl of Atholl, who now enjoyed the office of justice-general which until 1628 had been the hereditary perquisite of Argyll's predecessors. Atholl's commission ran from Dumbarton to Inverness. It did not cover the area of Argyll's justiciary, nor the far north, Ross, Sutherland and Caithness, the responsibility of the earl of Seaforth, another of Lauderdale's and Tweeddale's many cousins, who, like Argyll, was prepared to exploit his position for his own gain. He and

57 *RPCS* II, pp. 592–94.
58 There is a good account of Lochiel by E.M. Furgol in the *Oxford DNB*; see also P. Hopkins, *Glencoe and the End of the Highland War* (Edinburgh, 1986), chaps 1 and 2.
59 A.I. Macinnes, 'Repression and Conciliation: The Highland Dimension 1660–1688, *SHR* LXV (1986), p. 172.

Argyll were now working together to profit from the extravagance of Angus MacDonald of Glengarry by buying up his enormous debts, although Seaforth was himself sufficiently delinquent in his own payments to the crown that Moray wondered why his rights in Lewis had not been reduced. Atholl was given broad police powers, the right to raise an armed force, £200 sterling for expenses, and the escheats of some of the convicted. Argyll was further annoyed because on the same day the council assessed him a total of £7,082 Scots because of the depredations his tenants had committed on the lands of Lady Drum: they had stolen oxen and sheep. His defence, that he could be held liable only if his complicity in the thefts could be proved, was manifestly mistaken; the council properly rejected it.[60] Moray was not convinced that Atholl's force would accomplish much, but in fact it worked well enough. Its purpose was not to stamp out lawlessness in places like Lochaber, but to protect the Lowlands from the caterans. 'The country hath been kept as quiet and free from all depredations as at any time heretofore,' wrote the earl of Linlithgow in February 1668.[61] The council thought so too, and in March it expanded Atholl's authority by creating a special six-man court to try the offenders he arrested and charged, in order to avoid the inefficiency of the numerous local jurisdictions.[62]

Throughout much of 1668 the council's chief preoccupation in the Highlands was not Lochaber, however, but the messy situation in the far north, where Argyll's feckless brother-in-law, George Sinclair, earl of Caithness, had fallen under the influence of his violent kinsman William Sinclair of Dunbeath. Dunbeath, the sheriff-depute of Caithness, pursued a long-standing feud with the Mackays of Strathnaver; large-scale cattle raids over Sutherland and Caithness were the result. In February 1668 the council, acting on Caithness's complaint of a long string of such raids, dating back to 1653, appointed a four-man committee to meet in Thurso in June to try to find a settlement. Caithness, meanwhile, blotted his copybook by threatening to try some members of Rothes's troop of soldiers, sent north as tax collectors and quartered in Thurso, for alleged misbehaviour. The council

---

60 *RPCS* II, pp. 324–32. Hopkins, *Glencoe*, pp. 42, 49. A.I. Macinnes, *Clanship, Commerce and the House of Stuart, 1603–1788* (East Linton, 1996), p. 127. 16 Mar. 1669, Moray to Kincardine, *Moray Letters*, pp. 261–62. The council took pains with this decision. It ruled that Lady Drum, who asked for more than £7,750, had overstated her losses. In Dec. 1668 the council reaffirmed its support for Lady Drum; *RPCS* II, p. 564.
61 BL Add. Mss 23128, f. 334. 3 Aug. 1667, Moray to Lauderdale, BL Add. Mss 23127, f. 178.
62 *RPCS* II, pp. 412–15, 421–23.

sent a messenger to Caithness with orders forbidding this; the earl was to appear in Edinburgh to answer for the behaviour of the magistrates of Thurso. Caithness threatened to hang the messenger.[63] For this the council warded him in Edinburgh Castle on 23 July for his various acts of violence; they regarded his excuses as lame.[64] Within a week he had found bond and was released. Argyll had asked Lauderdale to intervene with Rothes to 'lenitie' his brother-in-law, and Tweeddale admitted that the soldiers had practised extortion and had not been very efficient at collecting the back taxes. A militia, once established, would be far better at such a job, in his opinion. The council appointed a committee to adjudicate the dispute between Caithness and the Sutherland men and adjourned the case until December.[65] The overburdened Tweeddale was a member of the committee – 'we have had our hands full with him [Caithness]', he complained to Moray in August.[66] An agreement was patched together by December, but the troubles in the north continued owing to Dunbeath, who had fled from Edinburgh in August and continued his career of violence. Tweeddale suspected that he was backed by Seaforth, also a troublemaker, who was 'hugely discontent' and was accessory to Dunbeath's 'pranks'.[67]

Lauderdale was concerned. He wanted no major outbreak in the north that would come to Charles's notice and tarnish the regime's reputation. 'Our wise cousin Caithness' was playing the fool, but he ought to be preserved, if possible, from the consequences of his stupid and violent nature.[68] At the same time as the December agreement between Caithness and Strathnaver was reached the council put Dunbeath and his accomplices to the horn. It was not until April 1669 that the council finally removed Dunbeath as sheriff-depute.[69] In July the council commissioned John Campbell of Glenorchy to pursue him. Glenorchy seized Dunbeath House but could not lay hands on its elusive owner, who had more friends amongst the Sinclair gentry than did the earl. Glenorchy did leave a garrison in Dunbeath House and at the Sinclair castle at Berriedale, and

63 Ibid., pp. 404–06, 457–58, Hopkins, *Glencoe*, pp. 53–54.

64 *RPCS* II, pp. 496–99. 23 July 1668, Tweeddale to Lauderdale, BL Add. Mss 23129, f. 249.

65 *RPCS* II, pp. 502, 510–11. 11 July 1668, Argyll to Lauderdale, 4 Aug., Thomas Hay to Lauderdale, BL Add. Mss 23129, ff. 211, 264. 12 Sept., Tweeddale to Moray, NLS Ms. 7024, f. 117.

66 NLS Ms. 7024, f. 108.

67 15, 24 Oct. 1668, Tweeddale to Lauderdale, BL Add. Mss 23130, ff. 72, 78.

68 15 Aug., 22 Oct. 1668, Lauderdale to Tweeddale, NLS Ms. 7023, ff. 192, 210. Caithness was indeed a cousin. His mother, Jean Mackenzie, the sister of Lady Balcarres, was, like Lauderdale and Tweeddale, the grandchild of Lord Chancellor Dunfermline.

69 *RPCS* II, pp. 566–67, 574. 5 Dec. 1668, Tweeddale to Lauderdale, BL Add. Mss 23131, ff. 7–8.

explained to the council that he had scattered Dunbeath's collection of ruffians, some of whom had fled as far as Orkney. The council thanked him for his services.[70] In October it resolved to pursue Dunbeath for treason at the forthcoming parliament. In the following February Glenorchy in his turn was the subject of complaint on the part of some of the landlords he and Caithness had imprisoned in the course of their campaign against Dunbeath. They described Caithness's new deputy as an outlaw. The council decided that in future it would deal with these landlords itself.[71]

Glenorchy, an ambitious, experienced, and wily troubleshooter, was at this stage of his long and devious career the ally of his cousin Argyll. The latter was now setting out to implement his plan to use his position as justiciar in Argyll and the Western Isles to squeeze his debtors and restore his feudal superiorities in the area, while at the same time using that court to protect himself from his own creditors.[72] The lord advocate raised objections to the hereditary grant of the office; Tweeddale suggested that Charles, if he granted it only for life, would give the earl an incentive to behave well. This proposal greatly upset Argyll, though he got the hereditary grant.[73] By the summer of 1669 he was barely on speaking terms with Tweeddale. He would not take part in public business nor discuss it with him, Tweeddale wrote in July. Argyll thought Tweeddale was partial to Atholl, though, Tweeddale said, he had backed Argyll when he and Atholl differed. He thought Argyll was jealous of his power, and dated the decay of their friendship from 'his last amours', a Delphic phrase – Argyll was recently widowed and would marry Lady Balcarres in January 1670.[74] Lauderdale replied that he regretted the 'dryness' between the two, hoped it was not serious, and would do his best to reconcile them when he arrived in Scotland. Argyll's churlish behaviour did not abate. He blamed Tweeddale for the delay in his grant. The treasury commission was dunning him for £2,000 sterling which he owed the king. In August he wrote indignantly to Lauderdale about the

70 20 Sept. 1669, Glenorchy to Tweeddale, 25 Sept., Glenorchy to Linlithgow, NLS Ms. 7003, ff. 162, 164. *RPCS* III, pp. 87, 93–95.
71 17 Aug. 1669, Argyll to Lauderdale, BL Add. Mss 23132, f. 77. *RPCS* III, pp. 85, 134–38. Hopkins, *Glencoe*, pp. 53–55. Macinnes, *Clanship*, pp. 48–49.
72 On Argyll's machinations see Macinnes, *Clanship*, pp. 135–37.
73 8 Sept. 1668, Tweeddale to Lauderdale, 30 Sept., 10 Dec., Argyll to Lauderdale, BL Add. Mss 23130, ff. 12, 53–54, 23131, f. 22. 7 Jan. 1669, Lauderdale to Tweeddale, and to the lord advocate, Paton, 'Lauderdale', pp. 187–89. For the lord advocate's views see NLS Ms. 7033, f. 133.
74 29 Aug. 1668, Lauderdale to Tweeddale, NLS Ms. 7023, f. 197. 20 July 1669, Tweeddale to Moray, NLS Ms. 7024, f. 168. 22 July, Tweeddale to Lauderdale, *Laing Mss* I, pp. 372–74.

plight of his sister Lady Caithness. She and Caithness were at Inveraray; they dared not go home without an armed escort because of Dunbeath's continued violence. His 'incurable fanatic peevish humour' with Tweeddale continued, encouraged, according to Mackenzie, by Rothes out of dislike of Tweeddale, and further fuelled by his failure to obtain the wardship of the new marquess of Montrose, aged twelve, which he badly wanted. Tweeddale resolved to be patient until Lauderdale arrived.[75]

By the beginning of 1669 there was trouble again in Lochaber. Troops sent there to collect cess were being kept out and/or assaulted, especially by Clan Cameron, according to the earl of Moray, the sheriff of Inverness, who insisted that the lawbreakers be punished lest matters get completely out of hand. The council summoned some of the Highland lairds and once again ordered Highland landlords to find caution for the behaviour of their tenants and vassals. Charles endorsed this action and seemed unconcerned about 'the Loquaber (*sic*) rogues' prank', Lauderdale wrote, 'yet he said Earl Clarendon would have made a rebellion of it'.[76] At the same time the council praised the work of Atholl, whose commission was about to expire, and resolved to reimburse him for his overexpenditure of his allowance.[77] The earl of Moray continued to complain about conditions in Lochaber, but in June the council ordered him to produce his own sheriff-depute for Inverness, who was at the horn for withholding tax money he had collected.[78] The earl of Seaforth's friends boasted that if he were given a regiment he could pacify the whole area. Tweeddale was still suspicious of him, and besides 'some say he is troublesome amongst their wives'. Tweeddale was nevertheless angry when the council, against his advice, not only exonerated Lord Macdonald, whom Tweeddale regarded as a lawless ruffian, of a charge of mistreating a messenger executing a warrant of Seaforth's because such mistreatment was not specifically prohibited in the landlords' band, but also ordered Seaforth to pay Macdonald's expenses – Seaforth, after all, was the crown's agent in the far north.

75 BL Add. Mss 23131, ff. 99–100, 144. 26 Dec. 1668, Tweeddale to Moray, NLS Ms. 7024, f. 139. 3 Aug. 1669, Lauderdale to Tweeddale, Paton, 'Lauderdale', pp. 217–20. 10 Aug., Tweeddale to Lauderdale, BL Add. Mss 23132, ff. 61–63. Mackenzie, *Memoirs*, pp. 179–81. Kincardine also warned Lauderdale about Argyll's bad mood, BL Add. Mss 23132, f. 65. 12 Aug., Argyll to Lauderdale, BL Add. Mss 23132, f. 77.

76 *RPCS* II, pp. 586–88, 599–602. 23 Jan. 1669, Lauderdale to Tweeddale, Paton, 'Lauderdale', pp. 194–95. 24 Jan., earl of Moray to Tweeddale, NLS Ms. 7003, f. 118.

77 *RPCS* II, pp. 594–95.

78 NLS Ms. 7003, f. 134. *RPCS* III, pp. 10–11, 31, 66–67.

Tweeddale attributed the council's unusual disregard of the government's wishes to mischief-making on the part of the duke of Hamilton.[79]

Highland matters hung fire while Tweeddale was in London in the spring of 1669. Kincardine expected trouble there during the summer, so that Tweeddale, when he returned, should bring a letter from Charles pressing the council to keep the Highlands quiet. The letter Tweeddale did bring back commended Tweeddale's report on the Highlands; on the day the council received it, it renewed its Highlands committee – Tweeddale and Kincardine, inevitably, were on it – and instructed it to get the necessary bonds from both Argyll and Atholl and to do something about the MacGregors.[80] It also issued a long proclamation reiterating previous legislation on the obligations of landlords and clan chiefs, and included a list of those who had to appear annually in Edinburgh to renew their bands to keep the peace.[81] It was the formula as before. How little it was likely to accomplish is suggested by the fact that, two weeks prior to the issuance of the decree the council informed the laird of Macintosh, the hereditary baillie of Lochaber, that he would be held responsible only for his own tenants, since he was being violently prevented from executing his office.[82] Troops were again sent north to collect arrears of cess. The council's new direction did not depend on either Argyll or Atholl, whose commission was not renewed. Tweeddale nevertheless sounded cautiously optimistic in a letter to Moray on 2 August: if it worked, 'they will be better bairns thereafter'.[83]

The administration's new peacekeeper for the Highlands was James Campbell of Lawers, whom the council commissioned on 2 September to collect bands of caution in Lochaber and Badenoch and pursue various Highland lawbreakers, a list of whom the council gave him in January 1670. Lawers did an effective job over the next two years, or so the council declared when it renewed his commission in February 1672.[84] Kinsman though he was, Argyll resented Lawers's appointment and was extremely

---

79 25 Feb., 13 Mar. 1669, Tweeddale to Moray, NLS Ms. 7024, ff. 153, 157. 13 Mar., Tweeddale to Lauderdale, BL Add. Mss 23131, ff. 111–12. *RPCS* II, pp. 622–23.

80 17 June 1669, Kincardine to Lauderdale, BL Add. Mss 23131, f. 186. *RPCS* III, pp. 36–37.

81 *RPCS* III, pp. 36–37, 52–59.

82 Ibid., p. 44.

83 31 July 1669, Tweeddale to Lauderdale, BL Add. Mss 23132, ff. 42–43. 2 Aug., Tweeddale to Moray, NLS Ms. 7024, f. 169.

84 *RPCS* III, pp. 73–76, 115, 471. For the terms of his commission see *RPCS* III, pp. 87–90. His annual stipend was £300 sterling; Atholl had received only £200. R.A. Lee, *Government and Politics in Scotland, 1661–1681* (PhD diss., University of Glasgow, 1995), p. 172.

uncooperative.[85] And Atholl had dragged his feet about giving the sureties required of Highland landlords. He and two other magnates whose possessions lay on the fringes of the Highlands, the earls of Perth and Tullibardine, objected to the clause the council had added to the band on the deforcing of messengers in the wake of the Seaforth–Macdonald controversy – small wonder that Tweeddale hoped that Lawers's success would turn the two earls into better bairns. In June 1669 Kincardine, commenting unfavourably on Atholl's behaviour, hoped that Tweeddale would be home soon: 'till he come we shall get nothing done to purpose' in the Highlands.[86]

Keeping order in the north, the southwest, indeed everywhere would, Tweeddale hoped, be better done by the militia once it was properly established. The recent incidents in Lochaber and Caithness had made the shortcomings of the regulars only too apparent, and maintaining security was vital. The cousins had used the Pentland Rising to push Rothes out of power and obtain it for themselves; they could not afford to be surprised and caught short in their turn. Hence Tweeddale's nervous reaction to the attempt on Archbishop Sharp. Lauderdale had not been enthusiastic about his request for the levying of extra troops, which in any event would not have been available in August 1668 when intelligence arrived of a possible subversive gathering in the west. The council ordered Linlithgow to collect forces and go to Glasgow, but at the moment there were only forty men there. So Tweeddale decided to sound the alarm and let the conspirators scatter, rather than let them meet and try to seize them. Better, he thought, to 'scare the rogues' than 'be taken napping as Col. Turner was the other year' – tactics that met with the king's approval, and that apparently worked. Once the militia was settled the area would, Tweeddale hoped, be as quiet as Edinburgh now was.[87]

So, starting in the summer of 1668, Tweeddale and his fellow councillors busied themselves with getting the militia up and running, determining who should command and how the necessary money should be raised, a contentious issue in many shires. In August Charles, reversing the position he had taken in May, authorised the creation of a militia in Dumfriesshire

---

85 10 Aug. 1669, Tweeddale to Lauderdale, BL Add. Mss 23132, ff. 61–63. Hopkins, *Glencoe*, pp. 49–50.

86 *RPCS* II, p. 622. 17 June 1669, Thomas Hay to Lauderdale, BL Add. Mss 23131, f. 188. 24 June, Kincardine to Lauderdale, BL Add. Mss 23131, ff. 192–93.

87 *RPCS* II, pp. 518–19. 10, 29 Aug. 1668, Lauderdale to Tweeddale, NLS Ms. 7023, ff. 190, 197. 13, 15 Aug., Tweeddale to Lauderdale, BL Add. Mss 23129, ff. 276–77, 288–89.

and troops of horse in the other western shires. The council reported on 3 September that it would issue the necessary orders, gave an upbeat assessment of progress elsewhere, though only four shires had held rendezvous as yet, and recommended that militia units be added in the northern shires in the spring. Charles agreed.[88] Tweeddale was very hopeful: if it were properly and promptly paid, 'I am confident it will prove as good as any standing army ever was in Scotland.' All sober and peace-loving people were for it, Kincardine 'passionately' so. With a little money and the magazine being created in Edinburgh Castle the militia would allow Scotland to 'signify somewhat' in the king's service and impress the neighbours. Scotland's militia differed greatly from that of England, since the parliamentary Act authorising it allowed the king to send it anywhere – 'in effect a standing army, with less burden to the country and less charge to the king'.[89] On this last point Tweeddale was certainly right. The amount spent annually on militia officers' pay was only about £200 more than the cost per month of Linlithgow's regiment of regulars.[90] It was not clear, however, that its members would willingly accept being sent abroad.[91] Tweeddale wanted to know how the English militia was organised and paid: there might be some useful models there to copy. Money was, inevitably, a worry. Tweeddale hoped that the creation of the militia might lead to the dissolution of Rothes's troop of horse: the money thus saved could be used to pay militia officers. Rothes baulked, however, and Lauderdale would not force him. The secretary informed his colleagues that Charles was pleased with their proceedings but that they must not expect any money from him. He had not paid anything to the English counties for their militias during the recent war.[92]

By early 1669 the council felt confident enough about the militia to use it to enforce the laws against conventicles in the west – but it also ordered troops from Linlithgow's regiment sent there.[93] And soldiers were still being used to collect customs and excise, and arrears of cess in the Highlands, where only about one-third of what was owed had been paid. Not everything went smoothly, of course. Tweeddale was hesitant about creating militia

---

88 *RPCS* II, pp. 520–22, 525, 536–37, 540–41, 547–48.
89 10, 12 Sept., 12 Nov. 1668, Tweeddale to Moray, NLS Ms. 7024, ff. 116–17, 131.
90 Lee, *Government and Politics*, p. 172.
91 See, e.g., 29 Oct. 1668, Kincardine to Tweeddale, NLS Ms. 7003, f. 108.
92 10, 12 Sept. 1668, Tweeddale to Moray, NLS Ms. 7024, ff. 116, 117. 25 Sept., Tweeddale to Lauderdale, BL Add. Mss 23130, f. 46. 6 Oct. 1668, 27 Feb. 1669, Lauderdale to Tweeddale, NLS Ms. 7023, f. 206, Paton, 'Lauderdale', pp. 205–06.
93 *RPCS* II, pp. 618–21. See also 20 Feb. 1669, Tweeddale to Moray, NLS Ms. 7024, f. 150.

units in the north until the government could get a better sense of whom it could trust with the commands there. So Charles authorised levies only for Elgin and Nairn; the northernmost counties would have to wait until there was greater order there, and improved returns from the cess.[94] A lieutenant of the Perthshire militia was convicted of extortion: he had refused to enrol eligible recruits, and pocketed the payment he insisted the heritors make for the upkeep of the phantom soldiers.[95] But Tweeddale was pleased enough. On 12 August he wrote to Lauderdale that he had held a meeting of the commissioners of the Haddingtonshire militia the day before, and, having got it into the best possible shape, formally turned over his baton to 'nostre fils', who had accompanied him back from London in July.[96] When parliament met in the autumn of 1669 it ratified the government's actions and authorised payment for the men: 6s a day for the foot, 18s for the horse, to be paid by the shire's heritors, who could pass on the cost to their tenants.[97] This was, in effect, a new tax to help pay for the country's armed forces. How efficient these forces might be in case of trouble remained to be seen.

III

Money was always much on Tweeddale's mind, and on those of his fellow treasury commissioners. There were thorny little technical problems. The assayer of the mint, one of Halton's underlings, was in jail for debt; in March 1669 the council had to let him out temporarily to conduct an assay of the new coinage. In November 1668 Tweeddale worried that the pension list was getting out of hand again. It now totalled £27,000 sterling; no more should be handed out until £2,000 worth of pensioners died, he warned, if the treasury's credit was to be maintained. Lauderdale replied that the commissioners should write to him to that effect; he would speak to the king. Yet it was difficult to stop the flow of largesse. In July 1669 the minutes of the treasury commission listed a total of £12,900 sterling paid out from the proceeds of the forfeited estates; Tweeddale himself pocketed over £800 sterling. He had hoped to use the proceeds from these estates to reward those deserving folk who hitherto had received nothing, but most of the beneficiaries were the usual suspects. One notable exception was Tweeddale's old foe

94 *RPCS* II, p. 596, III, pp. 6, 36–37, 41–44. 13 Mar. 1669, Tweeddale to Lauderdale, BL Add. Mss
    23131, ff. 111–12.
95 *RPCS* III, pp. 60–61.
96 BL Add. Mss 23132, f. 71.
97 *APS* VII, pp. 554–55.

Lady Wemyss. The king told her that her pension would not be altered; 'she took it ill and her daughter worse'. Some of these payments were book-keeping transactions: the duchess of Hamilton's £2,000 reduced what her husband owed in arrears of the taxes for which he was responsible as collector – he was not very diligent – which amounted to c. £70,000 Scots. In August 1669 Tweeddale commented that the amounts bid thus far for the forfeited estates would not cover half the precepts drawn on them. The commissioners had paid off all they could, and there was no cash left.[98]

The branch of the king's revenue most susceptible of expansion was that of the customs and foreign excise. With the end of the war increased trade should bring about that expansion; the unprecedentedly large sum bid by the customs farmers in October 1667 reflected that hope and expectation. But, as Lauderdale had feared, the hope proved illusory. On 21 August 1668 Tweeddale informed Moray that the farmers could not continue. They would make no more than £26,000 and hoped that the king would not hold them to their £31,000 contract. What this showed to Tweeddale was that direct collection, which would end the repeated arguments over defalcations, would be superior to farming. Kincardine also thought so, he added, provided that honest collectors could be found.[99]

By November Tweeddale, with his usual diligence, had plunged into a detailed discussion of their accounts with the farmers. He wanted to treat them leniently, or 'put it under collection, it being hard to keep gentlemen in such hazard' – in other words, to deal with their accounts as though they were collectors rather than farmers. He fended off the efforts of the lord advocate and the president of the court of session to bring charges of illegal behaviour against them.[100] He urged Moray to use all the arguments he could think of to turn the farm into a collection for the future. He would rather be banished than have the farm continue another year, he wrote, with considerable hyperbole. At the same time he realised that if direct collection did not bring in as much as the farm, it would go hard on those

---

98 *RPCS* II, p. 623. 14, 19 Nov. 1668, 4 Feb., 7, 10 Aug. 1669, Tweeddale to Lauderdale, BL Add. Mss 23130, ff. 112–13, 118, 23132, ff. 58, 61–63, NLS Ms. 7024, ff. 147–48. 23 Nov. 1668, 3 July 1669, Lauderdale to Tweeddale, Paton, 'Lauderdale', pp. 120–21, NLS Ms. 7023, f. 217. 25 Feb. 1669, Tweeddale to Moray, NLS Ms. 7024, f. 153. NAS E6/1, pp. 182–85. On 14 Nov. 1668 William Sharp wrote that the commissioners had signed off on £1,000 for the earl of Dunfermline, even though there was no cash to cover it. BL Add. Mss 23130, f. 116. For Hamilton's laxness see 10 July 1669, Tweeddale to Lauderdale, BL Add. Mss 23132, ff. 111–12.

99 NLS Ms. 7024, f. 112.

100 31 Oct., 8 Dec. 1668, Tweeddale to Moray, ibid., ff. 129, 135. 10 Nov., Tweeddale to Lauderdale, BL Add. Mss 23130, f. 106.

who had advocated it.[101] Lauderdale endorsed Tweeddale's proceedings and told him not to worry: the farmers would be 'eased of their farm' in the way Tweeddale suggested. Charles would agree to direct collection, as 'for this there seems a necessity'. But he stressed to Tweeddale that 'the king is not in . . . general for collections; he is more for farms' – an admonition Tweeddale should have taken to heart.[102]

Before the farm could end and direct collection begin, the farmers' accounts had to be settled, a task which occupied the treasury commission throughout December. There were complications having to do with prizes taken during the war – the negotiations over Seaton's malversations were still going on – and the unresolved question of the salt tack, which Seaton had not yet surrendered. Tweeddale wanted collection to start right away, since the settlement was proceeding so slowly; Lauderdale decided that collection must wait until the accounts were settled.[103] Finally, on 13 January 1669, the treasury commission issued its report to the king, approving the farmers' accounts, cutting some of their requests for defalcations, and forwarding their formal request to be relieved of their tack.[104] On the 23rd Charles formally approved the report and the inauguration of direct collection. Three collectors were appointed, with a salary of £1,000 sterling to be divided among them – Tweeddale had wanted £200 more. Two of them, Patrick Murray of Ettrick, the chief of the commission, and Sir James Hay of Linplum, had been members of the five-man syndicate of farmers. They were Tweeddale's men, as was the third collector, Archibald Murray of Blackbarony.[105] And the king rewarded Tweeddale directly, with a bonus of £1,000 sterling, which he had certainly earned.[106]

101 24 Nov., 22 Dec. 1668, Tweeddale to Moray, NLS Ms. 7024, ff. 132, 138. 24 Dec., Tweeddale to Lauderdale, BL Add. Mss 23131, ff. 54–55. Moray apparently produced a paper listing seventeen arguments in favour of collection. On 7 Jan. 1669 Tweeddale wrote that it had never arrived, and asked for another copy, even though it was no longer necessary: collection had won out. BL Add. Mss 23131, f. 142.

102 1, 5, 31 Dec. 1668, Lauderdale to Tweeddale, Paton, 'Lauderdale', pp. 171–72, 175–76, 183–85.

103 The progress of the discussions of the farmers' accounts in December 1668 and January 1669 can be followed in Tweeddale's letters to Moray, NLS Ms. 7024, ff. 135–44, and to Lauderdale, BL Add. Mss 23131, ff. 16–55, and Lauderdale's to Tweeddale, Paton, 'Lauderdale', pp. 171–86.

104 BL Add. Mss 23131, f. 76.

105 23 Jan. 1669, Charles to the treasury and exchequer commissioners, Warrant Book 1660–1670, NAS GD 90/2/260, no pagination. NLS Ms. 3136, f. 86. 2 Jan., Tweeddale to Moray, NLS 7024, f. 140. 23 Jan., Lauderdale to Tweeddale, Paton, 'Lauderdale', pp. 194–95.

106 21 Jan. 1669, Lauderdale to Tweeddale, Paton, 'Lauderdale', pp. 193–94. Lauderdale also announced the christening of their second grandson, named John after both his grandfathers – the first boy had been named Charles, after his godfather, the king.

The treasury commission drew up a detailed set of instructions aimed at enforcing the existing rates on customs and foreign excise, prohibiting abatements, and inspecting vessels arriving from foreign ports. Proceeds were to be forwarded to the cashkeeper in quarterly instalments, and provision was made to prevent conflict of interest, especially in the wine trade. The commission estimated the fees and salaries of the collectors' staff at about £2,435 sterling.[107] The collectors were not universally admired. While Tweeddale was in London in May his wife wrote to him concerning complaints about the collectors' high salaries. If they were to be put in charge of the rest of the revenue – i.e., the inland excise and the cess – 'as I think they should', and make still more money, 'you may judge what will be said'. Lady Tweeddale's response to the grumblers was that the collectors could not work for nothing. The complaints, she felt, were designed to 'scare you from doing good to your friends'.[108] Tweeddale was worried, but when he got home he found that 'the collection looks not so desperately as I feared', and that Patrick Murray was being badly misrepresented.[109] Unhappily for the collectors, responsibility for the inland excise, including its extensive arrears, went to Lauderdale's man, the cashkeeper William Sharp, who in the 1670s was to make a fortune out of it.[110]

In March 1669 Sir Walter Seaton finally surrendered his salt tack, and the question of what to do about the salt duty became a live issue. The duty was lucrative, but massively evaded. Foreign salt used for curing fish for export was duty-free; the difficulty was that a great deal of the salt allegedly imported for this purpose was in fact used otherwise, which cut into the profits of Scottish salt-producers, such as the now very influential Kincardine. He wanted penalties imposed on violators and pressure applied to customs officials to enforce the law.[111] With Seaton's surrender of the tack those officials were Tweeddale's newly-appointed collectors; on 18 March Tweeddale wrote that Patrick Murray was busy going up and down the coast visiting the salt pans.[112] Salt was an obsession with

---

107 9 Feb. 1669, Tweeddale to Moray, NLS Ms. 7024, f. 146. NAS E6/1, p. 156. The instructions are summarised in R.W. Lennox, *Lauderdale and Scotland: A Study in Scottish Politics and Administration 1660–1682* (PhD diss., Columbia University, 1977), pp. 319–20.

108 NLS Ms. 14402, f. 13.

109 6 July 1669, Tweeddale to Moray, NLS Ms. 7024, f. 165.

110 21 Aug. 1669, Tweeddale to Lauderdale, BL Add. Mss. 23132, f. 81. Lennox, *Lauderdale and Scotland*, pp. 199, 324–25.

111 26 Oct. 1668, Kincardine to Tweeddale, NLS Ms. 7003, f. 108.

112 NLS Ms. 7024, f. 159.

Kincardine, who constantly raised it with his colleagues. By the spring of 1669 he and Moray had worked out a plan, which had been germinating for some months, to turn salt into a royal monopoly: the crown would buy all salt, domestic and imported, for 42s a boll for resale. This would render moot the issue of duty on foreign salt, since the crown did not pay customs duties. Moray argued that the proposed price was fair under current market conditions, and would treat all manufacturers equitably, by keeping individual saltmakers from undercutting their competitors by selling cheap. Moray hoped that Cashkeeper Sharp might turn his office into a sort of bank, by giving saltmakers a note, payable on demand, in return for their product.[113] The plan generated considerable discussion while Tweeddale was in London in May and June. It was necessary to reach some sort of accommodation with English saltmakers; if the Scots undersold their English counterparts, the English parliament would exclude them from the English market. This would be counterproductive: 'it is not fit the king buy salt to throw it away'.[114] Kincardine thought that the English were being unreasonable. They needed Scottish salt, which was better than theirs for some purposes, yet had raised the duty on it and would not bargain. If we retaliate, he wrote, English merchants would suffer: we can get everything cheaper abroad save tin, lead, alum and fuller's earth.[115] Nothing was settled over the summer, though discussions went on apace. Tweeddale finally wrote on 18 September that a settlement would have to await Lauderdale's coming and, in all likelihood, action in parliament; Lauderdale had indicated that the king's instructions would cover both salt and coal exports.[116]

IV

As the trade negotiations with England, over coal and salt and many other matters, trickled to a halt in the late summer of 1668 the prospect of union negotiations loomed ever larger. Union between England and Scotland, the

113 See Moray's letters of 4 Nov. 1668, 9 Mar., 5 May 1669 to Kincardine, *Moray Letters*, pp. 259–61, 262. Lauderdale referred to 'the King's design of salt' in December 1668; Paton, 'Lauderdale', pp. 175–76.

114 25 May, 19 June 1669, Moray to Kincardine, *Moray Letters*, pp. 264–65.

115 29 Oct. 1668, Kincardine to Tweeddale, NLS Ms. 7003, f. 108. Moray commented in a letter of 3 Sept. that Scottish salt, being harder, drier and bigger-grained than English salt, was superior for meat, while English was better for 'butter and other such domestic uses'. *Moray Letters*, p. 259.

116 31 Aug. 1669, Lauderdale to Tweeddale, Paton, 'Lauderdale', pp. 220–22. 18 Sept., Tweeddale to Moray, NLS Ms. 7024, f. 177.

fond dream of King James VI and I, embraced by Covenanters and Royalists alike in the 1640s, loathed in Scotland when Cromwell's dragoons forcibly imposed it, was once more under serious discussion. As early as 1663 Moray had told Charles, who was not happy about the protectionist policies of both his parliaments, that protectionism was an old issue, going back to King James's time, and that James had promoted union as a solution to this and much else.[117] The link between the issues of trade and political union was well established; hence Tweeddale's comment in September 1667 that 'This business of trade . . . will I hope fairly introduce the consideration of an union.' In Clarendon's time such negotiations would have got nowhere unless Scotland was reduced to the status of a viceroyalty like Ireland; now, the makeup of the committee Charles appointed to consider whether there should be trade negotiations – all the major English officials were members – greatly encouraged Tweeddale.[118] He did not say so, but he knew that political union would be palatable to many Scots only if trade, particularly to the plantations, were freed up. If the negotiations fail, 'the Hollanders will wither all', and the hope of a union would vanish.[119]

In October 1667 Lauderdale raised the subject of union with Lord Keeper Bridgeman. The idea was new to Bridgeman, who wanted to think about it, but at first glance 'he was hugely pleased with it'.[120] When the trade negotiations began the English commissioners requested a copy of the union proposals of King James's time;[121] as they were drifting into stalemate, in June 1668, Bridgeman discussed union with the English commissioners, who, he assured Lauderdale, were 'most earnest for it'. Lauderdale added that 'This discourse of the union will, I am confident, advance and not retard the matter of trade.'[122] What the English commissioners apparently had in mind was 'an entire Union' like that between England and Wales,[123] which not even the most ardent Scottish unionist could possibly accept. It would be Cromwell come again, only worse. Lauderdale's letter crossed one from Tweeddale, who hoped to see Lauderdale in Scotland soon, bringing 'a good "ischew" of this business of trade which will make way for the

117   7 Sept. 1663, Moray to Lauderdale, BL Add. Mss 23120, ff. 8–9.
118   21 Sept. 1667, Tweeddale to Lauderdale, BL Add. Mss 23128, f. 56.
119   28 Sept. 1667, Tweeddale to Lauderdale, ibid., f. 76.
120   8 Oct. 1667, Lauderdale to Moray, NLS Ms. 7023, f. 100.
121   NLS Ms. 2955, f. 22.
122   4 June 1668, Lauderdale to Tweeddale, NLS Ms. 7023, f. 165.
123   NLS Ms. 14492, pp. 108a–112.

union proposed, both adding much weight to persuade it.[124] Tweeddale's priorities were correct. In 1668, as in 1707, the selling point for the Scots had to be economic. English concessions on trade were the only way to make union palatable to the smaller kingdom. Tweeddale knew this; Lauderdale, absent from Scotland for so many years, did not, and, confronted with English commercial intransigence, chose the opposite approach.

At all events nothing could happen until both parliaments agreed to authorise union negotiations. In the meantime Lauderdale and Bridgeman occasionally discussed trade, but Bridgeman was ill, and spent July 1668 in Tunbridge Wells. Lauderdale and his wife were also drinking the waters – 'an universal waterdrinking', he wrote – and 'nothing or little to be done when all the world is in the vacation gone into the country'.[125] Tweeddale, much though he wanted the union, was gloomy. 'I have small hope of the trade with England, and I apprehend the matter of union was proposed to divert it,' he wrote in September.[126] The bright spot was the prospect of revived Scoto-Dutch trade, 'which makes a great noise here', Lauderdale replied, and may help the union negotiation, which, he wrote on 22 September, 'is now pressed warmly'. Tweeddale's hopes revived: 'Oh, that the king would mind it.' A year previously Tweeddale had hoped that successful trade negotiations would lead to favourable consideration of union; now, he had fallen in line with Lauderdale's thinking. 'I am glad to hear the union looks so hopeful,' he wrote to Lauderdale on 15 October, 'for then the trade needs not trouble you much.'[127]

Lauderdale became gradually more optimistic. He had successfully cultivated the mercurial Buckingham, and Bridgeman remained zealous for it. Lauderdale prodded him: England should make some temporary gesture on trade, or the Scots would never accept union. Lauderdale adopted a deliberately laid-back attitude to let the English make the running. On 27 October he could report that the king, having spoken to Bridgeman, Buckingham and Albemarle, who were all keen for union, had ordered a proposal prepared.[128] Tweeddale was impatient. He worried about the possibility of Anglo-Irish union negotiations, which Lauderdale assured

124 9 June 1668, Tweeddale to Lauderdale, BL Add. Mss 23129, f. 146.
125 18 June, 4 July 1668, Lauderdale to Tweeddale, NLS Ms. 7023, ff. 170, 177.
126 BL Add. Mss 23130, ff. 18–19.
127 17, 22 Sept. 1668, Lauderdale to Tweeddale, NLS Ms. 7023, ff. 203, 204. 24 Sept., 15 Oct., Tweeddale to Lauderdale, BL Add. Mss 23130, ff. 42, 70.
128 6, 22, 27 Oct. 1668, Lauderdale to Tweeddale, NLS Ms. 7023, ff. 206, 210, 212.

him would not happen, and he thought that Lauderdale might have discussed matters more thoroughly with Bridgeman during the king's absence at Newmarket, 'but it seems you are becoming fond of hunting and taking the air, two things you were not accustomed to, but I hope it will not become a laboratory fondness', like Moray's, hinting at a parallel between Elizabeth Murray and Moray's niece as distractions. Lauderdale replied that the reason he had delayed 'was not my love of hunting and air but because I would not begin it without the duke of Buckingham, (who is most zealous in the matter)'.[129]

Preliminary discussions began on 17 November 1668, but there was little immediate progress. Lauderdale sent some tentative proposals to Tweeddale along with an account of the meeting at which they were discussed and instructions to gauge Scottish opinion. He enclosed a generalised, upbeat sort of letter to Rothes which Tweeddale was to use if he saw fit.[130] As Tweeddale was considering the papers Argyll, with whom Tweeddale's relations had not yet soured, came in; Tweeddale showed him the proposals. They agreed that far too few Scottish peers – only ten – were to sit in the combined parliament: there must be at least twenty. It was Scotland's bad luck to have such a numerous nobility; they dominated the Scottish parliament and would never accept the exclusion of so many. 'You must either prevail for a greater number or get some assurance of calling more speedily.' Lauderdale's first reaction was unconcern: not even ten would show up, he observed, since they would get no expense money. Tweeddale decided to keep the papers confidential, but he later changed his mind and showed a revised version, mentioning twenty peers, to Rothes, who copied it and began to show it to his friends.[131]

The king's decision in December to prorogue the English parliament until October 1669 caused the union 'to sleep a while', in Tweeddale's phrase. Both he and Kincardine wanted to return to the matter of trade,[132] but that issue, too, slept a while, as Tweeddale and his colleagues dealt with all the other items on their plate: the messy religious situation in Burnet's

129 7, 12 Nov. 1668, Tweeddale to Lauderdale, BL Add. Mss 23130, ff. 104, 108. 17, 24 Nov., Lauderdale to Tweeddale, Paton, 'Lauderdale', pp. 169–71.

130 3 Dec. 1668, Lauderdale to Tweeddale, Paton, 'Lauderdale', pp. 172–75, 237–38. Paton misdates the second letter, which is undated.

131 8 Dec. 1668, 6 July 1669, Tweeddale to Lauderdale, BL Add. Mss 23131, ff. 16–17, NLS Ms. 7024, f. 166. 15 Dec., Lauderdale to Tweeddale, Paton, 'Lauderdale', pp. 179–80.

132 12 Dec. 1668, Lauderdale to Tweeddale, Paton, 'Lauderdale', pp. 177–79. 17 Dec., Kincardine to Lauderdale, 19 Dec., Tweeddale to Lauderdale, BL Add. Mss 23131, ff. 36, 42–43.

archdiocese, disturbances and delinquent taxpayers in the Highlands, forcing the capitulation of Sir Walter Seaton, and establishing the direct collection of customs and foreign excise. And there were other matters too: whether to purchase the Bass Rock, which Tweeddale still did not think worth having, what to do about the lists of Papists handed to the council by the archbishops – Tweeddale and Kincardine were on a committee to make recommendations – student riots in Aberdeen, where the denizens of Kings and Marischal Colleges roughed each other up. The council wished to promote a Scottish musket-making industry, and in March 1669 banned the further importation of muskets to that end.[133] And then there were family matters. Halton proposed a marriage between his son and his and Lauderdale's niece, their sister's eldest daughter: what did Lauderdale think about it?[134] And both Lauderdale and Tweeddale were appalled by the behaviour of Moray and *his* niece, Lady Sophia; Lady Balcarres, Sophia's mother, is 'mad' if she does not 'cut off this infamous scandal'. Tongues were wagging in both Scotland and England, including that of Gilbert Burnet, whose questions Moray regarded as impertinent. He thought it best to write to the duchess of Hamilton that 'I neither am married nor do intend it.' On 3 July Lauderdale was relieved to be able to report that, according to Moray, Lady Sophia, whose health was still bad, was leaving for home.[135]

Then, in May 1669, while Tweeddale was in London, the union became a major issue once again. On 31 May the foreign committee of the English privy council, the inner ring of Charles's advisers during the Cabal years, discussed Lauderdale's draft proposal. Commissioners would be appointed for both kingdoms to work out a plan, which both parliaments must then ratify. There was to be an inseparable union. The subjects of each kingdom would have the same privileges in both. Prejudicial laws would be repealed. There would be a single bicameral parliament, with thirty Scottish MPs in the Commons, the same number as in the parliaments of the Protectorate. The issue of peers was finessed: the king would summon whatever Scottish nobles and bishops he chose, and determine their precedence. Customs duties, excise and poll taxes, and the currency would be standardised.

133   *RPCS* II, pp. 597, 603–07, 618. 9 Feb., 13 Mar. 1669, Tweeddale to Lauderdale, NLS Ms. 7001, pp. 208–10, BL Add. Mss 23131, ff. 111–12.
134   BL Add. Mss 23131, ff. 183–85. The match did not take place.
135   17 Apr., 3 July 1669, Lauderdale to Tweeddale, NLS MS. 7023, ff. 215, 217. 29 May, Moray to Kincardine, *Moray Letters*, pp. 264–65.

When other taxes were voted, England would pay 70 per cent, Ireland 18 per cent, and Scotland 12 per cent – an interesting comment on the perceived relative wealth of the three kingdoms. The legal and ecclesiastical systems would remain separate, but in future there might be a law code for all of 'Great Britain', the new-old name of the united kingdom. The only issue that raised doubts was that of the peerage, which was 'to be chewed over yet further'. On 9 June Tweeddale was admitted to the English privy council; on the following day a small meeting of the foreign committee in Arlington's lodgings – all three of the cousins were present – agreed to send the plan to Charles for his approval.[136] Charles was expecting it: on 27 May Sir Joseph Williamson, Arlington's secretary, through whose hands most of the latter's correspondence passed, noted in his diary that the king had taken the initiative, 'expressing great desire to have all his subjects conspire to one another's happiness under his reign'.[137] Tweeddale's instructions were quickly prepared. As in 1604, a parliament was necessary to authorise the meeting of the commissioners; it would meet on 19 October, at the same time as the English parliament. Tweeddale was to consult with Rothes and others about an agenda, and draw up a proper commission for Lauderdale on the model of those used for Middleton and Rothes. The new commissioner would preside in person over the forthcoming meeting.[138]

Word of the meeting of parliament preceded Tweeddale's return to Scotland. There was much speculation as to its purpose; 'the rich men fear their purses', Kincardine observed. He informed Lauderdale that the parliament house was in bad shape. The cloth of state was 'pitiful', the roof leaked, and there was no furniture, thanks to Lady Middleton, who apparently had appropriated it at the end of her husband's kleptocratic regime.[139] It was not the only structure needing repairs. In August 1669 one of Lauderdale's correspondents pointed to 'the marks of Oliver's fingers' all over Edinburgh, in the still-defaced regalia insignia at Holyrood, the market cross, and the Netherbow gate as well as the parliament house.[140] The chief culprit was the master of the works, Moray's brother William, who was honest but incompetent. In July 1668 Tweeddale grew impatient at the slow pace of the work at Edinburgh Castle and urged Moray to

136 Minutes of the Foreign Committee, PRO SP 104/176, ff. 155, 157, 161. NLS Ms. 597, f. 232.
137 PRO SP 29/253, f. 45.
138 NLS Ms. 14488, f. 67. *RPCS* III, p. 35.
139 17, 22 June 1669, Kincardine to Lauderdale, BL Add. Mss 23131, ff. 186, 190–91.
140 *Laing Mss* I, pp. 374–76.

'quicken' his brother, which he did. But the work still dragged, and by February 1669 Lauderdale agreed that William should be forced out and the office suppressed in order to save the salary. The negotiations took some time: it was necessary to proceed delicately, since the family's reputation was at stake. In August William was persuaded to announce that he was weary of his place and would retire if he got the arrears of his pension and fees; on 1 October the treasury commission, which had overall responsibility for repairs to royal palaces and castles, so ordered.[141]

By 6 July, when Tweeddale got back to Scotland, there had been much talk about the union plan. The figure of twenty peers was being spread around, he reported, in order to create dissatisfaction amongst the nobility.[142] On 15 July he wrote Moray that the union was 'mightily spoken against here'. He himself kept quiet, on the theory that when the English learned that the Scots disliked it they would like it better, and anyway 'the humour will evaporate before the parliament'. Kincardine saw the difficulties: 'In the affair of the union you [Lauderdale] will have many humours to please.'[143] Lauderdale professed not to worry about opposition.[144] The major question to be settled before the meetings of the parliaments was how the commissioners were to be chosen. Was the king to appoint them, or were the parliaments to elect them? This was not a serious issue in Scotland, but in England it was. The English parliament had elected the members of the trade commission, with unhappy results; Lauderdale wanted no more Downings. In a meeting of the foreign committee on 29 June, the last before Tweeddale left for Scotland, Lauderdale strongly urged royal nomination, which, he asserted, had been the procedure in 1604; 'if ye Parliaments name them, nothing is like to come of it'. The English members agreed, but heeded Ashley's caution that no one should be named ahead of time: the commission was to be drawn up for parliament to consider and the names left blank.[145] As usual, nothing much happened during the summer, but in late August there developed what Lauderdale called a 'stumble'. Bridgeman discovered from the records that

---

141 Tweeddale's problems with William Moray can be followed in his letters to Robert Moray between July 1668 and Aug. 1669 in NLS Ms. 7024, ff. 96ff. See also 4 Feb. 1669, Lauderdale to Tweeddale, Paton, 'Lauderdale', pp. 199–200, 4 Aug., Tweeddale to Lauderdale, BL Add. Mss 23132, ff. 52–55, NAS E6/1, p. 204, and NLS Ms. 597, ff. 147–48.

142 6 July 1669, Tweeddale to Lauderdale, NLS Ms. 7024, f. 166.

143 Ibid., f. 167. BL Add. Mss 23132, f. 65.

144 13 July 1669, Lauderdale to Tweeddale, Paton, 'Lauderdale', p. 213.

145 PRO SP 104/176, ff. 176–77.

in 1604 the parliaments had chosen the delegates.[146] This was disconcerting but did not alter the government's policy. The parliaments were to be asked to leave the appointments to the king.

The failure of the trade negotiations had certainly given impetus, for Tweeddale at least and probably for Moray and Kincardine as well, to the idea of union. Tweeddale believed in the principle; it was not for nothing that he had served in Cromwell's parliaments. For Kincardine the considerations were economic: he would support whatever would enhance the profits of the family's coal and salt business. The union was the only remedy for Scotland's present and future ills, he wrote in November 1669, during the meeting of the parliament.[147] Moray, who had seen far more of the world than any of the other three, seems to have believed that both countries could benefit, and that the Stuart monarchy's hand would be strengthened in its dealings in the dangerous world in which French political power and Dutch economic strength far overshadowed those of Charles's multiple kingdoms. Lauderdale was far more ambivalent. For all his almost permanent absence from his native land he was a good Scottish patriot, 'a man very national', in the words of the Covenanting minister Robert Law.[148] He had experienced the Cromwellian union only from the inside of an English prison, which could hardly have commended the experiment to him. Could Scottish identity survive union, no matter what its terms?

But now he wanted it, because the king did: the initiative was the king's, as Williamson had noted in his diary. The question is why – and why now. There is no clear-cut answer. Charles is the most enigmatic ruler of his dynasty. He certainly had one purpose as king: not to go on his travels again. What his other objectives might be, or even if he had any, have been the subject of much inconclusive debate. Some years ago this writer expressed the view that Charles wanted to enhance the power of the crown, which meant that the great obstacle, parliament, had to be made either pliable or irrelevant, and that during the Cabal years he tried to accomplish this.[149] His effort, which had to be conducted surreptitiously, behind the façade of the easy-going, pleasure-loving gentleman which in fact he was, ended in failure for many reasons, some of which were beyond his control.

---

146 Ibid., f. 194. 31 Aug. 1669, Lauderdale to Tweeddale, Paton, 'Lauderdale', pp. 220–22.
147 NLS Ms. 7003, f. 172.
148 Quoted in M. Lee, Jr, *The Cabal* (Urbana, 1965), p. 30.
149 Lee, *Cabal, passim*.

He then reverted, with the primacy of Lord Treasurer Danby in the mid-1670s, to a regime that in some ways resembled that of Clarendon. It is coincidental that the Cabal years, which saw Charles's larger initiative, were also the years of the cousins' effort to reform and revitalise the Scottish government. And it was on this point, the idea of a union, that the two initiatives came together.

It is hardly a coincidence that Tweeddale had been in London for about two weeks when, on 27 May, Williamson made that note in his diary. Tweeddale had always been the chief proponent of union. 'He really drove at the union, as a thing which he thought might be brought about' wrote Gilbert Burnet.[150] Charles had summoned him to London to discuss the restoration of the outed ministers, but it is very likely, though there is no documentation to prove it, that he discussed the union with Charles. It was a propitious moment. Lauderdale had kept the king apprised of the course of the trade negotiations and their collapse; Charles had recently used his prerogative to end the English duty on imported Scottish cattle. Charles was concerned that Scotland prosper, for the sake of his pocketbook, not that of the Scots; his Scottish officials were now telling him that union could solve the impasse over customs duties and the Navigation Act. There was also the larger political consideration. The English parliament, the principal obstacle to whatever plans Charles harboured for increased royal power and independence of action, had control of the purse, which made it indispensable to Charles. There were two possible solutions: either to create a loyal and subservient majority in the Commons, or to expand the crown's ordinary income to the point where it no longer depended on parliamentary votes of supply. Union with Scotland would add Scottish members to the Commons – reliable Scottish members; Lauderdale would see to that. There would be Scottish peers as well, which would be helpful in the Lords, especially if the king had the naming of them, as was now being proposed. The last session of the English parliament, early in 1668, had been difficult, and had broken down over an acrimonious legal dispute between the two houses. Some of Charles's advisers urged him to dissolve it, but the king feared that a new House of Commons might be even more awkward to manage.[151] Union could go a long way toward solving the problem. Small wonder that the plan was attractive to Charles.

---

150 Burnet, *History* I, pp. 486–87.
151 K.D.H. Haley, *The First Earl of Shaftesbury* (Oxford, 1968), p. 272.

So Lauderdale prepared to go to Scotland to carry out his master's wishes respecting the union and much else. He spent some time in July drinking the waters at Epsom to strengthen himself, and then – on his physician's advice, he said – four or five more days at Ham House, where he was spending more and more time.[152] He sent Tweeddale home at the end of June with a 'to-do' list, and followed him with a letter while Tweeddale was en route. He intended to put on an impressive show as commissioner. He would take up residence in Holyrood, as his predecessors had. Five sets of hangings would be necessary – he wanted the dimensions of the rooms – and also a good bed and chairs, and a pewter dining service. Would it be necessary to buy damask table linen and a tun of Rhenish wine in Holland? Coach horses were much too expensive in London; he wanted Kincardine, who had many connections there, to obtain seven or eight from Holland or Oldenburg, as well as a coachman, and a coach of crimson or figured velvet from The Hague. Lauderdale would bring with him his own cook, footcloth and liveries, and a supply of canary; other cooks, the butler, the caterer, and the sherry, beer and French wine Edinburgh could supply. He would need a stable, of course – and how about glassware?[153] Tweeddale set to work. Four days after his return he sent the measurements of the rooms to Lauderdale and wanted to know how far off the floor he wanted the hangings. Get a cloth of state and a riding horse from the king, he wrote, and buy the coach in London. Letters for the coach horses were on their way to Holland.[154]

There was a hitch over the accommodations in Holyroodhouse. The duchess of Hamilton, the hereditary keeper of the palace, baulked at vacating her rooms for Lauderdale's benefit – or so Lauderdale heard from her confidante, Lady Margaret Kennedy. Lauderdale was annoyed. He needed the public rooms, and the 'two rooms where I lay last'. Rothes, who as chancellor had lodgings in the palace, offered them to Lauderdale, who politely declined. In the end it all turned out to be a misunderstanding. Hamilton left the keys with Tweeddale when he went out of town and said that his wife was near her time and could not occupy the rooms anyway. This storm in a teacup consumed the month of July.[155] In the meantime the

---

152 13 July 1669, Lauderdale to Tweeddale, from Ham House, Paton,' 'Lauderdale', p. 213.

153 BL Add. Mss. 23131, f. 200. 3 July 1669, Lauderdale to Tweeddale, NLS Ms. 7023, f. 217.

154 BL Add. Mss 23132, ff. 11–12.

155 20, 24 July, 3 Aug. 1669, Lauderdale to Tweeddale, Paton, 'Lauderdale', pp. 214–20. 24, 27, 29, 31 July, Tweeddale to Lauderdale, BL Add. Mss 23132, ff. 28, 32–33, 36, 42–43. 30 July, Lady Hamilton to Lauderdale, a very apologetic note, BL Add. Mss 23132, ff. 38–39. She gave birth to a daughter, who died young.

other preparations went forward. The appropriate commission was duly drafted. Kincardine dealt with Holland for the horses and undertook to get the coach house and stables built. William Sharp sent an inventory of the goods in Holyroodhouse, and wanted to know about Lauderdale's cook's requirements for the kitchen. Tweeddale and his wife would look after hiring the servants. Lauderdale ordered his coach and liveries, and shipped his hangings, chairs and stools in late July; they arrived at Leith by 7 August. Moray promised to send the king's portrait to hang in the council chamber; the treasury commission, Tweeddale said, would pay for it if the privy purse would not. The furniture in Holyroodhouse was, so Sharp said, not in the best of shape, like the old hanging with Lauderdale's arms on it that he found to adorn the guard room.[156] It would, nevertheless, be a splendid show, and an expensive one. The treasury commission authorised £2,000 sterling on 9 July. There was considerable correspondence between Tweeddale and Lauderdale on the matter, with comparisons being made with the outlays for Middleton and Rothes. Lauderdale's attitude was that 'I ought not to be a loser', since he provided so much himself, whereas Rothes 'had £2,000 and yet bought nothing'. Loser he was not: he eventually collected £6,000 for his expenses, along with an allowance of £50 per diem while he was in Scotland and, unprecedentedly, £10 a day after his return.[157]

As for the agenda, Lauderdale wanted Tweeddale to send him material for his instructions. The union proposal was the key to the session; if it went forward, Lauderdale anticipated a very short first session, which Tweeddale hoped for also, but there were other matters to consider.[158] On 2 August Tweeddale wrote himself a note about what was to be done. An Act was needed to reassert royal authority over the church and that of the royal commissioner over the national synod should that body ever meet. The projected Act of Supremacy, which was designed, among other things, to put an end to any questions abut the legality of the indulgences, was a matter of great urgency to Tweeddale. It must happen before the union

156 20 July 1669, William Sharp to Lauderdale, BL Add. Mss 23132, f. 23. 10, 31 July, 7, 12 Aug.,
     Tweeddale to Lauderdale, BL Add. Mss 23132, ff. 11–12, 42–43, 58, 71. 22, 27 July, Lauderdale
     to Tweeddale, Paton, 'Lauderdale', pp. 215–17. Tweeddale had reminded Lauderdale to send
     the king's portrait as long ago as November 1668. BL Add. Mss 23130, f. 108.
157 3 Aug. 1669, Lauderdale to Tweeddale, Paton, 'Lauderdale', pp. 217–20. NAS E6/1, pp. 181–83.
     See also 10 July, 10, 21 Aug., Tweeddale to Lauderdale, BL Add. Mss 23132, ff. 11–12, 61–63, 81.
158 22, 27 July 1669, Lauderdale to Tweeddale, Paton, 'Lauderdale', pp. 215–16, 217. 26 Nov. 1668,
     Tweeddale to Moray, NLS Ms. 7024, f. 133.

negotiations got under way, or the argument would be made that it should be left to the newly combined parliament, and such a delay would be very unfortunate. Furthermore, it would have a useful impact on the factions in the church: 'Their smelling Erastianism strikes terror in both parties.' The king wanted to look into the status of the militia, and the restructuring of the court of session and the high court of justice. There were also questions of creditors and debtors, foreign trade, the export of bullion, the sumptuary laws and the vexing issue of salt, on which Tweeddale wanted Charles's instructions. Publicity about some of these matters, Tweeddale thought, would show the world that the regime cared for the welfare of the people. He also wanted a list of the nobles whom the bishops would be instructed to elect to the Committee of the Articles.[159]

The work of preparing Lauderdale's instructions went slowly. Tweeddale and his associates, chiefly Kincardine and Lord Advocate Nisbet, thought Moray's draft of religious legislation too general, open to too many constructions. Lauderdale thought it windy, full of references to the kings of Israel and Judah, 'all which he is fond of'.[160] Tweeddale wanted Charles to write to the president of the session, the lord advocate, and other officials respecting legal reform, and sent drafts, which Charles approved.[161] Tweeddale was desperately tired and needed a few days' rest. Lauderdale grew impatient, but by 28 August 'nostre fils' had arrived with the draft of the instructions, most of which Lauderdale and Moray found satisfactory save for the ecclesiastical legislation. So they suggested to Charles that his instructions be very general, and that any religious legislation be sent to him for approval instead of being left to Lauderdale as commissioner to approve, 'which he liked very well'. Tweeddale reminded Lauderdale that this was Yester's first serious mission; he hoped that Charles would reward the young man with £500 sterling, which would enable him to buy a piece of property priced at 8,000 merks Scots, which £500 would comfortably cover. Otherwise Tweeddale would buy it for him, but he would have to borrow to do so. Lauderdale agreed that Yester had behaved 'extraordinarius', and would get the money for him; unfortunately Charles had left

159 NLS Ms. 14488, ff. 70, 72, 74, 79–80. 22 July, 5, 19 Aug. 1669, Tweeddale to Lauderdale, *Laing Mss* I, pp. 372–74, BL Add. Mss 23132, ff. 56, 79–80. 4 Aug., 23 Sept., Tweeddale to Moray, NLS Ms. 7024, ff. 171, 178.

160 4 Aug. 1669, Tweeddale to Moray, NLS Ms. 7024, f. 171. 24 Aug., Lauderdale to Tweeddale, NLS Ms. 14406, f. 105.

161 19 Aug. 1669, Tweeddale to Lauderdale, BL Add. Mss 23132, ff. 79–80. 26 Aug., Lauderdale to Tweeddale, NLS Ms. 7023, f. 224.

town five hours before Tweeddale's letter arrived. In the end Charles's instructions were extremely general. There was a list of items to consider, above all the union and the royal supremacy, about which there was a lot of speculation in Scotland. Charles in effect left matters in Lauderdale's hands. Curiously, one matter that concerned him was the order of the riding, the formal procession for the opening of parliament, because he thought the previous arrangement, that of 1633, slighted the archbishops, and so the order was changed.[162]

Lauderdale was now anxious to get away, but he could not leave until after the king returned to London in mid-September. In the meantime he held some informal meetings with English officials about the union and drafted documents about salt and the restructuring of the high court of justice. Tweeddale had warned him that a lot of people planned to go as far south as Newcastle to meet him; Lauderdale firmly discouraged this. He also did not want Edinburgh officialdom to meet him on horseback; 'they are far more themselves in their formalities at the Watergate'.[163] At last he could announce that he would leave on 27 September, after a final series of meetings with Arlington, Bridgeman, Clifford and Secretary Trevor, and of course the king. He would reach Morpeth, on the English side of the border, on 5 or 6 October, 'where I hope to meet you and nobody else'.[164] Everything was in readiness for the lord commissioner's triumphant return to the land where he was now a virtual viceroy, to usher in what was to be the most successful parliament of the cousins' regime.

162 7, 19, 24 Aug. 1669, Tweeddale to Lauderdale, BL Add. Mss 23132, ff. 58, 79–80, 83. 7 Sept.,
     Tweeddale to Moray, NLS Ms. 7024, f. 176. 31 Aug., Lauderdale to Tweeddale, Paton,
     'Lauderdale', pp. 220–22. The parliament of 1633 was the last at which bishops were present at
     the opening.
163 4 Aug. 1669, Tweeddale to Lauderdale, BL Add. Mss 23132, ff. 52–53. 2, 14 Sept., Lauderdale to
     Tweeddale, NLS Ms. 14406, ff. 110, 112. In his letter Tweeddale also wondered if the commis-
     sioner's throne in the parliament house was too high, and if there should be a sermon at the
     opening of parliament – Tweeddale thought not. Details, details!
164 21 Sept. 1669, Lauderdale to Tweeddale, Paton, 'Lauderdale', pp. 222–23. See also his letter of
     10 Sept., NLS Ms. 7023, f. 227.

CHAPTER SEVEN

Supremacy and Union, 1669–1670

I

King Charles's instructions for the holding of parliament, formally approved on 15 September 1669, undoubtedly reflected Lauderdale's thinking as he set out later that month. There was a long list of things to do, but only three items were mandatory: the union, a new Militia Act, and an Act fully spelling out the royal supremacy in ecclesiastical affairs. Only the last required Lauderdale to get the king's approval before he formally touched it with the sceptre. On all other matters he could act without submitting the text to London. It was a measure of Charles's trust in his commissioner that he gave Lauderdale such wide latitude. On some items Lauderdale chose not to act. He postponed until 1670 the voting of a tax to pay the expenses of the members of the union delegation: if, as Kincardine had speculated, rich men feared for their purses when they heard that parliament was to meet, their fears were allayed. Almost nothing was done about the situation of debtors and creditors. The proposed overhaul of the court of justiciary waited until 1671. On the other hand there was considerable economic and social legislation, one item of which proved to be seriously controversial.[1]

Lauderdale arrived in Edinburgh early in October.[2] His reception in Scotland was as spectacular as he had intended. Tweeddale rode to Durham to meet him. The treasury commission provided for trumpeters to meet him at the border; from there various militia regiments escorted him to the capital. 'At his entry into Edinburgh he was saluted by the Magistrates in their gowns at the water-gate,' an unprecedented gesture. 'He has been more numerously received than any previous Commissioner, the crowds of people being very great and expressing much satisfaction.'[3] The elections had gone well. There were a lot of new members: twenty-two representatives from the thirty-one shires and thirty from the sixty-eight burghs had not sat before. And there were only four disputed elections,

1 Charles's instructions are in BL Add. Mss 23132, f. 93.
2 He was present in the privy council on 11 Oct.; *RPCS* III, pp. 80–82.
3 Mackenzie, *Memoirs*, pp. 141–42. *CSPD 1668–69*, pp. 527–28. NAS E6/1, p. 205. Tweeddale, 'Autobiography', p. 97.

from three shires and the burgh of Cromarty.[4] The government made no effort to manipulate elections: it was not necessary. A newsletter of 4 October reported that the burgh of Annan declined to elect a candidate who refused to subscribe to the declaration against the Covenant, though he was willing to make an oral commitment; another was chosen in his stead.[5] On 12 October Lauderdale reported to the king on the elections and gave a glowing account of six militia regiments, including his own and Yester's, which were ready to go when and where the king wished. 'All your commands are to me above all human laws.'[6]

Lauderdale also indicated in this report that he would carry out Charles's orders as to 'the insolent, impertinent Glasgow paper'. He was as good as his word. He spent the week prior to the opening of parliament greasing the skids under Archbishop Burnet, whose removal would await the passage of the Act of Supremacy. A committee of the council, which of course included Tweeddale, as well as Kincardine, Rothes and Hamilton, considered the documents that had emerged from the Glasgow synods and interrogated the dean of Glasgow cathedral. The officials of the archdiocese refused to admit to Burnet's initiative, and Sharp attempted to argue that the Peebles meeting was not a synod, but merely a gathering of concerned individuals. Lauderdale brushed all this aside. On 16 October the council formally condemned Burnet's paper and confined him to his diocese; he would not be present at parliament.[7]

On 19 October Lauderdale opened parliament as scheduled. It was a busier and more contentious day than he had anticipated. The members heard a prayer from Bishop Leighton, now the regime's favorite bishop, rather than a minister who might take the opportunity, as Lauderdale put it, to 'tell God almighty news from the debates'.[8] The king's letter was then read. It laid stress on his great 'desire to settle union between our kingdoms and request you, on these and other matters, to give full credence to our commissioner'. Lauderdale's own speech underlined the king's plan 'to pros-

---

4 G. MacIntosh, 'Arise, King John: Commissioner Lauderdale and Parliament in the Restoration Era', in K.M. Brown and A.J. Mann, eds, *Parliament and Politics in Scotland, 1567–1707*, (Edinburgh, 2005), pp. 168–69.

5 *CSPD 1668–69*, p. 517.

6 BL Add. Mss 23132, f. 115.

7 Ibid., ff. 119, 120. *RPCS* III, pp. 82, 84. 16 Oct. 1669, R. Mein to Williamson, *CSPD 1668–69*, p. 533. 24 Oct., Tweeddale to Moray, NLS Ms. 7024, ff. 183–84. For Burnet's paper see above, chap. 6, pp. 175–76.

8 19 Oct. 1669, Lauderdale to Charles, BL Add. Mss 23132, f. 121.

ecute a closer union between the kingdoms than that brought about by King James', and emphasised that the church as currently constituted would be upheld, and conventicles and other unlawful meetings stamped out.[9] Next on Lauderdale's agenda, after the tendering of the necessary oaths, was the election of his hand-picked Committee of the Articles. Here difficulties arose. Lauderdale blocked an attempt to defer the choice of the committee until after the settling of the disputed elections: it would have involved three days' delay, he thought, and he was in a hurry to get the union business settled. So the sorting-out of the electoral disputes was handed over to a parliamentary committee. Then there was further dispute over the choosing of the shires' and burghs' members of the Articles: were they to be elected by the already-elected members of the first two estates, as Lauderdale wanted, or by all the bishops and nobles? Lauderdale was clear that an Act of the previous parliament had settled the issue, 'but now the Chancellor could not remember it and the Register could not find the Act and the duke of Hamilton cried out against it'. Lauderdale angrily told the clerk-register to 'break up the door where the record lay (for he pretended not to have the key)'. At last Archbishop Sharp produced a copy, Lauderdale was proved right, and the election proceeded as he had planned, following a list he gave to the bishops.[10] 'If they be amiss,' he reported to the king, 'blame me, for I wrote the lists, and not a man was altered.'[11] To make sure that he maintained his grip, he prohibited members of parliament not on the committee from attending its meetings, lest, as Sir George Mackenzie put it, they become 'tumultuary'; the prohibition had the additional advantage of preventing leaks.[12] All in all, it had been a successful, though wearying, day. Lauderdale was hoarse from having to speak so often and, so said Tweeddale, at the top of his voice. But he had reason for concern. Hamilton's attempts at obstruction were to be expected, but that Rothes, who had presided over the parliament in 1663, could not remember the Act regulating the election of the Articles was a warning signal.[13] Those outside the cousins' inner circle were disgruntled.

9 19 Oct. 1669, R. Mein to Williamson, *CSPD 1668–69*, p. 538. *APS* VII, pp. 551–52.
10 19 Oct. 1669, Tweeddale to Moray, NLS Ms. 7024, f. 182.
11 BL Add. Mss 23132, f. 121.
12 Mackenzie, *Memoirs*, pp. 142–43. R.S. Rait, *The Parliaments of Scotland* (Glasgow, 1924), p. 382. Parliament had permitted non-members to attend the Articles in 1662. On the matter of leaks see 6 Nov. 1669, R. Mein to Williamson, *CSPD 1668–69*, p. 570.
13 The Act in question in is *APS* VII, p. 449. For the activities of this first day see Lauderdale's and Tweeddale's letters, notes 8 and 10 above. For what follows on the union see M. Lee, Jr, *The Cabal* (Urbana, 1965), pp. 54–59.

In his report on the opening of parliament Lauderdale promised the king that he would get it to act on the union in two days. He was almost as good as his word; it took three. By the morning of 21 October the Articles approved a draft reply to the king's letter, favouring the union in principle and authorising him to appoint the Scottish commissioners. When the draft reached the floor it became clear that a number of members were uneasy; so Lauderdale, knowing that he had the votes, allowed the debate to proceed, 'that the humour might evaporate and he might better know the temper of the house', as Tweeddale put it. He intervened only to issue a 'sorry reprimand' to Sir George Gordon of Haddo, who 'impertinently' wanted to know who would wear the crown of Scotland if the line of King James should fail. There was unease over granting the king the right to name the commissioners without parliamentary approval. Hamilton backed a proposal, which Tweeddale labelled 'a wild proposition', that parliament have the power to veto any of the king's choices and add other commissioners. The most effective speech, 'long-winded', said Tweeddale, was that of Sir George Mackenzie of Rosehaugh, who urged going more slowly, waiting for the English parliament to act, and wanting parliament to be consulted, not only on the membership of the commission, but also on its proceedings. The nature of the proposed union had not been made clear; parliament must take care to protect Scottish liberties and law, as had been done in 1604. Mackenzie nowhere said that he opposed the union, but he saw no reason for such haste. The English parliament, he said, 'must not think that we are weary of our liberties'. The speech irritated Tweeddale, who complained that 'such long discourses were intolerable, especially where they intended to persuade the Parliament not to comply with his Majesty's desires'.[14] The debate ran through the evening of the 21st and the morning of the 22nd; then with all the 'ridiculous motions being laid aside', Lauderdale got the vote he wanted. The king could name the commissioners, who would in due course report back to the house. Mackenzie cast the only negative vote.[15]

The near-unanimity of the vote disguised the fact that, as Williamson's correspondent Robert Mein put it, there had been 'much dispute'.[16]

14 Mackenzie, *Memoirs*, pp. 149–55.
15 *APS* VII, pp. 552–53, App., p. 107. The best account of the proceedings, from which the quotations in this paragraph are taken, is Tweeddale's letter to Moray, 22 Oct. 1669, Paton, 'Lauderdale', pp. 223–26. The impertinent Sir George Gordon became lord chancellor and earl of Aberdeen in 1682, the long-winded Mackenzie lord advocate in 1677.
16 *CSPD 1668–69*, p. 546.

Lauderdale recognised the significance of the debate, and pointed out to the king that the union was not popular. Opposition could not be laid exclusively at the feet of the cross-grained and factious duke of Hamilton, as Tweeddale insinuated in his report. Now that he was on the spot, Lauderdale became aware of the true state of Scottish opinion. So he stressed in his report to Charles that the next step, namely, the draft of the commission and the scope of its powers, must come from England. He explained that he expressly avoided raising this question because it would have caused delay and debate, and might have led to backlash in the English parliament, but whatever the latter adopted 'shall, I hope, pass easily here'. And Charles must be sure to get the right to nominate the English commissioners as well. If the English parliament chose the delegates, 'I shall despair of success.'[17] He remembered Sir George Downing.

It was important that the English parliament act promptly. As Sir Alexander Fraser, the king's physician, currently a shire representative and a member of the Articles, reminded Arlington, 'our people are not so wise or patient'. The longer the English took to act, the happier the disaffected in Scotland would be, and the more their numbers would grow.[18] Moray did his best to get Charles to speed things up, but the king was dilatory about speaking to Lord Keeper Bridgeman, and, indeed, about writing to his commissioner, though Moray kept reminding him to do so. And it was clear that the English parliament would not move quickly. On 26 October it even adjourned for eight days. During the adjournment Moray floated to the king a suggestion of Sir Thomas Clifford, whom Tweeddale, his friend, regarded as the most enthusiastic supporter of the union in Charles's inner circle. Since, Clifford said, it was inconvenient for the Scottish parliament to sit for a long time, let it authorise the king to draft a commission under the great seal. Then, when its other necessary business was done, it could adjourn until spring. Lauderdale, if he approved, could draft the necessary instructions for Charles to sign. Ashley thought well of this plan, Moray added. This letter was written on 28 October. Moray evidently had not seen, or not heeded, Lauderdale's report to Charles, whose attitude was remarkably casual – he finally got around to speaking to Bridgeman, after a great deal of prodding, and he had to be reminded of his instructions to

---

17 22 Oct. 1669, Lauderdale to Charles, BL Add. Mss 23132, ff. 123–24.
18 4 Nov. 1669, Fraser to Arlington, *CSPD 1668–69*, pp. 566–67. Fraser was, of course, a non-resident. His situation, and that of other lairds, was regularised by an enactment on 26 Oct. that non-resident heritors could both vote and be elected. *APS* VII, p. 553.

the Scottish parliament before he authorised the printing of his letter to them. For Charles, preoccupied as he now was with the negotiations with France that were to result in the treaty of Dover, the plan for union was no longer as important to him as it had been some months earlier.[19]

Moray's suggestion about the commission arrived in Edinburgh on 2 November. Lauderdale was appalled, and wrote him a furious letter. 'I thought I had clearly enough in one to his Majesty declared against our going a step further, and that the commission must be done there' – and now this! The union was immensely unpopular in Scotland, owing to 'the endeavour to have made us slaves by garrisons and the ruin of our trade by severe laws . . . To press more before England take notice of the matter would render the proposer most odious as the betrayer of his country.'[20] Tweeddale, writing on the same day, said much the same thing, in less vehement language. One of the major drawbacks to Moray's plan, which he evidently had not considered, was that any proposal for a commission would lead to a debate on placing limitations on the commissioners, a debate that Tweeddale wanted to avoid at all costs.[21]

Lauderdale was doubly aggrieved and shocked by Moray's initiative because things had gone so well until now. Two days earlier he had expressed his delight that Charles had approved of his opening moves, and modestly protested that he did not think his speech worth printing.[22] Worse was to come. Moray did not wait to find out how Lauderdale viewed his proposal. On 2 November, the same day as Lauderdale's vehement letter, Charles sent an order to his commissioner to have the Scottish parliament endorse the proposal. Worse still, the order was sent by express rather than in the ordinary post, which caused all sorts of rumour and conjecture. Lauderdale was shaken again: he had sent an express to the king explaining his opposition to the move. On 9 November he wrote an obsequious letter to Charles stating that he could not 'in faithfulness and duty to your service' carry out his command until he confirmed it after considering Lauderdale's objections, contained in the letter which he would write to Moray. This letter, which complained 'heavily' of the use of the express, said that he had consulted the leading members of the Articles, fifteen in all, including

19 26, 28, 30 Oct. 1669, Moray to Lauderdale, BL Add. Mss 23132, ff. 131, 133, 137. 26 Oct., Arlington to Lauderdale, BL Add. Mss 23132, f. 129.
20 Ibid., f. 143.
21 NLS Ms. 7024, f. 186. Tweeddale made this point more emphatically four days later; NLS Ms. 7024, f. 188.
22 BL Add. Mss. 23132, ff. 139–40.

Tweeddale. They all opposed the blanket authorisation. Scottish honour was at stake. Lauderdale repeated that the union was very unpopular because of the 'ruin of our trade . . . these nine years past'. He explained again in great detail why Moray's proposal was a bad idea. Parliament would accept the English draft of a commission, but would pass nothing more until England acted. The tone of this letter, which was designed for the king's eyes, was carefully restrained. A covering letter accompanying it was much less so. Lauderdale scolded Moray again for using the express. Show my letter to the king, he went on, and let him send what order he pleases. But if he repeats his instructions, 'it destroys the business'.[23]

On that same day, 9 November, Moray reported to Lauderdale that the king had drawn back. He understood Lauderdale's objections to the blanket commission, and he did not mean to be peremptory. He would await Lauderdale's advice before deciding on what to do. Moray explained that the original order, for which he did his best to blame Clifford, had been issued because Clifford had argued in the foreign committee of the English privy council that the English parliament was not apt to act until December at the earliest.[24] The king said – again – that he would do what he could to prod parliament into action, but those of his principal advisers who were the strongest proponents of the union, Clifford, Bridgeman and Arlington, were dubious. Moray still hankered after his proposal: it would be a 'string to your bow'. Four days later he reported on another meeting of the foreign committee. Its members reiterated that the English parliament would not be hurried; 'even the aid is slow', Clifford remarked. There was some speculation about dissolving the Scottish parliament rather than adjourning it to a particular date, in the interests of flexibility. There was, in fact, an impasse, and Lauderdale's advice would certainly be solicited. At the end of his letter Moray returned to the blanket authorisation, which would be valid only if the English parliament failed to act before its session ended. If Lauderdale pulled this off, 'the king would think this a noble piece of service. I think I guess how you will relish this. Disappoint me.'[25]

Lauderdale ignored the suggestion. He was pleased, he wrote to Moray, 'that I shall not be chid[ed] for not obeying the command you sent me BY THE EXPRESS'.[26] To the king he expressed his gratitude that Charles had

23 9 Nov. 1669, Lauderdale to Charles, and to Moray, ibid., ff. 145, 147–48, 149.
24 31 Oct. 1669, minutes of the foreign committee, PRO Ms. 104/176, f. 210.
25 Ibid., ff. 217–18. 9, 13 Nov. 1669, Moray to Lauderdale, BL Add, Mss 23132, ff. 150–51, 159–63.
26 13 Nov. 1669, Lauderdale to Moray, BL Add. Mss 23132, f. 153. In the printed version of the letter in *LP* II, pp. 158–59, the editor did not capitalise 'by the express'.

countermanded the order: 'I was afflicted above measure to have so great a business miscarry in my hand by precipitation, which will go well here if we meet with any suitable return'.[27] In both his and Tweeddale's opinion there was nothing to do but mark time until the English parliament acted, if it ever did. Lauderdale was not optimistic. Either here or there, he wrote, the union was 'choked'.[28] Moray's hopes were fading also. On 20 November, he observed that the Commons' doings, which Charles found very difficult to deal with, made it most unlikely that he would even try to raise the question of union.[29] Moray was right. The Commons were preoccupied with the inquest into the failures of the recent war and their quarrel with the Lords in the case of Skinner vs the East India Company. The king prorogued parliament in December with no mention of the union.[30]

So Lauderdale avoided the embarrassment of a certain parliamentary confrontation, and a possible defeat, over the commission. But the whole episode disturbed him profoundly. He had had no idea of how unpopular the idea of union was in Scotland; it was no part of his political agenda to inaugurate his career as commissioner by promoting a cause to which his countrymen felt so hostile. After all, his good political reputation amongst them hinged on his being perceived as 'a man very national', and his countrymen had, as he discovered, 'a great jealousy [fear] of uniting with England'. His enthusiasm for the union began to wane. He disclaimed personal responsibility: 'What is done is purely in obedience to his Majesty.' The hostile James Kirkton wrote that Lauderdale on his return to court early in 1670 told Charles that Scotland was 'as pliant as a glove toward the designed union and the altered parliament'.[31] It is unlikely that he said any such thing. He felt blindsided. He had not been warned, and Tweeddale, the union's great proponent, had to be responsible.

Moray's behaviour was even worse. He had floated a proposal that Lauderdale found completely unacceptable, and then, without waiting for Lauderdale's reaction, he had persuaded the king to accept it. As the commissioner angrily observed, 'You have taken much pains to bring me into a great difficulty',[32] from which with much ado he had extricated

27 16 Nov. 1669, Lauderdale to Charles, BL Add. Mss 23132, f. 156.
28 16 Nov. 1669, Tweeddale to Moray, NLS Ms. 7024, f. 191. 18 Nov., Lauderdale to Moray, BL Add. Mss 23132, f. 158.
29 BL Add. Mss 23132, f. 159.
30 R.F. Hutton, *Charles II, King of England, Scotland and Ireland* (Oxford, 1989), p. 269.
31 2, 9 Nov. 1669, Lauderdale to Moray, BL Add. Mss 23132, ff.143, 147–48. Kirkton, *History*, p. 177.
32 9 Nov. 1669, Lauderdale to Moray, BL Add. Mss 23132. f. 149.

himself. The sending of Charles's instructions by express added to Lauderdale's difficulties. Moray also kept pestering Charles to write to Lauderdale – three times today as well as twice or thrice before, he wrote on 28 October.[33] Lauderdale instructed him not to push the king this way. There was no need, and Charles disliked writing letters: Lauderdale himself never urged the king to do so when he was in London. Moray rather defensively replied that Charles had never complained about his importunings.[34] Charles was always polite, and in Lauderdale's view Moray should have known better. He was the king's intimate; his discussions with Charles frequently took place in the chemical laboratory in which Charles had established him.[35] Because of this relationship Moray was enormously useful to Lauderdale, and would continue to be – as long as he did not take any initiatives: Lauderdale wanted no independent agents. His confidence in Moray was badly shaken. Tweeddale too had blotted his copybook by misreading, or, worse, wilfully ignoring popular hostility to the union, though he had, rather belatedly, mentioned it, especially that of the nobility, in some of his letters to Moray.[36] Lauderdale was beginning to wonder about the judgment, and the long-term usefulness, of both Moray and his 'dearest brother'. But for the moment he kept his own counsel; there was much work to be done.

Once parliament accepted the union Lauderdale turned to the other two major items on Charles's agenda, the Militia Act and the Act of Supremacy. The militia bill was brought in first. Parliament had authorised the militia – 20,000 foot and 2,000 horse – in 1663; the issue now was how to pay for it. The rates were set; the heritors were to pay.[37] The only debate occurred over the best way to deal with delinquents: by quartering, or by distraint of their goods. The Articles, after much debate, decided for quartering, but when the bill was brought in, many 'bogled' at this. So Lauderdale pulled the bill, and the Articles then devised a method of distraint as swift and severe as quartering: goods could be seized for non-payment and sold after six days. The bill passed on 30 October with only one dissenting vote. What Lauderdale called the 'odium' of quartering had been avoided. As Tweeddale later explained to Moray, using the militia for quartering on the source of their emoluments was impractical, nor could

33 Ibid., f. 133.
34 6 Nov. 1669, Lauderdale to Moray, 13 Nov., Moray to Lauderdale, ibid., ff. 144, 154–55.
35 See, e.g., 22 Oct. 1669, Moray to Lauderdale, ibid., f. 127.
36 See, e.g., those of 15 July, 2, 30 Nov. 1669, NLS Ms. 7024, ff. 167, 186, 195.
37 See above, chap. 6, pp. 184–86.

they be kept too long from their employments.[38] This relatively uncontroversial piece of legislation caused more friction between Lauderdale and Moray, who, evidently not understanding that the Act had already passed, proposed changes in it. Lauderdale was annoyed.[39] The king, Moray reported, was pleased with the Act. 'He . . . put it in his pocket, and say other people what they list, thinks it is for his no small advantage that the 22,000 Scots are by Act of parliament to march whither he pleases within his dominions.' Many Englishmen did not agree. The Act of 1663 had attracted little notice in England; this one did. The notion that the king could authorise a Scottish army to march south in case of trouble was disquieting, to say the least. Lauderdale remarked on the 'strange prejudices' that arose against him on account of it; happily, they did not last long – or so he thought.[40] In time he would be undeceived.

The next item on Lauderdale's to-do list, the supremacy bill, would be a good deal trickier. The bishops, who disliked the indulgence, could be expected to do all they could to block or emasculate it. Sharp tried a preemptive strike through a sermon before parliament which purported to describe what the king could not do, including ordaining or suspending ministers, going on 'at a wild rate little better than the western paper'. Tweeddale was amused, Lauderdale less so. He demanded an explanation, and Sharp had to provide a 'clarification' on the following Sunday.[41] Lauderdale's line, as he put it in a letter to the king, was that the bill represented no change in policy; it simply filled lacunae in the Supremacy Act of 1662.[42] This was disingenuous. Sharp, in his earlier complaints about the indulgence, had implied that that Act required the consent of the clergy for the king to take actions such as the indulgence, which was why Tweeddale had argued for the need for new legislation.[43] Lauderdale spun out the debate in the Articles in an effort to reach consensus. When Sharp saw the text of the bill he was very alarmed at the removal of all 'clogs' on royal power, and told Tweeddale 'all King Henry the 8th ten years' works was

38 28, 30 Oct. 1669, Lauderdale to Moray, BL Add. Mss 23132, ff. 135–36, 139–40. 13 Nov., Tweeddale to Moray, NLS Ms. 7024, f. 190. APS VII, pp. 554–55, App., p. 107. Parliament approved the Act on 30 Oct., but the formal vote was recorded on 16 Nov.

39 11 Nov. 1669, Lauderdale to Moray, BL Add. Mss 23132, f. 152.

40 30 Nov. 1669, Moray to Lauderdale, ibid., f. 165. 15 Feb., 1 Mar. 1670, Lauderdale to Tweeddale, NLS Ms. 7023, f. 231, 14406, f. 125.

41 26 Oct. 1669, Tweeddale to Moray, NLS Ms. 7024, f. 185.

42 22 Oct. 1669, Lauderdale to Charles, BL Add. Mss 23132, ff. 123–24.

43 22 July 1669, Tweeddale to Lauderdale, Laing Mss I, pp. 372–74.

now to be done in three days'. Tweeddale tried to calm him down, but he insisted on seeing Lauderdale. If the king wanted the bill as drawn, he said, the bishops would accept it, but he suggested adding the phrase 'as it is settled by law' to the clause granting the king the power to determine the external government of the church. Since this would put all the 'clogs' back, Lauderdale refused. So Sharp subsided, and when, in the discussion in the Articles, one of his fellow bishops suggested such a clause, Sharp 'snapped him up'. The Articles then unanimously approved the text, which was sent to the king accompanied by a plea from Lauderdale that Charles change nothing in it, or else 'we are thrown into the mere'. Lauderdale wanted Moray to be watchful: an effort might be made to reach Archbishop Sheldon and stir up opposition among the English clergy, 'though I am sure the law of England gives the king as much'.[44] He was very nervous. 'My heart is vexed,' he wrote nine days later. Charles could alter the supremacy bill of course, 'but alterations will, I think, make it never pass.'[45]

Lauderdale's worry was unnecessary. Charles, having read 'every word' of Lauderdale's letter of 2 November, approved the bill as it stood.[46] Sharp made one final effort to block it. He complained to Tweeddale that the bishops had not been consulted, as the law of 1662 required, and gave him a paper to show Lauderdale which Tweeddale described as 'Presbyterian trew blew': under such a law a pagan prince could determine the fundamentals of the Christian religion. Lauderdale paid no heed, and the bill passed unanimously. The earl of Dumfries, a former ally of the late Chancellor Glencairn, who was now trying rather half-heartedly to ingratiate himself with the cousins, praised the bill, saying that the king's authority was now greater than that of either pope or presbyter. When he sat down he whispered to Tweeddale that 'the king had now got in between God and the bishops': there would be no *jure divino* episcopacy in Scotland.[47] This was not an altogether irrelevant comment. In the discussion in the Articles Sharp had talked about the divine right of bishops and alleged that the king believed that no ministerial ordination was valid without them. Tweeddale commented that the archbishop had no business pronouncing on the king's views without a warrant.[48]

---

44 28 Oct., 2 Nov. 1669, Lauderdale to Moray, BL Add. Mss 23132, ff. 135–36, 139–40.
45 Ibid., f. 152.
46 9 Nov. 1669, Moray to Lauderdale, ibid., ff. 150–51.
47 16 Nov. 1669, Tweeddale to Moray, NLS Ms. 7024, ff. 192–93. Dumfries had been deeply involved in the attempt to billet Lauderdale in 1662.
48 6 Nov. 1669, Tweeddale to Moray, ibid. f. 189.

Lauderdale was cock-a-hoop. He gleefully wrote to the king that 'I found the old spirit of Presbytery did remain with some of the bishops (so unwilling are Churchmen, by what name or title soever they are dignified, to part with power).' They wanted a conference, which Lauderdale refused: 'I would not alter a syllable in the Act.' He also frightened them out of any thought of protest on the floor. After its unanimous passage Lauderdale immediately touched it with the sceptre: it was the law of the land. At the same time he touched the Militia Act. So, Lauderdale cheerfully concluded, Charles could now do whatever he liked in the church, and have 20,000 men at his disposal to make good that power. 'Never was king so absolute as you are in poor old Scotland.'[49] Kirkton declared that the Act gave the king more power 'to establish a new confession of faith, or a new religion, than to impose one 'penny upon our bread or drink.'[50] Charles, Moray reported, was delighted by the Act, and amused at Lauderdale's account of his silencing of the bishops. Moray, too, was delighted. 'What would King James have given for such an Act 3 or 4 score years ago?'[51] The Act might have delighted King James, but in fact he did not need it. His church was broadly acceptable to his people, at least until his decision to impose the Five Articles of Perth. The Act of Supremacy was an admission, and a recognition, that Charles's church was morally bankrupt and politically impotent. Only royal authority could make it viable, and only minimally viable at that.

Lauderdale made immediate use of the Act to get rid of Archbishop Burnet. The divisions in the church made the situation 'almost desperate', in Tweeddale's view. His conversations with Robert Douglas made it clear to him that even the moderates among the nonconformists were more hostile to the bishops than ever. Gilbert Burnet's reports from the west indicated that the Presbyterians there hoped that the archbishop's behaviour might produce sufficient backlash to force Charles to jettison bishops altogether. The indulgence, on which Tweeddale had pinned his hopes of reconciliation, seemed not to be working very well there. The best course now was to replace Burnet with 'short-faced Dunblane', who had been able to persuade the clergy of his diocese to attend presbyteries – one of the most serious counts against Burnet was his punishing of clergymen whose only fault was their refusal to do this. So, Moray asked Charles, now that he

---

49 16 Nov. 1669, Lauderdale to Charles, BL Add. Mss 23132, f. 156. The Act is in *APS* VII, p. 554.
50 Kirkton, *History*, p. 176.
51 22–23 Nov. 1669, Moray to Lauderdale, BL Add. Mss 23132, f. 161.

had the power to do so, how about Tweeddale's suggestion of Short Face for L.F.? Charles said he thought well of the idea.[52]

So the wheels began to turn. Lauderdale made the action more palatable to the clergy through legislation, passed, noted Mackenzie, on St Andrew's Day, ratifying the privy council's acts for the security of ministers, against conventicles, and asserting the parish's responsibility for restitution if the perpetrators of offences against the minister were not caught. He also ordered troops to Dumfries and Kilmarnock on account of some 'insolencies' there, which involved ordinary robberies as well as the harassing of ministers.[53] On 30 November Tweeddale wrote that Charles's commands on Burnet and the approval of Leighton as his successor were 'daily expected'. Tweeddale had provided the necessary drafts, and in due course Charles signed them. 'All that know', wrote Moray, 'how he [Leighton] hath brought in all the ministers in his present diocese will mightily approve of the king's choice.'[54] Charles's warrant stipulated that if Burnet refused to resign he would be suspended and charged with fomenting popular discontent: misprision of treason. The archbishop put up little or no resistance, though he did ask Lauderdale to discuss the matter with the other bishops. Lauderdale consulted four of them. Sharp muttered 'faintly' something about the indelible character of a bishop. Lauderdale abruptly replied that, whether or not that was so, the exercise of his office 'was not *Jure Divino*, but depended solely upon the supreme Magistrate'.[55] Burnet was granted an annuity, freedom from any financial obligation to his predecessor's heirs, and immunity from prosecution for the allegedly seditious paper of the Peebles synod. On 24 December, the day after parliament adjourned, he resigned, 'being sensible that my service . . . hath not been . . . acceptable to his Majesty'.[56]

While Burnet was being eased out of office the work of the parliament had gone on. Some useful legislation was relatively uncontroversial. Orkney and Shetland were re-annexed to the crown after formal ratification of the

52 2, 4, 16 Nov. 1669, Tweeddale to Moray, NLS Ms. 7024, ff. 186, 187, 191. 22 Nov., Moray to Lauderdale, BL Add. Mss 23132, f. 161. 29 Nov., Gilbert Burnet to Tweeddale, NLS Ms. 7121, f. 5.
53 *APS* VII, pp. 556–57. Mackenzie, *Memoirs*, pp. 162–63. 28 Oct. 1669, Lauderdale to Moray, BL Add. Mss 23132, ff. 135–36. 6, 16 Nov., Tweeddale to Moray, NLS Ms. 7024, ff. 189, 191.
54 30 Nov. 1669, Tweeddale to Moray, NLS Ms. 7024, f. 195. 30 Nov., 10–11 Dec., Moray to Lauderdale, BL Add. Mss 23132, ff. 165, 178–79.
55 16 Dec. 1669, Lauderdale to Moray, BL Add. Mss 23132, f. 186. The warrant, in Tweeddale's hand, is in BL Add. Mss 23132, f. 168.
56 Ibid., ff. 197, 199. 24 Dec. 1669, Tweeddale to Moray, NLS Ms. 7024, f. 201. J. Buckroyd, 'The Dismissal of Archbishop Alexander Burnet, 1669', *Records of the Scottish Church History Society* 18 (1974), pp. 149–55.

court of session's voiding of the contracts of alienation to the earl of Morton. Lauderdale, anticipating possible difficulty, slid the bill through quickly and silenced subsequent discussion by touching it with the sceptre, 'which made Earl Tweeddale laugh', he wrote Moray, 'for there was no more to be said'. The privy council was authorised to levy tolls on bridges and ferries for their upkeep, to naturalise Protestant aliens if they had some property or intended to set up manufacturing, to punish justices of the peace who neglected their obligation to maintain highways, and, after some discussion, to set the prices of ale, beer and bread and punish violators. The bishops did not like the Act declaring that quot silver, the fee for recording a testament, was to be levied on the net worth of an estate after the decedent's debts were paid rather than on its total value at death, but they swallowed it. Gordon of Haddo and Mackenzie of Rosehaugh, those two regular nay-sayers, did not like the Act authorising the trial *in absentia* of some of the recent rebels, arguing that only parliament could conduct such trials. The lord advocate and the president of the session successfully refuted them; Whitehall approved.[57] After Lauderdale brushed aside an attempt by Haddo to waive the collection of arrears of taxation, parliament decreed that people in the northern shires still owing such arrears on 1 June 1670 would have to pay double, 'which,' wrote Tweeddale, 'I believe will pinch the Highlanders'. Export duties on corn were slashed, and, to make the Act revenue-neutral, import duties on tar and iron substantially raised. And an attempt was made to persuade importers to pay duty in bullion instead of coin.[58]

The one controversial piece of legislation was the treasury commission's proposal for revision of customs and excise.[59] The issue was salt. The commission, prompted by the increasingly influential Kincardine and his fellow coal and salt magnates, including Lord Chancellor Rothes, wanted an end to the exemption provided by the legislation of 1662 for foreign salt imported to cure fish for export. A lot of salt was being imported: 24,204 bolls in 1668–69. The manufacturers argued, quite accurately, that large amounts of salt allegedly imported under the exemption were being diverted for domestic uses, and their business was suffering. They wanted the duty to be collected on all imported salt, with rebates granted for salt

57 *APS* VII, pp. 559, 562–63, 566–68, 574–77. 16, 18 Dec. 1669, Lauderdale to Moray, 23 Dec., Moray to Lauderdale, BL Add. Mss 23132, ff. 186, 191, 197. 21 Dec., Tweeddale to Moray, NLS Ms. 7024, f. 200.

58 *APS* VII, pp. 559–61, 568, 577–78. 4 Dec. 1669, Lauderdale to Moray, BL Add. Mss 23132, f. 170. 24 Dec., Tweeddale to Moray, NLS Ms. 7024, f. 201.

59 2 Nov. 1669, Tweeddale to Moray, NLS Ms. 7024, f. 186.

legitimately used on exported fish, chiefly salmon, herring and white fish –
Scottish salt was no use on oily fish like salmon and herring.[60] Opposition
was widespread, especially among the burghs and their merchants, who
benefited from the lax administration of the existing statute. Tweeddale's
account of the discussion in the Articles was gloomy. The duke of
Hamilton, apparently acting on the principle that the aristocracy should
not be taxed at all, made difficulties but was voted down and left the
meeting in a huff. His language suggested that he believed that the purpose
of the legislation was to benefit Kincardine and his salt-maker allies.
Lauderdale made a concession on the wine duties and got the bill through
the committee. People mistakenly thought that the bill added to their tax
burden, wrote Tweeddale; what it did was to end fraud.[61]

Opposition to the bill continued when it reached the floor. The burghs
lobbied effectively against it, and attracted support from some shire representatives and nobles. The vote was so close that the clerk pronounced it a
tie, to the surprise of those who thought it had been defeated. Lauderdale
quashed the demand for a second vote, and Rothes as chancellor broke the
tie. Lauderdale had won – barely. He had been caught by surprise. 'We were
confident and neglected' to do the necessary arm-twisting, he wrote to
Moray. During the debate he allowed his bad temper to show: if the bill
failed the king would act by prerogative, which drew the rejoinder from
Mackenzie of Rosehaugh that the prerogative could not be used in specific
contravention of a statute. Because the vote had been so close Lauderdale
decided to delay giving the royal assent until he had explored his options.
He would have much preferred to act by prerogative, but in the end he
concluded that he could not do so. Mackenzie was right: two of Middleton's
'damned Acts' stood in the way. The Act had passed on 17 November; on
15 December, Lauderdale officially approved it. The only gainers by it, in
Mackenzie's view, were Kincardine and his fellow salt-makers.[62]

Mackenzie was right once again. On 8 April 1670 the treasury commission
authorised the three collectors of customs and excise to buy up all salt,
foreign and domestic, for the king's use for seven years 'and longer if his
Majesty please'. On 11 May the privy council officially endorsed this and

---

60 C.A. Whately, *The Scottish Salt Industry 1570–1850* (Aberdeen, 1987), p. 5. The figure on imports
   is in NLS Ms. 7033, f. 164. See also the minutes of the treasury commission, NAS E6/1, pp. 216–18.
61 16 Nov. 1669, Tweeddale to Moray, NLS Ms. 7024, ff. 192–93.
62 18 Nov., 16 Dec. 1669, Lauderdale to Moray, BL Add. Mss 23132, ff. 158, 186. *APS* VII,
   pp. 563–565. See the good brief summary by Gillian MacIntosh in Brown and Mann,
   Parliament and Politics, pp. 175–77. Mackenzie, *Memoirs*, pp. 167–71.

prohibited all Scots other than the collectors from importing foreign salt.[63] It took some time for them to act on their authority. They wanted to get agreements from all the major producers, and this was not easy. The dowager Lady Elphinstone, in particular, was obstinate; Patrick Murray could not persuade her. Kincardine was enraged. He had bought up a large quantity of salt in anticipation of selling at a higher price after the final settlement, and now he was stuck with his huge inventory. 'It is a hard matter to be yoked with fools that understand not reason,' he lamented to Tweeddale. Perhaps Lauderdale could make her see reason.[64] Since the young Lord Elphinstone had just married Halton's eldest daughter, Lauderdale was not likely to put too much pressure on the lady. There was also difficulty with English customs officials, who were treating Scottish salt as foreign and forbidding its import, though Lauderdale had obtained an order in council against this.[65] Clearly the scheme was off to a stumbling start.

If the union did not happen, wrote Lauderdale to the king on 16 November, 'I hope you will allow us to do something for our trade,' though he admitted to Moray that nothing much could be done until the Scots knew what England would do about the union. Tweeddale, too, hoped that Charles would actively promote Scottish trade, since parliament had been so eager to do as he wished – 'that he be well pleased with what is done is the height of our ambition and desire'. There were some discussions, and some legislation to switch the burden of customs duties from exports to imports. There were proclamations against the importing of Irish cattle, horses, and victual, a clandestine trade almost impossible to extinguish. There was even discussion of a foreign plantation, but the parliamentary commission on trade, which continued to meet after the adjournment, wisely decided that this was too great an undertaking.[66]

Among other proposals was that for a fishery company, a panacea of the 1630s, discussed in 1667, and now revived in part, wrote Tweeddale, to 'let see we mind not the union so much as not to provide as if it were never

63 NAS E6/1, pp. 255–56. *RPCS* III, p. 166. Whately, *Salt Industry*, pp. 83–84. The collectors received an extra £450 a year for the additional responsibility.
64 28 Apr., 19 May 1670, Patrick Murray to Tweeddale, 14, 21, 24 May, Kincardine to Tweeddale, NLS Ms. 7004, ff. 35, 48–50, 55, 57–58. 12 May, Thomas Hay to Lauderdale, BL Add. Mss 23134, f. 3.
65 5 July 1670, Patrick Murray to Tweeddale, NLS Ms. 7004, f. 120.
66 2, 7, 30 Nov., 24 Dec. 1669, Tweeddale to Moray, NLS Ms. 7024, ff. 186, 194, 195, 201. 16 Nov., Lauderdale to Charles, 2 Dec., Lauderdale to Moray, BL Add. Mss 23132, ff. 156, 167. On Irish cattle see *RPCS* III, pp. 145–46, 1 Mar. 1670, Thomas Hay to Lauderdale, BL Add. Mss 23133, f. 31.

to be'.[67] In mid-June 1670 the company was formally established. The king granted it various tax exemptions and monopolistic privileges, and headed the subscription list, with £5,000 sterling, to be taken from current arrears of taxation. Lauderdale contributed £400, Rothes and Tweeddale £300, and other aristocrats and government supporters lesser amounts. Charles was enthusiastic, and was prepared to supply a warship to protect the as-yet-unassembled fishing fleet. He also talked of building a new town in the north, perhaps in Lewis, to aid its operations – Argyll's father's opposition had wrecked a previous attempt to build such a town, perhaps out of jealousy of the Mackenzies, who dominated the island.[68] The Dutch, predictably, made difficulties. They would not sell any ships, which the company had hoped to buy from them, and fined and imprisoned a man who was prepared to send some people with expertise in net-making and curing herring to Scotland. But there was optimism at the launching – Tweeddale thought they could undersell the Dutch in both the Baltic area and France – and in July Kincardine reported that the ships fishing among the Hollanders were doing very well. But in the end the company, like its predecessors, was a failure. It 'became little more than a means to extract dues from fishermen and merchants' – it was entitled to £6 on every last of exported herring – and was finally formally dissolved in 1690.[69]

In the waning days of the parliamentary session Tweeddale was much occupied with the reports of the collectors of customs and foreign excise. They delighted him: the crown would net £25,000 sterling, remarkable for a bad trade year. He crowed over his pessimistic colleague Cochrane, now earl of Dundonald, who had thought that the net would be only £10,000. Farmers could not have done better: Patrick Murray and his colleagues had exposed the 'ignorance and knavery' of previous collectors. Any others would have brought in £5,000 less. He hoped that the results would please Charles. The estimate was in fact optimistic. The government's increased expenses and the uncertainty of improved trade – in May 1670 Murray

---

67 11 Dec. 1669, Tweeddale to Moray, NLS Ms. 7024, f. 196. 11 Nov. 1667, Argyll to Lauderdale, *Argyll Letters*, pp. 89–90.

68 26 Apr. 1670, Moray to Kincardine, *Moray Letters*, pp. 268–70.

69 *RPCS* III, pp. 175–78. 28 Dec. 1669, Moray to Lauderdale, BL Add. Mss 23132, f. 202. 15, 18, 27 Jan., 15 Feb. 1670, Tweeddale to Moray, NLS Ms. 7025, ff. 4, 5, 9, 12. 8 Feb., Lauderdale to Tweeddale, NLS Ms. 7023, f. 230. 5 Apr., Tweeddale to Lauderdale, BL Add. Mss 23134, f. 6. 24 May, 5 July, Kincardine to Tweeddale, NLS Ms. 7004, ff. 57–58, 121. W.R. Scott, 'The Fiscal Policy of Scotland before the Union,' *SHR* I (1904), p. 175. The quoted phrase is that of Bob Harris, 'Scotland's Herring Fisheries and the Prosperity of the Nation, c. 1660–1760,' *SHR* LXXIX (2000), p. 44.

predicted a decline in the take on wine imports – prompted Tweeddale to urge a suspension of pensions for a year, 'to recruit us'. This did not happen. Tweeddale was mystified that Kincardine, his fellow treasury commissioner, had spoken to Treasurer-Depute Bellenden about reviving the farm. All that could be said against the collectors, he declared, was that they were his people, a comment that revealed his basic naivety. As he would learn, for his 'dearest brother' that was precisely what was wrong with the system of direct collection.[70] For the moment, however, there was no change. In April 1670, the collectors' commission was renewed until November, and a new book of rates was issued which Tweeddale praised as much clearer than its predecessor. As yet he had no inkling of any future rift with Lauderdale. He wrote to Moray on 30 November 1669 that Lauderdale's expenses as commissioner far exceeded what Charles had thus far paid him. He should have a *douceur* of £2,000 sterling, which Middleton had got, and a Garter, which Middleton had never received, to quiet his detractors and fuel Scottish pride in their leader. On 1 January 1670 Tweeddale wrote that Lauderdale was leaving Scotland 'in as good and quiet a condition as it has been these 40 year'.[71]

On 17 December 1669 Lauderdale read to the assembled members of parliament Charles's letter (which Lauderdale himself drafted) thanking them for their good work on the union. Since the English parliament had not yet acted, and Charles was not disposed to hurry them, he authorised an adjournment once parliament's immediate business was done. Adjournment, not dissolution. Dissolution, wrote Lauderdale, would look like an abandonment of the union in the face of English inaction.[72] On the 23rd the adjournment, until 8 June 1670, took place. Lauderdale gave the members a dinner beforehand and then went off to supper at his brother's lodgings 'with good company'.[73] He had good reason to feel satisfied. There had been difficulties, but he had done what he had set out to do. From London there had come a steady stream of praise, not only from the one man whose opinion mattered to Lauderdale, but also from everybody else. If progress on the union was minimal, that was not his fault. He could not

---

70 For Tweeddale's comments on the customs collection see his letters of 30 Nov., 4, 11, 15, 24 Dec. 1669 to Moray, NLS Ms. 7024, ff. 195–97, 199, 201. 19 May 1670, Patrick Murray to Tweeddale, NLS Ms. 7004, f. 50. Lennox, *Lauderdale and Scotland*, pp. 230–32, 316–17.

71 NLS Ms. 7024, f. 195, 7025, f. 1. NAS E6/1, pp. 253–55. 15 Feb. 1670, Tweeddale to Moray, NLS Ms. 7025, f. 12.

72 BL Add. Mss 23132, f. 180. 2 Dec. 1669, Lauderdale to Moray, BL Add. Mss 23132, f. 167. Charles had left the decision to Lauderdale; 30 Nov., Moray to Lauderdale, BL Add. Mss 23132, f. 165.

73 *APS* VII, pp. 565–66. 23 Dec. 1669, Lauderdale to Moray, BL Add. Mss 23132, f. 192.

compel the English parliament to act, and neither, apparently, could the English government. On 11 December Charles prorogued it, 'very ill pleased with almost everything [that] was done', wrote Moray. Arlington, arguably *primus inter pares* amongst the Cabal, was also displeased. Lauderdale's achievement was 'cried up to the skies' at court, and the king 'said everything there is wonderful, as well as he can wish'. Two weeks later he 'brags that now Scotland hath the best laws in the world'. Moray wanted multiple copies of the printed Acts for distribution.[74]

The lord commissioner was tired. He had been working virtually non-stop since his arrival, and had had bouts of bad health throughout the session. At the end of the contretemps over Moray's proposal of the blank commission he was 'weary of this grinning honour; fain would I be at Whitehall again', since the king 'is now master here over all causes and all persons'.[75] But it was six more weeks before he was able to pronounce the adjournment. He had to wait on the English parliament, whose behaviour disgusted him as much as it had the king: 'sure they spent as much time as we, and done just nothing'. Once parliament adjourned he was anxious to leave as soon as possible. But he could not go immediately. He would not travel in Christmas week, there were festivities – the town of Edinburgh gave him a banquet – and a day of private business, more trouble, he thought, than ten days of public business. 'I am old and begin to grow crazy, so cannot come fast . . . where the pitcher breaks, there is an end.' Furthermore the weather was terrible, bad enough to keep the youthful Yester from leaving with the parliament's formal responses to the king's letter of commendation and adjournment, certainly bad enough to make it impossible to travel by coach or 'riding for such an unwieldy creature as I am' – Colonel Lockhart 'broke his leg going out of town on horseback'.[76] It was not until the latter part of January 1670 that he was able to leave.

Tweeddale too was weary, and rather more apprehensive than Lauderdale about the Scottish reaction to the legislation that the commissioner had pushed through. The Act of Supremacy would raise fears as well as hopes, and further legislation on the church would have to await the next session of parliament. Moray thought that Tweeddale should come to London for a policy discussion on religious issues. His letter crossed one from Tweeddale saying that he could not possibly leave Edinburgh for two months after

74 10–11, 25, 28 Dec. 1669, Moray to Lauderdale, BL Add. Mss 23132, ff. 178–79, 200, 202. 26 Oct., 14 Dec., Arlington to Lauderdale, BL Add. Mss 23132, ff. 129, 183.
75 13 Nov. 1669, Lauderdale to Moray, ibid., f. 153.
76 16, 23, 28, 30 Dec. 1669, Lauderdale to Moray, ibid., ff. 186, 192, 204, 205.

Lauderdale himself departed. 'We must see how the country settles after this physic'.[77] He himself needed physic: like Lauderdale he was desperately tired. His letters to Moray in December are full of his longing for solitude and 'a retreat'. He was weary of parliaments and of business, and the humours of unreasonable men, he wrote on 28 December. He asked Moray to train Yester when the young man arrived in London, to lighten some of his load – a previous such request to Lauderdale, 'a virtuous master' for Yester, had gone unanswered.[78] His own affairs suffered from neglect. His election as president of the council was not much solace. And, just after Christmas, his baby son Gilbert died. It had been a very difficult year.[79]

The last days of the session had been hard for both Lauderdale and Tweeddale. There was grumbling because there was so little legislation on debtors and creditors, which many landowners wanted. The only general enactment stipulated that no one's goods could be seized for debt without proper notification – cold comfort indeed for the debtor class. Specific relief was granted to only one small class of debtors, those who had stood surety for the government borrowing of 1638–41.[80] Lauderdale, because he had promised that he would, jammed through a ratification of the restoration of the earl of Argyll, which irritated the many foes of that acquisitive and greedy gentleman. Tweeddale himself did not support it. He was still at odds with Argyll, and his kinsman the earl of Erroll, who was very poor and not a recipient of royal largesse, stood to be a loser by it. Furthermore, Argyll refused to pay the dowry of his sister Jean, the wife of Lord Newbattle, whom Mackenzie described as Tweeddale's 'minion and cousin'. Matters became still more difficult a month later, when Argyll married Lady Balcarres. Both Tweeddale and Lauderdale opposed the match because they feared that the interests of her children, the young earl of Balcarres, now eighteen, and his sister Sophia, of whom Moray was so fond, would suffer. According to Mackenzie it was Tweeddale who prodded Lauderdale into opposing the marriage, but he also says that Lauderdale was so fed up with Argyll that he vowed that obtaining the ratification was the last favour he would do for him. Argyll was quarrelling with everybody, including his sister Lady Caithness, who was casting about for a solution to her foolish and improvident husband's financial problems.

---

77 16 Dec. 1669, Moray to Lauderdale, ibid., f. 189. 14 Dec., Tweeddale to Moray, NLS Ms. 7024, f. 198.
78 7 Nov. 1668, Tweeddale to Lauderdale, BL Add. Mss 23130, f. 104.
79 RPCS III, p. 127. Tweeddale's letters in December are in NLS Ms. 7024, ff. 196–202. See also that of 23 Jan. 1670. NLS Ms. 7025, ff. 6–7.
80 APS VII, pp. 556, 578.

One consequence of Argyll's quarrelsomeness was that Lauderdale began ostentatiously to favour his rival Atholl, who in January 1670 inherited the earldom of Tullibardine from his cousin. That cousin had been sheriff of Perthshire; Atholl got the office and wrote Lauderdale a gushing letter of thanks for his help. Since he was already sheriff of Fife, gratitude was in order. He also became colonel of the life guards, replacing the ailing earl of Newburgh. Atholl was being co-opted into the cousins' regime.[81]

II

The sacking of Archbishop Burnet had some unexpected consequences. In the first place, Bishop Leighton proved surprisingly unwilling to move into the vacant archbishopric. He told Tweeddale that the situation in Glasgow was hopeless and that he was unfit to remedy it. Tweeddale told him that it was his duty to try; he and Lauderdale 'assailed him with that fury as well nigh made him cry'. After Lauderdale left for London Tweeddale and Lothian continued the assault. Leighton was equally stubborn, and equally lachrymose, a few days later. Tweeddale was convinced that only a direct order from the king would suffice. He tried to soften Leighton up by saying that if he declined the job the policy of indulgence would end, and it would be his fault. This made some impression. At a meeting with some of the indulged ministers, which Tweeddale arranged in Rothes's lodgings with various important councillors present, Leighton stressed that all he wanted was peace within the church, and to Tweeddale's great relief said nothing about his unwillingness to take the job.[82] But he continued to waver. Lauderdale did not like the form of *congé d'élire* that Tweeddale sent him and thought it unnecessary anyway, given the Act of Supremacy; the royal patent was held up because Tweeddale wanted a holograph letter from the king to 'the little pope' – Lauderdale's term.[83] The delay, Tweeddale wrote in late February, had started the rumour that the English clergy were unhappy about Burnet's ouster and that he would be restored; 'and we return to our

---

81 Ibid., pp. 581–84. Mackenzie, *Memoirs*, pp. 177–81. 5 Mar. 1670, Lady Caithness to Lauderdale, BL Add. Mss 23133, f. 38. For Erroll see 21 Sept. 1669, Lauderdale to Tweeddale, Paton, 'Lauderdale,' pp. 222–23, and 8 Apr. 1670, John Patterson (a future archbishop of Glasgow) to Tweeddale, NLS Ms. 7004, f. 37. 11 July 1670, Atholl to Lauderdale, BL Add. Mss 23134, f. 67. The best contemporary account of the parliament is that of Mackenzie, *Memoirs*, pp. 137–82. Mackenzie's judgments are sometimes open to question. For example, he says (p. 156) that Tweeddale had acquired an 'absolute ascendant' over Lauderdale. One wonders why he thought so.
82 8, 11, 15, 23 Jan. 1670, Tweeddale to Moray, NLS Ms. 7025, ff. 2, 3, 4, 6–7.
83 8 Feb., 17 Mar. 1670, Lauderdale to Tweeddale, NLS Ms. 7023, ff. 230, 236.

vomit', which Burnet himself thought might happen. Yester, now back in London, reported that Lauderdale and Archbishop Sheldon, who thought Burnet had been badly treated, had a row about it; happily, Yester continued, the king was very displeased with Sheldon.[84]

Finally, on 22 March 1670, Lauderdale dispatched the patent and the royal letter, with the hope that 'our little friend does not after all this shame us all by refusing', and wanting a blank patent for a new bishop of Dunblane.[85] Leighton seemed surprised at the king's order; he thought his previously expressed unwillingness to take the job had ended the matter. But he did not change his mind: he was old, ill and unworthy, and he intended not only to decline the Glasgow see but also to resign his own bishopric, since he and his colleagues 'have occasioned so much trouble and done so little or no good, now these seven or eight years since the restitution of our order'.[86] The pressure on him did not, however, cease. By June, after a summons to London to get a direct order from the king, he finally consented to administer the Glasgow archdiocese, not as archbishop but as coadjutor. This decision disappointed Moray, who had hoped that a nonconformist might be induced to accept the bishopric of Dunblane if it became vacant, which 'would be of vast use'.[87] There was a condition to Leighton's agreement to administer Glasgow: he must be allowed to implement his accommodation scheme, which, he hoped, would lead to the withering away of nonconformity in a generation. His plan differed from the policy of indulgence in that it required concessions from the bishops rather than merely their acquiescence in the presence in their dioceses of ministers who disregarded some of the customary rules. He proposed to persuade ministers to accept bishops as 'chief presbyters' only for the sake of peace in the church, and to attend diocesan synods in which the bishops had no veto power. Bishops were to ordain only candidates approved by the parish in which they were to serve and to ordain them in that parish, and such ministers could say that they were ordained by the chief presbyter, thus avoiding the toxic term 'bishop'. A triennial provincial synod would have the right to try, and to censure, bishops. A greatly relieved Kincardine, temporarily in charge in Edinburgh while Tweeddale was in London,

84 25 Dec. 1669, Moray to Lauderdale, BL Add. Mss 23132, f. 200. 22 Feb., 22 Mar. 1670, Tweeddale to Moray, NLS Ms. 7025, ff. 13, 16. 22 Mar., Yester to Tweeddale, NLS Ms. 14403, f. 40.
85 NLS Ms. 7023, f. 237.
86 5 Apr. 1670, Tweeddale to Lauderdale, 6 Apr., Leighton to Lauderdale, BL Add. Mss 23134, ff. 6, 10–11.
87 25 Dec. 1669, Moray to Lauderdale, BL Add. Mss 23132, f. 200.

expressed his pleasure that Leighton was 'engaged upon any terms', given the situation in the archdiocese.[88]

The second unlooked-for consequence of the sacking of Burnet was the outbreak of a wave of conventicles. There were other contributing factors: the indulgence (five more ministers were added in March), the Act of Supremacy, removing as it did any shred of independent authority the bishops might have claimed to possess, the release in December 1669 of a number of lairds Burnet had jailed for scrupling at signing the bond to keep the peace,[89] an ostentatious crackdown on Papists which the council launched in January,[90] rumours from England about government permissiveness there. All these developments persuaded many dissenters that episcopacy in Scotland was tottering and would soon collapse either of itself or by royal fiat. Tweeddale's distaste for bishops and Lauderdale's contempt for them were hardly secrets, whatever they might say in public. The indulged ministers contributed to the dissenters' new confidence by resuming the practice, followed after the abolition of episcopacy in 1638, of lecturing on scripture before the sermon instead of merely reading the lesson. Lauderdale was irritated; the council ordered them to stop, on pain of being ousted if they persisted. The ministers were 'mightily startled', wrote Kincardine, and protested that their congregations would shrink as a result, but the order stood. Many compromised: they would 'read many chapters and say little on them'.[91] The west country, Tweeddale wrote, was swarming with fanatics and conventicles in spite of the cold weather: 'we shall fill prisons as fast with them as we do pulpits', and will soon 'have a magazine of ministers for foreign plantations', to which convicts were regularly deported. That 'mad generation', he was told, sent expectants to England and Ireland to be 'ordained' at presbyteries; he asked Moray to find out if this were true. 'I be weary of taming this shrew'.[92]

The really alarming aspect of the conventicling was that it was not confined to the west and southwest. The illegal meetings cropped up everywhere – in Perthshire, in Fife, in the area between Edinburgh and

---

88 D. Allen, 'Reconciliation and Retirement in the Restoration Scottish Church', *Journal of Ecclesiastical History* L (1999), p. 257. M. Greig, 'Gilbert Burnet and the Problem of Nonconformity in Restoration Scotland and England', *Canadian Journal of History* 32 (1997), p. 5. 2 July 1670, Kincardine to Tweeddale, NLS Ms. 7004, f. 117.

89 BL Add. Mss 23132, ff. 162, 177, 206, 207, 23133, f. 34.

90 *RPCS* III, pp. 119–23. 1 Jan. 1670, Tweeddale to Moray, NLS Ms. 7025, f. 1.

91 *RPCS* III, p. 123. 15 Jan., 3 Feb. 1670, Tweeddale to Moray, NLS Ms. 7025, ff. 4, 10. 21 Apr., Kincardine to Tweeddale, NLS Ms. 7004, f. 33.

92 27 Jan., 3, 10 Feb. 1670, Tweeddale to Moray, NLS Ms. 7025, ff. 9–11.

Glasgow. Edinburgh itself was not immune: Provost Ramsay and the other magistrates had to pledge again to eliminate them, on penalty of a £50 fine for each violation.[93] The peccant ministers refused to pledge not to hold conventicles or to leave town. So the provost, reacting to Tweeddale's prodding, expelled them by public proclamation, forbade the leasing of houses to them, and sent soldiers to occupy their houses and supervise their moving out.[94] This had some effect, even though, according to William Sharp, some of them went no further away than Dalmeny and Queensferry. Edinburgh was quiet. But Ramsay worried that the rumours from London about government permissiveness would encourage the nonconformists. And on 23 June Thomas Hay informed Tweeddale of a large conventicle near Dunfermline that drew participants from Edinburgh, which greatly worried Rothes and Archbishop Sharp. A week later Rothes, in describing the council's sending troops westward to hunt conventicles, added that on that night two companies of the king's regiment of foot would search Edinburgh. It was difficult to catch the participants, he acknowledged.[95] Indeed it was. He and Halton wrote rather alarmist accounts of one conventicle that carefully planned a retreat into a bog when pursued by Newburgh's horse. They 'laughed at the party', wrote Rothes, and shouted 'that they were for the king, but so long as they had life, they should never be quiet so long as there were fourteen bishops in Scotland'.[96]

The privy council issued repeated proclamations against conventicles and, in March, one against Quakers, whose activities were a growing cause of concern. Twenty-three members of the sect were seized at a meeting in Edinburgh, along with two books full of useful information.[97] But the government's principal focus was still the west, increasingly unsettled in the absence of an archbishop. On 7 April the council appointed a seven-man committee, headed by Hamilton and Kincardine, to go west to

93 1 Mar. 1670, Thomas Hay to Lauderdale, BL Add. Mss 23133, f. 31. *RPCS* III, pp. 150–51.

94 23 Apr. 1670, Sir Charles Erskine to Tweeddale, 28 Apr., Patrick Murray to Tweeddale, NLS Ms. 7004, ff. 27, 35.

95 7 May 1670, William Sharp to Tweeddale, 23 June, Patrick Murray to Tweeddale, NLS Ms. 7004, ff. 47, 107. 23 June, Hay to Tweeddale, NLS Ms. 7023, f. 243. 30 June, Rothes to Lauderdale, BL Add. Mss 23134, ff. 46–47.

96 14 June 1670, Halton to Lauderdale, 16 June, Rothes to Lauderdale, BL Add. Mss 23134, ff. 40, 42–43.

97 3 Mar. 1670, Tweeddale to Lauderdale, BL Add. Mss 23133, f. 34. Two days later Kincardine sent Lauderdale a long and fascinating account of their activities, gleaned from the prisoners and their papers. BL Add. Mss 23133, f. 42. The crackdown pleased Charles; 10 Mar., Lauderdale to Tweeddale, NLS Ms. 7023, f. 235.

enforce the legislation against conventicles, end what they regarded as the disorderly baptisms of children, and consider ways to protect the orthodox ministers there.[98] For once Tweeddale was not named, owing to his imminent departure for London. The committee convened in Glasgow on 27 April and spent a little over two weeks in Glasgow and Ayr, collecting information and imprisoning some who 'positively refused to hear their own preachers' and others who rioted against their ministers. They also ordered one minister to be tried by his presbytery for bad behaviour. They paid attention to complaints of absenteeism, and ordered ministers to stay at home and preach every Sunday.[99] William Primrose, a member of the committee, wrote to Tweeddale from Ayr that they had heard complaints from 8 a.m. to 8 p.m. He believed that many were justified, and that people would go to the official church if pious and sober men were in charge.[100] The committee declined to hear charges of scandalous behaviour against individual clergymen, lest the publicity cause the ministers' collective reputation to sink still further, although they did take testimony in some egregious cases. Kincardine, on his return to Edinburgh, was very discouraged. The clergy were a seedy lot. The minister of Maybole was 'a naughty man', but Burnet had put him in charge of the presbytery. In Ayrshire the gentry were the more delinquent group; in Clydesdale the common people were. Kincardine wondered if Leighton was tough enough to ride herd on these contumacious folk. The committee should have stayed longer, to keep people in awe; now that they were no longer there, the people were 'as ill conditioned as ever'. He wished that Scotland had its own plantations where all the troublemakers could be dumped – after a whipping – and perhaps be made useful. In June: 'Our west country grows madder and madder'; force was the only solution. In July he was advocating an increase in the size of the guard and an overhaul of the officer corps of the army, to improve efficiency against conventicles.[101]

The duke of Hamilton's reports in June bore out Kincardine's judgment. Conventicles were starting up again. He sent soldiers after a large gathering

98 *RPCS* III, pp. 157–60.
99 30 Apr. 1670, the committee to Lauderdale, NLS Ms. 7034, f. 3.
100 6 May 1670, Primrose to Tweeddale, NLS Ms. 7004, f. 44.
101 The letters of Kincardine and other committee members to Tweeddale from late April to early July 1670 are the best evidence for the committee's doings. NLS Ms. 7004, ff. 25ff. See also 30 Apr., William Lockhart to Tweeddale, NLS Ms. 7004, f. 41. The 'naughty man' in Maybole, John Jaffray, was eventually hauled up before the council on charges of oppression and drunkenness; by February 1672 he was ousted. *RPCS* III, pp. 363–65, 431.

west of Hamilton; they broke it up but could catch no one. It was alarming that some of the conventiclers were people from parishes served by indulged ministers. Soldiers in Glasgow caught a few but let them escape; 'they were the greatest rogues in all our country'. Sending the militia after them was useless: the mere act of summons would sound the alarm. Hamilton wanted more soldiers employed – which, no doubt, he would command. The ministers stirred people up by telling them 'how highly conventicles are kept at London', but he did not fear a major outbreak unless there was a war. Nor did Rothes.[102] Archbishop Sharp was predictably gloomy. 'Implacable persons', he wrote, are holding armed meetings and attacking ministers. Kincardine tried to cheer him up, without much success.[103] Only Patrick Murray played down the problem. The conventicles were nowhere near as large as the reports asserted they were, and the militia could cope. There was no need to add to the regular army.[104]

Tweeddale, to his great alarm, discovered that his own reputation was in jeopardy. On 4 June Kincardine informed him that Provost Ramsay was showing around a letter Tweeddale had written to him asking him to keep the malcontents quiet for a month or two, by which time there would be a general indulgence 'or some such thing'. Tweeddale hurriedly retrieved the letter, which in fact said nothing like that.[105] There were those in Scotland who believed that Tweeddale's career was at stake. The problem had to be solved, and in fact it seemed to be getting worse, though some on the council, notably Rothes, wanted to play it down so as not to fuss the court.[106] What Lauderdale and Tweeddale told Charles about the conventicles is not clear, but he did express his satisfaction with the council committee's doings in the west.[107] What incensed him was the report of a Popish funeral openly conducted in Aberdeen, complete with Highlanders carrying torches and swords; he wanted the perpetrators punished. 'I never saw him in greater passion,' wrote Lauderdale from Dover, where the king was meeting his beloved sister. Small wonder: while Charles was

---

102 13, 30 June 1670, Hamilton to Tweeddale, NLS Ms. 7004, ff. 87, 115–16. 30 June, Rothes to Lauderdale, BL Add. Mss 23134, ff. 46–47.
103 30 June 1670, Sharp to Lauderdale, NLS Ms. 2512, f. 134. 23 June, Kincardine to Tweeddale, and to Lauderdale, NLS Ms. 7004, ff. 109, 112.
104 5 July 1670, Murray to Tweeddale, NLS Ms. 7004, f. 120.
105 Ibid., ff. 74, 101, 103.
106 16 June 1670, Andrew Murray to Tweeddale, ibid., f. 91.
107 24 May 1670, Kincardine to Tweeddale, ibid., ff. 57–58.

concluding the secret treaty which was in so many ways the most crucial single event of his reign, there must be no suspicion of any softness on Popery.[108]

In February 1670, shortly after Lauderdale's return from Scotland, the English parliament reconvened. After the disappointments of the autumn session expectations in Scotland were low. Tweeddale thought that Charles made a tactical mistake in talking of union in his opening speech, since the parliament had been so scornful about it at the end of the previous session, but if nothing came of it, 'God be blessed', Scotland could manage alone. In his pessimistic mood he worried that the talk of union might upset the progress on trade represented by the new book of rates.[109] To his surprise and delight parliament was most accommodating. Agreement in principle was reached early in March with little opposition, and a final bill, vetted by Lauderdale and entirely satisfactory to him, adopted early in April, after which the king vanished to Newmarket. The session had been a great success in other ways as well, including a vote of supply, and Charles could now look forward with confidence and pleasure to his sister's arrival. The success was due in part to Charles's decision in March to attend the House of Lords to follow the progress of the Roos divorce case, which he said was better than going to a play.[110]

It had been expected that if the union legislation passed in England Tweeddale would be summoned to London to discuss what would happen next: the timing of the meeting of the Scottish parliament, currently adjourned until 8 June, to authorise Charles to appoint commissioners, who those commissioners should be, and when they should meet with their English counterparts. Charles did order Tweeddale to come to court, and Lauderdale told him to hurry: speed was essential if the 8 June deadline was to be met.[111] But there was another reason for Lauderdale's

---

108 12 May 1670, Thomas Hay to Lauderdale, BL Add. Mss 23134, f. 31. 20 May, Lauderdale to Tweeddale, NLS Ms. 7023, f. 297. The council jailed the laird of Drum because 300 of his tenants had shown up with weapons at the funeral, and he was insolent. 16 June, Rothes to Lauderdale, BL Add. Mss 23134, ff. 42–43. Lauderdale was at Dover only briefly; by 25 May he was back at Ham House, NLS Ms. 7023, f. 244.

109 22 Feb., 27 Mar. 1670, Tweeddale to Moray, NLS Ms. 7025, ff. 13, 17.

110 The progress of the union bill through the English parliament can be followed in Lauderdale's letters to Tweeddale in February and March, NLS Ms. 7023, ff. 232–38. See also his letter of 7 Apr. 1670, Paton, 'Lauderdale', p. 236. Hutton, *Charles II*, pp. 269–70. For the Roos divorce case see Lee, *Cabal*, pp. 110–11; L. Stone, *Road to Divorce* (Oxford, 1990), pp. 309–13.

111 NLS Ms. 7102, nos 8, 9.

impatience to see his dearest brother that had nothing to do with the destiny of kingdoms.

On 19 February Lauderdale wrote urgently that Tweeddale, when he came to London, must bring Lady Tweeddale with him. The secretary's marriage had fallen apart. Lady Lauderdale had finally had enough of her husband's affair with Lady Dysart, and she was going to France, ostensibly for her health, on the recommendation of Sir Alexander Fraser. 'I assure you,' wrote Lauderdale, 'my wife will go 20 of March, and I swear I will neither dissuade nor stay her.' The household at Highgate would break up, and the children needed looking after. 'Your son and daughter are but ill governors for babes, and I am a worse nurse.'[112] All Lauderdale's letters for the next six weeks urged Tweeddale to hurry – and Lady Tweeddale too. She was prepared to come, wrote Tweeddale on 3 March, even though his affairs were in disorder, since the family's needs came first.[113] Bad weather delayed Lady Lauderdale's departure for some days; her husband, apologising for missing a few posts, blamed business and 'some recreation (which you know must be allowed me, though now it is neither gaming nor plays)'.[114] At last she left, taking her very valuable jewellery with her. On 7 April Lauderdale wrote that he had played with the children for two hours that evening, and offered the Tweeddales the use of the house if they wanted it. 'Haste you.'[115]

Tweeddale intended to leave on 11 April, but bad weather – it snowed on 9 April – and Lady Tweeddale's toothache delayed them. Once they left, she fell ill on the road, occasioning further delay.[116] They finally arrived late in the month. Lauderdale and Yester rode out to meet them, and Lauderdale took Tweeddale promptly to the king, who approved his report of the council's actions against conventicles.[117] It was necessary, now, to postpone the opening of parliament, since the king was preoccupied with his meeting with his sister at Dover, and his approval of the necessary instructions had to await his return. On 5 May, Charles officially postponed the

---

112 NLS Ms. 7023, f. 232.
113 BL Add. Mss 23133, f. 34.
114 22 Mar. 1670, Lauderdale to Tweeddale, NLS Ms. 7023, f. 238. This letter contains a long account of Charles's decision to attend the House of Lords.
115 Paton, 'Lauderdale', p. 226.
116 19 Mar., 5, 9 Apr. 1670, Tweeddale to Lauderdale, BL Add. Mss 23133, f. 54, 23134, ff. 6, 13. 7 May, Moray to Kincardine, Moray Letters, p. 271.
117 24 Apr. 1670, Lauderdale to Tweeddale, Paton, 'Lauderdale', pp. 226–27. 30 Apr., Charles to Hamilton, Warrant Book 1660–1670, NAS GD 90/2/260, no pagination.

meeting from 8 June to 20 July, and, later, to 28 July.[118] While the cousins were preparing for the parliamentary session Lady Tweeddale was packing up the family for their move back to Scotland. Lady Dysart was most helpful and friendly. She suggested that the Tweeddales stay at Ham House while the king was at Dover, and she presided over a supper at Lauderdale's Whitehall lodgings. Present at the supper was Richard Maitland, Halton's eldest son, whom Lady Dysart praised as 'a well favoured and proper young man', the first hint that she was thinking of young Richard as a husband for her eldest daughter, an idea from which much was to follow, though that marriage never took place.[119] The packing-up was finally done. Yester, who had been serving his apprenticeship by reporting on the doings of the English parliament for his father,[120] accompanied his mother, wife and children back to Scotland early in July, leaving Tweeddale behind to accompany the lord commissioner as soon as all was in readiness.[121]

Once Charles returned from Dover it was possible to draft the royal instructions for the session of parliament. They were quickly enough done, though delayed by the appalling news of Henrietta's sudden death. Charles wanted the session kept short. Business left over from the last session might be dealt with – in the event there was none, since the commission on the justiciary was not yet ready to report. There were to be no private Acts. Lauderdale was told to get everything finished and be back at court by 1 September.[122] So his instructions were brief and straightforward in all respects but one. Parliament was to authorise the meeting of the Scottish union commissioners with those of England; Charles would name them and set the quorum. It was to vote three months' cess to pay their expenses; if anything was left over it could be used to repair royal residences. These two items were the only ones on Lauderdale's original agenda,[123] but the outburst of conventicling required more. So there was to be legislation against conventicles and schismatical withdrawals from church. Before parliament met Lauderdale was to convene the council to draft legislation

118 *RPCS* III, pp. 165, 187–88.
119 25 May 1670, Lauderdale to Tweeddale, NLS Ms. 7023, f. 244. NLS Ms. 14546, pp. 2–3. Tweeddale, 'Wrangs', p. 282.
120 See, e.g., NLS Ms. 14403, ff. 41, 44.
121 5 May 1670, Moray to Kincardine, *Moray Letters*, pp. 270–71. 5 July, Kincardine to Tweeddale, NLS Ms. 7004, f. 121.
122 11 June, 2 July 1670, Kincardine to Tweeddale, NLS Ms. 7004, ff. 85, 117. 28 July, Lauderdale to Moray, BL Add. Mss 23134, f. 76.
123 12 Mar. 1670, Lauderdale to Tweeddale, NLS Ms. 7102, no. 9.

to this end and for the punishment of people who assaulted ministers. Heritors and their tenants must give security that they would attend the parish church, on pain of forced sale of property, eviction and exile. Those who officiated at conventicles were to be imprisoned or banished. The militia could be used if necessary, and parliament could raise troops for quartering in people's houses. Archbishop Sharp, who was wringing his hands as usual, was to be told to allow transfers of ministers to the Glasgow archdiocese, to improve matters there. In some respects Charles was prepared to be lenient. Those born since 1640, and therefore too young to have been forced to swear to uphold the Covenant, did not have to take an oath against it. Ministers who disapproved of episcopacy were to be left alone if they behaved themselves and kept quiet. Charles also approved a set of general instructions for the government of the church: rules for national synods (none ever held), monthly meetings of presbyteries and annual meetings of diocesan synods, episcopal preaching and residence, and the ordination of ministers, matters which the Act of Supremacy allowed him to determine. Charles was clearly worried about conventicles, and so were his officials on the spot. Kincardine's letters to Tweeddale in these months were full of reports of meetings. At one point in June he thought it might be possible to cut the size of the companies of foot to save money. Three weeks later he reversed himself and wanted them increased, if the government could afford it. When Lauderdale arrived the council discussed whether to raise another troop of eighty horse to police the west. Tweeddale was not keen on the proposal. It would simply fill the prisons and eat up the funds which might otherwise be used to provide for the appointment of more outed ministers. The council left the decision to parliament, which did nothing.[124]

In mid-July Lauderdale and Tweeddale set out for the north. They reached Edinburgh a few days before parliament was due to open. En route Lauderdale amused himself with the captain of the Carlisle garrison, an 'abominable newsmonger' who imagined conspiracies, no doubt to inflate the importance of his position.[125] An aristocratic delegation headed by Lord Chancellor Rothes met them at the border; from that point on there was a sort of triumphal procession to the capital. On 28 July Lauderdale

124 The king's instructions, dated 7 July 1670, are in BL Add. Mss 23134, ff. 53–59. See also BL Add. Mss 23134, ff. 51–52. 30 June, Sharp to Lauderdale, NLS Ms. 2512, f. 134. 28 July, Tweeddale to Moray, NLS Ms. 7025, f. 19.
125 18 July 1670, Lauderdale to (?Moray), BL Add. Mss 23134, f. 68.

opened parliament as scheduled, a few hours late because he forgot to bring the king's letter with him and had to send Yester back to his lodgings to fetch it. His own speech, which Tweeddale called eloquent, declared that the first order of business was to authorise Charles to issue a commission to negotiate the union, as the English parliament had done, and to appoint the commissioners. But the main emphasis of the speech was on the religious issue. The episcopal polity was ringingly reaffirmed. What Lauderdale wanted of parliament was more severe legislation on conventicles and crimes against ministers of the church.[126]

Though Lauderdale complained midway through the session that 'no galley slave hath a worse life than I have from morning to night save that I am not beaten',[127] everything went very smoothly, perhaps precisely because he worked so hard. The union legislation took only two days to be approved. In sending it Lauderdale asked the king to sign off on the list of commissioners, which he promptly did. It was Lauderdale's list, and notably did not include the duke of Hamilton, who apparently blamed Tweeddale for the snub; the latter was unrepentant.[128] The king had asked for a levy of three months' cess to pay the commissioners' expenses; Lauderdale got five, £30,000 sterling instead of £18,000. This recommendation had squeaked through the Articles by one vote owing to difficulties raised by Hamilton, who argued that the nation was poverty-stricken, but in the full house it passed easily enough. After some debate on how to assess the levy Lauderdale opted for the traditional structure. He was acting without instructions on this point, he explained to Moray. He hoped Charles would not be angry, but it made the passage of the tax much easier.[129] Charles was delighted. Moray's letters in August regularly reported that the king and the leading members of the English government heaped praises on the commissioner.

In his letter of 11 August to Moray Lauderdale wrote that the council had discussed a 'clanking Act against conventicles'.[130] Historians have alighted on

---

126 28 July 1670, Lauderdale to Moray, ibid., ff. 76–77. 28 July, Tweeddale to Moray, NLS Ms. 7025, f. 19. Tweeddale sent a copy of the speech to Moray with a request that he ask the king to authorise its printing. There is a very good account of this parliament in G. MacIntosh, *The Scottish Parliament under Charles II 1660–1685* (Edinburgh, 2007), pp. 105–13.

127 11 Aug. 1670, Lauderdale to Moray, BL Add. Mss 23134, f. 95.

128 30 July 1670, Lauderdale to Moray, 6 Aug., Moray to Lauderdale, ibid., ff. 80, 84. 29 Aug., Tweeddale to Moray, NLS Ms. 7025, f. 24.

129 2, 9 Aug. 1670, Lauderdale to Moray, BL Add. Mss 23134, ff. 81, 88.

130 Ibid., f. 95.

this vivid phrase to describe the religious legislation of this parliament, which is unfortunate. It suggests a policy of unalloyed repression, but in fact that policy was considerably nuanced. There were several pieces of legislation, adopted over a span of more than two weeks in August. The first dealt with those 'fanatics' who refused to testify under oath, several of whom were languishing in irons in Edinburgh. Refusal to answer now meant fines and imprisonment or banishment to the plantations. To encourage informing, no one could thus 'infer against himself' loss of life or limb, or banishment. Mackenzie and Gordon of Haddo 'played the fanatics' and strung out the debate, but it passed overwhelmingly.[131] The 'clanking Act', passed on 13 August, prescribed very severe penalties for attendance at field conventicles, including execution for those who preached at them, a 'summary' execution 'without any process', in Lauderdale's words, and fines double those levied on attenders at household conventicles. Preachers at house conventicles could be imprisoned and forced to find caution of 5,000 merks for future good behaviour, or else be banished. The governments of royal burghs where the latter were held could be fined. There were rewards for those who seized preachers, and for sheriffs and stewards of regalities who broke up the open-air gatherings, which the government was most concerned to suppress. The Act was to run for three years unless the king chose to extend it.[132] Other legislation made it a capital offence to assault or rob a minister, and prescribed a scale of fines for irregular baptisms and for non-attendance at the parish church for three consecutive Sundays. Any landholder who absented himself for a year could be summoned to the council to take the oath against rebellion, on pain of banishment and the loss of his estate. This proposal aroused enough misgivings in the council that Lauderdale redrafted it before it went to the Articles, but there was no difficulty for any of the legislation when it reached the floor. The Act against conventicles produced only one negative vote, that of the young earl of Cassillis, 'according to the laudable custom of his father', that stiff-necked Presbyterian who resigned as justice-general in 1661 for refusing to take the oaths of allegiance and supremacy. The commissioner oozed self-satisfaction. He had moved things along, he boasted to Moray, where no one else could have.[133]

131 2 Aug 1670, Lauderdale to Moray, ibid., f. 81. 4 Aug., Tweeddale to Moray, NLS Ms. 7025, f. 20. *APS* VIII, p. 7.
132 *APS* VIII, pp. 9–10.
133 Ibid., pp. 8–9, 10, 11–12. 13, 16 Aug. 1670, Lauderdale to Moray, BL Add. Mss 23134, ff. 96, 104.

This was ferocious legislation, especially for a regime that had come to power because of the failure of a repressive religious policy and had recently got rid of a repressive archbishop whose putative successor favoured a policy of accommodation. In the view of Julia Buckroyd, the most recent historian of church and state in Scotland, Lauderdale's purpose was to effectuate the king's principal objective, maintaining peace and order, rather than to punish wrongful belief.[134] The penalties were severe, but in September Charles and Lauderdale instructed Tweeddale to accept the offer of the friends of two conventicling ministers, in their name, of £500 sterling security that they would hold no more conventicles. The ministers expressed unwillingness to sign the bond themselves – 'some of that gang will not subscribe to the lord's prayer if asked of them,' wrote Tweeddale – but they evidently did, since the king made signing a precondition for his approval.[135] Leighton's plan of accommodation must be given a chance, with the 'clanking Act' held over the dissenters' heads. Leighton himself had set to work, holding synods in Glasgow and Peebles, and preaching in his new archdiocese. He seems hearty and 'no way desperate', wrote Lauderdale on 2 August. The implication of the three-year limit on the Act was that the government expected that it would then no longer be necessary. In Lauderdale's view the situation was nowhere near as dire as had been reported. There was no likelihood of a rising, he wrote to Charles on 11 August, and the disaffected 'are afraid and much broken'. Tweeddale, who on his return to Scotland had grumbled about the expense of keeping 'unpeaceable' dissidents in prison, echoed Lauderdale's sentiment. 'The fanatics,' he wrote to Moray, 'are lower than ever.' When Leighton complained about the severity of the Act, Tweeddale assured him that it was not intended to be enforced.[136]

The political situation in England was also much on Lauderdale's mind. This legislation might serve to reassure the English bishops worried about the ouster of Archbishop Burnet, and the English parliamentarians who had, in their recent session, passed their own draconian legislation against conventicles. In making policy for Scotland Lauderdale could not afford to be too out of step with prevailing English opinion, whatever it might

---

134 For the 'clanking Act' and Lauderdale's purposes see J. Buckroyd, *Church and State in Scotland 1660–1681* (Edinburgh, 1980), pp. 91–95.

135 15, 27 Sept. 1670, Tweeddale to Lauderdale, BL Add. Mss 23134, ff. 120, 125–27. 22 Sept., Lauderdale to Tweeddale, Paton, 'Lauderdale', pp. 229–30.

136 Burnet, *History* I, pp. 506–07. BL Add. Mss 23134, ff. 81, 94. NLS Ms. 7025, ff. 19, 23.

be, and for the moment orthodox Anglicanism appeared to be in the ascendant. Lauderdale knew nothing about the contents of the treaty of Dover.

Once the last of the religious legislation was passed the work of the parliament was essentially done. Lauderdale wrapped it up after two more days, on 22 August. It had been a successful session. On 2 August, perhaps anticipating that success, the treasury commissioners provided *douceurs* for all its own members save, interestingly, Lord Chancellor Rothes.[137] In spite of the king's prohibition some private legislation was enacted, notably the gift of the estate of the late earl of Dundee, escheated for lack of male heirs, to Lauderdale's brother, who in July had become a member of the court of session despite his lack of legal training. He was also confirmed in his office of master general of the mint, and his son Richard, Lady Dysart's prospective son-in-law, was joined with him in it, making it in effect hereditary.[138] This was an indication of Lauderdale's decision to make greater use of his brother in government, a decision that would be ruinous in the short run for Tweeddale and in the long run for Lauderdale himself.

Once parliament was over Lauderdale was in a hurry to get back to London to start the meetings on the union. The English parliament was due to meet in October, and the English commissioners wanted to have everything done by then. The invaluable cashkeeper, William Sharp, loaned the Scottish commissioners £5,000 sterling for their expenses.[139] On 23 August, the day after the adjournment, Lauderdale wrote to Moray that he would go to Yester House on Saturday the 27th for the weekend and leave for London on Monday.[140] While at Yester House he engaged in an astonishing piece of play-acting for the benefit of his unsuspecting hosts: he had left an important document in the wrong suit of clothes.

As Lord Yester later recalled it, he had a disquieting conversation with his father-in-law in January 1670. Lauderdale's estranged wife was angry with Yester because he apparently had no objections to Lauderdale's relations with Lady Dysart, and indeed was himself a frequent visitor at Ham House. She therefore might 'out of the pique she had at me defraud my wife

137 NAS E6/1, p. 269.

138 *APS* VIII, p. 45. May 1670, *Warrant Book 1660–1670*, NAS GD 90/2/260, no pagination.

139 17 Sept. 1670, Andrew Murray to Tweeddale, NLS Ms. 7004, f. 151. NAS E6/1, p. 275. Lennox, *Lauderdale and Scotland*, p. 197. In December 1670 Charles appointed Sharp receiver-general of the recently voted cess; he could reimburse himself out of the take, and collect a fee of £300. Lennox, *Lauderdale and Scotland*, p. 199.

140 BL Add. Mss 23134, f. 105.

and children' out of what they could expect to inherit from her – and she was very wealthy. This was especially likely to happen if Lauderdale should predecease her and she 'be preyed upon for that end by strangers and people about her'. Lauderdale had consulted with the lord advocate, who suggested that he might give Yester a bond for £10,000 sterling (or 200,000 merks Scots, slightly over £11,000 sterling, in another version of Yester's account), which would indemnify him if Lady Lauderdale attempted to disinherit Mary and the children. As a mere formality Yester should give him a backbond of £10,000, 'only for the fashion, that being the usual form in such cases'. The backbond would be payable to Lauderdale or the person he named, and would cover the payment of his debts and the relief of his estate. The documents would be drawn up in Scotland, so that Lady Lauderdale would not find out about them. This could be done when Lauderdale returned to Scotland for the session of parliament that summer. And so it was done. The exchange of documents was to take place at Yester House as Lauderdale was leaving for London. When the moment came Yester produced his backbond. Lauderdale fumbled and made excuses: 'he pretended the bond was not upon him having shifted his clothes that morning, but that he would deliver it'. He pocketed Yester's backbond and left for London. His own bond was never delivered.[141]

What was Lauderdale up to? Simply put, it was he, not his wife, who was planning to rob their daughter. Lady Lauderdale's health was bad; it was foolish to suppose that he would predecease her. And when she died he would marry Lady Dysart and give her what he could of Lady Lauderdale's property, especially her jewellery, worth, by one estimate, £13,000 sterling.[142] And his own property would be hers, including his title, which would pass to his brother and then to Halton's eldest son Richard, the likely lad who was marked out as the future husband of Lady Dysart's eldest daughter. (She had a son who would become earl of Dysart.) Mary's marriage contract provided that the second son of her marriage to Yester would take the Maitland name and inherit Lauderdale's title and estates. But there was an escape clause: Lauderdale, by payment of a rose noble, could nullify that provision, in which case his brother would inherit. Should Lauderdale do this, that second son would be entitled to £7,000

141 NLS Ms. 14547, ff. 141–44, 14549, f. 138. See also Tweeddale, 'Wrangs', p. 288, and M. Lee, Jr, 'The Troubles of a Family Man: The Earl of Tweeddale and his Kin,' in *'Inevitable' Union*, pp. 256–57.
142 NLS Ms. 14548, f. 84.

sterling from Lauderdale's estate when he died. And Lauderdale paid the rose noble, though exactly when is not clear. The necessary paperwork was finally executed in April 1672, though it may have been drawn up earlier. Tweeddale evidently learned of it from the earl of Lothian, who saw the documents in William Sharp's bedchamber.[143] It is clear, however, that Tweeddale knew nothing of all this in September 1670.

However fishy Lauderdale's story might have seemed, Tweeddale and Yester had no reason to distrust him. Everything was going well in Scotland, Lady Dysart was writing warm and friendly letters to Lady Tweeddale, and Yester had just been made a privy councilor.[144] Lauderdale knew his son-in-law; he knew that Yester was both foolish and gullible. And Tweeddale would certainly be reluctant to think ill of his 'dearest brother' and patron. It would not be long before he was undeceived.

143 Tweeddale,'Wrangs', p. 283. NLS Ms. 14549, ff. 113, 219–20.
144 On 25 July 1670. RPCS III, pp. 195–97.

CHAPTER EIGHT

The Triumvirate Comes Apart, 1670–1671

I

Having successfully accomplished his sleight-of-hand at Yester House, Lord Commissioner Lauderdale set out for London accompanied by several of the union commissioners. By the night of Monday 12 September 1670 he was back at court, having spent an agreeable weekend with Lady Dysart at her sister's house at Little Easton in Essex.[1] Two days later a formal session of the union commissioners heard the reading of the commissions, during which, Lauderdale reported in a rather deadpan tone, they all took off their hats. The first business session convened on the 17th. All the members of the Cabal were there, as were Lord Keeper Bridgeman and the future earl of Danby, and, among the Scots, Rothes, Kincardine and Moray. Tweeddale, however, was not, although he was expected. Nor were the two bishops on the Scottish commission, Sharp and Leighton: Charles had ordered them to stay at home and mind the shop while everyone else was away. These meetings had been over two years in the making; in six weeks the project, 'a plot as wise as it was just, and as successful as it was wise', in the words of James Kirkton, was dead, and everyone knew it.[2] What had happened?

What had happened was that the king was no longer interested in pursuing it, and could now convey his changed view to Lauderdale. For Charles the union was a means of controlling a combined parliament by adding reliable Scottish members to both houses in Westminster, but particularly to the Commons. In the preliminary discussions at the end of 1668 the plan had been to add some Scottish members to each house, 'by the rule of quota as to both houses', as Lauderdale put it in December.[3] A year later, after he became aware of the unpopularity of any form of union in Scotland, especially amongst the peerage, he began to have second

1 1 Sept. 1670, Lauderdale to Moray, 13 Sept., Lauderdale to Tweeddale, Paton, 'Lauderdale', pp. 227–28.

2 15 Aug. 1670, Charles to Lauderdale, BL Add. Mss 23134, f. 103. 15 Sept., Lauderdale to Tweeddale, NLS Ms. 14406, f. 164, Kirkton, *History*, p. 178. For the union negotiations see Mackenzie, *Memoirs*, pp. 193–211, and the record of the formal sessions in C.S. Terry, ed., *The Cromwellian Union*, SHS (Edinburgh, 1902), pp. 187–218.

3 Paton, 'Lauderdale', pp. 179–80.

thoughts. It would be very difficult to limit the number of peers to ten, or even twenty, as had been thought in 1668.[4] For Charles the issue, and the union, became irrelevant in the summer of 1670 with the treaty of Dover and the projected destruction of the Dutch republic, which the combined Anglo-French attack would surely achieve. The resulting enormous expansion of English trade, and of customs revenues, would make Charles financially independent of parliament. He would not attempt to govern without it, but he could ignore it if he chose to do so: those reliable Scottish votes would no longer be necessary. In the summer of 1670 Lauderdale – and Ashley and Buckingham – knew nothing of this: only Arlington and Clifford knew of the treaty, with its potentially explosive Catholicity clause. A second treaty, without that clause, had to be negotiated for Protestant consumption. So Buckingham was sent to France, to represent Charles at his sister's funeral and to negotiate the treaty, which he successfully did, triumphantly overcoming all the 'obstacles' and 'opposition' in his way. By 9 September he was back in London,[5] preening himself on his success, and forgetting that he had left that delicious French cupcake, Louise de Kerouaille, awaiting transportation in Dieppe. She cooled her heels there for a fortnight before Arlington sent a yacht to rescue her. Louise was a maid of honour to Charles's deceased sister; she had caught the king's eye at Dover. Now Louis XIV sent her to Whitehall to bind Charles to French interests, which in some manner she did.[6] The new version of the alliance, formally signed on 21 December, contained terms more favourable to England than those agreed on at Dover.[7]

Lauderdale and Buckingham arrived back at court within a few days of each other. Now, if not before, Lauderdale was made aware of Charles's changed view of the union. The king was not opposed to a union if satisfactory terms could be worked out, but he no longer cared. He made his indifference perfectly clear by going off to Newmarket for a fortnight in late September, in the middle of the negotiations. So Lauderdale prepared to adopt an unyielding attitude toward the English commissioners. If he

---

4 See above, chap. 6, p. 193.
5 Lauderdale mentions the date in his letter of 13 Sept. 1670 to Tweeddale, Paton, 'Lauderdale', pp. 227–28.
6 There is an amusing account of Buckingham's mission in J.H. Wilson, *A. Rake and His Times* (New York, 1954), pp. 164–72.
7 R.F. Hutton, *Charles II, King of England, Scotland and Ireland* (Oxford, 1989), pp. 270–73. For the treaty of Dover see M. Lee, Jr, *The Cabal* (Urbana, 1965), pp. 96–112.

could get everything he wanted, the union would happen, but if not, not. This stance took the English commissioners by surprise. They had assumed, and Lauderdale had repeatedly said, that the Scots would accept what the king wanted, and they also assumed that the king would endorse only what was acceptable to them.

Before the king left for Newmarket the commissioners met three times. Charles's instructions listed five items for them to deal with; they agreed to start with the question of the succession to the throne of what would be the kingdom of 'Great Britain'. The English proposed that the crown be vested in 'the king, his heirs and successors'; the Scots objected, pointing to the statute of Henry VII to the effect that no one be punished for following a successor who was a usurper. Furthermore in 1604 the agreed-upon phrase had been 'the king and his posterity'. The English eventually gave way because, as Bridgeman put it, 'they were so unwilling to differ'. The word 'successors' was dropped. 'The king and his heirs', the English agreed, meant the heirs of the body of James VI and I. The Scots had made their point.

Bridgeman then wanted to know whether they should next take up the question of the parliaments, or that of securing the laws of each country. The Scots opted for the latter. It was less contentious, and Lauderdale did not want to discuss the parliamentary issue in the king's absence – he was to leave for Newmarket on 26 September.[8] So on the 24th the commissioners began discussing the laws. Here the sticking point was the fact that in England the parliament was the final court of appeal, whereas in Scotland no appeal lay to parliament from the decisions of Scottish courts. The Scots were unwilling to change this, even with a combined parliament: distance, and English ignorance of Scottish law, would make a fair and reasoned judgment almost impossible. The English rejoined that if there were no appeals from Scottish courts, Scottish peers would sit in judgment on English cases but not vice versa, and if Scottish peers were excluded in such cases, the result would be 'a house within a house'. Buckingham was prepared to accept the Scots' argument, but Ashley and the lawyers objected. So a committee was to be named to consider the issue, but, Kincardine observed, it was so ticklish that no one wanted to sit on such a committee, 'and so all is delayed', and the commission adjourned until mid-October. In the end the issue was postponed, since everything hinged

---

8   22 Sept. 1670, Lauderdale to Tweeddale, Paton, 'Lauderdale', pp. 230–33.

on what sort of parliament would emerge. Sir John Baird, one of the lords of session among the commissioners, commented to Tweeddale that if Lauderdale did as well in future as hitherto, 'there will be no reason for any to doubt of the good success of the affair'. But he hoped that Tweeddale would come to London for the rest of the meetings. The legal question was 'very tender', and the Scottish commissioners would need 'all the help we can get'.[9]

Once the week's work was over Lauderdale betook himself to Ham. From there he wrote Tweeddale a letter very critical of the lord advocate, Sir John Nisbet, who had argued in a meeting of the Scottish commissioners that to propose a union, and subvert parliament, was treasonable. Lauderdale was contemptuous: 'as if, forsooth, he had a negative vote, or as if his vote in such a business were worth 3 pence, let be 200£ and 40 p. per diem'. He concluded the letter by telling Tweeddale, 'If you mean to come at all, now is the time, for on 13 Oct. we will fall on our great and difficult points.'[10] Tweeddale had been kept very well informed: no fewer than five different commissioners, not including Lauderdale, had written to him about the first business meeting on 17 September. He was not sure that he should go. He was expanding the house he had bought from Sir William Bruce in Edinburgh, for which he wanted Moray to find some marble chimney-pieces, and remodelling Yester House, now that his son's family was living with them.[11] He was also troubled about the state of opinion in Scotland. The Act against conventicles was being deliberately misconstrued, and aversion to the union was growing and being stoked by the querulous duke of Hamilton, whose public refusal to attend council meetings was causing trouble. Tweeddale was even more worried because Hamilton's

---

9 24 Sept. 1670, Kincardine to Tweeddale, 24 Sept., Baird to Tweeddale, NLS Ms. 7004, ff. 161–62, 163. Baird, who a week earlier (NLS Ms. 7004, f. 157) had thought Buckingham opposed to the union, was now convinced of his enthusiasm for it. Given Buckingham's temperament, both judgments could have been correct.

10 27 Sept. 1670, Lauderdale to Tweeddale, NLS Ms. 7023, f. 246. Kincardine in his letter of 24 Sept. (above) also commented on Nisbet's attitude. There is a curious statement in Mackenzie's *Memoirs*, pp. 212–13, that when Baird asked Lauderdale if he would write for Tweeddale to come to London, 'Lauderdale, in a huff, answered that if he pleased he might come, but he would write for none', which was hardly the case. Baird's description of his treatment of Tweeddale after his arrival, on the other hand, does comport with what Tweeddale later wrote to Lady Dysart. See below, pp. 249–50.

11 15 Sept. 1670, Tweeddale to Lauderdale, BL Add. Mss 23134, f. 120. 15 Sept. 1670, 2 Feb. 1671, Tweeddale to Moray, NLS Ms. 7025, ff. 26–27, 43. 22 Sept. 1670, Moray to Tweeddale, Paton, 'Lauderdale', pp. 233–35.

level-headed duchess had also taken umbrage. She accused him of stirring up trouble between the duke and Lauderdale. He did his best to pacify her, without much success. According to the duchess, he admitted to having done wrong and promised amendment, but the tone of her letter makes it clear that her suspicions were not entirely allayed.[12]

On the king's orders Tweeddale went to Glasgow, where Gilbert Burnet's preaching was well received 'by the greatest fanatics',[13] in order to attend a meeting between Bishop Leighton and some of the dissenting ministers. It did not go well. The ministers insisted that any meeting to discuss Leighton's accommodation scheme should be attended by all the outed ministers, which, Tweeddale felt, would play into the hands of the radicals. The churches there were currently staffed by 'insufficient, scandalous, impudent young fellows', and the resentment stirred up by the quartered soldiers was more damaging than the helpfulness of the security they provided.[14] Nevertheless the quartering continued; troops were sent to Glasgow and Ayr. Tweeddale let it be known that if the accommodation failed, the indulged ministers might be confined to their parishes and their stipends put to other uses, 'to supply the defect of their withdrawing their concurrence from ecclesiastic government, so much conducing to the quiet of the civil', a threat Lauderdale endorsed.[15]

Tweeddale nevertheless decided to go to London. He left on 10 October, and so was present at the decisive meetings at the end of the month on the issue of the parliaments. Mackenzie in his *Memoirs* states that Lauderdale's plan was to maintain the two separate parliaments and have them meet together in emergencies,[16] of which, of course, the king would be the judge. But the way Lauderdale put it in an informal session at which the king was present was that all of both parliaments should be permanently joined: it was unreasonable that only a part of the Scottish parliament should join the entire English parliament. The Scottish parliament, he said, would never agree to the disenfranchisement of any part of itself. The English did not dispute the logic of the Scottish position; they simply said that neither

12 6 Sept. 1670, Tweeddale to Moray, NLS Ms. 7025, f. 25. 14 Nov., Lady Hamilton to Lauderdale, BL Add, Mss 23134, f. 144. Tweeddale's own letters mention no such apology.

13 15 Sept. 1670, Tweeddale to Moray, NLS Ms. 7025, ff. 26–27.

14 27 Sept. 1670, Tweeddale to Lauderdale, BL Add. Mss 23134, ff. 125–27. Tweeddale, 'Autobiography', p. 98.

15 29 Sept. 1670, Tweeddale to Lauderdale, BL Add. Mss 23134, f. 133. 6 Oct., Lauderdale to Tweeddale, NLS Ms. 7023, f. 247.

16 Mackenzie, *Memoirs*, pp. 207–08.

house of the English parliament would accept such a proposal. The king offered some expedients, but they went nowhere. So he adjourned the meetings until the following week, when 'I think the difficulties will appear so great that no further progress can be made at this time.' Lauderdale, describing all this in a carefully worded letter to his son-in-law, declared that all the Scottish commissioners now know that 'for zeal to a union I am as far from betraying the rights of Scotland as any of them'. Your father, he added, will not stay long; 'I hope it for her [Lady Tweeddale's] satisfaction and fear it for my own.' And, indeed, he had written to her in an almost apologetic tone about having to keep Tweeddale in London for the critical phase of the negotiations.[17]

Lauderdale in his letter to Yester pointed out that his father had spoken in favour of the proposal on the parliaments. In his own letter to his son Tweeddale indicated that there had been no yielding on either side. At the next meeting there would be either an advance or a 'fair retreat';[18] perhaps the proposal that the combined parliaments meet only in emergencies, as indicated by Mackenzie, who was not a commissioner but had his information from Baird. But there were no more meetings or discussions, only adjournments. Tweeddale, in spite of his eagerness to get home,[19] stayed in London, evidently hoping for a break in the deadlock; he did not leave until 1 December.[20] The month of November is basically a blank: there is nothing in the record of that month to indicate what he was doing or thinking. The failure of the union negotiations had to be a grave disappointment.[21] Ever since his days as a member of the parliaments of the Protectorate Tweeddale had believed in union. He had been its most strenuous advocate in the Scottish establishment, his 'dearest brother' had been so encouraging, it had seemed so close to achievement – and in a trice all his hopes had gone up in smoke. He never stopped believing in it. When union again looked to be possible in the wake of the revolution of 1689 he pushed hard for it, only to be defeated by English indifference.[22] He did not live to see it

17 29 Oct. 1670, Lauderdale to Yester, NLS Ms. 7023, f. 248. 25 Oct., Lauderdale to Lady Tweeddale, NLS Ms. 14406, f. 181. An anonymous tract of 1670, NLS Ms. 31.7.13, very hostile in tone to the union, makes precisely Lauderdale's argument; one wonders if he had seen it.

18 27 Oct. 1670, Tweeddale to Yester, NLS Ms. 7025, f. 31.

19 7 Oct. 1670, Tweeddale to Moray, 22 Oct., Tweeddale to Yester, ibid., ff. 29, 30.

20 6 Dec, 1670, Lauderdale to Tweeddale, NLS Ms. 7023, f. 252.

21 Yester said as much in a memorandum of 1672, NLS Ms. 14547, ff. 141–42.

22 P.W.J. Riley, *King William and the Scottish Politicians* (Edinburgh, 1979), pp. 51–55. Riley takes a dim view of virtually all of them but makes an exception for Tweeddale.

come about, but it seems likely that he would have applauded it, and been a far more effective advocate than his well-meaning but inept son.

What made matters worse was his deteriorating relationship with Lauderdale, which was certainly due in some measure to his advocacy after Lauderdale's attitude changed. While he was in London Lauderdale had been positively unpleasant. He 'called me in derision his tutor, saying he would not be tutored in England as he had been in Scotland', ostentatiously making much of his brother, and bringing Halton together with Kincardine and Rothes. At the end of his stay, however, Lauderdale had been slightly more friendly.[23] So when he got back to Yester House in mid-December he tried to build on this and put the disappointments of his London sojourn behind him. He wrote a cheerful account of how he was 'encompassed with children striving who should be most made of'. There were the grandchildren, Charles and John and Anne; 'my little daughter Jean, when she saw me make more, as she thought, of the rest than her, said I am a bairn too'.[24] Lauderdale had always been fond of his grandchildren; Tweeddale thought by this to return to the old footing. And Mary was pregnant again. This would be her first child not born at Highgate. Her mother was worried, Lauderdale wrote, because she would be lying in in the country: Lady Lauderdale remembered that her niece, the countess of Argyll, had died in childbirth for lack of proper medical attention. Tweeddale replied that they were only three hours from Edinburgh and that the (male) midwife was excellent. Lauderdale dismissed his wife's 'impertinences . . . Your lady need not notice them'. Dr Fraser recommended that Mary stay at Yester. At the end of March she was safely delivered of a boy, to Lauderdale's great relief.[25] But by that time the relationship between the 'dearest brothers' had become very rocky indeed.

Tweeddale found considerable business awaiting him when he got home. For one thing, the faculty of advocates was on strike. In March 1670 the commission on reform of the judiciary took note of the fact that cases before the court of session dragged on for an unconscionably long time. Advocates spun them out to increase their fees, and judges connived at this behaviour. In short, the system was corrupt. The commission drew up a table of maximum fees advocates could charge each class of litigant, and

23 NLS Ms. 7001, pp. 314–22.
24 15 Dec. 1670, Tweeddale to Lauderdale, BL Add. Mss 23134, f. 157.
25 26 Jan., 7, 9, Feb., 4 Apr. 1671, Lauderdale to Tweeddale, NLS Ms. 7023, ff. 258, 262, 294, 272. 2 Feb., Tweeddale to Lauderdale, BL Add. Mss 23134, f. 189.

demanded that advocates take an oath to adhere to it. They refused, and on 10 November they collectively withdrew from the courts. The council, perhaps because of the absence of its most important members, side-stepped the issue by writing to Lauderdale to ask the king to intervene. Charles endorsed the judges' stance.[26] Tweeddale was worried, unnecessarily, as it turned out. The dean of the faculty of advocates, Sir Robert Sinclair, a 'very prominent and unscrupulous' lawyer, had hopes of promotion to the office of lord advocate in the reshuffle of judicial offices that would follow the expected resignation of Lord President Gilmour, who was dying. Sinclair took the lead in signing the oath, and gradually the other advocates followed suit. By January 1671 the strike was over.[27] The reorganisation of the court of justiciary, another of the cousins' administrative reforms, was complete in January, and caused far less flap. The court was to consist of the justice-general (the earl of Atholl), the justice clerk, and five lords of session, who were to meet every Monday during the term of the court of session and go on circuit in April or May. While on circuit the judges were either to make decisions in difficult cases or to remit them to a full meeting of the justice-court; they were not to refer them to the council. The office of justice-depute was abolished. The new structure, far more professional despite the fact that its presiding officer was an aristocratic politician with no training in law, was a considerable improvement on what had gone before, and was ratified in parliament in 1672.[28]

Another problem awaiting Tweeddale was a mutiny of soldiers whose pay was in arrears that had broken out in November in the Canongate. According to the council's report the men had received only 2s a week since March 1669; they were entitled to 3s 6d. The council's chief concern was to prevent trouble spreading to the west. Linlithgow was hurriedly dispatched there, money was borrowed from the magistrates of Glasgow, and the duke

---

26 10 Nov. 1670, Yester to Lauderdale, BL Add. Mss 23134, f. 138. 17 Nov., Charles to Lord President Gilmour, *Warrant Book 15 Aug. 1670–30 Apr. 1672*, NAS SP 4/1/20.

27 20 Dec. 1670, Tweeddale to Moray, 20, 29 Dec., Tweeddale to Lauderdale, NLS Ms. 7025, ff. 35, 70, 72. 5 Jan. 1671, Kincardine to Lauderdale, 7 Jan., Rothes to Lauderdale, BL Add. Mss 23134, ff. 172, 168. J.M. Pinkerton, ed., *The Minute Book of the Faculty of Advocates I (1668–1712)*, Stair Society (Edinburgh, 1976), intro., pp. xiii–xiv. There is a brief account of the dispute in A.J.G. Mackay, *Memoir of Sir John Dalrymple, First Viscount Stair* (Edinburgh, 1873), pp. 94–99. The description of Sinclair is P. Hopkins's: *Glencoe and the End of the Highland War* (Edinburgh, 1986), p. 75.

28 14 Jan. 1671, Lauderdale to Tweeddale, NLS Ms. 7023, f. 256. *RPCS* III, pp. 282–84, 301–03, 332. *APS* VIII, pp. 87–88. *An Introduction to Scottish Legal History*, Stair Society (Edinburgh, 1958), p. 411.

of Hamilton instructed to call out three troops of militia in case of need. Fortunately they were not needed. Linlithgow's prompt action averted trouble, though, as he ruefully commented in his report, his enemies were using the incident to slander him, and his own pay was eight months in arrears. He asked the council to investigate the charges against him. In December it heard the quartermaster, who cleared Linlithgow of all charges. Hamilton in his report to Lauderdale seized on the occasion to jab at Tweeddale for setting unrealistic rates on oats and straw for the horse guards and to air a number of other complaints. He felt neglected. Lauderdale rather snippily replied that the rates were set by the council, and that the king had commended the council's prompt action. The affair was trivial and all over very quickly. In the end the council decided, on 5 January 1671, to file criminal charges against only two of the ringleaders, and keep six others, 'profligate and deboshed persons', in prison for the time being; all but one were eventually sent to France. The principal result, Tweeddale observed, was an acute shortage of ready money; half of last term's pensions remained unpaid.[29] Another result was Hamilton's nervous and rather defensive attempt to placate Lauderdale. He had never said anything against the union in parliament – Lauderdale had charged him with opposing it – but only raised the question of the methods adopted to pursue it. And he certainly never meant to suggest that the king had neglected him, but 'if I have not met with it from others than his Majesty . . . many are mistaken as well as I am'.[30] His annoyance with Tweeddale had not abated. Moray's efforts to smooth matters over, particularly with Duchess Anne, were not very successful. She remained suspicious of Tweeddale in spite of what she described as his apology, and wrote to Lauderdale that as long as he was her friend she really did not care whether Tweeddale was. Lauderdale assured her that he was indeed her friend.[31]

Tweeddale could endure the enmity of the duke of Hamilton, which was nothing new. What he could not surmount was the changed attitude of Lauderdale, which was manifested in the first instance by his ostentatious favour to his brother. At long last Treasurer-Depute Bellenden was prepared

---

29 *RPCS* III, pp. 241–49, 255–56, 257–58, 261, 262, 293. 14 Nov. 1670, Hamilton to Lauderdale, 24 Nov., Linlithgow to Lauderdale, 10 Dec., Borthwick to Lauderdale, BL Add. Mss 23134, ff. 142–43, 151, 155. 24 Nov., Lauderdale to Hamilton, NAS GD 406/1/2703. 29 Dec., Tweeddale to Moray, NLS Ms. 7025, f. 36.

30 16 Dec. 1670, Hamilton to Lauderdale, BL Add. Mss 23134, f. 161.

31 4 Oct., 12, 23 Nov., 5 Dec. 1670, Moray to Lady Hamilton, 24 Nov., Lady Hamilton to Lauderdale, 26 Nov., Lauderdale to Lady Hamilton NAS GD 406/1/6102, 6105–07, 8422, 8434.

to resign, under intense pressure and on account of failing health, in return for a doubling of his pension from £500 to £1,000 sterling. When he notified his colleagues of his resignation, wrote Kincardine, 'There was a silence amongst us, and so within a little he made a leg and exit.' Tweeddale later remarked that 'I hear he wept for days for demitting the treasurer-depute's place.' His crankiness and bad temper would not be missed; his competence and honesty would be. Halton replaced him, both in his office, the office Tweeddale still longed for,[32] and on the treasury commission. Halton received gifts of the estate of the late earl of Dundee, who had died without heirs in 1668, and of the arrears of excise from May 1661 to August 1663.[33] He also became an ordinary lord of session, and, quite unprecedentedly, took a seat between the lord president and the justice-clerk, which allowed him to cast the first vote. Tweeddale was scandalised.[34] There was also a new lord president of the session: Sir John Gilmour resigned in December 1670. His place was earmarked for Lord Advocate Nisbet, but he declined on financial grounds. 'He is not one to lose £500 sterling a year for a small advancement,' was Kincardine's comment. So the office went to Sir John Dalrymple, Lord Stair, a member of the union commission, who had formulated the argument opposing appeals from Scottish courts to parliament that the Scottish commissioners employed in the discussions. He had been on the court since 1661 – indeed, since 1657: he had been a friend of Monck's. He had transferred his loyalty to Lauderdale and remained the secretary's faithful follower. He was also Kincardine's and Rothes's candidate. Gilmour feared that he would not maintain the independence of the court, and opposed the appointment. But Stair proved to have a mind of his own, and a first-rate legal mind it was. He was to have a distinguished career.[35]

Tweeddale bemoaned the change in the political atmosphere. He lamented to Moray that he could not be as useful in the king's business as he had been. Past and future obstacles – Halton's rise? – made it impossible,

---

32 On this point see 31 Jan., 16 Mar. 1671, Lady Dysart to Lady Tweeddale, Doreen Cripps, *Elizabeth of the Sealed Knot* (Kineton, 1975), pp. 93–95.

33 *Warrant Book 15 Aug. 1670–30 Apr. 1672*, NAS SP 4/1/29–32, 38–44, 45–46, 305. 5 Jan. 1671, Kincardine to Lauderdale, BL Add. Mss 23134, f. 172. 24 Apr., Tweeddale to Lauderdale, NLS Ms. 7025, f. 86.

34 4 Jan. 1671, Tweeddale to Yester, NLS Ms. 7025, f. 38. It is doubtful that he would have written in this way to anyone other than his son.

35 6 Dec. 1670, Lauderdale to Tweeddale, NLS Ms. 7023, f. 252. 20, 22 Dec., Tweeddale to Lauderdale, NLS Ms. 7025, ff. 70, 71. 10 Jan. 1671, Kincardine to Lauderdale, BL Add. Mss 23134, ff. 174–75. Mackenzie, *Memoirs*, pp. 214–15. G.M. Hutton, 'Stair's Public Career', in D.M. Walker, ed., *Stair Tercentenary Studies*, Stair Society (Edinburgh, 1981), pp. 5–6, 11–14.

and anyway his own affairs were in such disorder that he had to pay some attention to them. Moray in his turn commented to Lady Hamilton that Tweeddale's diminished political activity would be costly to the country: 'Things, I am afraid, will go the worse for it.' At the end of January Tweeddale learned from Kincardine that Lauderdale had written 'a most kind letter' to Hamilton; 'you may imagine what measures I take from this.' Even the lame-duck Bellenden was sniping at him. Moray, ever the peace-maker, nevertheless hoped that Tweeddale and Hamilton could work together, even though they were not friends – after all, Tweeddale and Rothes had managed an armed truce for years.[36] Tweeddale tried to conduct business as usual. He wrote to Lauderdale about the technicalities of the new appointments, Bishop Leighton's unsuccessful meetings with various outed ministers, the renewal of Campbell of Lawers's commission for policing the Highlands, the price the king should pay for the Bass Rock,[37] as well as the progress of Mary Yester's pregnancy – and Lauderdale replied in neutral and guarded language save where his unborn grandchild was concerned. What is notable in the surviving record, though perhaps Tweeddale was not yet fully aware of it because he spent so much time at Yester House rather than in Edinburgh, was that Kincardine was now Lauderdale's principal correspondent. It was Kincardine who reported on the doings of the treasury and exchequer commissions. Tweeddale was gradually being pushed to the periphery of affairs.

In Tweeddale's letterbook there is an undated letter to Lady Dysart, written probably in April, lamenting that Lauderdale's 'way with me is altogether changed and growing to a distance . . . scarce consistent with friendship'. Some had noticed this after the end of the first session of parliament in 1669, he went on, and it was talked of before Lauderdale's latest visit. Since then Lauderdale's correspondence had not had the same freedom and confidence it once had, and Tweeddale's apprehension on this score was one reason for his decision to attend the union negotiations. He could not imagine why Lauderdale was so cool to him – surely not on account of any supposed 'aversion' he had to Halton's becoming treasurer-depute:

---

36 5, 27, Jan. 1671, Tweeddale to Moray, NLS Ms. 7025, ff. 40–42. 9 Jan., 3 Feb., Moray to Lady Hamilton, NAS GD 406/1/6111–12.

37 In January Charles authorised the treasury commission to pay £4,000 sterling for the Bass Rock – Kincardine thought he should pay no more than £1,200 – and later appointed Lauderdale its keeper and commander of an 18-man garrison. *Warrant Book 15 Aug. 1670–30 Apr. 1672*, NAS SP 4/1/76, 259, 262–63. *RPCS* III, p. 392. 2 Feb. 1671, Kincardine to Lauderdale, BL Add. Mss 23134, f. 185.

Lauderdale knew that he had always promoted Halton's interests. Some evidently think, he went on, that he was in correspondence with 'my lady in France' or that he was too eager in his pursuit of Sir Walter Seaton. This last story may have come from William Sharp, he guessed; but he was only doing his duty. He had no doubt about Lady Dysart's friendship – she had, in fact, written urging that he not come to London for the union negotiations because, as she explained to Lady Tweeddale, 'the matter of the union is not ripe for his journey'. But her letter arrived too late. If Lady Dysart could help him, he would be most grateful. Lady Dysart wrote a friendly reply, urging him to say no more about any of this, and he agreed that he would not.[38]

Tweeddale's letter was that of a deeply worried man, who could not understand why his formerly assured position in the Scottish power structure was slipping away. That slippage had become more apparent in early February, when Halton, now installed as treasurer-depute, informed his colleagues that the king wanted to put an end to direct collection of customs and foreign excise and reinstate tax farming, and to do so immediately, a decision that Kincardine, though not Tweeddale, knew was coming. One of the reasons for it, apparently, was that the revenue from Irish customs and foreign excise was much greater than Scotland's.[39] Tweeddale had heard rumours – on 29 December he had written to Moray that there was much talk of a new tax farm and so 'a total change of servants and what else you please to imagine'.[40] He was shocked, not so much by Charles's decision – he was aware that the king had always preferred farming to direct collection – as by the fact that Lauderdale had kept him completely in the dark. His isolation was apparent. 'Canny men will hardly be seen with me, especially in a coach,' he wrote to Moray on 7 February, while Kincardine, that lucky man, had received a gift of all wardships till next May, and a couple had fallen in worth 40,000 merks. Sir William Bruce's syndicate was apt to get the contract for the farm at the auction, he went on; there was no competition.[41] Two days later Tweeddale sent an account to Lauderdale of the excellent performance of the collectors in their first year, when trade was in great decay: only £2,000 sterling

---

38 NLS Ms. 7025, ff. 77–78, Ms. 7001, pp. 311–12. Cripps, *Elizabeth*, pp. 90–91.
39 10 Jan. 1671, Kincardine to Lauderdale, BL Add. Mss 23134, ff. 174–75. On the Irish customs see
      28 Mar. 1671, Moray to Tweeddale, NLS Ms. 7005, f. 11.
40 NLS Ms. 7025, f. 36.
41 Ibid., f. 44.

less had come in than in the previous year. Of the king's other revenue all but £7,000 Scots had been paid in, and much of that was owed by 'such as never will pay till they be compelled'. He also commented adversely on the bargain with the saltmasters: it would be expensive for the crown.[42] He wrote to Moray on the same day that the crown's revenue 'is the best collected and counted for revenue . . . as is in Europe, and whatever change is made I am very sure shall be to the worse'. He was planning a brief comparison of the current situation with that of four years ago, 'to compare with what may come'.[43] Patrick Murray, the chief of Tweeddale's group of collectors, hoped that collection might continue at least until November, when their contract expired, but if not, he and his syndicate would consider whether to make a bid for the farm. If they did, he assured Tweeddale, they would make the farm dear for anyone else.[44] As he feared, the treasury commission on 14 February ordered an auction on 8 March. Rothes commented that 'there was only one of our number for the continuing of the collection'.[45] He was delighted that farming was to resume, no doubt in part to discomfit Tweeddale. In the treasury commission, which he used to dominate, Tweeddale was now a minority of one.

In his frustration and genuine anger at Lauderdale for writing about anything and everything in his letters except the customs farm, Tweeddale sent a most injudicious letter to his 'dearest brother'. He was surprised, he wrote, when Halton announced the king's decision, since he had heard nothing from Lauderdale about it. He recounted, at length and with figures, the excellence of the collectors' work, and their absolute honesty. They are my friends, he went on, and they have followed my directions. 'I have known that to be no bad character with you, and I am conscious to myself not to have offended you in the least . . . I have kept a friendship the most exact and most sincere that mortal man may be capable of.' Since he had never put his interests and reputation ahead of Lauderdale's, he wanted to know why 'you expose me thus, for so I account the using of those I trusted and was answerable for'.[46] He was deeply wounded. For years he had been Lauderdale's chief confidant and chief agent, they had their

---

42 BL Add. Mss 23134, f. 201.
43 NLS Ms. 7025, f. 45.
44 12 Feb. 1671, Murray to Tweeddale, NLS Ms. 7005, f. 5
45 14, 28 Feb. 1671, Rothes to Lauderdale, BL Add. Mss 23134, ff. 208, 224.
46 NLS Ms. 7025, ff. 73–74. In this letterbook the letter is dated 13 Feb.; Lauderdale's reply (see below) dated it 14 Feb., which no doubt was the date Tweeddale put on it.

grandchildren in common, and now, all at once and quite inexplicably, he was out of the loop and out in the cold. He was resentful, certainly of Halton and possibly of Kincardine, the recipient of so many recent favours. Kincardine was busily playing the courtier. On 23 February he informed Lauderdale of the birth of his daughter, named Elizabeth, 'you may guess after whom'. Had it been a boy, 'I guess it had been called John'. Kincardine reminded Lauderdale in this letter that the union commission had been adjourned until the end of March and advised an adjournment *sine die*, which accordingly was done.[47] The project on which Tweeddale had set his heart was now officially dead.

Perhaps Tweeddale was resentful of Lady Dysart as well, although she had done nothing to provoke it save to be who she was, the supplanter of Mary Yester's mother in her father's affections. Lady Dysart was also the recipient of a number of favours, including a special precept the treasury commission signed on 4 February, 'the first she ever had from this country which she has so much obliged', as Rothes obsequiously put it.[48] Tweeddale may not have thought so well of her – we can only guess as to what he had heard about her from his pregnant daughter-in-law at Yester House. Only Moray could be trusted now; he also favoured direct collection, and told Lauderdale so. Regarding the customs farm Tweeddale wrote to Moray that he did not know what the upshot would be, 'but sure I am I have an uneasy life here, and all my designs and endeavours are broke and overturned with all the obloquy imaginable'. Lauderdale was confiding in Kincardine and Halton now, a way of telling him he should meddle no more – and so he would not.[49]

Lauderdale's reply to Tweeddale was measured and conciliatory. Tweeddale's letter amazed him, he said, because he had given Tweeddale no occasion for jealousy. Halton had carried the king's instructions regarding the customs farm, to be sure; since everyone, including Tweeddale, knew that the king preferred a farm to direct collection, he saw no reason to alert everyone else about the change. This was in no way a reflection on the collectors, whom Lauderdale praised. He also praised Tweeddale's work in dealing with Seaton, and he knew that they shared the wish that the king

47 BL Add. Mss 23134, f. 216. 2 Mar. 1671, Lauderdale to Tweeddale, NLS Ms. 7023, f. 266. *RPCS* III, p. 306.
48 4 Feb. 1671, Rothes to Lauderdale, BL Add. Mss 23134, f. 193. In Dec. 1670 she received a regrant of the earldom of Dysart to herself and her heir, whom she would name. *Warrant Book 15 Aug. 1670–30 Apr. 1672*, NAS SP 4/1/28.
49 16, 25 Feb. 1671, Tweeddale to Moray, NLS Ms. 7025, ff. 46, 47. 24 June, Moray to Yester, NLS Ms. 7005, f. 38.

should have the largest possible income. Lauderdale could not understand why Tweeddale took the change of policy as a personal affront and an 'exposure'. 'You was [*sic*] very jealous here last, I dealt frankly with you and thought I had satisfied you. Now you express greater jealousies but I cannot imagine any true ground.' To please Tweeddale he went to the king and asked him to postpone the auction of the farm until the regular time, but Charles would not. There was no more that Lauderdale could do.[50] It was an eminently reasonable letter, the letter of a man unjustly accused, and, as regards the king's known views, substantially correct. But so, also, were Tweeddale's suspicions.

Two days after writing his aggrieved letter Tweeddale had re-collected himself. He wrote a long account of the discussion in the treasury commission on the relative merits of farming and direct collection. The collectors had offered to farm the customs and the salt for £24,000 sterling, or £21,000 without the salt, since, they were told, the importing of foreign salt was to be prohibited. He argued again for continuing the collection until the end of the collectors' contract in November, on the ground that the farmers would gouge if they were to take over at once.[51] But he quickly backed down when he received Lauderdale's letter: if the king wanted a farm, so did he. If it did well, fine; if not, he would bear no blame, though he was surprised at the unusual timing. But he would expostulate no more, since he was not the target of anyone's displeasure. He also wrote to Lady Dysart, thanking her for helping to clear the air.[52] Even before he received this letter Lauderdale decided to make peace, though not before he had written a stinging letter to his son-in-law, who had written to him echoing his father's complaints.[53] On 2 March he informed Tweeddale that Charles had adjourned the meetings of the union commission *sine die*, and asked for Tweeddale's views about parliament, which stood adjourned to 11 May and in fact would be adjourned four times before meeting in June 1672. Nine days later he wrote that he was pleased to see, from Tweeddale's last two letters, that he had stopped expostulating; it would have been easier for

---

50 21 Feb. 1671, Lauderdale to Tweeddale, NLS Ms. 7023, f. 264.
51 NLS Ms. 7025, ff. 75–76, 77. See also his letter to Moray on 16 Feb., NLS Ms. 7025, f. 46. In his letterbook there is an undated memorial arguing that starting the farm in mid-term would cause confusion and was unfair to the collectors. NLS Ms. 7025, f. 98.
52 Ibid., ff. 78–78b. These letters are undated in the letterbook. That to Lauderdale was written on 2 Mar. 1671, that to Lady Dysart later in the month.
53 4 Mar. 1671, Lauderdale to Yester, NLS Ms. 7023, f. 308. The letter has no year date; the content indicates that it was written in 1671.

both if he had not gone on so long about it. If Tweeddale had an alternative suggestion respecting salt, Lauderdale would be glad to hear it – he had thought Tweeddale supported the crown's monopoly. Tweeddale's last letter had been all about the affairs of the duke of Monmouth, who had just come of age: what would happen to his wife's enormous estate, of which both he and Lauderdale were curators? On this point Lauderdale had no news to report – 'God send good from Yester,'[54] which would soon come.

Since the king would not budge on the timing of the auction of the customs farm it went forward as planned, on 8 March. Before it was held Tweeddale and Cochrane, now earl of Dundonald, made an effort to have salt included in the farm; the rest of the commission refused. The effort prompted a vehement attack on Dundonald from Kincardine. Dundonald, he said, had publicly stated that the king was being cheated in his purchase of the Bass Rock, and that he regretted being on the treasury commission.[55] Kincardine wanted no obstacles to his plans for a salt monopoly for himself, and on the day before the auction he wrote that Tweeddale had acquiesced in salt's exclusion from the tack. The treasury commission specifically excluded, besides salt, wine imported for nobles' use, materials for manufacture excluded by Act of parliament, and whitefish and herring exported by the fishery company. The successful bidder on 8 March was Sir William Bruce's group, the chief member of which was the enterprising Linlithgow merchant Alexander Milne. They outbid the current collectors and the ever-hopeful Walter Seaton, whose recent troubles had not dulled his optimism. The farm went for £26,000, without salt. Kincardine crowed that many of them, including Sir William, were his relatives, and most were his friends. If they got their fingers burned, as he had predicted they might, the syndicate was so large that no one would be ruined. The treasury commission stipulated that there were to be few grounds for abatement: only war, prohibitions and huge import taxes. No tacksman would ever again be allowed the latitude granted to Sir Walter Seaton. It was, for the new majority of the commission, a most successful outcome. In due course the privy council officially banned the importation of foreign salt, and Kincardine obtained his salt monopoly, for a rental of £2,000 sterling a year. The principle of farming was extended to the rest of the king's revenues – to Orkney, for example, where Kincardine hoped to get £2,000 sterling a year.

54 Ibid., ff. 266, 267. See also his letter of 21 Mar. 1671, ibid., f. 269. *RPCS* III, pp. 318–19, 383–84, 496–97, 524.
55 4 Mar. 1671, Kincardine to Lauderdale, BL Add. Mss 23135, ff. 5–6.

Ironically, by February 1672 Kincardine was expressing irritation at Bruce and the rest of the farmers for asking for abatements. Kincardine regarded the requests as unjustified, but they were eventually granted. Perhaps, he mused, direct collection was better.[56]

So ended Tweeddale's experiment in direct collection of customs and foreign excise. His campaign for reform and rooting out of corruption ended also, since he no longer controlled the treasury commission. R.W. Lennox, in his study of Restoration finance, put it well: 'Tweeddale possessed the vision to realize that in the long run a permanent collection would be more advantageous to the Crown than farms . . . but he lacked the political insight to comprehend that the king preferred the security and consistency of farms more than the promise of future reward.' He also failed to see that Lauderdale would regard a financial administration that did not depend directly on him as a potential threat. Like so many other empire builders, Lauderdale preferred loyalty (i.e., Halton) to competence if he had to choose. With the advent of the Dutch war Lauderdale and Kincardine reverted temporarily to collection, owing to the difficulty of gauging what a farm was worth in wartime, with their man Bruce, not Tweeddale's man Murray, as collector.[57]

So by the spring of 1671 two of Tweeddale's major policy initiatives, reform of the Scottish fiscal and financial structure, and the union as a solution to divers economic and political problems, had collapsed. The third, the attempt to win over the outed ministers and thus make the episcopal system viable, was in parlous condition. In December 1670 Leighton held yet another meeting with the outed ministers. Tweeddale wished 'he had forsworn it. They are sought too much and grow insolent upon it.' Leighton may have had the better of the argument, but that would probably induce bitterness and greater hostility, and cause Leighton to contemplate retirement again.[58] The major issue was attendance at presbyteries, which had always been an integral part of the reformed kirk, whether or not there were bishops in it. Compromise might have been possible in 1661, but no

---

56 23 Feb. 1671, Charles to the treasury commission, NLS Ms. 7023, f. 265. 28 Feb., 7 Mar., Rothes to Lauderdale, BL Add. Mss 23134, f. 224, 23135, ff. 9–10. 28 Feb., 7, 9, Mar., 6 Apr. 1671, 6 Feb. 1672, Kincardine to Lauderdale, BL Add. Mss 23134, f. 226, 23135, ff. 17–18, 32–34, 49, 143–44. NAS E6/1/305–07, 312. 14 Mar. 1671, Tweeddale to Moray, NLS Ms. 7025, f. 49. The collectors bid £22,000, Seaton, £25,800. *RPCS* III, pp. 310–11. C.A. Whately, *The Scottish Salt Industry 1570–1850* (Aberdeen, 1987), p. 84.

57 R.W. Lennox, *Lauderdale and Scotland: A Study in Scottish Politics and Administration 1660–1682* (PhD diss., Columbia University, 1977), pp. 233, 317.

58 20, 29 Dec. 1670, Tweeddale to Moray, NLS Ms. 7025, ff. 35, 36.

longer. One of the ministers declared that episcopacy was unscriptural, and so no activity that suggested any sort of acceptance of that damnable institution could be countenanced.[59] The parties agreed to exchange arguments in writing, but no one, including both Tweeddale and Lauderdale, expected anything useful to result. The conference was, in fact, a failure. In January 1671 the council reacted by ordering that outed ministers who had been admitted to preach but refused to attend presbyteries and synods be confined to their parishes. There was discussion of withholding their stipends, but this drastic step was not taken. There was also discussion of how to fill the vacant parishes in the west. It was a measure of the government's discouragement that it decided not even to attempt to fill the eight or nine most disorderly ones, those whose inhabitants 'would not receive angels if they committed the horrid crime of going to presbyteries and synods', as Leighton later put it. He was understandably discouraged, but agreed to stay on as long as he felt he could be useful.[60]

Lauderdale approved of the council's actions, but was becoming impatient with the 'unsatisfied' ministers – 'I mean to trouble my head no more with them' – and with Leighton's dithering. He should allow himself to become archbishop, which would then make it possible to fill other episcopal vacancies and have the added advantage of ending the hankering of religious conservatives on both sides of the Tweed for the restoration of Archbishop Burnet.[61] It was not until October that Leighton finally agreed to become archbishop. One reason for his delay, he told Tweeddale, was that he felt that it would be more difficult for him to resign if he thought that his service had become unprofitable. Tweeddale reassured him on this score, and pointed out that his forbearance had not made much of an impression on the dissenters, whereas his acceptance of the archbishopric would strengthen the hand of the episcopal clergy.[62] Leighton's acceptance was a relief to everybody concerned, although his wavering had caused a great deal of exasperation. Lauderdale was weary of his 'melancholy insinuations of retreat'; Moray thought that he 'should be cudgelled out of those whimsies . . . that are unworthy of a man of spirit'.[63] Leighton's behaviour was

59 28 Dec. 1670, John Law to Lady Cardross, *LP* III, App., pp. 233–34.
60 *RPCS* III, pp. 277. 27 Jan. 1671, Tweeddale to Moray, NLS Ms. 7025, f. 42. 1 Dec., Leighton to Lauderdale, BL Add. Mss 23135, f. 112.
61 19 Jan., 4 Feb. 1671, Lauderdale to Tweeddale, NLS Ms. 7023, ff. 257, 261, 26 Jan., Lauderdale to Sharp, Dowden, 'Letters', p. 265.
62 7 Oct. 1671, Tweeddale to Lauderdale, NLS Ms. 7025, f. 62.
63 19 Oct. 1671, Lauderdale to Tweeddale, NLS Ms. 7023, f. 282. 18 Oct., Moray to Tweeddale, NLS Ms. 7005, f. 62.

indeed damaging. His unwillingness to accept the archbishopric for almost two years after Burnet's resignation hardly indicated confidence in the polity he was trying to persuade the dissidents to accept. He was a terrible salesman. But Lauderdale and Tweeddale really had no option. All the dissidents detested Sharp, and Leighton, in the words of the Restoration episcopate's most sympathetic historian, was its 'only member . . . who made a serious effort to solve the problem of nonconformity on any basis other than repression'.[64] It was a Hobson's choice.

Sharp was unhappy with Leighton for precisely that reason: he had offered so many concessions to the dissenters that there would be nothing left to the office of bishop but the name.[65] Kincardine, who now undertook to deal with Sharp while leaving the delicate task of handling Leighton to Tweeddale,[66] found Sharp very exasperating. The archbishop dragged his feet over episcopal appointments, partly because he wanted, and got from Lauderdale, 1,000 merks from the income of the bishopric of the Isles for a library for St Leonard's College, St Andrews. He also insisted on the public burning of a seditious book, *Jus Popoli Vindicatum*, smuggled in from Holland, which, Kincardine thought, would simply make people curious about it.[67] He did not believe that Sharp should be consulted on vacancies: he had no judgment. His most recent appointment in divinity at St Andrews 'looks liker a boy than a master, and sure can have no authority'.[68] In March the council had to instruct Sharp to be helpful in filling vacancies in western parishes if a patron from outside the St Andrews archdiocese wished to summon a minister from there.[69] By May Kincardine was describing Sharp as 'insolent' and reminding Lauderdale that the only way to deal with him was to bully him.[70] The primate was not happy about Leighton's elevation, but, perhaps mollified by Charles's granting him the right to name the judges of the commissary court in Edinburgh, informed Lauderdale that he accepted it, 'though I differ from the new Archbishop as to his proposals for accommodation, not having the habitude of parting by my own consent with the rights of the episcopal order'. He

64 W.R. Foster, *Bishop and Presbytery: The Church of Scotland 1661–1688* (London, 1958), p. 54. See also 20 Oct. 1671, Gilbert Burnet to Lauderdale, NLS Ms. 3648, ff. 9–10.

65 2 Feb. 1671, Sharp to Lauderdale, BL Add. Mss 23134, f. 187.

66 See, e.g., 7 Oct. 1671, Tweeddale to Lauderdale, NLS Ms. 7025, f. 62.

67 14 Jan., 2, 18 Feb., 15 Mar. 1671, Sharp to Lauderdale, NLS Ms. 2512, ff. 136, 138, 140, BL Add. Mss 23134, f. 157. *RPCS* III, pp. 296–97. 9 Feb., Kincardine to Lauderdale, *Laing Mss* I, pp. 381–82. *Warrant Book 15 Aug. 1670–30 Apr. 1672*, NAS SP 4/1/147.

68 23 Feb. 1671, Kincardine to Lauderdale, BL Add. Mss 23134, f. 216.

69 *RPCS* III, pp. 311–12.

70 BL Add. Mss 23135, f. 71.

also spoke of 'the growing disorders and unsettlement of this church',[71] though in fact there was less disorder than the government had anticipated. Earlier in the year it had been bracing for a new outbreak of conventicling with the warmer weather. The ministers who presided over the illegal gatherings were returning from Ireland and other lurking places, Kincardine informed Lauderdale in February.[72] The council ordered the western sheriffs and the circuit judges to enforce the law against conventicles and against lecturing by the indulged ministers, as well as to be on the lookout for irregular baptisms.[73] All was surprisingly quiet. The indulged ministers were behaving well, and Leighton declared that there was very little conventicling. In August Tweeddale informed Lauderdale that the treasury commission felt able to defer until November a request to look into reports of conventicles and irregular baptisms. What Lauderdale wanted, he wrote to Sharp in August, was to keep matters peaceful until next spring, when he planned to come to Scotland himself.[74] In October 1671, when Leighton accepted the archbishopric, there were still many problems to solve – e.g., the filling of a number of episcopal vacancies, including Edinburgh, a critical appointment. There was no immediate crisis, but in spite of the temporary quiet, the policy of accommodation was clearly on life support.

II

In the aftermath of the issue of the customs farm an uneasy truce prevailed for several months between Tweeddale and his colleagues in the government, even though, as he lamented to Moray, whenever he made a suggestion someone always spoke against it. There was, for example, an aged minister confined to his parish for failure to attend presbyteries. He wanted to come to Edinburgh for medical help; Tweeddale supported his plea. Halton 'argued mightily against it', but no one backed him, 'so I had my desire'.[75] The detailed letters that Tweeddale used to write to Lauderdale on government business now came occasionally from Rothes but mostly from

---

71   23 Nov. 1671, Sharp to Lauderdale, ibid., f. 103.

72   BL Add. Mss. 23134, f. 185. See also 2 Feb. 1671, Rothes to Lauderdale, BL Add. Mss 23134, f. 183. 16 Feb., Lauderdale to Tweeddale, NLS Ms. 7023, f. 263.

73   *RPCS* III, pp. 300–01, 312, 347–48. 7 Mar. 1671, Thomas Hay to Lauderdale, BL Add. Mss 23135, f. 19.

74   NLS Ms. 7025, ff. 56–57. Dowden, 'Letters', pp. 266–68. 8 June 1671, Moray to Tweeddale, NLS Ms. 7005, f. 34. 27 July, Kincardine to Lauderdale, BL Add. Mss 23135, f. 75.

75   14 Mar. 1671, Tweeddale to Moray, MLS Ms. 7025, f. 49.

Kincardine, who was getting on very well with Halton. On 7 March 1671, for example, Kincardine touched on religious issues, the adjournment of parliament, whether to include salt in the customs farm, the exchequer commission's handling of the duke of Hamilton's accounts, and the earl of Argyll's attempts to avoid paying Lady Mowat what he owed her.[76] Most of the 'dearest brothers" correspondence now dealt with other matters. In April Tweeddale offered to sell Pinkie House to Lauderdale. He had a chance to buy Clerk Register Primrose's estate at Linton, which Yester wanted and which would have been a good purchase for him – or so both Moray and Lauderdale thought. The sale of Pinkie would have allowed Tweeddale to buy Linton, and he offered to sell to Lauderdale at a good price, so that it would remain in the hands of a grandchild of Lord Chancellor Seton, whose favourite house it had been. Lauderdale thanked him but declined: he had too many houses, and was land-poor. Sir William Bruce was currently at work renovating Thirlestane, which may help account for his refusal.[77] Lauderdale in his letters wrote much about the grandchildren, their ailments, and his own. He sent Mary a bracelet after her safe delivery, a fashionable one, wrote Lady Dysart, modelled on one Queen Catherine wore. Perhaps it was a christening present – there was an elaborate ceremony at Yester, attended by the Edinburgh political establishment.[78] There was much discussion of health, physic, purges, taking the waters – physic, in Lauderdale's view, was very necessary for 'us who have full bodies'. Lady Tweeddale suffered a miscarriage in July – Lady Dysart recommended asses' milk – and in September Tweeddale commiserated with Lauderdale about having a tooth pulled.[79] The one political recommendation Tweeddale made in the summer of 1671 was that of his Haddingtonshire neighbour, Sir Robert Sinclair, for the vacant office of justice-clerk. The two men were friendly, and had travelled together to and

76 BL Add. Mss 23135, ff. 17–18. It is a boon to scholarship that Kincardine rather than Halton, with his horrible handwriting, was Lauderdale's chief correspondent.

77 22 Apr. 1671, Tweeddale to Lauderdale, NLS Ms. 7025, ff. 84–85. 2 May, Lauderdale to Tweeddale, NLS Ms. 14406, f. 212. 7 May, Moray to Yester, NLS Ms. 7023, f. 275. Tweeddale's colleague Dundonald showed some interest in buying Pinkie, but his children objected. 16 Aug., Tweeddale to Lauderdale, NLS Ms. 7025, f. 57b. Pinkie remained in the family until 1728. For Thirlestane see 3 Jan., Bruce to Lauderdale, BL Add. Mss 23134, f. 170.

78 11 Apr. 1671, Tweeddale to Lauderdale, NLS Ms. 7025, f. 76b. 19 Apr., Yester to Lauderdale, BL Add. Mss 23135, f. 54. 27 Apr., Lady Dysart to Lady Tweeddale, Cripps, *Elizabeth*, pp. 96–97.

79 4 Apr. 1671, Lauderdale to Tweeddale, NLS Ms. 7023, f. 272. 27 July, Lauderdale to Yester, 7 Aug., Moray to Tweeddale, NLS Ms. 7005, ff. 45, 46. 7 Aug., Lady Dysart to Lady Tweeddale, Cripps, *Elizabeth*, p. 103. 20 Sept., Tweeddale to Lauderdale, NLS Ms. 7025, f. 58.

from the London union meetings. Lauderdale turned Sinclair down. Sir James Lockhart of Lee had far more experience, Lauderdale explained. Indeed he did: he was over seventy, and had been on the court of session since the Restoration. Given Sinclair's dubious behaviour – he was currently trying to take advantage of the feckless financial behaviour of his kinsman, the childless earl of Caithness, to shoehorn himself into the earldom – Lockhart was a much better choice.[80]

Throughout the spring and summer of 1671 Tweeddale was nervous about the Buccleuch estate, since Monmouth was now of age and could make his own decisions about it. At Tweeddale's behest Lauderdale warned Monmouth against farming it, which would inevitably lead to the gouging of the tenants, and told him that it was time he took some responsibility for his own affairs.[81] But the duke was a heedless young man. He might have left the management of the estate to his curators, of whom Tweeddale was one. Instead, under pressure from his formidable mother-in-law, he appointed a commission to this end; its leading members were Rothes, Wemyss and Bellenden, none of them Tweeddale's friends. According to Patrick Murray, Lady Wemyss and Rothes told him to do this or 'give it over forever'.[82] Tweeddale was very unhappy. 'Consider the club,' he wrote to Lauderdale on 24 April. 'A malicious mother seeking the ruin of the family, a stepfather who refused to be curator with other honest men, Langshaw [Patrick Scott of Langshaw] an old ignorant knave . . . and the chancellor to supervise and laugh at other men's misfortune if he make his advantage of it,' which he would certainly do if he could.[83] Tweeddale was afraid that he and the other curators would be accused of peculation; 'I am sure none of us has had a sixpence by meddling.'[84] The new commissioners were mishandling the estate by planning to replace all the chamberlains and baillies, in some cases with Wemyss's old servants as a way of paying them off. There were 'evil rumours' going around that Tweeddale had enriched himself in his capacity as curator – Lady Wemyss was saying that her daughter the duchess had told her so. This was a base calumny; he had never acted alone, without the other curators. Lauderdale reassured him:

---

80 NLS Ms. 7025, f. 56, 7005, f. 45. For Sinclair's manoeuvres see 9 Mar. 1671, Kincardine to Lauderdale, BL Add. Mss 23135, ff. 32–34.
81 26 Jan., 16 Feb. 1671, Lauderdale to Tweeddale, NLS Ms. 7023, ff. 258, 263.
82 19 Apr. 1671, Patrick Murray to Tweeddale, 29 Apr., Moray to Tweeddale, NLS Ms. 7005, ff. 21, 23.
83 NLS Ms. 7025, f. 86.
84 16 Feb. 1671, Tweeddale to Lauderdale, ibid., ff. 75–76.

the king is 'very sensible of the causeless malice against you'. Tweeddale was grateful, but he still worried that Rothes and Lady Wemyss, out of malice to the curators, would damage and loot the estate – and there was evidence that tenants' rents were being raised substantially. Tweeddale was content to have no further part in its management, but it should be entrusted to people more suitable than those currently in charge, one of whom had been a jailkeeper in Hull for his father, the local hangman. Moray thought that Clifford could be helpful in this business, and urged Tweeddale to keep in touch with him.[85]

Tweeddale did have some cause to worry. He had paid no part of the debt he had acknowledged owing the Buccleuch estate in 1667, and the king, now that Monmouth was of age, had launched an inquiry into the legal status of Monmouth's marriage contract: could Lady Tweeddale challenge it as a violation of her brother Earl Francis's entail?[86] Tweeddale moaned in a letter to Clifford that many people wanted to overthrow that entail, and were telling Monmouth that he was not really in charge of the Buccleuch estate unless he could cut Lady Tweeddale out altogether.[87] For Tweeddale to approach Monmouth now on the question, 'in the temper and disposition he now is', would be counterproductive. All he could do was to rely on Charles's favour and his sense of justice.[88] According to a legal opinion Charles received in February 1672, Lady Tweeddale had a legal case, but she could not go to court before Duchess Anna reached her majority. There was, however, to be an inquiry. In April 1672 Tweeddale received a formal summons to produce whatever documents he had relating to the entail.[89]

In his currently highly nervous state of mind Tweeddale wanted some tangible indication that he still stood well with Lauderdale and the king. So when he learned that Earl Marischal, lord privy seal, was ill and not likely to recover, he wrote to Lauderdale that he would like to have the office, which was really a sinecure. Perhaps if Lauderdale spoke to the king, other

85 See Tweeddale's letters in April and May 1671, ibid., ff. 83–94. 9 May, Lauderdale to Tweeddale, NLS Ms. 7023, f. 274. 4, 7 July, Moray to Tweeddale, NLS Ms. 7005, ff. 40, 42. On the raising of rents see 2 May, Sir Francis Scott of Mangerton to Dundonald, NLS Ms. 7005, f. 29.

86 22 Jan. 1671, Charles to Rothes, Sir William Fraser, *The Scotts of Buccleuch*, 2 vols (Edinburgh, 1878), I, pp. 428–29.

87 21 Apr. 1671, Tweeddale to Clifford, NLS Ms. 7025, ff. 81–82.

88 4 July 1671, Tweeddale to Lauderdale, NLS Ms. 7025, f. 55.

89 NLS Ms. 14544, ff. 49, 63. The matter of the entail and the marriage contract is very complicated. See M. Lee, Jr, 'The Buccleuch Marriage Contract', in *The 'Inevitable' Union* (East Linton, 2003), pp. 223–45.

suitors might be deterred, 'but it may be I go too far'.[90] In his letters to
Lauderdale he was very diffident in his phrasing, but he made it clear to
Moray that he really wanted the job. The difficulty was that his uncle
Dunfermline also had a claim. In 1646 Charles I had promised him the
position when it became vacant; in 1660 Lauderdale had tried to get it for
him, but Clarendon had persuaded the king to appoint Marischal.
Lauderdale reminded Tweeddale of all this in reply to Tweeddale's first
approach,[91] but Tweeddale pressed on. In his letters to Moray he ridiculed
Dunfermline's claims and irritated his friend with his insistence that Moray
make his case for him with Lauderdale and Charles.[92] When Tweeddale
first raised the question Moray gave him sensible advice. Dunfermline
believed that he had a valid claim. He would push for it, and Lauderdale
was obligated in some sense to help him get it. Do not let personal disappointment cause you to alter your behaviour, Moray went on. Treat
Lauderdale as you always have, unless you get 'some flat check', so that he
cannot blame you for altering your relationship.[93] But Tweeddale would
not be deterred. His standing in the eyes of the world, and in his own,
depended on his getting this appointment.

   So when Marischal finally died, at the end of October, he asked
Lauderdale to recommend him to Charles, not because the office was
'invidiously lucrative, but a mark of the king's favour, which I design chiefly
in it'. He would make a settlement with Dunfermline if the king so wished.
He also wrote to Moray in a tone of desperate eagerness. 'I wrote you my
thoughts of E. Dunfermline's pretensions, which are the same to everything
he has a mind to.' His own claim to be an officer of state was better than
Dunfermline's; he would rather give up his place in the treasury than fail in
this.[94] The dispiriting answer came soon enough. On 7 November Moray
wrote that he had seen Charles, who did not say that he had disposed of the
office, but made it clear that in his view Dunfermline had a right to it.
When Moray said that Tweeddale would do better service, Charles said
nothing and left the room. Moray tried to console his friend: Dunfermline
was old and not in the best of health, and Tweeddale would surely be next.[95]

90 20 Sept. 1671, Tweeddale to Lauderdale, NLS Ms. 7025, f. 58.
91 29 Sept. 1671, Lauderdale to Tweeddale, NLS Ms. 7023, f. 281.
92 See, e.g., 5 Oct. 1671, Moray to Tweeddale, NLS Ms. 7005, f. 58.
93 25 Sept. 1671, Moray to Tweeddale, ibid., f. 54.
94 31 Oct. 1671, Tweeddale to Lauderdale, BL Add. Mss 23135, f. 101, and to Moray, NLS Ms. 7025,
    ff. 64–65.
95 NLS Ms. 7005, f. 69.

Two days later Lauderdale wrote to say that he had showed the king Tweeddale's and Dunfermline's letters, and the latter's claims; the king gave the office to Dunfermline. Tweeddale must understand, he went on, that he could not conceal Dunfermline's claim.[96] Tweeddale wrote a quiet letter of acceptance of the king's decision[97] – he could do no other – but it was a bitter blow. He had never been an officer of state, nor would he be, until long after all the others concerned in this affair were dead.

While the disposition of the privy seal was under discussion there was another unfortunate exchange of letters between Tweeddale and Lauderdale. The secretary was in a touchy and difficult mood. The Anglo-French attack on the Dutch, a war which he knew would be immensely unpopular in Scotland, was planned for the spring of 1672. Charles intended to precede it by issuing a declaration of indulgence in the hope – vain, as it turned out – of reconciling dissenters in England to a war against a Protestant state in alliance with the most powerful and feared Catholic power in Europe. Lauderdale knew all this, and was planning to come to Scotland in April to get parliament to vote a tax for the war, and possibly to deal with the intractable religious problem. Lady Dysart was coming too, either separately or in his company. And by that time she might be Lady Lauderdale. Lauderdale's wife's health was deteriorating; when she died Lauderdale intended to waste no time in marrying the fascinating Elizabeth. His skittishness was understandable. On 7 October Moray wrote a ten-page letter to his friend the duchess of Hamilton about the secretary's mood. He must be delicately handled: 'a very small provocation will make him fly quite off the hinges'. He cannot take criticism, and 'the turning over of a straw may serve to lose his friendship, so little is he master of his humour'. If her husband has any issue with him, he should speak quietly and in private, and 'not show any heat'. And remember to treat Lady Dysart carefully: 'what humours not her will certainly put him out of humour'. Moray's own relations with Lauderdale were precarious. The duchess had asked him if he was going to accompany Lauderdale to Scotland. He replied that he did not believe that Lauderdale wanted him there, though the secretary would be happy if he were not here, in London.[98] It was an extraordinary letter. Moray obviously had great faith in the duchess's discretion and friendship for him. He was not mistaken.

---

96 NLS Ms. 7023, f. 285. Dunfermline's letter is in NLS Ms. 2955, f. 39. The king's formal gift is dated 16 Nov. 1671. *RPCS* III, pp. 407–08.

97 NLS Ms. 7025, f. 65.

98 NAS GD 406/1/6129.

Tweeddale's unfortunate letter to his now trigger-tempered 'dearest brother' was caused by the gossipy Gilbert Burnet. Burnet was currently writing his book on the first two dukes of Hamilton, Duchess Anne's father and uncle, which would appear in 1677. She had given Burnet access to the family papers; he was going back and forth to London to consult with Lauderdale and ask the secretary to correct his draft chapters, which Lauderdale did. Lauderdale commented to the duchess in August that Burnet's work was good, on the whole, but that there were errors in the account of events after Charles I left Scotland in 1641.[99] Both Hamiltons thanked him profusely for his help.[100] While he was in London Burnet saw Moray, who wrote to Tweeddale on 29 August that Burnet, when he saw Tweeddale, would 'say things that need not be told till then. Only in general JR [Lauderdale] says often it will be SS's [Tweeddale's] fault if they live not still as they used to do.'[101] Burnet did indeed say these things to Tweeddale; hence Tweeddale's letter, written on 24 October. It began with family news, and then said that Burnet had 'called here [Yester] as he passed' and said that you had told him to tell me 'that it should be my fault if it were not as well betwixt us as ever'. Mistakes are made, Tweeddale said, and he corrected them once he knew what they were, 'after I have suffered all I can by them'. Jealousies he remitted to God.[102]

Lauderdale's response was chilling. He denied having commissioned Burnet to deliver any message to Tweeddale: 'it were strange if I would have chosen him for a mediator betwixt you and me'. He did not know what mistakes Tweeddale was talking about, or what sufferings, of which 'I am wholly ignorant . . . till you shall be pleased to inform me'. He was equally ignorant of 'those jealousies . . . of which you commit the removal to God'. The letter ended abruptly: 'Here are (sic) no considerable news.'[103] Tweeddale could read between the lines of such a message. Lauderdale did not deny the accuracy of Burnet's comment, merely that he had ordered Burnet to make it. His subsequent professions of ignorance were disingenuous at best. Small wonder that Tweeddale did not reply.

Lauderdale's next letter, two days later, was to inform Tweeddale that Charles was granting the privy seal to Dunfermline, to which Tweeddale

99 NAS GD 406/1/2709.
100 BL Add. Mss 23135, ff. 88, 107.
101 NLS Ms. 7005, f. 50. Moray repeated the comment three days later, NLS Ms. 7005., f. 52.
102 NLS Ms. 7025, f. 63.
103 The letter is dated 4 Nov. 1671, NLS Ms. 7023, f. 284. It is also printed in Paton, 'Lauderdale', pp. 238–39.

responded accepting the king's decision. Otherwise there is no indication in the Lauderdale or Yester archive of any exchange of letters. On the other hand the Lauderdale papers are full of letters from Kincardine on the subjects Tweeddale used to write of: the exchequer accounts, the Highlands, the appointment of bishops. Lauderdale's next letter to Tweeddale, on 16 December, described Lady Lauderdale's burial at Clarenton, in France; she had died earlier in the month. Lauderdale feared that his daughter would 'overgrieve'; he would write to her soon. He was currently taking physic at Ham.[104] The letter was belated. Yester had already heard the news from his uncle, William Hay of Drumelzier, Tweeddale's younger half-brother, who was in France; Tweeddale expressed surprise that Lauderdale had not yet written either to him or to Mary.[105] No matter: the future had arrived, and Tweeddale's world would very soon be overturned.

104 NLS Ms. 7023, f. 287.
105 Tweeddale to Moray, NLS Ms. 7025, f. 100. The letter is undated; the context makes it clear that it was written in mid-December 1671.

CHAPTER NINE

Family Feud, 1672–1673

At the turn of the year 1672 the privy council and the treasury commission had the usual sort of administrative business on their plates. Cameron of Lochiel was charged with another assault on the MacDonalds and with violently occupying the lands of Alexander Robertson of Struan. The council ordered his imprisonment when he failed to find caution to keep the peace. The minister of Auchinleck was assaulted and robbed. A council committee investigated and decided that the parishioners would have to pay compensation unless they caught the perpetrators, which they did not; in March they were assessed 3,500 merks. The king granted an additional tax on tobacco for thirteen years to Sir John Nicolson of Lasswade, one of Lauderdale's followers – he was the lieutenant-colonel of Lauderdale's militia regiment – ostensibly to repay the debt owed to his grandfather, Sir William Dick of Braid, for loans made in the 1640s. The auditing of the earl of Crawford's accounts as lord treasurer was finally finished – he had left office in 1662 – and sent off to London. Lauderdale had to remind Hamilton that he had not finished accounting for the arrears of the taxation of 1633, of which his father-in-law, the first duke, had been the collector. The council rejected a challenge to the monopoly of Andrew Anderson as king's printer, but limited it in a way that satisfied all but one Glasgow printer, 'a most obstinate fellow', in Kincardine's opinion. The bishopric of Edinburgh needed filling. Leighton's inauguration as archbishop of Glasgow had to be appropriately staged. Sharp was being difficult, as usual: Kincardine asked Lauderdale to order him to preside over the inauguration. And in February the council decided to cancel the circuit courts, scheduled for the spring in accordance with the recent reorganisation of the court of justiciary, since parliament was due to meet in April. The postponement became an annual event; the judges never went on circuit until the early eighteenth century.[1]

Among other matters the council on 14 December duly noted Lauderdale's appointment as its president, a post Tweeddale had previously

---

[1] For the activity of the council and the treasury commission in these months see *RPCS* III, pp. 416 ff., and Kincardine's letters to Lauderdale in Dec. 1671, BL Add. Mss 23135, ff. 114–15, 118, 120–22. 30 Jan. 1672, Lauderdale to Hamilton, NAS GD 406/1/2711. For Nicolson's grant see NAS SP 4/1/314–20.

held in the absence of Lord Chancellor Rothes, who was himself now superseded.² Tweeddale scarcely noticed, save to chide Moray for not letting him know about it.³ His all-consuming preoccupation, now that Lady Lauderdale was dead, was to safeguard Mary's inheritance. This meant sending Yester to London at once, both to condole with his father-in-law and to look after his wife's interests. Mary was pregnant again, and could not go herself. Moray urged haste, and hasten Yester did. He arrived early in January, and proceeded to play into Lauderdale's hands.

On the first news of his wife's illness Lauderdale sent an agent, Patrick Vaus, and then his secretary, Andrew Forrester, to Paris. Their objective was to lay hands on Lady Lauderdale's jewels and movables, which she bequeathed to Mary in her will. They coerced her companion, Lady Boghall, into handing them over, on the ground that by French law Lady Lauderdale could not make a valid will without her husband's consent. It might have been possible to argue this point, since for centuries, thanks to the Auld Alliance, Scots had such privileges as denizens of France. But practically it was impossible: the courts of Louis XIV were not going to hand down a judgment that would offend one of King Charles's principal ministers on the eve of the launching of the long-planned war against the Dutch. Vaus and Forrester had the invaluable help of Sir George Douglas, the commander of a regiment in French service, who was made a gift of Lady Lauderdale's coach and horses for his trouble. Douglas was useful in another way: his mistress, Mlle du Four, helped Vaus to assemble the future Lady Lauderdale's wedding clothes. The best material available was being used. 'What fine lady his lordship intends to regale is not known, but it is probable that she will be of my Lady Dysart's stature, for I am told for certain that the gowns were made to her measure . . . It seems that my L. Lauderdale intends that somebody shall rejoice, mourn who pleaseth.'

These were the comments of William Hay of Drumelzier in separate letters to Tweeddale and Yester written on 27 January.⁴ He wrote an account of Lady Lauderdale's funeral to Yester, and offered to help in whatever way he could. But he received no instructions from Yester until it was too late – after Lauderdale's death Yester claimed that Lauderdale had intercepted his letter to Drumelzier. Forrester and Vaus seized everything and were back in London by mid-January. Marshal Schomberg, who had offered to keep

2 *RPCS* III, pp. 416–17. The king's order was dated 24 Nov. 1671.
3 26 Dec. 1671, Moray to Tweeddale, NLS Ms. 7005, f. 91.
4 Drumelzier to Tweeddale, ibid., f. 97, and to Yester, NLS Ms. 14414, f. 15.

Lady Lauderdale's jewels instead of Lady Boghall, said that there was now no point in trying to accomplish anything in France. What Yester must do was deal directly with Lauderdale in London.[5] Those dealings were hardly very helpful. Lauderdale was smooth as butter, and Yester allowed himself to be taken in. Mary's entail had not been disturbed, Lauderdale said. His late wife's will was of questionable validity, but he expected to get a gift of all of her property directly from Louis XIV. (He had been in touch with Colbert about this, according to Drumelzier.) Lauderdale preferred, he said, to give the jewels to Mary himself. It was indeed true, he told Yester, that he intended to wed Lady Dysart in February, before Lent, when it would not be possible to marry, but the marriage would in no way diminish his affection for his daughter and grandchildren. Mary would in fact get more good things directly from him than she would have got from her mother. He wanted to take his new wife with him to Scotland for the impending session of parliament: hence the rapid marriage, according to Lady Dysart.[6] Yester professed himself satisfied, and told Lauderdale that he would leave everything in his hands. As he explained to his parents, there was really nothing else he could do. Those parents were not at all pleased. They berated him for his weakness and stupidity in allowing his resentment at Lauderdale's behaviour to show, and told him to come home before he did anything really stupid.[7] He hastily assured them that he had signed nothing. But he was not much bothered by Lauderdale's extremely generous marriage contract and his stalling over the backband when Yester asked for it. He went home in February apparently entirely unworried.[8]

So Tweeddale was compelled to put the best face possible on the family's relations with Lauderdale under the new circumstances. He took some encouragement from the fact that Lauderdale's December letter announcing his wife's death was more familiar and friendly in tone than the chilling putdown of 4 November. He did his best to butter up the new Lady Lauderdale, wrote a congratulatory note to her husband when Charles gave him a Garter and a dukedom, and got a correct thank-you for

---

5 Drumelzier's letters to Yester from France in Dec. 1671 and Jan. 1672 are in NLS Ms. 14414. ff. 1–15. Schomberg's comment is in that of 14 Jan., ff. 11–12. See also Tweeddale, 'Wrangs', pp. 286–87, and 18 Jan. 1672, Lauderdale to the duchess of Hamilton, NAS GD 406/1/8426. For Yester's claim see NLS Ms. 14549, ff. 209–10, and also Ms. 14547, ff. 143–44.

6 23 Jan. 1672, Lady Dysart to Halton, quoted in D. Cripps, *Elizabeth of the Sealed Knot* (Kineton, 1975), pp, 110–11.

7 They both wrote on 16 Jan. 1672; NAS Ms. 14413, ff. 12–13, 22–23.

8 Yester's letters to his father in Jan. and Feb. 1672 are in NLS Ms. 14403, ff. 48–70.

his pains.[9] Moray kept urging him to come to London. He was entirely sympathetic to Tweeddale; he regarded the breach as Lauderdale's doing, 'groundlessly made and unjustly kept up'. Before Lady Lauderdale's death he had urged that Tweeddale 'should take more pains to keep right' with the secretary by being very careful not to take offence and writing as before: 'all might quickly fall right again'. But at this point Moray could not act as mediator and involve the king unless Tweeddale were in London.[10] His own influence with Lauderdale was gone. In a long and bitter letter to the duchess of Hamilton he indicated that Lauderdale had cut him off. 'You know well enough the Commissioner stands as high in his pride as any creature can do,' and turns on all those who are not sufficiently deferential to his brother.[11] Mackenzie, followed by many modern scholars, attributes the break between the two to Moray's opposition to Lauderdale's remarriage.[12] How Mackenzie knew this is not clear. None of the principals was likely to confide in him, and he was not in London. It seems more likely that Lauderdale's treatment of Tweeddale, and of his daughter and Yester, Moray's protégé, was responsible.

Tweeddale did not go to London. Yester did, however; he arrived there in June, by which time Lauderdale had left for Scotland, in order to deal with the real estate Mary had inherited, one part of her mother's property on which Lauderdale could not lay his hands. Lauderdale was slow to relinquish the houses, not doing so until 28 September. In the meantime he collected the rents and provided no maintenance. The house in Highgate, which Moray urged Yester to sell, was in particularly bad shape. There would be large bills for repairs, both there and at the Aldersgate Street properties. Among other things, according to Yester's subsequent account, Lauderdale had dug up the fruit trees at Highgate and moved them to Ham House.[13]

Tweeddale made a tactical mistake in not taking Moray's advice. Fatherly affection seems to have caused him to overestimate his son's capacities, an error he was frequently to repeat. Getting Yester to act vigorously was 'like

9 9 May 1672, Lauderdale to Tweeddale, Paton, 'Lauderdale', pp. 239–40. See also NLS Ms. 7025, ff. 101–03b.

10 1 Dec. 1671, Moray to Yester, 1 Feb., 9, 13 Apr. 1672, Moray to Tweeddale, NLS Ms. 7005, ff. 79, 99, 126, 130.

11 The letter was written on 19 June 1672, NAS GD 406/1/6136.

12 Mackenzie, *Memoirs*, pp. 217–18.

13 NLS Ms. 14547, ff. 141–42, 145–46, 171, 178–86, 196–97. See also 17 Oct. 1672, Andrew Hay to Lady Tweeddale, NLS Ms. 7005, ff. 188–89, and n.d., Moray to Yester, NLS Ms. 7023, f. 301.

digging with a wet sponge'.[14] He had reason, however, not to leave
Edinburgh: the impending war. In January Charles indicated that the
Scottish government should find 1,000 soldiers to serve in England. The
treasury commission protested: the government simply could not afford
the expense. Money was scarce, and would be scarcer still in wartime: the
last war, said the commission, had cut revenue by one third. The coast
would need defending, and the enemy would stir up the religiously disaffected.[15] The pleas got nowhere. On 22 February Charles formally issued
the order, accompanying it by a promise that the crews of Scottish
merchant ships would not be pressed into service in the English navy.[16] So
the council issued the necessary instructions, and also ordered the
mustering of the shire militias. Shires were given quotas of men to raise.
They were to be given 'blue coats lined with white, and have hats', and
rendezvous at Leith or Burntisland on 1 May. When war was officially
declared in March Charles ordered that an additional 500 men be drafted,
sailors this time – the council apportioned them amongst the burghs – and
that they and the soldiers be sent by land to Newcastle.[17] The council
demurred. The men should go by ship: there were no guards available, and
too many would desert during an overland march. They asked Lauderdale
to be sure that the sailors on the ships transporting the draftees not be
pressed, a very necessary request, which Charles granted, since it turned
out to be impossible to find 500 sailors. In the end some 1,100 men were
sent by sea in mid-May. The council fined the shires and towns that failed
to meet their quotas. The earl of Linlithgow had to supply 200 men from
his own regiment, which he was plainly reluctant to do.[18] Charles was not
altogether happy, and in August, after parliament had voted the tax money
he wanted for the war, he demanded 200 men to help make up the shortfall; in March 1673 he wanted 900 more.[19] This new war, with one of
Scotland's major trading partners, was generating no enthusiasm.

14 The phrase is from P.W.J. Riley, *King William and the Scottish Politicians* (Edinburgh, 1979),
   p. 50, commenting on Tweeddale's entrusting Yester with a mission to King William in 1689.
15 18 Jan. 1672, the treasury commission to Lauderdale, BL Add. Mss 23135, f. 132.
16 *RPCS* III, pp. 473–74. 29 Feb. 1672, Kincardine to Lauderdale, BL Add. Mss 23135, ff. 147–48.
17 *RPCS* III, pp. 478–80, 487–90, 499–503, 510.
18 Ibid., pp. 510–16, 522–23, 527–32. 8 Apr. 1672, Andrew Murray to Tweeddale, NLS Ms. 7005,
   f. 124. 17 Apr., the council to Lauderdale, 23 Apr., Linlithgow to Lauderdale, BL Add. Mss 23135,
   ff. 155, 160.
19 *RPCS* III, pp. 579–80, 594, IV, pp. 33–34.

If the war was less than popular, the king's declaration of indulgence, which accompanied its formal beginning in mid-March, caused the government positive alarm. The declaration suspended the penal laws against non-Anglicans, granted Protestant nonconformists the right to hold public worship on receipt of a licence, and Catholics the right to worship privately in their homes. It applied only to England; Lauderdale had argued in vain in the foreign committee for a document that would apply to all of Charles's kingdoms. Had he prevailed the Scottish church would have been enormously changed. 'Indulgence' in Scotland had meant bringing dissident ministers (and their followers) into the church by law established. Charles's indulgence legitimated services outwith the established church – almost, but not quite, the licensing of conventicles. No wonder it caused a stir, and raised hopes, in an unsettled polity. The council was concerned about conventicles in Glasgow, though Leighton was encouraged by his recent conferences with dissenting ministers. Some of them had indicated that they might be willing to attend presbyteries, though not synods. But there was the Auchinleck affair, and Papist activity in the northeast: Mass held openly, baptisms, marriages 'with a bagpiper before them', wrote Kincardine. He was not hopeful that anything could be done in religious questions until Lauderdale arrived in Scotland.[20] The council ordered a crackdown on both Papists and Quakers. It imprisoned Lord Sempill for sending his second son to the seminary at Douai; he was released after finding caution of 10,000 merks to send his third son to Glasgow University.[21]

As might have been expected, the news of the indulgence caused 'wild and disaffected persons' to agitate for a toleration for Presbyterians, in Scotland as in England.[22] Archbishop Sharp, on this occasion understandably gloomy, wrote to Lauderdale that he counted on the secretary's continuing support for the bishops, fearing the 'great depression of the episcopal order by the late publication of his majesty's pleasure in matters of religion'. Places previously quiet may witness disturbances now, he added. And he once more expressed his distaste for the Scottish indulgence, which, he said with gross exaggeration, gave considerably more to nonconformists than the king's recent proclamation.[23] On one point at least Sharp was entirely

---

20 See his letters of 6 and 29 Feb. 1672, BL Add. Mss 23135, ff. 143–44, 147–48; n.d., Leighton to Lauderdale, BL Add. Mss 23135, f. 189.
21 *RCPS* III, pp. 463–64, 476, 480–82.
22 W. Mackay, ed., *Chronicles of the Frasers*, SHS (Edinburgh, 1905), pp. 499–500.
23 6 Apr. 1672, Sharp to Lauderdale, NLS Ms. 2512, f. 148.

wrong: Charles's declaration allowed Catholics to worship freely in private, which was never permitted in Scotland. It can be argued that this permission merely recognised existing practice, in Scotland as well as in England, but the king's saying so made all the difference. The declaration 'appears to have been a deep Popish design to procure indulgence to Presbyterians that they might make way for toleration of Popery', wrote the diarist Alexander Brodie.[24]

Moray, who complained to Tweeddale that Lauderdale told him nothing about anything, was extremely curious about Scottish reaction to the declaration. What the king had granted to English nonconformists should be handled differently in Scotland, he thought. Once again he urged Tweeddale to come to London before Lauderdale left for Scotland, in order to discuss the religious issue, and bring Leighton with him. He knew that Tweeddale would be sympathetic to the principle of the indulgence, which would please Charles. And then, perhaps, he and Lauderdale could get back on the old footing again. But he must hurry: Lauderdale would be leaving soon, and after that there would be no hope of adjusting their differences, though Moray would not 'give over what I think fit to be done till the roof tree fall'. He thanked Tweeddale for his information about the receipt of the indulgence. Charles's 'mind is either little known there or not considered', he thought. Those who talk wildly against it should be 'taken up roundly'. On 6 April Tweeddale wrote once again that it would be impossible for him to leave until May, perhaps because Mary was due then, and he seems to have resorted to a curious ploy. He later claimed that he received no answers to his letters of 2 and 6 April, although Moray's replies, dated 9 and 13 April, are in the Yester papers.[25] Moray thought that they might have been intercepted, a not unreasonable supposition, given Lauderdale's attitude to the two men. By 23 May, when Moray floated this speculation, it was too late: Lauderdale and his duchess were about to depart. He had one more piece of gloomy news for Tweeddale. Uncle Dunfermline, so recently elevated to lord privy seal, had died earlier that month. Moray spoke to the king on Tweeddale's behalf as soon as he heard the news. Charles said that he would 'look about him before he dispose of his place' – a polite way of saying no.[26]

24 D. Laing, ed., *The Diary of Alexander Brodie*, Spalding Club (Aberdeen, 1863), p. 327.
25 Moray's letters to Tweeddale after the issuing of the indulgence, dated 16 Mar., 6, 9, 13 Apr., and 23 May 1672, are in NLS Ms. 7005, ff 100, 122, 126, 130, 143–44.
26 Ibid., ff. 143–44.

Moray's letter of 23 May had one more piece of intelligence for Tweeddale: Kincardine had arrived in London. He was so busy at court that Moray had had no time to talk to him at any length, but, said Moray, he spoke well of you. Kincardine was busy receiving instructions. He was to take Moray's place as secretary while Lauderdale was in Scotland,[27] an indication of how completely Lauderdale had broken with his old friend and colleague. Moray was sad that Kincardine, a still older friend, had not told him of this, perhaps out of embarrassment. Moray was philosophical: the job was burdensome and unprofitable, and gave him no more access to the king than he already had. He understood Kincardine's situation: his estate was on the brink of ruin, and if he did not want to leave his children beggars he had to curry favour with Lauderdale. If he lost that favour, which was not easy to keep, 'he is undone'. For all that, Moray concluded, he believed that Kincardine liked him better than he did Lauderdale.[28]

It was high time that Lauderdale went to Scotland. With Tweeddale no longer in charge the administration was drifting. Halton complained to his brother that the council seemed unwilling to do much of anything about the problems in the west. Hamilton refused to serve on the commission to look into the Auchinleck affair, and had a waspish exchange with him about it. There was also a slanging match on the subject between Archbishop Sharp and the earl of Dumfries. Halton had told Rothes that he should work at holding the council together, and would be blamed if things went wrong. Rothes shrugged this off, and wanted to know what it was that he was doing wrong. Lauderdale must come to Scotland this spring: Halton could not do everything by himself, and he had no one to talk with but Kincardine. What Halton's letters showed very plainly was that he could not keep his colleagues on the council in line.[29] Kincardine in his turn sounded much the same note. 'Tis a hard matter that men for their private grudges will neglect (to say no worse) the king's service and hazard their country's quiet,' he wrote à propos of his colleagues' neglect of the religious situation in the west.[30] In May Rothes did bestir himself to write to Tweeddale and ask him to come to Edinburgh for the meetings of the treasury commission. Without him there was no quorum,[31] since

---

27 Charles summoned him on 11 April, NAS SP 4/1/421.
28 14 May 1672, Moray to the duchess of Hamilton, NAS GD 406/1/6133.
29 23, 25 Jan. 1672, Halton to Lauderdale, BL Add. Mss 23135, ff. 135–37.
30 6 Feb. 1672, Kincardine to Lauderdale, ibid., ff. 143–44.
31 9 May 1672, Rothes to Tweeddale, NLS Ms. 7005, f. 138.

Kincardine by this time was on his way to London. The council did attempt to do something about Highland lawlessness, giving a new commission to the earl of Seaforth to pursue criminals, especially MacLeod of Assynt, who was holed up in his fortified house and defying the sheriff of Sutherland.[32] And in May it appointed a large commission of Border landowners to pursue lawbreakers in that area; there was an indication that a joint commission with English landholders might be created.[33] The council's principal concern was to provide the men for the war, and it was having limited success. More energy and direction were badly needed.

Lauderdale and his duchess left for Scotland toward the end of May. While he was en route, before parliament met, Moray wrote to his two friends with counsel and advice. To Tweeddale he urged patience and moderation, and not to neglect public business. It was rumoured in London that Tweeddale was planning not to attend parliament; both Moray and Andrew Hay, his London agent, urged him to go and, as Hay put it, concur in measures for the king's service. It would be very badly taken if he stayed away: he must act as if there were no differences between him and Lauderdale. Moray was doing his best to cheer up his friend – he was not being bad-mouthed at court, Moray assured him.[34] To the duchess of Hamilton Moray wrote that Kincardine had got a warrant from Charles authorising her husband to reimburse himself for the debt the crown still owed him, £13,000 sterling, out of the unpaid tax money for which he was collector. The warrant had not been delivered to the treasury commission; the duke should be friendly to Lauderdale and Kincardine and pretend not to know that the warrant had been issued.[35] Lauderdale was holding up the warrant – behaving shamefully, Moray wrote, but there was nothing Hamilton could do about it. Lauderdale spoke for the king, after all. If Hamilton followed his conscience and opposed any war tax on the ground that the country could not afford it, he would hopelessly alienate the king, and he would not get his warrant. There was no point in being a martyr and ruining himself and his family, but if he played his cards right he could smooth things over. Tweeddale's difficulties with Lauderdale 'will not be so

---

32 *RPCS* III, pp. 483–85.

33 Ibid., pp. 507–08, 517–20.

34 23 May, 6 June 1672, Moray to Tweeddale, NLS Ms. 7005, ff. 1439–44, 14414, f. 21. 25 June, Andrew Hay to Tweeddale, NLS Ms. 7005, f. 159.

35 29 May 1672, Moray to the duchess of Hamilton, NAS GD 406/1/6134. The warrant is dated 25 May, NAS SP 4/2/19.

easily composed', he ruefully added.[36] Hamilton followed Moray's advice and remained quiet. It seems likely that Lauderdale leaked the existence of the warrant in order to achieve precisely this result. On 17 September, after parliament had adjourned, the treasury commission received the warrant.[37]

The result, for Lauderdale, was a successful session of parliament. His instructions, dated 23 May, directed him to explain the reasons for the war. The king was not going to ask for a war tax, but since there was the possibility of invasion, or sedition stirred up by the enemy, Charles recommended that parliament take measures (read: vote money) for these purposes. Lauderdale was to assure parliament that Charles would maintain the existing religious polity and suppress conventicles. He was also authorised to approve of the acts of the commission to regulate judicial proceedings. He could also approve a sumptuary law, which indeed was adopted and broadmindedly made an exception for actors.[38] In his private instructions Charles authorised Lauderdale either to extend the indulgence or remove or shuffle around nonconformist ministers in the interest of religious peace – what amounted to carte blanche in religious policy. If Lauderdale judged that more troops were necessary the Scots would have to pay for them, and for the deployment of the militia. What these instructions boiled down to was that Charles wanted money and religious peace. He left it to his commissioner to decide how to get them.[39]

The parliamentary session ran for three months, from 12 June to 11 September. Near its beginning, on 27 June, the council issued a proclamation prohibiting slanderous speeches. People must not 'meddle with the affairs of state in their common and ordinary discourses'. Following Middleton's precedent in 1662, Lauderdale filled vacancies on the Committee of the Articles by appointment; there seems to have been no objection. According to Mackenzie, Lady Lauderdale and some of her companions were present on opening day, an unprecedented spectacle that raised the 'indignation of the people very much against her'.[40] One wonders: Lady Lauderdale certainly prompted a great deal of indignation

---

36 19 June 1672, Moray to the duchess of Hamilton, NAS GD 406/1/6136.

37 NAS E 6/2/5.

38 *APS* VIII, pp. 71–72. Also excepted were servants who got hand-me-downs, heralds, pages and lackeys.

39 The instructions are in BL Add. Mss 23135, ff. 168–70. No additional troops were in fact raised; R.A. Lee, *Government and Politics in Scotland, 1661–1681* (PhD diss., University of Glasgow, 1995), pp. 152–53.

40 *RPCS* III, pp. 538–39. Mackenzie, *Memoirs*, pp. 219–20.

in later years, and Mackenzie may well have been reading later feelings back into 1672. As Moray observed, at this point she was being polite: she 'can compose her spirit to what is prudent'.[41] Her influence over her new husband was very obvious, however, and duly noted by all those who wanted favours from Lauderdale. Begging letters were addressed to her as well as to the king and Lauderdale.[42] John Campbell of Glenorchy, who had got a conveyance of the Caithness estates, wanted to succeed the childless and insolvent earl in return for paying some of his debts. If that was not possible, he offered Lady Lauderdale £1,000 for her daughter Catherine's dowry if she would be helpful in getting his money back, and some other title, to salvage his wounded ego. Nothing happened immediately, but four years later, when the earl died, Glenorchy paid her £2,000 sterling and got the earldom.[43]

The king's letter to parliament asked for support for the war but not directly for a subsidy, and lavishly praised Lauderdale. The latter followed with a long speech, a litany of Dutch offences going back to the days of the Commonwealth, which made the war 'unavoidable'. Parliament must act now, he went on, to protect the country against invasion and sedition. All this evoked a loyal reply, promising to be of service and praising Charles for elevating their commissioner to a dukedom.[44] Money, of course, was Lauderdale's main objective. He prompted Atholl, who had been working very hard to ingratiate himself with Lauderdale, to make the necessary motion in the Articles, which, after some debate, agreed to recommend twelve months' cess, £864,000, to be collected over two years. This was a very large sum. To assuage landowning debtors, who would be paying the tax, it was agreed that they could keep one-sixth of their interest payments for a year.[45] This annoyed the creditor class, mostly in the burghs; they were relieved when Lauderdale blocked a suggestion to tax financial assets as well as personal and real estate. So the tax was voted. To ease its passage

41 19 June 1672, Moray to the duchess of Hamilton, NAS GD 406/1/6136.
42 See, e.g., the letters of Lady Montrose, who said she was dying, on behalf of her 'orphans', BL Add. Mss 23135, ff. 222–26.
43 12 Dec. 1672, 8 Mar., 9 Apr. 1673, and n.d., Glenorchy to Lady Lauderdale, ibid., ff. 220–21, 236, 257, 263. Lady Caithness, Argyll's sister, also wrote her asking for support, ibid., ff. 255, 259–60, 265, 268. P. Hopkins, *Glencoe and the End of the Highland War* (Edinburgh, 1986), pp. 55–56, 61–62.
44 *APS* VIII, pp. 57–58. BL Add. Mss 23135, ff. 175, 177.
45 As an example of the problems of the landowning classes: in July 1672 the council cut the £16,000 liferent of the dowager countess of Moray; the earl's income was only £10,000, less than the £12,000 annual interest on his debt. *RPCS* III, pp. 562–63.

Lauderdale stressed that the money would be used strictly for defence; in August he turned aside a royal request for 2,000 men to join in a projected landing in Holland that, in the end, never took place. Atholl received his reward: in November he became lord privy seal, one more indication of Tweeddale's fall from grace. Before the king acted Moray told Tweeddale that his name had been mentioned, as before; the answer 'was an avisendum'. Atholl was profusely grateful.[46]

Lauderdale in his speech had promised to defend the church and stifle sedition. The chief measure to this end was the renewal of the Conventicle Act, due to expire in 1673, for three more years. Unlawful ordinations would be punished, and the parents of children who did not have them baptised by legally ordained ministers fined. In a renewal of previous legislation a committee was set up to value teinds and make it possible for heritors and life-renters to collect and buy up their own teinds. An Act for regulating the militia provided, inter alia, that all officers be members of the established church.[47] Sharp and his colleagues could complain of none of this legislation, of course, but it dodged the main question of the indulgence, and with respect to unlawful ordinations it set a date behind which the law would not inquire: 1661. The main issues would be dealt with elsewhere.

Three major pieces of legislation passed this parliament that were to have long-lasting effects. Parliament ratified the work of the judicial commission, creating the High Court of Justiciary and imposing the limitations on advocates' fees previously mentioned,[48] though not without some grumbling by the president of the session in the Articles and, unsurprisingly, Mackenzie of Rosehaugh on the floor. He complained about the way the package of laws was voted on and the ignorance of the drafting commission.[49] Secondly, the monopoly of foreign trade that the royal burghs had enjoyed was shattered. Henceforth their monopoly was limited to the importation of wine, wax, silks, spices and dyestuffs. Foreign trade was otherwise open to anyone who chose to engage in it. The principal gainers were the burghs of regality and barony and the aristocrats who

---

46 *APS* VIII, p. 62. NAS SP 4/2/123. G. MacIntosh, *The Scottish Parliament under Charles II 1660–1685* (Edinburgh, 2007), p. 118. 14 Dec. 1671, 9 Jan. 1673 Atholl to Lauderdale, BL Add. Mss 23135, ff. 116–17, 246. Aug 1672, Charles to Lauderdale, BL Add. Mss 23135, f. 198. Lee, *Government and Politics*, p. 218. 17 Sept. Moray to Tweeddale, NLS Ms. 7005, f. 182.

47 *APS* VIII, pp. 58–59, 71, 72–73, 89.

48 See above, chap. 8, pp. 245–46.

49 *APS* VIII, pp. 80–88. MacIntosh, *Scottish Parliament*, pp. 119–20.

controlled them – e.g., Lauderdale with his burgh of Musselburgh. These burghs could export their own manufactures and import a long list of raw material such as timber and iron. Lauderdale and his aristocratic colleagues had their own interests in mind, to be sure, but the monopoly was anachronistic and increasingly unenforceable. The royal burghs protested, not least because the burghs of regality and barony were not obligated to help pay the burghal share of national taxation. Predictably a few royal burghs attempted to change their status, without much success. The Act passed without too much trouble, since only the burghs opposed it. And it was helpful to trade. T. C. Smout's conclusion is that 'The Scottish legislature must be given credit for their (sic) wisdom . . . in curtailing the privileges of the royal burghs.'[50]

Finally, there was a statute on vagabondage that Gordon Donaldson regards as 'the foundation of the Scottish poor law until 1845'.[51] The legislation of 1663[52] requiring vagabonds to be put to work and poor children assigned to masters was to be enforced, and, as before, parishes were to pay. But now, designated burghs had to provide correction houses for the shire, paid for by the parishes (heritors, tenants and occupiers, that is). Sturdy beggars would go to the correction houses or be put to work; the impotent poor, the object of *pro forma* solicitude, could obtain a licence to beg. The excise commissioners in each shire were to report twice annually to the privy council on the working of the law.[53] If there was a safety-net in this legislation, it was a safety-net for the rich against the threat of riot. The unemployed, the 'sturdy beggar' of the seventeenth century, inspired fear rather than sympathy.

Throughout the session Lauderdale was concerned to look out for the interests of the landowning classes, perhaps because they were the ones who had to pay the cess. There was another enactment against the importation of Irish foodstuffs, which the council undertook to enforce. Burghs could not arrest non-residents for debt without having gone through the courts. On the other hand Lauderdale killed Kincardine's proposal to end the summer session of the college of justice, which gratified Edinburgh, in spite of the opposition of many of those who had to find lodging in the

---

50 APS VIII, pp. 63–64, 68, 77–78. T.C. Smout, *Scottish Trade on the Eve of Union* (London, 1963), p. 17. See also R.S. Rait, *The Parliaments of Scotland* (Glasgow, 1924), pp. 259–62.
51 G. Donaldson, *Scotland: James V – James VII* (Edinburgh, 1965), p. 399.
52 APS VII, pp. 485–86.
53 APS VIII, pp. 89–91.

capital in order to attend.[54] There were goodies for those in favour. The summer's warrant book contained new pensions for Rothes and Kellie, £500 sterling for Kincardine for his services as secretary while Lauderdale was in Scotland, and forgiveness of feu and tack duties for Argyll and his stepson Balcarres. At the end of the session there was a large number of private ratifications and Atholl got the privy seal and, in January, a seat on the court of session, Kincardine the contents of a Dutch ship seized in Orkney, and Halton, the retrospective gift of the wardship and marriage of his son-in-law Lord Elphinstone. He also became sheriff of Edinbugh for life. Hamilton, since he had behaved himself, got a lucrative wardship as well as his warrant. The earl of Wemyss, now evidently in favour since Tweeddale was not, got the right to pass on his titles to his daughter Margaret if he had no sons. His wife, who loathed Tweeddale, was busily making up to Lady Lauderdale. There was even something for Tweeddale: the reduction of cess on Haddingtonshire parkland for his benefit – and Lauderdale's.[55]

But Lauderdale had given hostages to fortune. His behaviour as commissioner was, to say the least, overbearing. When one burgh representative, during the discussion of the cess, suggested that members be given time to consult their constituencies, not a Scottish practice, Lauderdale overreacted violently. He accused the peccant member of subverting the constitution and forced a humiliating public apology.[56] His legislative programme, whatever its merits, had alienated the legal profession, never a good idea, and the royal burghs, the only burghs represented in parliament. And he had bought peace for this session with the duke of Hamilton by surrendering his hold over that perennially discontented troublemaker. He would learn soon enough, if he did not already know it, that gratitude did not loom large in Hamilton's scale of values.

As for the commissioner's 'dearest brother', he had been very circumspect, earning Moray's praise for behaving properly in public questions and frankly in private ones. Moray still hoped that he and Lauderdale could reach a better understanding, 'for time does many unlikely

54 Ibid., pp. 61, 69–70. *RPCS* IV, pp. 19–20. Mackenzie, *Memoirs*, pp. 225–26.

55 NAS SP 4/2/15–17, 39–40, 92, 98, 103–04, 107, 118. 27 Aug. 1672, Lady Wemyss to Lady Lauderdale, BL Add. Mss 23135, ff. 196–97. There is a complicated story behind the Wemyss grant. The couple's only son died in 1671, so Lady Wemyss persuaded her husband to disinherit his daughter by an earlier marriage in favour of their daughter Margaret. See M. Lee, Jr, *The Heiresses of Buccleuch* (East Linton, 1996), pp. 77–78.

56 See MacIntosh, *Scottish Parliament*, pp. 118–19.

things."[57] Lauderdale's behaviour, however, did not hold out much hope of that: he increased the pressure on his daughter. He had formally redeemed his estate – i.e., broken Mary's entail – by the payment of the rose noble, though he had not granted it to his brother or anyone else.[58] What he wanted now from Mary was a formal renunciation of anything that she might claim from her mother except the London real estate, and of all claims on his estate as well. The three – Tweeddale, Yester, Mary – felt that they had to sign. There was the threat that he might take them to court, and there was no way that they could win such a case against the all-powerful royal commissioner. He still had the backband to hang over their heads, and he had stacked the court with four ignorant (in Mackenzie's view) non-lawyers, including his brother and the unpopular Provost Ramsay of Edinburgh.[59] So they signed. Mary and Yester renounced anything she might claim from her mother save the London houses, and from her father's estate except the £7,000 sterling to which she was entitled by the terms of her marriage contract if she was not, in fact, his heir. In return Lauderdale relieved them of any financial obligations arising from Mary's mother's estate, an empty gesture since there were none.[60]

Tweeddale was unhappy. He even lashed out at Moray for giving Yester bad advice, a charge Moray resented. And he later claimed that Mary was so upset by her father's behaviour that she almost died, and never really recovered her health, a dubious statement, since she lived another thirty years. Lauderdale's actions could hardly be called paternal, but he continued to promise 'that his daughter should have a considerable share of all, and that the bond and backband should be destroyed', and this in front of witnesses.[61] From London Andrew Hay applauded Tweeddale's and Yester's decision. Yester was right to defer to 'so great a father-in-law' who, believing that he had law and equity on his side, would so persuade others. He advised continuing to show 'obsequious respect'.[62] The duchess, who, Hay thought, wanted to compose all these differences, was gracious when Lady Tweeddale visited her at Lethington. Lady Tweeddale pressed Lauderdale about the backband, which circumstances clearly had rendered irrelevant, but Lauderdale would not give it up. According to Yester he lied

57 17 Aug. 1672, Moray to Tweeddale, NLS Ms. 7005, f. 177.
58 NLS Ms. 14549, f. 113.
59 25 June 1672, Andrew Hay to Yester, NLS Ms. 14417, f. 3. Mackenzie, Memoirs, p. 240.
60 NLS Ms. 14548, ff. 102–03, 104. NLS Ms. 14546, pp. 9–14.
61 Tweeddale, 'Wrangs', p. 289.
62 17 Aug. 1672, Andrew Hay to Tweeddale, NLS Ms. 7005, f. 175.

to Lady Tweeddale, saying that he had given it to Yester, and afterwards refused to talk about it at all, referring the question to the lawyers. As Tweeddale later ruefully wrote, Lauderdale was 'valuing himself upon his overreaching the earl of Tweeddale and his goodson [son-in-law, i.e., Yester] by their exuberant trust of him'.[63] They continued wishfully to hope that Lauderdale meant what he said.

As parliament was winding down Lauderdale came to what can only be described as an impatient decision on religious policy. Given the concerns and expectations which the English declaration of indulgence had aroused, he could not simply do nothing. Conventicles continued to be troublesome, despite the council's best efforts – it even fined the countess of Wigtown for attending one, but turned the money over to the earl. Clifford, writing from London in July, asked Lauderdale to arrest five Scottish preachers who had taken part in a 'dangerous assembly' at Flodden and had probably gone back home.[64] So on 3 September the council published a list of some eighty outed ministers, who were simply assigned to parishes, mostly in western shires where vacancies troubled Archbishop Leighton, and also in Linlithgow and Argyll, apparently without consultation. They were appointed in twos, or even in threes, to vacant parishes, and twenty-six were assigned to parishes where an indulged minister had already been appointed. The total was 'some 136 indulged ministers, or approximately half of those . . . deprived in 1663'. A conciliar committee was authorised to move any of the listed ministers within six months; after that there would be no further changes. The ministers were to give communion only to parish residents, preach only indoors, not to marry or baptise anyone from outside the parish, and leave it only with the permission of the bishop.[65] Gilbert Burnet claimed in his *History* that he sold this policy to Lauderdale on the ground that the appointed ministers, confined to their parishes, would be kept from 'going round the uninfected parts of the kingdom'. But Burnet is not a reliable witness respecting Lauderdale. The secretary was perpetually enraged, wrote Burnet; he wanted a rebellion in order to bring over an army of Irish Papists – which did not exist – to crush it.[66]

---

63 NLS Ms. 14547, ff. 143–44. 25 June 1672, Andrew Hay to Yester, NLS Ms. 14417, f. 3. Tweeddale, 'Wrangs,' p. 289.

64 BL Add. Mss 23135, f. 182. *RPCS* III, pp. 545–47, 549–51, 555, 559–61, 583–85. See also 31 May 1672, James Turner to Hamilton, NAS GD 406/1/8904.

65 Ian B. Cowan, *The Scottish Covenanters 1660–1688* (London, 1976), p. 79. *RPCS* III, pp. 586–91. For Leighton's views see BL Add. Mss 23135. f. 189.

66 Burnet, *History* I, pp. 520, 591.

What Lauderdale expected to come of this policy is hard to know. His latest biographer describes it as 'a lazy measure by a government tiring of the whole time-consuming business of conciliation',[67] which seems about right. Perhaps the indulgence would work, perhaps not. But Lauderdale hardly seemed to care. His visit to Scotland leaves the impression that he was no longer interested in the details of Scottish government. The enthusiasm and hopes and expectations of the new brooms of 1667 had trickled away; the failure of the union was the death-knell of reform in Charles's ancient kingdom. And now the king, who never much cared what went on north of the Tweed anyway, was embarked on the great gamble of his reign, the war that was to ruin the Dutch and give him an income which would make him independent of parliament. To what extent Lauderdale was in Charles's confidence is unclear – he certainly did not know about the treaty of Dover. Once again, Burnet: Lauderdale, he says, asked Atholl, his point man on the tax of 1672, to speak to Hamilton about the tax. Hamilton asked how the English parliament felt about the war; Atholl replied that 'there was a settled design to have no more parliaments in England'.[68] If Atholl ever said this – and there is no corroborating evidence – Lauderdale must have been his source. The war, his new wife, his cooling relations with Moray and with his daughter and the Tweeddale family, all meant that from now on Lauderdale, like his master, wanted Scotland to remain quiet and offer no challenge to his authority. He counted on his new principal agents, Kincardine and Halton, to accomplish this. Unlike Tweeddale they were not apt to press Lauderdale to take any initiatives. That now suited Lauderdale very well.

The haste and sloppiness of the indulgence legislation is clear evidence of how anxious Lauderdale was to get home once the parliamentary session was over. 'The Cabal are all impatient for your return,' wrote Clifford on 7 September.[69] He and the duchess travelled in style; his expense account for a twenty-five day journey came to £776 7s 11d sterling.[70] They got back on 25 October. The king was pleased with him, and the largesse that had flowed at the end of the parliamentary session continued. Kincardine's general gift of the wardships was extended to 11 August 1674. In March 1673 Cashkeeper Sharp obtained a farm of the inland excise for £29,325

67 R.C. Paterson, *King Lauderdale* (Edinburgh, 2003), pp. 200–01.
68 Burnet, *History* I, pp. 586–88.
69 BL Add. Mss 23135, f. 203.
70 NLS Ms. 577, f. 70.

sterling per year, with a salary of 2,000 merks, a very good bargain for Sharp.[71] Halton's son-in-law Lord Elphinstone was granted the right to seize foreign brandy, a prohibited import. What he in effect did was to sell exceptions to the prohibition, which flooded the market with cheap liquor. According to Mackenzie it caused a decline in both customs and excise revenues because less Spanish wine was imported and the price of barley fell because whisky production declined.[72] The financial corruption against which Tweeddale had fought flourished anew under Lauderdale's brother. Lauderdale himself received an exoneration for whatever offences he might have committed as commissioner in the last three parliamentary sessions. The king also decided to turn the Bass Rock into a prison, for which the newly-voted tax would help to pay; Lauderdale, as its captain, would find ways to profit from it.[73]

Even before he got back Lauderdale was being pressed by problems in Edinburgh, where there was opposition to the re-election of his ally Sir Andrew Ramsay as provost. The leader of the opposition, Francis Kinloch, a former dean of guild, argued that Ramsay could no longer be provost because he now sat on the court of session. There were riots in the streets. Lauderdale's correspondent, the dean of St Giles' Cathedral, blamed a group of fanatics – his characterisation – and thought Lauderdale should do something. Charles ordered an investigation. The council committee, which included Tweeddale, in effect did nothing. According to Mackenzie, who acted as Kinloch's lawyer, it unfairly refused to allow him and his colleagues to question witnesses. And, said Mackenzie, there really was no tumult; it was an invention of Ramsay's people to keep their grip on power. The committee collected documents, which in January 1673 it sent to Lauderdale, who, wrote the council, could inform the king: that was preferable to their offering their own opinion. Ramsay stayed in office, and Charles later ordered the firing of the town clerk, who was one of Ramsay's opponents.[74]

71 NAS SP 4/2/173–74, E 6/2/67, 97. R.W. Lennox, *Lauderdale and Scotland: A Study in Scottish Politics and Administration 1660–1682* (PhD diss., Columbia University, 1977), pp. 199–200.

72 NAS SP 4/2/129–30, 133–34. MacIntosh, *Scottish Parliament*, p. 124. Mackenzie, *Memoirs*, pp. 243–44.

73 NAS SP 4/2/113–116, 134–35, E 6/2/58–59.

74 *RPCS* III, pp. 605–06, IV, pp. 4–5. NAS SP 4/2/316–17. BL Add. Mss 23135, ff. 207, 232, 234–35. 18 Jan. 1673, Mackenzie to Lauderdale, BL Add. Mss 23135, f. 248. MacIntosh, *Scottish Parliament*, pp. 122–23. Mackenzie, *Memoirs*, pp. 246–50. *Laing Mss* I, pp. 389–90. One of the reports said that Kinloch on the night before the vote was canvassing some of the electors in Edinburgh's taverns. *Plus ça change ...*

The religious problem could not be solved so readily. The new indulgence was not going well. On 11 November Hamilton wrote to Lauderdale that some of the outed ministers were urging the new appointees to refuse their appointments, and the people to boycott those who did accept. And the conventicling went on. Lauderdale's response was to order Rothes to seize the malcontents and suppress conventicles.[75] In February 1673 Kincardine urged Lauderdale to put pressure on Ramsay to act against conventicles in Edinburgh: he was conniving at them to keep in well with the citizenry.[76] The council did what it could. It ordered nonconformist ministers in Edinburgh to give assurances that they would not hold conventicles, or else move out of town. Heritors must report conventicles, and sheriffs must suppress them.[77] Then, at the beginning of March, the king's policy of indulgence in England collapsed. On 8 March 1673 Charles, faced with an angry parliament, personally tore the seal from his declaration, in spite of the opposition of his brother, Lauderdale, Clifford and Shaftesbury, three members of the Cabal.[78] At the end of the month Rothes wrote to Hamilton, asking him to show up at the next council meeting to discuss the indulgence. Lauderdale expected him to attend: it was necessary to do something 'suitable to what length they have gone in England', a Delphic phrase. Hamilton excused himself. He was too busy to come, an act of defiance that Rothes ignored.[79] Lauderdale and his colleagues were handling Hamilton very carefully. The secretary regretted that he had failed to get the suddenly deceased duke of Lennox's 'blue ribbon' for Hamilton, but he did get the baillery of the regality of Glasgow for him. The secretary instructed William Lockhart, his London man of business, who was about to go to France, to look after Lady Hamilton's business there. Hamilton was always polite and grateful, but he always wanted more – the captaincy of Dumbarton Castle, for example, which he did not get.[80] He was, in a word, difficult.

The situation in the west continued to deteriorate. Ian Cowan estimates that over fifty of the nonconformists named to parishes in 1672 refused to

---

75 NAS GD 406/1/2717, 2731. Lauderdale sent Hamilton a copy of his letter to Rothes.
76 BL Add. Mss 23135, ff. 253–54. Kincardine blamed nonconformist women who influenced their husbands.
77 *RPCS* IV, pp. 30–31, 37–39.
78 R.F. Hutton, *Charles II, King of England, Scotland and Ireland* (Oxford, 1989), pp. 297–98. Arlington supported Charles's decision; Buckingham wavered.
79 *Hamilton Mss*, pp. 85–86.
80 14 Jan. 1673, Lauderdale to Hamilton, NAS GD 406/1/2675. 23 Jan., 20 Feb., 13 May, Hamilton to Lauderdale, NAS GD 406/1/2719, 2720, BL Add. Mss 23135, f. 269.

serve.[81] On 29 April 1673 Charles ordered troops sent to the west, both to suppress Covenanters and to secure the area against possible trouble from the Dutch[82] – the fears were much the same as they had been in the previous Dutch war. On 31 May the king instructed the council to offer the ministers who had refused appointment another parish, or to get assurances that they would live peaceably where they were. At the suggestion of Leighton, currently at court, he named a five-man committee to watch the Glasgow archdiocese and call in troops if necessary. Hamilton's was the first name on Charles's list; Tweeddale's was not on it. On the same day Lauderdale wrote Hamilton, sending a copy of the king's letter, stressing Charles's confidence in Hamilton, talking cheerfully of Prince Rupert's naval victory (which in fact had not happened) and of a speedy peace, and regretting that he could not persuade the king to make the baillery of Glasgow a hereditary appointment – Charles was not making such appointments any more.[83]

Hamilton's reply was hardly cooperative. He regretted that Charles had asked him to undertake this assignment, which was both dangerous and above his capacity. The king was asking five men to accomplish what the whole council had been trying to do for ten years; better to put the business into the hands of the officers of state and the armed forces.[84] This was, in fact, what the council had done. Three of the five appointees held public office, among them the earl of Linlithgow, the commander of the armed forces. In effect Hamilton was refusing to do the king's bidding, though his letter was, as usual, careful and polite. He did keep Rothes informed about conventicling in Lanarkshire and his activity in fining those attendees he caught. He seemed to take some pleasure in reporting on irregular baptisms and the failure of most indulged ministers to celebrate 29 May, which was both the king's birthday and the date of his entry into London in 1660.[85] There is evidence that Kincardine, at least, had lost his patience; he had to write to the duke denying the allegation that he had called Hamilton 'mutinous and so unfit for public things'. The five-man commission, he explained, was designed to keep Hamilton from bearing the burden, and the odium, of sole responsibility for maintaining order and

81 Cowan, *Scottish Covenanters*, pp. 79–80.
82 *RCPS* IV, pp. 45–47.
83 Ibid., pp. 56–57. NAS GD 406/1/2722.
84 9 June 1673, Hamilton to Lauderdale, NAS GD 406/1/2723.
85 See, e.g., 11 June 1673, Hamilton to Rothes, *Hamilton Mss*, p. 86. The council confiscated half the stipend of such ministers; *RPCS* IV, pp. 71–72.

decorum in the Glasgow diocese.[86] The council acquiesced in Hamilton's defiance, however, and in effect bought his argument. On 25 July 1673 it wrote to Charles suggesting that the whole council, or a larger committee with more officials, would be more effective than the five men Charles named to deal with a problem which had been 'a great part of the Council's employment these ten or twelve years past'. The letter was signed by four of the five nominees and a number of other councillors, including Tweeddale and Yester.[87] Hamilton's behaviour in this matter was a warning signal that Lauderdale did not heed.

Archbishop Leighton, the man upon whom Lauderdale's policy depended for its success, was becoming discouraged. Bishop James Ramsay of Dunblane, Leighton's successor in that see, wrote to Lady Lauderdale on 21 May that Leighton was on his way to court, probably to resign. Hamilton reiterated this view four days later in a letter to Tweeddale. Leighton needed encouragement, and he got some there, from Moray at least. Bishop Ramsay thought that if the king ordered him to stay on, he would, and that is what in fact happened: he promised Charles that he would stay on for a year and then retire.[88] But he was not happy. In a letter to Lauderdale, undated but probably written at about this time, he put it this way: 'Truly I believe that the utmost that is to be expected [from the new indulgence] is the preventing of mischief and keeping things from running to extreme confusion . . . for church order and cordial agreement I confess I have given over to look for it in those parts for our time . . . It was unhappily and I fear irrevocably lost, at first setting out, by too high and too hot and hasty counsels.'[89] Leighton was quite right. Middleton's precipitancy in 1662 and 1663 had permanently poisoned the well. Less than half of those outed in those years had been reconciled to the episcopal regime in any way, and even amongst the reconciled there was great discontent. Many of those who had accepted the first indulgence were offended by the haphazard methods of the second. As Ian Cowan observed, 'The policy of Indulgence had done little or nothing to ease the conventicling problem and may even indeed be held to have promoted it.' With Tweeddale no longer in a position of influence, and only Kincardine left, it appeared increasingly likely

---

86 24 July 1673, Kincardine to Hamilton, NAS GD 406/1/2673.

87 *RPCS* IV, pp. 81–82. BL Add. Mss 23135, f. 278.

88 BL Add. Mss 23135, f. 272. NLS Ms. 7006, f. 16. 17 June 1673, Moray to Tweeddale, NLS Ms. 7006, f. 30. NAS SP 4/2/270.

89 Quoted in Paterson, *King Lauderdale*, p. 201.

that Lauderdale would revert to repression.[90] So too would politics in England: the passage of the Test Act in March 1673, the resignation of Tweeddale's friend Clifford, the Catholic supporter of indulgence, as lord treasurer in June after only seven months in office, and his replacement by the future earl of Danby, who in 1674 would adopt a policy of high Anglicanism in order to pacify the Cavalier Parliament. As was the case in the Clarendon years, Lauderdale had to accommodate to the prevailing tone of the English administration.

Gilbert Burnet, writing of the changing face of Scottish politics with the rise of Halton in 1671, said that Tweeddale 'was resolved to withdraw from business'.[91] Tweeddale's withdrawal was hardly altogether voluntary. There were no more letters from his dearest brother. The breach between them was no secret; indeed Tweeddale wrote about it, not only to colleagues like Kincardine, who thought that healing was only a matter of time, but also to Lauderdale's own people. William Lockhart was sorry to hear about Tweeddale's trouble with 'my lord duke whom I serve', and wanted to help.[92] Andrew Hay from London kept urging either Tweeddale or Yester or both to come to London, if only to look after the houses that Lauderdale had finally turned over to his daughter. In December 1672 he had an interview with Lauderdale, who, wrote Hay, said kind things about Yester and opined that his son-in-law was not paying much attention to his affairs![93] Moray, who was desperately anxious to bring the two men back into some sort of relationship, really did not know what to do. His letter of 25 November 1672 was bleak. No great person was prepared to be helpful to Tweeddale, he wrote. There was no point in talking to Charles: what would he tell Lauderdale to do? 'To bid them to live well together signifies nothing.' He had spoken to Ashley, but really had nothing to suggest to him. Nothing could be done unless Tweeddale or Yester came to London; if anything arose that might be a reason for a summons, he would try to effectuate it. Moray speculated about the possibility that Charles might appoint a lord treasurer in Scotland, since he was about to do so in England, elevating

---

90 Cowan, *Scottish Covenanters*, p. 81. See also J. Buckroyd, *The Life of James Sharp, Archbishop of St Andrews* (Edinburgh, 1987), p. 96, and *Church and State in Scotland 1660–1681* (Edinburgh, 1980), pp. 106–07. She entitles her chapter on 1672–75 in the latter book 'The Slide to Severity'.

91 Burnet, *History* I, p. 519.

92 19 Oct. 1672, Kincardine to Tweeddale, 14 Nov., Lockhart to Tweeddale, NLS Ms. 7005, ff. 192, 197.

93 28 Nov., 10, 28 Dec. 1672, Hay to Yester, NLS Ms. 14403, ff. 9, 11, 12. 28 Nov., Hay to Tweeddale, NLS Ms. 7005, f. 205.

their friend Clifford, but he thought it unlikely. He was concerned that their letters might be intercepted – Halton was likely to do that sort of thing – hence the use of 'this human packet',[94] a practice Moray would continue to employ.

The new year brought no improvement. Moray continued to canvass Clifford and Ashley, who was now lord chancellor and earl of Shaftesbury, especially the latter, who, like everyone else, said that Tweeddale had to come to London if anything was to be done for him.[95] The difficulty was that neither Clifford nor Shaftesbury was in a position to be helpful. The Test Act, passed on 29 March, would drive Clifford from office; Shaftesbury's support of it helped to turn his once friendly relationship with Lauderdale to bitter enmity and cause the king to lose confidence in him. Lauderdale's mood made Moray very gloomy about the possibility of resuming a working relationship; he was chilly to all his old friends. Andrew Hay also felt that present circumstances – March 1673, the month of both the end of the indulgence and the Test Act – were not encouraging for a visit, though sooner or later Tweeddale or Yester must come, to deal with the problem of the Highgate house. Hay, strikingly, described the political atmosphere as a less intense version of that of 1642.[96] Under the circumstances it is not surprising that Shaftesbury failed sometimes to carry out his promises to Moray to speak to Charles about Tweeddale. He had far more urgent matters to deal with.

Those promises, which Moray detailed in a very long letter written over a two-week period, from 17 June to 1 July,[97] were undertaken in a very different context. In April Tweeddale's patience finally snapped. There was no single episode that caused this, but rather an accumulation of disappointments and slights.[98] He continued to serve on committees of the council. He faithfully attended the meetings of the treasury commission – his last recorded appearance in the *sederunt* is 8 December 1673 – but the commission was no longer making policy, as it had in the years when it was first established. In February Moray had urged him to try to do something about the problem of brandy: complaints were surfacing about Elphinstone's commission and Provost

94 NLS Ms. 7005, ff. 201–02.
95 See, e.g., 3 Feb. 1673, Moray to Tweeddale, NLS Ms. 7006, ff. 6–7.
96 4 Mar. 1673, Moray to Tweeddale, 18 Mar., Hay to Tweeddale, ibid., ff. 10–11, 14.
97 Ibid., ff. 30–32.
98 There is a copy of Lauderdale's will of 1673, leaving his title to his brother and his movables to his wife, in the Yester papers, NLS Ms. 14548, f. 141, but no evidence as to when Tweeddale obtained it.

Ramsay's smuggling.[99] There is nothing in the commission's minutes about brandy; if Tweeddale tried, he failed. Elphinstone's gift was symptomatic of the new regime under Halton's aegis. On 15 April Tweeddale unburdened himself to both Moray and Andrew Hay. It was time, he wrote to Moray, to forget about accommodation with Lauderdale and set to work to assess how to rein in present evils – 'you may imagine them like '67' – and prevent worse ones. To Hay he wrote about Highgate and Lauderdale's deplorable treatment of Yester. He would not give up the backband, which could be very dangerous to Yester 'if it fall in ill hands, as it is like enough to do'. It would be a good thing 'if God would make him sensible of his dealings with the young man'. Neither he nor Yester was coming to London just now. He asked Hay to consult with Moray to consider what might be done.[100]

Tweeddale now had to reconfigure his political alliances. He proposed using a cipher for the names mentioned in his correspondence with Moray, and sent one to him. Moray acknowledged that 'opening of letters is in fashion', but thought a cipher useless, since the context would make clear who was meant. He would write only what could be seen by anyone, unless the letter was to be carried by someone who could be trusted. Tweeddale could not see how his good friend Clifford and Lauderdale could get along, but this was wishful thinking, as Moray pointed out in June. Clifford and Lauderdale had been together in urging Charles to defy parliament over the indulgence. Clifford valued Lauderdale's friendship, wrote Moray, and anyway he was leaving office. Shaftesbury was the man: he and Lauderdale had quarrelled, and to all appearances he stood well with Charles – appearances that were deceiving. Amongst possible allies in Scotland, Moray wondered, would Rothes be useful? He had heard that Rothes 'was not with J.R. [Lauderdale] as formerly'. Tweeddale saw no indication of disagreement.[101]

On the other hand – a wonderful illustration of the cliché about politics and bedfellows – there was a sudden rapprochement between Tweeddale and Hamilton, whom he and Moray had scorned and despised for years. Hamilton was vastly irritated with Halton, who as treasurer-depute was dragging his feet about the final clearance of Hamilton's accounts for 1633. In February he had complained to Lauderdale about the slowness of the

99 NLS Ms. 7006, ff. 6–7.
100 NLS Ms. 7025, ff. 106–07.
101 24 Apr., 24 May 1673, Moray to Tweeddale, NLS Ms. 7006, ff. 23, 25. 25 Apr., 10 May, Tweeddale to Moray, NLS Ms. 7025, ff. 107–09.

treasury commission, whose behaviour did not improve; in August he would write of the 'unkindness (I shall not say injustice)' he had received from Halton. His wife wrote a similar letter to Lady Lauderdale, and added that she feared that Halton was trying to turn Lauderdale against her husband.[102] Tweeddale knew all about this, of course, from his seat on the treasury commission. He took advantage of Hamilton's manifest annoyance and met with him. On 7 June he wrote cheerfully to Moray that he and Hamilton 'are in better correspondence than ever'. According to one of Yester's correspondents Hamilton in his turn spoke very highly of him and his father.[103] It was an alliance that would endure, between a solipsistic aristocrat who had felt unappreciated, scorned and neglected for years, who had never received the deference to which, in his opinion, his position entitled him, and one of those who had scorned him, a public servant who on personal and political grounds felt insulted, cheated and outraged. What bound them together was hatred of Lauderdale.

In the latter half of June Moray was in almost daily contact with Shaftesbury, going round and round on the question of when and how Shaftesbury should approach the king and whether Tweeddale should come to London without a summons from Charles. Shaftesbury thought not: if Tweeddale did appear, all of Lauderdale's many enemies here would hope and believe that he was coming with information that would ruin the duke, who, they believed, was hated in Scotland. Moray did not think that that should stop Tweeddale from coming. There was speculation that Lauderdale would go to Scotland to meet parliament, now scheduled for November,[104] in order to get him out of the public eye in London. There was another argument 'in the junto' which widened the breach between Shaftesbury and Lauderdale, over the law involved in filling the lord admiral's place – the Test Act had driven the duke of York from office. Lauderdale was going on about how a clause in the commission for the new lord admiral 'was agreeable to the laws of England . . . and the Chancellor told the king that he hoped his Commissioner for Scotland would not be allowed to teach the Chancellor of England the laws of England and so the debate ended'. On the first of July Moray wrote that Lauderdale and his duchess were going to Bath for a month, leaving Kincardine behind to act

102 20 Feb., 18 Aug. 1673, Hamilton to Lauderdale, 25 Aug., Lady Hamilton to Lady Lauderdale, NAS GD 406/1/2720, 2724, 8793.

103 NLS Ms. 7025, f. 112, Ms. 14414, f. 25. For this paragraph see also J. Patrick, 'The Origins of the Oppositon to Lauderdale in the Scottish Parliament of 1673', SHR LIII (1974), pp. 18–19.

104 RPCS IV, pp. 54–55.

as secretary; Shaftesbury decided to wait until Lauderdale left before speaking to the king.[105]

On 4 July Moray dined with Shaftesbury. He returned to his lodgings in Whitehall, was overcome by a fit of choking, 'and died suddenly, being choked with phlegm and endeavouring to vomit', according to Robert Hooke the chemist, who went on to write that 'he is lamented by all'. 'He was sixty-five years old. Charles ordered that his old friend be buried in Westminster Abbey. His funeral, on 6 July, was well attended by his colleagues in the Royal Society; he was laid to rest in what is now the Poets' Corner. Andrew Hay saw to it that his letters did not fall into the wrong hands. They were sealed, and Charles ordered that they be burned without being read.[106]

One man did not lament Moray's death. On 7 July Lauderdale wrote to Kincardine that the news had surprised him. Had he died a year ago, Lauderdale went on, he would have been sorry, but not now. Moray had picked a quarrel with him over nothing, and never repaid a loan made twenty-five years ago. 'One use I shall make of it: I shall be very unwilling to dine with the lord chancellor, seeing his meat digests very ill.'[107] This ungracious comment was a measure of the animosity with which Lauderdale now regarded his colleagues in the triumvirate that had set out six years ago to bring Scotland a measure of good government and, perhaps, beneficial change. With Moray's death there was now no chance of bringing the dearest brothers back together. Lauderdale knew that he could never destroy Moray's friendship with the king, and he never tried. Moray's influence with Charles might some day be wielded against him; Moray was the one Scot whom Lauderdale could not overreach. Now that he was gone Lauderdale had no more worries. Tweeddale the ex-Cromwellian was not a threat – and Lauderdale had another weapon to use against him. The final stage of the brothers' fraught public relationship was about to begin.

---

105 All this comes from Moray's letter written from 17 June to 1 July 1673, NLS Ms. 7006, ff. 30–32.
106 *Moray Letters*, Intro., pp. 56–59. 22 July 1673, Hay to Tweeddale, NLS Ms. 7006, f. 39. Tweeddale's letters to Moray cited above come from Tweeddale's letterbook.
107 A. Robertson, *The Life of Sir Robert Moray* (London, 1922), pp. 146–47.

CHAPTER TEN

Dearest Brothers No More, 1673–1674

I

Moray's death was a sad blow to Tweeddale, personally and politically. Moray was an old and valued friend and ally. And now Tweeddale had no correspondent who had the king's ear, as Andrew Hay promptly pointed out. He should come to London, lest he 'be totally forgot by the world'.[1] Throughout the summer Hay kept urging him, or Yester, to come to the capital, if only to deal with Mary Yester's houses in Highgate and Aldersgate.[2] Tweeddale decided not to go, for now. It is possible to detect his hand in a letter to the king from the exchequer commission in August asking Charles to reconsider the gift to Kincardine of the pre-emption on salt, which he had come to regard as bad policy. The tack was costing the treasury a substantial amount of money, as Charles admitted in granting it for only £2,000 sterling per year. Kincardine profited from importing foreign salt, but consumption was down, especially of domestic salt, which was a glut on the market. The commission recommended, at the very least, an auction of the tack. Charles wrote a stinging reply. Prices were reasonable, he said, and the 'clamour' the commission mentioned was obviously being fomented. Kincardine's tack would remain in place.[3]

A few days later Charles wrote another stinging letter, this one to the privy council, scolding it for neglecting his instructions of 31 May regarding the outed ministers.[4] Too many of them were hanging around in Edinburgh, and the west still seethed with conventicles. The appointment of the special committee for the west did not mean that the council was to sit back and do nothing, Charles went on: he would be watching. The council bestirred itself. On 3 September, the day it received the letter, it ordered all outed ministers in Edinburgh to appear on 5 September, and planned a large meeting with other outed ministers for the 30th. Rothes wrote to Hamilton that he was to attend that meeting: absentees would be

1 12 July 1673, Hay to Tweeddale, NLS Ms. 7006, f. 35.
2 See, e.g., his letter of 2 Aug. 1673, ibid., ff. 46–47.
3 BL Add. Mss 23135, f. 280. NLS Ms. 7034, f. 24. Charles's reply, dated 24 Aug. 1673, is in NAS SP4/2/274–75.
4 RPCS IV, pp. 95–96. See above, chap. 9, p. 285.

reported to Charles.[5] Little enough came of this flurry of orders. Three of the Edinburgh ministers were horned for non-appearance; two did appear and accepted parochial assignments. Of the twenty-nine ordered to appear on the 30th, twenty-six of whom had refused to accept assignment, only two appeared and accepted parishes. The others were ordered to appear in November, at which point the whole business was put off again: the meeting of parliament was imminent.[6] The council had also ordered a long list of alleged attendees at conventicles to appear on 30 September. Very few did; the rest were horned for non-appearance.[7] Kincardine, who by now was back from London, was very worried. 'Private conventicles abound, where very dangerous persons preach dangerous doctrines', and there are 'very numerous field conventicles . . . at which . . . guards are kept by armed men'. He was glad that Lauderdale would be in Scotland soon. The disorders were so great that parliamentary action was necessary, and perhaps a greater armed force to keep the peace.[8] The policy of accommodation was in shambles, and something would have to be done about it.

Tweeddale for once was very unsure of his next step. In September he learned that Monmouth was going to pursue the Tweeddales at law, over Lady Tweeddale's claim to be the heir of her long-dead brother David. In October the situation became much worse. Monmouth and his duchess refused to ratify the 1667 agreement on Tweeddale's debt to the Buccleuch estate.[9] This agreement had been worked out in the early months of 1667, shortly after Yester's marriage to Mary Maitland, when Tweeddale was in high favour with both Charles and Lauderdale. It balanced Tweeddale's accumulated debt, now some £80,000, against his claim to the Buccleuch property of Easter Hassenden and his wife's claim to receive a substantial part of her brother David's estate.[10] The Tweeddales did not get all they claimed, but did get the debt reduced to £15,600. The king approved the settlement and agreed that the Monmouths would ratify it when they came of age.[11] In the course of the negotiations Tweeddale, or his lawyers, made

5 Ibid., pp. 96–97. *Hamilton Mss*, p. 87.
6 *RPCS* IV, pp. 100–02, 104–05, 108–09.
7 Ibid., pp. 106–07.
8 20 Sept. 1673, Kincardine to Lauderdale, BL Add. Mss 23135, f. 284.
9 8 Sept. 1673, Sir Archibald Murray of Blackbarony to Yester, 20 Oct., Dundonald to Tweeddale, NLS Ms. 7006, ff. 55, 56.
10 For the details of these claims see above, chap. 3, pp. 88–89.
11 *Warrant Book 1660–1670*, NAS GD 90/2/260, under date of 5 Mar. 1667; no pagination. NLS Ms. 14542, f. 4. NAS GD 224/524/43. There are slightly different figures in NLS Ms. 14544, ff. 17–18.

one very damaging mistake. They stated that Earl Francis, Duchess Anna's father and Lady Tweeddale's brother, had reached the age of twenty-five before he died, and had given a discharge to his tutors and curators, meaning that he laid no claim to his brother David's estate – David died in 1648, Francis in 1651.[12] The claim was false: Francis had not yet turned twenty-five when he died. This misstatement allowed the Monmouths' lawyers to argue that the agreement had been based on erroneous information. It was therefore invalid, and the king's guarantee not binding on him. Tweeddale would have to pay the full amount that he owed, which by Whitsun 1673 came to £86,468.[13]

This was a disaster; it is not unreasonable to suppose that Lauderdale had a hand in it. Tweeddale had to go to London before what he called the 'process' started;[14] the question was one of timing. Tweeddale felt that he would not be of any use at parliament, but he wanted to be there to see what Charles was going to ask it to do. Yester had important business in London, and his second son David wanted to go abroad. All three could travel together, and he wanted to get his business with Monmouth settled, but if they did this, Lady Tweeddale would be left alone all winter. Alternatively, they might wait until Lauderdale arrived, but then, Lauderdale might prevent him from going at all.[15] There was the further complication that Hamilton was himself thinking of going to London. They were planning an attack on Lauderdale when parliament met: should the king be made aware that something was planned, or should they keep the element of surprise and run the risk that Lauderdale would put his own spin on what happened? In the end Hamilton decided to stay and expose 'mismanagement and abuses'. If he failed, he would leave parliament and go to the king.[16]

Tweeddale was in some doubt that parliament would be held at all. When it became clear that it would be, he decided to attend it. He was very hopeful because, not having Moray to inform him, he misread the political situation in London. Shaftesbury, now openly antagonistic to Lauderdale, was still lord chancellor. Tweeddale had heard that Charles had laughed at

12 NLS Ms. 14544, f. 21.
13 What Tweeddale owed under the terms of the 1667 settlement was £21,528 by Whitsun 1673. He had never paid anything. NAS GD 224/924/44.
14 NLS Ms. 7025, ff. 124–25.
15 Undated, and 24 Oct. 1673, Tweeddale to Blackbarony, NLS Ms. 7025, ff. 117b, 121.
16 11 Oct. 1673, Tweeddale to Hamilton, 21 Oct., Tweeddale to Blackbarony, ibid., ff. 119, 118.

York and Lauderdale when they had urged the king to fire him. So Tweeddale believed that Charles kept Lauderdale on only because he 'believes he cannot do his affairs here without him, he being the darling and delight of the country'.[17] If Charles could be disabused of that notion, the great man would surely fall. Yester would go to London, strictly on family business, the sale of the houses and finding out if Monmouth would in fact ratify the agreement on Tweeddale's debt to the Buccleuch estate – Tweeddale had recently written him an unctuous letter.[18] Yester waited until Lauderdale arrived in Scotland in order to confront him about the backband. He had been advised to pursue a legal nullification, but wanted to have it out with Lauderdale first. He got nowhere, and left for London on 12 November, the day of the opening of parliament.[19]

The reason why Tweeddale thought there might be no parliament was the dicey political situation in England. The duke of York's public acknowl-edgment of his Catholicism, and his remarriage to a Catholic princess in October, had guaranteed a confrontation when the English parliament next met. It was rumoured in Edinburgh that it might be adjourned on account of the marriage, and the Scottish parliament delayed as well.[20] But it did meet, and, sure enough, the eruption came. On 30 October the Commons voted an address to the king against York's marriage and, a day later, made a wholesale attack on the French alliance and those who advised it. Sooner or later they would name names. So on 4 November Charles prorogued parliament until January, but not before one 'evil coun-sellor' was named: Lauderdale.[21] The secretary had a very bad reputation in England, as a believer in arbitrary government who was prepared to send Scottish troops to England against the king's enemies. 'De'il hoop his lugs [box his ears] that loves a parliament!' wrote a satirist in *The Dream of the Cabal* in 1672.[22] Shaftesbury, Moray's and Tweeddale's friend, was widely believed to be behind the opposition in the Commons. After the proroga-tion Charles fired him as lord chancellor, to Lauderdale's great delight. 'I

17 21 Oct. 1673, Tweeddale to Blackbarony, ibid., f. 118.

18 Ibid., f. 115. NLS Ms. 14413, ff. 39–43.

19 NLS Ms. 14413, ff. 39–43, 14548, ff. 105, 121. 11 Oct. 1673, Tweeddale to Hamilton, 12 Nov., Tweeddale to Charles, NLS Ms. 7025, ff. 119, 122.

20 21 Oct. 1673, Tweeddale to Blackbarony, NLS Ms. 7025, f. 118.

21 K.H.D. Haley, *The First Earl of Shaftesbury* (Oxford, 1968), pp. 338–39. M. Lee, Jr, *The Cabal* (Urbana, 1965), pp. 234–36.

22 Haley, *Shaftesbury*, pp. 340–41. G. deF. Lord, ed., *Poems on Affairs of State* I (New Haven, 1963), p. 193.

bore it with great moderation,' he wrote to his brother, 'but I could easily read in divers countenances what operation it had.'[23]

Lauderdale and his duchess left for Scotland in mid-October, before the meeting of the English parliament. They travelled in leisurely fashion and reached Lethington at the end of the month. He had left his brother behind as secretary – Tweeddale opined that he preferred to have Kincardine with him in Edinburgh to act as his lieutenant in parliament.[24] Lauderdale's letter to the king announcing his arrival sounded very confident. He was not planning to go to Edinburgh until two days before parliament opened: it was unnecessary. The king's instructions were 'only to quiet the minds and secure the peace of this your kingdom', and he foresaw no difficulties, even though the disaffected were 'spreading such news as your small friends at London would have them' – a punning jab at Shaftesbury.[25] And indeed Charles's formal instructions contained very little by way of a legislative agenda, save on the perennial issue of conventicles. There was no mention of a new liturgy, a subject which apparently had been under discussion in London: Charles told Halton that 'we must take care to keep all things right, so much the rather now when a great many endeavour to put them wrong'.[26] There was no suggestion that Lauderdale should ask for a tax. He was to stress that the existing church government would be maintained, and that there would be no further indulgences. What Charles wanted was a tighter and more efficient administration; if legislation was necessary on such matters as the militia, the courts and the economy, Lauderdale as usual had carte blanche to act.[27] It seems clear that for Charles there was less need for a session of the Scottish parliament than there was to get Lauderdale out of the line of fire when his faithful Commons gathered again at Westminster, as inevitably they must. It was a tactic Charles would later employ with his equally unpopular brother.

Tweeddale and Hamilton were making their preparations as well. After Lauderdale's arrival Tweeddale wrote to Hamilton, asking if the commissioner had shown him or Rothes the king's instructions, which Tweeddale had not seen. He described to Hamilton the raucous proceedings at Westminster on 27 October, when the Commons voted both to delay

23 BL Add. Mss 23136, ff. 18–19.
24 Oct. 1673, Tweedale to Blackbarony, NLS Ms. 7025, f. 115.
25 4 Nov 1673, Lauderdale to Charles, BL Add. Mss 23136, f. 7.
26 4 Nov. 1673, Halton to Lauderdale, ibid., f. 5. Halton stressed that he was quoting the king.
27 Charles's instructions are in ibid., f. 3.

answering the king's message and also on a motion to replace the speaker because he was a privy councillor.[28] This was an interesting anticipation of the tactics Hamilton was to employ when parliament met on 12 November. Lauderdale suspected that there might be trouble. He was aware of the widespread dislike of Kincardine's salt monopoly, Elphinstone's gift of the forfeitures of brandy, and Nicolson's gift of the tobacco tax, which Charles had renewed as recently as 28 May.[29] The convention of royal burghs, meeting a few days before parliament opened, elected as its clerk James Roughead, the town clerk of Edinburgh whom Charles had ordered fired because he was an opponent of Lauderdale's ally Provost Ramsay. Ramsay, the presiding officer, was furious, and walked out, which should have brought the session to an end. It did not: Ramsay had no support.[30] But when the parliamentary assault came it was so prompt, vehement and widespread that for once the resourceful commissioner was caught completely off guard.

Parliament opened as usual, with a reading of the king's letter, followed by the commissioner's speech. Charles spoke regretfully of the stubbornness of the Dutch, which meant that the war had to go on, and mentioned that the purpose of the session was to curb field conventicles. There was a hint that the crown needed money, but none was asked for. Lauderdale's speech stressed how well the last session of parliament had gone, and how necessary it was to curb the insolence of seditious people and maintain episcopacy.[31] But when he proposed that the Articles meet at once to prepare a reply to the king's letter, Hamilton, echoing the tactics of the English opposition, arose to demand that the redress of grievances be dealt with first, a ploy which, according to Mackenzie, he and his allies had decided on the night before.[32] Hamilton received a great deal of support. There followed a confused discussion which Lauderdale could not control, and which he described the next day in a letter to his brother. The opposition wanted the admission of the whole house to the meetings of the Articles. The discussion got very heated. Sir Francis Scott of Thirlestane

---

28 NLS Ms. 7025, f. 114. Tweeddale dated the copy of the letter 4 Oct. 1673, but the context makes clear that it was written a month later. This is one more example of Tweeddale's habit of misdating letters.

29 NAS SP 4/2/180–82.

30 G. MacIntosh, *The Scottish Parliament under Charles II 1660–1685* (Edinburgh, 2007), p. 128.

31 *APS* VIII, p. 210. BL Add. Mss 23126, f. 16.

32 Mackenzie, *Memoirs*, p. 253.

made a vehement speech against the war, which profited only the English and was very damaging to Scotland. The laird of Polwarth wanted a special committee of grievances. Lauderdale had very little support: his letter mentioned only Atholl, Argyll, Kincardine and Lord President Stair. His fellow treasury commissioner Dundonald finally bailed him out by moving to adjourn, a motion Lauderdale gratefully accepted. During all this argument Tweeddale remained very quiet, only intervening to suggest that delaying an answer to the king's letter was not unprecedented and that the opinions of those who were not members of the Articles should be taken into account. Lauderdale was suspicious. Tweeddale 'spoke very ambiguously', he wrote to Halton, but Scott and Polwarth are his 'creatures'.[33]

On the following day Lauderdale set about damage control. He called a meeting of 'the considerablest of all the 3 Estates' and gave way on the three major flash points. The salt, brandy and tobacco monopolies would be abolished – 'Kincardine most handsomely offered to lay down that lease [salt] . . . for the good of the kingdom.' On 17 November, when parliament reconvened, Lauderdale announced that the three monopolies would be dealt with in the Articles, and immediately adjourned for a week. He rebuffed Hamilton's efforts to bring up other grievances and paid no attention to the earl of Eglinton's complaint that 'we have no Articles' because they had not been properly constituted. When the Articles met 'the E. of Tweeddale, who was the father and mother of the preemption of the salt, is now the great haranguer against it.' Tweeddale commented to his son that ending the salt monopoly would net the crown £7,000 sterling a year, and £2,000 more from ending the gift of brandy – tobacco was worthless to begin with.[34] Lauderdale, in describing this meeting in a second letter to Halton, told him to assure the king that he would never allow any damage to be done to the constitutional position of the Articles, which Charles regarded as 'one of the best flowers in his crown of Scotland',[35] and to ask Charles for authority to abolish the three monopolies. Now that Shaftesbury had been fired – Lauderdale learned the news on the 16th – he felt free to underline the connection between the fallen lord chancellor and Tweeddale.[36]

---

33 There is an excellent description of this scene in MacIntosh, *Scottish Parliament*, pp. 125–26. 13 Nov. 1673, Lauderdale to Halton, BL Add. Mss 23136, ff. 14–15. See also NLS Ms. 7034, ff. 31–32.

34 20 Nov. 1673, Tweeddale to Yester, NLS Ms. 14413, f. 43.

35 13 June 1674, Lauderdale to Sharp, Dowden, 'Letters', pp. 269–72.

36 18 Nov. 1673, Lauderdale to Halton, BL Add. Mss 23136, ff. 18–19. Lauderdale's speech to parliament is in BL Add. Mss 23136, f. 20.

On 20 November Lauderdale wrote to the king, his first letter since that of 4 November announcing his arrival. In it he recapitulated what he told Halton, but with a shift of emphasis. Shaftesbury is now the principal plotter and Tweeddale his principal ally. Hamilton, who has always opposed obeying the king, on the union and almost everything else, is in this case a mere figurehead, 'brought in to lead the dance'; Tweeddale is the 'contriver and counsellor', behind the scenes at first, but now openly so. (Tweeddale himself described his interventions in debate as infrequent and moderate.)[37] Yester had left for London; he 'perhaps . . . went up upon these designs'. Shaftesbury has 'plotted long to get me out of this employment', and thought to install Monmouth in his place, but Monmouth refused. They want 'to hinder the parliament from paying their duty to you, and to make it appear that the kingdom is not united in your service . . . If they be suffered to prevail you will quickly see what work they will make'.[38] This was an extraordinarily skilful letter, designed to discredit Hamilton and Tweeddale in advance. Lauderdale calculated that when parliament was over they would go to London to appeal directly to the king. He was determined that they go as individuals, not as spokesmen for a disgruntled parliament, and that what they had to say would carry no conviction with Charles.

To achieve all this Lauderdale had to regain control of the parliament, which he did by acceding to the abolition of the three monopolies[39] and using his power of adjournment – there were six in a three-week span – to stifle debate and prevent opposition motions. Ending the monopolies pleased the royal burghs, whose support Lauderdale began cultivating after parliament's tumultuous opening day. He sent for Ramsay's Edinburgh opponents, Francis Kinloch and James Roughead, 'caressed them in the meanest manner that may be', and recommended Roughead's reinstatement as town clerk, which Charles promptly ordered, two months after he had fired him.[40] The burghs on 22 November sent a delegation to Lauderdale, thanking him for his action on the monopolies.[41] The opposition tried to regain their support by accusing their bête noir, Provost

---

37 28 Nov. 1673, Tweeddale to Yester, NLS Ms. 14413, ff. 51–52.
38 BL Add. Mss 23136, f. 24.
39 Charles authorised this action on 26 Nov. 1673. Ibid., f. 26.
40 13 Nov. 1673, Patrick Murray to Yester, NLS Ms. 7006, f. 64. NLS Ms. 7034, ff. 25–26. NAS SP4/2/362. Murray was delighted at Lauderdale's humiliation at the opening of parliament, and wished that Yester had been there to see it.
41 NLS Ms. 7034, f. 48. Charles ordered Lauderdale to thank them; 29 Nov. 1673, Halton to Lauderdale, BL Add. Mss 23136, f. 28.

Ramsay, of corruption and moving for his impeachment, which surprised Lauderdale but which he was able to block. The charges were eventually referred to the judges.[42] Having killed the impeachment, Lauderdale forced Ramsay to resign as provost and from the court of session.[43] His twelve-year reign in Edinburgh was over.

On 1 December, and again on the 3rd, Lauderdale wrote to Charles in a tone of considerable self-satisfaction about his handling of the parliament, which he adjourned on 2 December. He had dealt with the elimination of the monopolies in such a way as to be able to take credit for taking the initiative. And 'I have beat down . . . all extravagant motions and all manner of vote except to those acts which I moved . . . myself.' It was not easy. The opposition, of which 'Tweeddale is the head and heart', met daily, and 'the duke of Hamilton is content to appear the leader and driver'. Among the motions 'beat down' was one by Hamilton, 'moved irregularly (for no mortal can stop his tongue)' against the appointment of unqualified men to the court of session, and 'wild motions' by Dumfries on abuses in the mint, a slap at Halton. Lauderdale adjourned parliament until 28 January 1674, which would allow Charles time to decide, after the English parliament met on 7 January, whether he wanted to resume the session in Edinburgh. He had re-established his control: 'as soon as I took my hand from your sceptre' touching the last Acts approved, those abolishing the tobacco monopoly and repealing part of the sumptuary law of 1672, 'there was not a whisper after'. He planned to remain in Scotland, but urged Charles to make no decisions until after he had talked to Kincardine, whom he was sending to London immediately. You will know what to say to Hamilton and Tweeddale if and when they show up, he went on. They 'have no authority. They shall only come as private men'. Once again, as in his letter of 20 November, Lauderdale stressed that his difficulties had been 'advised and fomented at London, you know by whom [Shaftesbury]', from which Charles was to infer that the Scottish opposition was not widespread, and was the work of a handful of malcontents.[44]

Charles was pleased at his commissioner's handling of the situation, as was the duke of York. Some people here had hoped for trouble in Edinburgh, wrote Charles, but 'they are not so pert on that subject as they

---

42 They are spelled out in *APS* VIII, App., pp. 28–30. See also the account of the debate in NLS Ms. 7034, f. 33.
43 Mackenzie, *Memoirs*, pp. 260–62.
44 BL Add. Mss 23136, ff. 29–30, 35–36.

were'. Yester, 'who comes but seldom in my eye looks but melancholy upon it'.[45] When Yester finally got an interview with the king, he found Charles very chilly and very well informed about the goings-on in parliament. The king was angriest at Hamilton and at the proposal for a committee of grievances, which, he said, would 'overturn the foundation of the parliament'. Yester did his best to play down his father's role, and asked Charles to permit him to come to London to justify himself. The king 'put it off . . . saying you had better stay there to advance his service'. But he would listen to complaints. As for what Yester called the 'misunderstanding' between his father and Lauderdale, Charles 'said he concerned not himself therein, but that he expected you would have a care of his service . . . and bidding me beware of believing some persons who would be for the making that kingdom a province of the republic of England', remarkable language which indicated the depth of his resentment of the opposition and his memory of Tweeddale's and Shaftesbury's Cromwellian past. Yester hurriedly explained that he was in London on private business. He apologised to his father for his shortcomings, 'I being a little dashed, it being the first time'.[46]

Kincardine arrived in London with Lauderdale's reports on 15 December. He saw the king the next day, and wrote that Charles and York were very well satisfied, satisfaction which the brothers personally expressed in letters to the commissioner a few days later. Kincardine, who had a handful of letters to deliver to various important people in the administration, commented that people at court thought that strange things were going on in Scotland, and were surprised to learn from him that the fuss was caused only by a few people 'making noise and bustling'.[47]

Charles and his commissioner addressed each other as though the parliamentary session had been a success. It was, in fact, a complete failure and very nearly a disaster for them.[48] None of the king's admittedly meagre

---

45 29 Nov. 1673, Charles to Lauderdale, ibid., f. 29. See also 4 Dec., York to Lauderdale, ibid., f. 41.

46 4 Dec. 1673, Yester to Tweeddale, ibid., ff. 44–45. This is a copy of Yester's letter, which was intercepted, as was one from Polwarth to Yester on 6 Dec. saying that Tweeddale and Hamilton were leaving for London on the 9th. Ibid., f. 46.

47 9 Dec. 1673, Lauderdale to Charles, 16 Dec., Kincardine to Lauderdale, 21 Dec., Charles to Lauderdale, and York to Lauderdale, ibid., ff. 47, 49–50, 55, 57. The royal letters were carried north by Halton, who, now that Kincardine had arrived to replace him, was returning to Scotland.

48 There is an excellent account in MacIntosh, *Scottish Parliament*, pp. 124–32. See also J. Patrick, 'The Origins of the Oppositon to Lauderdale in the Scottish Parliament of 1673', *SHR* LIII (1974), pp. 1–21.

agenda had been adopted. Lauderdale kept control only by sacrificing the monopolies from which three of his allies profited. He also sacrificed another political ally, Provost Ramsay. He had to listen to attacks on his appointments to the bench and on his brother's misdoings at the mint, both altogether justified. The opposition, which owed much to the accumulated resentments of many years, was widespread. It was also well organised; undoubtedly Lauderdale was right in believing that responsibility lay with Tweeddale rather than with the solipsistic Hamilton. They held regular meetings 'in a most unheard-of manner' in Masterson's tavern, where, he reminded Charles, 'billeting was broached and members debauched under pretence then of your desire for it'.[49] Lauderdale was both surprised and shaken. Kincardine and Halton had not warned him. They had not seen trouble coming themselves, and the twisting and unreliable Rothes had said nothing. Parliament, he concluded, was no longer a dependable instrument of his government. 'You shall find me readier than all your enemies to rid you of the trouble of Scots Parliaments, which I swear are now useless at the best,' he wrote to Charles on 5 March 1674.[50] Between 1669 and 1673 Lauderdale had presided over four parliamentary sessions; he never met another. When the government needed money in 1678 a convention of estates was summoned: it could deal only with money, and was prohibited from discussing any other subject. It could not easily serve as a forum for an attack on his regime.

The failed parliament of 1673, which met no more after 2 December and was formally dissolved in May 1674, marks the end of a chapter in Scottish government and politics, a chapter corresponding to the Cabal years in England. By the end of 1673 Charles's grand design of those years was in ruins and the Cabal had broken up. Clifford was forced out of office by the Test Act and died before the end of the year. Shaftesbury was now in opposition, and Buckingham, everything by starts and nothing long, became his lieutenant. Arlington deflected the Commons' attacks on him and remained in office, but he 'was worn out by overwork, political exertion, and gout'.[51] He resigned in September 1674; his political influence rapidly waned thereafter. Only Lauderdale remained. Similarly in Scotland: the plans of the triumvirate to alter the complexion of affairs in 1667 had been dashed. Moray was dead and Tweeddale in opposition. There was, seemingly, a new

---

49 20 Nov. 1673, Lauderdale to Charles, BL Add. Mss 23136, f. 24.
50 Ibid., f. 115.
51 R.F. Hutton, *Charles II, King of England, Scotland and Ireland* (Oxford, 1989), p. 321.

triumvirate: Lauderdale, Kincardine and Halton, backed by Argyll and Atholl. But it had no agenda and it did not last. By the end of 1674 Lauderdale had pushed his brother into the background and broken with Kincardine, either because the duchess of Lauderdale turned against him (Mackenzie) or because he objected to Lauderdale's newly oppressive regime (Gilbert Burnet).[52] The mid-1670s were the years of Danby, whom Lauderdale was carefully cultivating. On 11 December he wrote a long letter to Danby describing his parliamentary success: only what he wanted passed was voted on, and there was no reflection on him, in parliament or out, 'whatever be the lies vented in London'. The king 'may do what he pleases in parliament or out of it here'.[53] Danby's regime, at least with respect to religious policy, resembled that of Clarendon. So Lauderdale's government became like those of Middleton and Rothes, and provoked an even more substantial rebellion, which, as with Rothes, greased the skids for his eventual fall from power.

II

It was Lauderdale's usual practice to leave for London as soon after the end of a parliamentary session as possible. This time, however, he did not, partly because parliament might reassemble on 28 January, partly because he knew that he would be attacked in the Commons once the English parliament came together. Kincardine reported that Danby, who was very supportive, expected that the Commons 'were like to begin where they left [off] concerning you'. Kincardine replied that what the English parliament said and did made no difference to Scotland, as long as the king remained firm.[54] Danby was correct. On 13 January 1674 the assault came. Sir Robert Thomas declared that Lauderdale 'has contributed as much to our misfortunes as any man'. Sir Thomas Littleton feared the army that he had at his disposal: 'a man of such principles is not fit to be trusted with such an army'. Another member accused him of a design to further Popery, and wanted him removed from the king's presence forever. There was even the suggestion that he be the subject of a bill of attainder. Some two weeks later the Commons voted unanimously to ask the king to receive an address

52 R.C. Paterson, *King Lauderdale* (Edinburgh, 2003), p. 215.
53 NLS Ms. 3420, f. 146.
54 18 Dec. 1673, Kincardine to Lauderdale, BL Add. Mss 23136, ff. 51–53.

asking for Lauderdale's removal.[55] Finding the king unresponsive, a Commons committee asked Kincardine to appear, evidently with a view to extracting information about Scotland; when he refused to answer their questions they desisted. Kincardine reported that he was 'civilly used', and told the committee that 'as a gentleman' he would be happy to provide information 'at another place' but not in a Commons committee room.[56]

On the day after the first attack on Lauderdale Charles wrote him a short note of thanks for his good work. 'It is hot at present,' he remarked, but when people stop to think, 'reason and justice will have the credit it (*sic*) ought to have.'[57] Kincardine, who wrote frequently and at length about the goings-on in parliament and at court, was not worried, given the support Lauderdale was getting from Charles, James, and Danby. In February the Commons returned to the charge. They were exercised about the Scottish militia being 'ready to march', which would violate an Act of King James's time prohibiting armed forces from going from one kingdom to another, and was therefore a treasonable proposal. Kincardine was dismissive, but he did feel that Lauderdale should answer the charge that he had said that 'the king's edicts are as good as laws', a story evidently being spread by Gilbert Burnet. Your friends are at a loss to know how to respond to this, Kincardine went on. If Lauderdale said it, the context was crucial, since royal proclamations could carry penalties with them, but Kincardine doubted that Lauderdale had said it at all. He had never heard Lauderdale use the word 'edicts', which, he said, is not a Scottish word. Kincardine's scepticism is shared by Lauderdale's most recent biographer, among others. Whether the commissioner actually said this – he later denied it, and the king backed him up – is unimportant. His recent behaviour certainly left the impression that he would carry out the king's wishes no matter what.[58]

There were matters other than the complaints of the House of Commons to concern Lauderdale in January 1674. There had been anti-Catholic riots in London on 5 November 1673, the anniversary of the Gunpowder Plot.[59]

---

55 Anchitell Grey, *Debates of the House of Commons* (London, 1769), II, pp. 236–44, 372–73. Paterson, *King Lauderdale*, pp. 212–14. The Commons also asked for the dismissal of Buckingham, who 'made such a hash of his speech that none of his friends dared to defend him . . . Charles obliged at once.' Hutton, *Charles II*, p. 316.

56 10 Feb. 1674, Kincardine to Lauderdale, BL Add. Mss 23136, ff. 83–87.

57 14 Jan. 1674, Charles to Lauderdale, ibid., f. 72.

58 12 Feb. 1674, Kincardine to Lauderdale, ibid., f. 91. NLS Ms. 597, f. 259. Paterson, *King Lauderdale*, p. 213.

59 Tim Harris, *Restoration: Charles II and his Kingdoms 1660–1685* (London, 2005), p. 81.

Fear of Popery was on the rise in England in the wake of the duke of York's marriage and the Dutch government's effective propaganda campaign. So Charles ordered a crackdown, instructing the Scottish privy council to work with his commissioner to suppress Popery and superstition. The council had indeed anticipated his request, issuing a proclamation recapitulating anti-Catholic legislation, ordering military commanders to report on Papists in the army and the bishops to produce a list of Papists in their dioceses by 1 May.[60] More immediately important to Lauderdale was the question of whether parliament should reassemble on 28 January. There were reports that troops were being moved back to Edinburgh from the west to overawe parliament if and when it did meet.[61] Lauderdale did not want it to resume, nor, for entirely different reasons, did Hamilton and Tweeddale, who were currently in London pressing their case for regime change. They wished to underline the fiasco of the November session, not to hurry home for a new meeting, while Lauderdale did not want a rerun of November.

There was, however, the question of money. It seems likely that Charles and Lauderdale had hoped to repeat in November 1673 what had worked so well in 1672: there would be no formal request for a tax, but the king's loyal subjects, i.e., Lauderdale's allies, would propose one. Money was in short supply, as usual. On 19 December 1673 the treasury commission wrote to the king asking that it be permitted to cover a shortfall of over £200,000 with the take from the 1672 tax. Charles refused: that money was earmarked for the war, and Charles would not grant the commission's request unless it told him how it would be repaid. He was unwilling, wrote Kincardine, 'to have that money meddled with'. Charles was also unwilling to dissolve parliament as long as the war continued, though on 17 January he authorised another short adjournment, to 3 March. By 24 January, when this order reached Edinburgh and was registered by the council, the king had received terms from the Dutch that sufficed, with the approval of the English parliament, to end the war. Peace was at hand.[62]

Lauderdale welcomed the adjournment. Tweeddale's friends in Edinburgh were disappointed. They anticipated being stronger in the new session, but William Hay, at least, was philosophical about the adjournment, both

60 *RCPS* IV, pp. 111, 117–23, 124–25. NAS SP 4/2/370.
61 7 Jan. 1674, Patrick Hume to Yester, NLS Ms. 7006, ff. 78–79.
62 3 Jan. 1674, Charles to the treasury commission, NAS SP 4/2/371–72. 3 Jan., Kincardine to Lauderdale, BL Add. Mss 23136, f. 64. *RPCS* IV, p. 130. Hutton, *Charles II*, pp. 316–17.

because of the bad weather and because he felt that Tweeddale wanted it.[63] Kincardine, interestingly, was not pleased, because he believed that Charles had ordered it 'at the importunity of his [Lauderdale's] declared enemies'. He told Charles so; the king replied that 'things were ill here, and we must not . . . have troublesome business both in Scotland and here together'. Kincardine rejoined that if Charles had been firmer with the commissioner's enemies there would have been no trouble in Scotland. If his account in his letter to Lauderdale is to be taken at face value, he was very argumentative with Charles. He then changed the subject, and discussed with Charles two other complaints the opposition had made in parliament. He refuted Tweeddale's charge that there were more non-lawyers than lawyers on the court of session. He also expected that the inquiry into misdoings at the mint would fizzle out: the 'clamour raised upon that affair' was aimed at Halton only because he was Lauderdale's brother. 'The king seemed to be very well pleased,' and in fact on 30 March the privy council gave the mint a clean bill of health. Kincardine would have wished for further discussions with Charles, but he 'is now so much taken up with affairs here that he can hardly think upon our affairs'.[64]

The peace with the Dutch, which was formally proclaimed in London on 28 February and in Edinburgh on 5 March, meant that there was no more need for parliament in Scotland. Charles thought it should be dissolved, but Kincardine persuaded him that dissolution would look as though he was doing so in order to put an end to Lauderdale's commission. It would be better to adjourn parliament and summon Lauderdale, 'who would probably propose the dissolution himself'. He also urged the king to fire Tweeddale, 'who was beloved by nobody', as Lauderdale wanted him to do. Charles declined to do this: he felt that Tweeddale would look like a martyr and Lauderdale be hurt. But he did accept Kincardine's advice respecting parliament. He adjourned it until 24 October – and prorogued the English parliament until November – and summoned Lauderdale for consultation.[65]

In his instructions to Lauderdale Charles directed him to redress outstanding grievances before his return.[66] One important constitutional issue, which was not precisely a grievance, arose early in 1674. Lord

63 7 Jan. 1674, Patrick Hume to Yester, 26 Jan., Hay to Tweeddale, NLS Ms. 7006, ff. 78–79, 80.
64 20 Jan. 1674, Kincardine to Lauderdale, BL Add. Mss 23136, ff. 74–75. *RCPS* IV, pp. 174–76.
65 10, 14, 28 Feb. 1674, Kincardine to Lauderdale, BL Add. Mss 23136, ff. 83–87, 99, 113. *RCPS* IV, pp. 146–47.
66 BL. Add. Mss 23136, f. 100.

Almond, having received an unfavourable verdict from the court of session in a lawsuit against the earl of Dunfermline, appealed the verdict on procedural grounds on the advice of his lawyers. The issue was political as well as legal: Dunfermline was Lauderdale's (and Tweeddale's) close cousin, while Almond was Hamilton's cousin by marriage. Lauderdale at once denounced the appeal as insolent and dangerous, and had the session write to Charles citing historical precedents to prove that no appeals were allowed from its decisions. Lauderdale declared that the appeal threatens 'the overthrow of your government' and urged Charles to write to the session indicating his displeasure and directing the court to find out who was responsible. Charles promptly did so.[67] The king also snubbed Hamilton when the latter complained about the session's verdict. 'What you say in this is as ill as anything you have said lately in parliament,' Kincardine quoted him as saying, 'and I believe nothing will satisfy you except the judges be all of your own choosing'. Historical precedent was on Lauderdale's side on this issue, which had arisen during the debates on the union. So too were the politics of it: the court was packed with Lauderdale's nominees. The lawyers were predictably unhappy with the outcome. Kincardine thought that if appeals were allowed there would be no end of lawsuits. Tweeddale, he correctly surmised, was in touch with the 'factious advocates'; Charles assured him that he would not listen.[68] The king's definitive decision came in the form of a letter to the court of session on 19 May: there would be no appeals, and the advocates must acquiesce, which, after some grumbling, they did.[69]

On 5 March Lauderdale wrote to the king expressing his pleasure that Charles had summoned him home and adjourned the parliament, 'where mad motions were prepared against your service'. He played cat-and-mouse with his opponents, who had organised a parade of coaches to the parliament house, and were deflated when the adjournment was announced. Hamilton, who had returned from London expecting parliament to reassemble, declared that the king had broken his word: he had promised to

---

67 7 Feb. 1674, Lauderdale to Charles, 7 Feb., the court of session to Charles, ibid., ff. 80, 81. 17 Feb., Charles to the session, NAS SP 4/2/380.

68 10 Feb., 10 Mar. 1674, Kincardine to Lauderdale, BL Add. Mss 23136, ff. 83–87, 119.

69 Mackenzie, *Memoirs*, pp. 274–310, gives a full account of this incident. See also R.S. Rait, *The Parliaments of Scotland* (Glasgow, 1924), pp. 475–77, and R.A. Lee, *Government and Politics in Scotland, 1661–1681* (PhD diss., University of Glasgow, 1995), pp. 242–45. For a review of the whole subject see J.D. Ford, 'Protestations to Parliament for Remeid of Law', *SHR* LXXXVIII (2009), pp. 57–107, esp. pp. 68–73.

allow parliament to reassemble and, after some days, to dissolve it. Lauderdale obviously enjoyed the scene. Tweeddale, he observed, 'does you much mischief there and here'; he urged Charles to 'dispatch' him and listen to no more complaints.[70] Efforts to patch up a truce between the two dukes got nowhere. Archbishop Sharp wanted Rothes to intervene to that end, but the chancellor, as always, was not prepared to take sides until he knew which would be the winner.[71]

In a memorandum for Kincardine a few days after the adjournment Lauderdale mentioned a proposal by Sir John Cochrane, not a member of the opposition, for the abolition of the arrears of the tax of 1633 and all other levies before 1660, as well as uncollected fines save those for keeping conventicles and other violations of the laws establishing and protecting the church.[72] Lauderdale pushed the idea in order to discomfit Hamilton, who was the collector of the 1633 arrears and was entitled to keep them. Charles accepted Lauderdale's recommendation and went still further, pardoning all fines before the date of the proclamation save those connected with the 1666 rebellion and capital offences. When the council took up the king's instructions Hamilton protested vehemently: his contract granting him the proceeds of the taxation could not legally be broken by a proclamation. Lauderdale as council president did not allow him to speak at the time, but since the proclamation had to be delayed by a day, Hamilton had time to mobilise his lawyers and present a petition to the council. A council committee recommended that the proclamation contain a clause that the cancellations did not prejudice Hamilton's rights, and it was so ordered. Hamilton had made his point. There was a further argument about the council's covering letter thanking the king for remitting the arrears and the fines, and praising Lauderdale for redressing grievances. Hamilton complained that Lauderdale had not, in fact, redressed grievances, which were in any case the business of parliament, and had misrepresented them to the king. He pointed to the scandalous cover-up of the behaviour of mint officials. Halton, at whom this was aimed, said that Hamilton should not speak to the king's commissioner thus; Hamilton snubbed him. The duke was told that the letter spoke only of Lauderdale's willingness to redress grievances, but he did extract one concession. The letter spoke of 'our' offer of lives and fortunes in the king's service rather

70 BL Add. Mss 23136, f. 115.
71 19 Mar. 1674, Lady Tweeddale to Tweeddale, NLS Ms. 14402, ff. 99–100.
72 BL Add. Mss. 23136, ff. 117–18.

than the kingdom's. Hamilton did not sign. He informed Tweeddale that five other councillors, four earls and General Drummond, also refused to sign, and that Rothes signed in his official capacity, 'it being carried by votes', not because he endorsed the praise of Lauderdale.[73]

One of Yester's correspondents commented to him in the wake of the parliamentary charade in March that Lauderdale's opponents were dithering and uncertain of their next move.[74] Hamilton's frustration showed in his letter of 28 March to the king. He only wished to serve the king, he wrote. Distempers were increasing. He knew that Lauderdale was on his way to London; he begged Charles to give him a hearing with Lauderdale present.[75] Charles wanted no part of this, and forbade him to come: 'it could do nothing but make more trouble and noise, and do hurt here as well as in Scotland'. Kincardine informed Lauderdale of Charles's decision on 11 April, and wished him a safe journey.[76]

It had all seemed so different when, in the aftermath of the adjournment of parliament in 1673, Hamilton and Tweeddale set out for London to lay their case before the king. They were accompanied out of Edinburgh by a huge following, twelve coaches and 300 horses; Hamilton sent the coaches back from Musselburgh. All but a very few people in Scotland supported them, according to Patrick Hume, and the first reports back to Edinburgh were that 'our patriots' had been well received.[77] The line they took was that parliament had been prematurely adjourned, leaving many things undone, the complaints about the lords of session and the mint especially; furthermore, what had been done was due to their prodding.[78] In addition Tweeddale prepared a long account of his difficulties with Lauderdale over the past three years. These he attributed to unnamed people looking for their own advantage, who aroused Lauderdale's jealousy of him by insinuating

---

73 For the discussion in the council see ibid., f. 125, NLS Ms. 7006, f. 124, and 19 Apr. 1674, Hamilton to Tweeddale, ibid., ff. 113–16. For the council's report and proclamation see *RPCS* IV, pp. 164–69. The council's letter, dated 26 Mar., is in NLS Ms. 7006, f. 118. The lawyers' opinion on Hamilton's rights is in NLS Ms. 7006, f. 121. Hamilton's letter to Tweeddale of 24 Mar. is in the Lauderdale papers, BL Add. Mss 23136, ff. 128–29. It evidently never reached Tweeddale.

74 NLS Ms. 14414, ff. 37–39.

75 NAS GD 406/1/2854.

76 BL Add. Mss 23136, ff. 131–32.

77 12 Dec. 1673, Hume to Yester, NLS Ms. 7006, f. 63. The letter is misdated 12 Nov. 6 Jan. 1674, Francis Scott to Yester, NLS Ms. 7006, f. 72.

78 Hamilton laid this out in a letter to one of Charles's equerries on 2 Dec. 1673, the day of the adjournment. *Laing Mss* I, p. 391.

that he monopolised business and was seeking to manage patronage. These nameless people persuaded Lauderdale to make use of Halton, whom he had previously regarded as 'a weak and insufficient person' who did not even deserve a pension – Tweeddale got him his first one. But now Lauderdale gave Halton all business to manage, made him a judge and treasurer-depute, and instructed him to farm the customs and excise at 'the most unseasonable time' at a cost to the government of £5,000 sterling.[79]

Hamilton and Tweeddale met a stone wall. The king was polite but 'somewhat warm' with them when they admitted that they had not discussed matters with Lauderdale or put their complaints in writing. They added another, non-parliamentary complaint, the gift of prospective ward-ships to Kincardine, which the king brushed off as 'no matter of grievance'. The duke of York was, if anything, chillier than his brother. Hamilton complained to him about the expense of the commissioner's office, £18,000 sterling a year, and that it was 'against the constitution of Scotland to be governed by a commissioner'. York replied that all kings 'governed their kingdoms . . . where they could not be themselves by one man'. Kincardine was anxious to have 'the affairs of those lords put to some period', and York agreed with him.[80]

Hamilton and Tweeddale were persistent. They kept seeking audiences with the king and York, and were sometimes kept waiting while Kincardine saw the king.[81] Their allies in Scotland, encouraged by the Commons' vote against Lauderdale, sent the earl of Dumfries, the leader in parliament of the campaign to investigate the mint, to reinforce them – 'to bawl against me', in Lauderdale's phrase. To York Lauderdale wrote that Dumfries had been involved in the billeting business, a deft way of insuring that the king would pay him no heed.[82] He accomplished nothing. Tweeddale was deliberately kept uninformed, by Charles's order, in the case of the treasury commis-sion's request to use the 1672 tax money to cover ordinary expenses – Tweeddale was a member of the commission. At the time of the parliamen-tary adjournment in March – Hamilton had returned to Scotland with Dumfries to attend that meeting that never was – Tweeddale opined to

79 NLS Ms. 7025, f. 127. This document, in the form of a letter to the king, is unfinished; it is not clear that it was ever delivered.
80 18, 25, 29 Dec. 1673, 10 Jan. 1674, Kincardine to Lauderdale, BL Add. Mss 23136, ff. 51–53, 60, 62–63, 68–69.
81 E.g., 10 Feb. 1674, Kincardine to Lauderdale, ibid., ff. 83–87.
82 1 Feb. 1674, Lauderdale to Charles, ibid., f. 78, and to York, ff. 78b–79. These two letters are copies of the originals.

Kincardine that parliament could not be dissolved except at a meeting. The latter was non-committal. He knew of the plan to dissolve parliament by proclamation, and did not want Tweeddale to 'have the least hint' of it.[83]

Following Lauderdale's instructions, Kincardine kept working to get Tweeddale fired. His persistence suggests that he resented Tweeddale's leadership in ending his salt monopoly. He had the backing of Danby and York, but found 'much more sticking than I expected'. He thought Arlington might be hostile.[84] Indeed the king, instead of firing Tweeddale, had him resume his seat on the English privy council after Hamilton returned to Scotland. Charles evidently valued his advice, particularly on economic issues. According to his own later account, Tweeddale persuaded the king to authorise the resumption of the meetings of the trade commission; Lauderdale quashed their projected report because it had been done without him. Tweeddale also reminded the king that Lauderdale's fee of £50 per diem, which, as Hamilton had pointed out, cost the treasury £18,000 sterling a year, obtained only when parliament was in session; during adjournments it was £10 a day. Charles accepted the argument and cut Lauderdale's fee to £10 as of 1 February. The commissioner was livid; he 'reckoned it as an unpardonable crime which made him implacable unto him [Tweeddale] ever thereafter'. Tweeddale's view was that he was merely doing his duty. He also temporarily persuaded Charles that no one should be commissioner for longer than five years, 'it being impossible for any man to continue in that situation 5 months and not give just cause of complaint against him'. Charles did not follow through on this. Whether Lauderdale knew about it, says Tweeddale, is uncertain, 'but if he did it was ground enough to provoke his revenge to the utmost'.[85]

Tweeddale later wrote that he stayed behind in London after Hamilton left 'to avoid further misrepresentation of him . . . at Court'.[86] He had a much more compelling reason: he desperately wanted either to persuade the duke and duchess of Monmouth not to pursue their case against him for the full amount of his debt to the Buccleuch estate, which they had indicated they would do in a letter to their commissioners in November 1673, or to persuade the king to uphold and enforce the agreement hammered out in 1667. His own finances were currently in bad shape, and his creditors

---

83 3 Jan., 14 Mar. 1674, Kincardine to Lauderdale, ibid., ff. 64, 121.
84 12, 14 Feb. 1674, Kincardine to Lauderdale, ibid., ff. 89–90, 93.
85 Tweeddale, 'Wrangs', pp. 291–93.
86 Ibid., p. 291.

were pressing him.[87] On 8 January he had an interview with the duchess that went badly. After what the duchess described as a tedious half-hour of compliments Tweeddale got to the point. He did not want a lawsuit, he said, and he thought the settlement was more than fair to the duke and duchess – he nattered on about how he had 'got too little abated him'. Anna replied coldly that in that case he would get justice. She expected him to try again, but she was not going to compromise, nor would she consult her commissioners, who in fact did nothing. She told Kincardine that she had a low opinion of Tweeddale, and of Hamilton too.[88] Lady Tweeddale hoped that some sort of a compromise might be reached, but by mid-February she concluded that the Monmouths were going to continue the legal process. Earlier that month the Monmouths' only child, a little boy, had died. The death brought Lady Tweeddale one step closer to the Buccleuch inheritance. But she grieved for Anna: she too had lost children. 'I pray God comfort his mother under so sad an affliction and preserve her from hurt by it in the condition she is in' – Anna was pregnant again. And when Anna was safely delivered in May, she wished Anna 'much joy and comfort in her son'.[89]

Lady Tweeddale was a kind and generous woman who would willingly have been friends with her niece. She had hopes that an interview with Yester, who was planning to see Anna before he left for France, might do some good. Yester told Anna that he held Lauderdale responsible for the Monmouths' suit, and was surprised that he should be so harsh to his own grandchildren. This rattled her, said Yester, but she collected herself and changed the subject. Lady Tweeddale was convinced that if Anna was listening to Lauderdale there was no hope: 'I shall never expect right or justice from him'[90] She wrote regularly to her husband while he was in London, keeping him abreast of developments and rumours in Edinburgh, and hoping that he would receive her letters – Tweeddale, Hamilton and the others were fearful, and rightly so, that their correspondence would be intercepted. She wavered a good deal about whether Tweeddale should come home. Hamilton wanted him to return, she wrote on 2 April, but she

87 Sir William Fraser, *The Scotts of Buccleuch*, 2 vols (Edinburgh, 1878), I, p. 435. 3 Feb. 1674, George Home to Tweeddale, NLS Ms. 7006, f. 91.

88 10 Jan. 1674, Kincardine to Lauderdale, BL Add. Mss 23136, ff. 68–69. For the commissioners' attitude see 21 Mar., Patrick Murray to Tweeddale, NLS Ms. 7006, ff. 99–100.

89 9, 17, 19 Feb., 1 June 1674, Lady Tweeddale to Tweeddale, NLS Ms. 14402, ff. 67, 71, 79, 167.

90 2 May 1674, Lady Tweeddale to Tweeddale, ibid., f. 140b. For Yester's interview see NLS Ms. 14407, f. 337.

did not, if Lauderdale left. Your enemies 'vaunt on all occasions their malice and revenge against you', she went on, but she professed not to be worried. When Lauderdale actually did leave, toward the end of April, she remarked that Tweeddale's friends wanted him to stay, lest it be said 'you dare not look that Sultan in the face'. But he would be snubbed if he waited on Lauderdale: 'If they [the duke and duchess] could not hear Yester spoke of where his daughter and grandchildren were without falling in passion, much less will they endure to see you.' Lauderdale, who used to be so fond of his grandchildren, now neglected them – and so, Lady Tweeddale added, did their mother. 'I may assure you they see that person [Lauderdale] so seldom that they can receive no prejudice by example if it come not by nature.'[91]

Lady Tweeddale's letters were full of Lauderdale's 'oppression, tyranny, and insolency': he was universally hated. He was responsible for the council's shabby treatment of Patrick Murray, the head of the group of customs and excise officials during the period when they were being directly collected, when he sought his arrears of salary and fees. Murray injudiciously told Dundonald that nothing like this had happened since Lauderdale's treatment of Yester over his executry. Dundonald repeated this to Lauderdale, who flew into a rage. So did Halton, who, said Murray, 'abused me pitifully with his tongue'. Lady Tweeddale thought that if the king knew of the treatment Murray had received, he would be displeased. But how could he know? Tweeddale might tell him, but would the king listen, in the face of Lauderdale's denials? 'That barbare', wrote Lady Tweeddale after Lauderdale left, reportedly said that Tweeddale would sweat for what his family and friends wrote to him: clearly their correspondence had been intercepted and read. She hoped their letters would not be construed as treasonable. 'I am astonished to think from whence all this hatred can come.'[92]

As Lauderdale was on his way to London Tweeddale received a long letter from Hamilton, who urged him, now, to remain and confront Lauderdale, to 'show you do not fear to face him'. If Tweeddale could not prevail, Hamilton was full of ideas of summoning other important folk to strengthen their case, especially Rothes, even though Rothes was showing

91 2, 7, 18, 25 Apr. 1674, Lady Tweeddale to Tweeddale, NLS Ms. 14402, ff. 109–10, 111–12, 119–20, 132–35.

92 29 Mar., 7, 19 Apr., 5 May 1674, Lady Tweeddale to Tweeddale, ibid., ff. 105–06, 109–10, 122–23, 144. 21 Mar., Murray to Tweeddale, NLS Ms. 7006, ff. 99–100.

no inclination to get involved. He himself planned a trip to Bath for his sciatica, and hoped for a summons to court. To that end he wrote to both York and Arlington, asking that they not judge him without a hearing.[93] Hamilton was being utterly unrealistic. When Lauderdale arrived at court he received what Hutton calls 'a hero's welcome'. The English privy council formally cleared him of the charges against him, and Charles gave him an English peerage.[94] And, on 18 May, the long partnership of the 'dearest brothers' was formally dissolved. Charles appointed a new privy council without Tweeddale; of Lauderdale's opponents only Hamilton remained on the council. Tweeddale's team of officials – Murray, Blackbarony and Hay of Linplum – lost their positions as receivers of the king's rents. Atholl and Argyll replaced Tweeddale on the new treasury commission; Argyll replaced him as an extraordinary lord of session. On the following day parliament was dissolved by proclamation. Before long Kincardine would replace Tweeddale on the English privy council; in January 1675 his and his son's militia commissions were voided.[95]

So when Tweeddale returned home to Yester House in July 1674 he was simply a private citizen. His last-minute pitch to the king, stressing his loyalty and service and stretching all the way back to the assertion that Charles I had made his father an earl because of his regard for the son, got nowhere, if, indeed, he was ever given the opportunity to make it. He scribbled what he intended to say to the king on the back of a letter of 2 June 1674 from Sir John Baird urging him to come home as, Baird said, Lady Tweeddale wished.[96] The latter was philosophical about what had happened but far from surprised. You will lose nothing by this, she wrote; rather, you will gain in esteem and affection. There was no point in importuning the king after the fact, she felt; in time he would see who did him the best service. This turned out to be a vain hope. In September William Hay advised Tweeddale not to involve himself in anything, since 'whatever might arrive by accident would be imputed to some deep design'.[97] Tweeddale followed his kinsman's advice. For the foreseeable future his political career was over.

93 19 Apr. 1674, Hamilton to Tweeddale, NLS Ms. 7006, ff. 113–16. 20 Apr., Hamilton to Arlington, NLS Ms. 7006, f. 122, and to York, NLS Ms. 7034, f. 53.
94 Hutton, *Charles II*, p. 322.
95 *RCPS* IV, pp. 186–92, 333. NAS SP 4/2/391–408. Lee, *Government and Politics*, p. 135.
96 NLS Ms. 7006, ff. 141–42.
97 30 May, 1, 7 June 1674, Lady Tweeddale to Tweeddale, NLS Ms. 14402, ff. 165, 167, 173–74. 3 Sept., Hay to Tweeddale, NLS Ms. 7006, f. 169.

In the aftermath of the political obliteration of Tweeddale and his allies the tendencies of the new regime became clear. Charles dissolved parliament and upheld the position of the judges respecting appeals to parliament from their decisions, as has been said, though he did ask the judges for suggestions as to how best to test the qualifications of future nominees.[98] He also restored Lauderdale's fee of £50 per diem as commissioner from 1 February until 30 April, while praising Lauderdale's self-sacrifice in offering to give it up (!) and issued an exoneration for all his actions as commissioner, even any that might be construed as treasonable. And he granted pensions to Lauderdale's allies Atholl and Argyll.[99] All this was to be expected. More telling, and more ominous for the future, was the new direction of religious policy. The king's decision in March 1674 to remit all fines save those imposed in connection with the 1666 rebellion and high treason had an unexpected consequence. Nonconformists regarded it, wrote James Kirkton, 'rather as an encouragement for the time coming than as a remission for what was past', and so there was a vigorous revival of conventicling.[100] By May it was flourishing, especially in the west, where, according to Gilbert Burnet, regular ministers were subject to violence and outed ministers occupied vacant churches. Lauderdale, he said, had done nothing about it while he was in Scotland, had, in fact, coddled dissent. By the end of May Burnet was writing that episcopal candidates for parishes dared not appear, the bishops were in despair, and there was even talk of renewing the Covenant.[101] Burnet and Leighton seem to have been behind a movement, first in the synod of Glasgow and then in that of Edinburgh, to petition for a meeting of a national synod to deal with the crisis in the church, a proposal vetoed by the bishop of Edinburgh.[102] Hamilton seized the opportunity to bring the petitions before the council on 6 May, together with a motion to inform Charles of the disorders in the kingdom. Lord Chancellor Rothes turned this aside, saying that they should first enforce the law; a public accounting of the divisions in the church would only encourage the conventiclers. The council then adjourned until June.[103] By the time it met again Hamilton had been stripped of his allies there, including Tweeddale; it would no longer be of use as a platform for the opposition.

98 NAS SP 4/2/422.

99 Ibid., pp. 414–15, 460–71.

100 Kirkton, *History*, pp. 201–02.

101 4, 25 May 1674, Burnet to Tweeddale, NLS Ms. 7121, ff. 10, 16–17.

102 J. Buckroyd, *Church and State in Scotland 1660–1681* (Edinburgh, 1980), pp. 108–09.

103 7 May 1674, William Sharp to Lauderdale, BL Add. Mss 23136, f. 136.

The prospect of a national synod appalled Archbishop Sharp. He called such a meeting divisive, destructive and ruinous to the authority of church and king. He thought Leighton was sending mixed signals about this proposal, but, he noted, among those ministers who supported it were those who had benefited from Tweeddale's patronage. Clergymen who supported it did so 'upon no other account but to shake off our yoke and break our bands asunder'. He begged Lauderdale to block it and raised the spectre of another 1638. Gilbert Burnet was much involved; Sharp recommended that he be sent to Inverness to preach to the Highlanders.[104] Lauderdale also found the proposal distasteful. He wrote a careful and not unfriendly letter to Leighton, explaining that a national synod had its uses, but not at the present time, since 'our Dissenters will have no manner of reverence' for it, and the orthodox clergy did not need it. He laid this out to Leighton because he was aware that the suggestion had come in the first instance from the Glasgow synod and because he was anxious that Leighton not carry out his repeated threat to resign. To Sharp he was much more blunt. The king would ignore all petitions to hold a national synod; the council must 'suppress those scandalous and seditious conventicles',[105] music to Sharp's ears. There would be no more thought of indulgence, nor could there be, given Lauderdale's dependence on Danby, the ally of the Anglican establishment. Archbishop Sheldon, after a number of years in the wilderness, was in favour once again, and Lauderdale on good terms with him. Sharp, who had never ceased to bewail concessions to dissent, was now a very important ally for Lauderdale, the more so because by the end of 1674 he had broken with Kincardine, the last member of the governing coalition who favoured the policy of accommodation.[106] And Lauderdale had also – famously because his *History* is famous – broken with Gilbert Burnet.[107]

Among the consequences of the renewal of the policy of religious repression was an increase in the size of the military establishment, starting in September 1674, and in the proportion of the crown's income spent on it.[108] The Scottish government in the mid-1670s came to resemble that of

---

104 See Sharp's letters of May and June 1674 to Lauderdale, NLS Ms. 2512, ff. 157, 159–60, *Laing Mss* I, pp. 396–97.

105 18 June 1674, Lauderdale to Leighton, BL Add. Mss 23136, f. 151. 13 June, Lauderdale to Sharp, Dowden, 'Letters', pp. 269–72.

106 Burnet, *History* II, pp. 118–19. See also Lee, *Government and Politics*, pp. 83, 85.

107 See Burnet's letter of 13 Oct. 1674 (misdated 1673) to Lauderdale, NAS GD 406/1/8909.

108 Lee, *Government and Politics*, pp. 136, 153–74.

continental monarchies rather than of England: an arbitrary regime dependent on military force. As before, the chief functions of that force were to suppress disturbances and collect taxes. Its misbehaviour and unpopularity provoked further trouble which in turn provoked more severe measures until, in 1679, another rebellion broke out. Ironically, the Scottish army, which in 1669 and 1674 had caused some fear in England that the king would order it to march south to suppress English liberties, now itself needed assistance to put this rebellion down.

Another ironic result of the change of religious outlook in Scotland was the restoration of Alexander Burnet to the archbishopric of Glasgow in September 1674, after Leighton was, at long last, allowed to resign the position he had never wanted and in which he had been a resounding failure. If Kirkton is to be believed, Burnet's restoration had its sordid side. Burnet's daughter, the widow of the heir to the Elphinstone estate, had substantial dower rights in the estate. The new heir wanted to marry Halton's daughter; Halton refused to consent unless the prospective bridegroom had property. So the deal was cut: Burnet's daughter surrendered her jointure, and her father resumed his archbishopric.[109] Kirkton's verdict on Halton has resonance: 'The man of all that ever I knew in power in Scotland who believed most perfectly his own pleasure to be righteousness.'[110] Burnet's years of enforced idleness had not changed his views. He remained the eager persecutor of dissent, and rose still higher: he spent the last five years of his life as archbishop of St Andrews after the murder of Sharp in 1679.[111] His rehabilitation put paid to all attempts to undo the fateful effects of Middleton's disastrous religious policy – it should properly be called Middleton's, though it had the approval of Charles and Clarendon. That policy was the not-so-hidden reef upon which every Scottish regime, including that of the cousins, was to shatter; it led to the awful military tyranny of the Killing Times.

III

The return of Long Face to his archbishopric is a convenient point at which to end this account of Scottish politics in the days of the cousins. Lauderdale remained in the saddle and prospered exceedingly, along with his wife and

109 Kirkton, *History*, p. 176.
110 Ibid., p. 183.
111 For religious policy after 1674 see Buckroyd, *Church and State*, pp. 115–36.

brother,[112] until, in 1680 a combination of advancing age, failing health, failing policies, some of which he adopted with reluctance, and an ever-narrowing circle of support in Scotland owing to his behaviour and/or that of his duchess forced him out of the office he had held for twenty years. He died two years later. Tweeddale remained out of office. He occasionally tried to hold out an olive branch to Lauderdale. There were times when the latter seemingly thawed, especially during his last visit to Scotland in 1677, when he saw his grandchildren and made a fuss over them. But in the end it all came to nothing; there never was a reconciliation. Halton, not Mary's second son, became the third earl – not duke – of Lauderdale, with a heavily encumbered estate because the duchess got most of the property. The lawsuits began almost at once. The Tweeddales took the duchess and the new earl to court on various charges, including the duchess's appropriation of the jewels that had belonged to Mary's mother. Their successes were minimal; some of the lawsuits dragged on into the next century. Tweeddale had no success at all in dealing with his other financial problem, his debt to the Buccleuch estate. The king steadily refused his pleas for help, and in the end he had to pay up. The settlement of 1667 stipulated that he owed £15,600; in 1679 he was forced to agree to pay £62,400; by 1690, when he made his last payment, he had paid over £71,000. He returned to public office in the 1690s, as lord chancellor, for two years. King William made him a marquess and renewed his lease of the lordship and regality of Dunfermline to recompense him for his payments to Duchess Anna, who mean-spiritedly complained about it.[113] He died in 1697.

The regime of the cousins was one of hopeful beginnings and missed opportunities, doubly regrettable because the Cabal years, from 1667 to 1673, were the only years of the Restoration era in which the men who ran the Scottish government had a comparatively free hand. These years did not resemble those of Clarendon and Danby, when the exigencies of English politics either determined or limited what the Scottish government could do. The Cabal was less a ministry than a collection of individuals. If one of the five was more important than the others, it was Arlington, and

---

112 For a summary of Lauderdale's profits from his various offices see R.W. Lennox, *Lauderdale and Scotland: A Study in Scottish Politics and Administration 1660–1682* (PhD diss., Columbia University, 1977), pp. 411–14.

113 NAS GD 224/924/41–44. For these matters see Lee, Intro. to Tweeddale, 'Wrangs', pp. 266–80, and 'The Troubles of a Family Man' in M. Lee, Jr, *The 'Inevitable' Union* (East Linton, 2003), pp. 246–67.

Arlington rarely showed any interest in Scotland. The initiatives of the cousins' first years were promising: better and more honest administration, improved finances, control of military expenditures, better order in the Highlands, a new flexibility in religious policy, above all the attempt to solve Scotland's serious economic problems by changing the relationship with England. Tweeddale was the driving force behind most of this, especially the union negotiations, which he desperately wanted to succeed. Their failure was the turning-point of the cousins' regime. The negotiations might have succeeded, as they did a generation later, had there been a determination in England to have them succeed. What drove them in Queen Anne's time were the succession question and its ramifications and the war with France; no such issues gripped Whitehall in 1670. Counterfactual history is always problematical, but if Charles II had been as determined as the Godolphin ministry, the union might well have taken place. None of his inner circle opposed the plan, and some, like Clifford and the lord keeper, Sir Orlando Bridgeman, were enthusiastic. But the king's political capital was only now beginning to recover after the disasters of the Dutch war. He was unwilling to spend it on what would certainly be a difficult effort to push union through a reluctant House of Commons, especially since the French alliance had opened up a much more attractive way of dealing successfully with that recalcitrant body. And so the union project collapsed.

So, too, in the aftermath, did the cousins' regime. Lauderdale cared nothing for the principle of union. He supported it wholeheartedly as long as the king did; when Charles's interest cooled, so did his. Tweeddale's enthusiasm never cooled. We do not know what sorts of conversations the 'dearest brothers' had as the negotiations foundered and then ended in the last months of 1670, but the result was plain enough. Tweeddale, in the statement he prepared for the king in January 1674, dated the souring of his relationship with Lauderdale from January 1671, followed, as it shortly was, by the appointment of Halton as treasurer-depute. There were, of course, other factors militating against the cousins' success. There was the intractable religious issue. The cousins' policies vacillated between attempts to placate moderate nonconformists and sporadic repression; neither worked for long. There was disagreement over the farming of the customs. There was the perennial shortage of money; the use of troops to collect arrears of taxation as well as to deal with religious unrest caused frictions that Tweeddale hoped to minimise but could not avoid. Moray's withdrawal from active political participation after his return to England in 1668 was unhelpful.

And then there was the bitter personal quarrel that erupted in 1672 over Mary Yester's inheritance. These might well have doomed the regime even if the union had succeeded. But the failure of the union was the beginning of the end. After the final rupture in 1673 Lauderdale's policy boiled down to keeping the lid on so that the king would not be bothered.

Lauderdale the agent and promoter of despotism has received a lot of bad press, both at the time (Gilbert Burnet, e.g.) and later. The secretary could be overbearing and arbitrary, and paranoid about any threat to his monopoly of power. His preoccupation with the welfare of his family coloured his policies to a greater extent than is commonly appreciated. His promotion of his brother crippled the possibility of fiscal reform. His support of his nephew Argyll's grasping and expansive tactics in the Highlands was very disruptive; the policies of the duke of York and his officials in the early 1680s, after Argyll was forfeited and had fled, were effective in curbing disorders there.[114] And of course Lauderdale's enthusiasm for his 'dearest brother' was overwhelmed by his far greater enthusiasm for Lady Dysart, with, for Scotland, most unfortunate consequences. But not all of Lauderdale's problems were of his own making. His power ended because, like Sharp and Rothes before him, he provoked religious revolt. But it is worth noting that the Presbyterian Kirkton, whom Lauderdale's government was pursuing as an outlaw in the mid-1670s, wrote of him, 'He was neither judged a cruel persecutor nor an avaricious executor (excepting his brother and wife's solicitations) all the times of his government.'[115]

On the other hand Tweeddale, the anti-Lauderdale, the most prominent political victim of the secretary's wrath, has perhaps been more highly praised than his career has warranted. Tweeddale was honest. He was also far-sighted, as his opposition to tax-farming and support of union show: whatever the nature of the 'bargain' of 1707, it eventually solved the commercial and economic problems that so concerned Tweeddale during his years of power. But he was prickly and difficult to work with, he often did not pay enough attention to the damaging religious issue, and he never did come to grips with the cardinal reality of his political position: that he was completely dependent on Lauderdale for his position in the government.

There is a sad irony in the relationship of the 'dearest brothers'. The marriage that bound them together, and a happy marriage it was, served in the end to drive them apart, thanks to Lauderdale's own second marriage,

114 Harris, *Restoration*, p. 358.
115 Kirkton, *History*, p. 211.

to a woman who has received an even worse press than he. Tweeddale's own very happy marriage, to the sister of the wealthiest noble in Scotland, in the end brought him to the verge of financial ruin, as his implacable niece extracted the last penny of the debt he owed the Buccleuch estate. As this extended foray into the politics of Restoration Scotland has demonstrated, aristocrats dominated the political scene. This had always been true, of course, but it was even more true during the reign of an absolute king whose attitude to his ancient kingdom was one of distaste and indifference. And aristocratic political behaviour was always conditioned, and sometimes dominated, by family considerations. It is not possible to understand the course of Scottish politics in the late 1660s and early 1670s without a knowledge of the implications of the Buccleuch marriage contract and the fate of Lady Lauderdale's jewellery.

Index of People

Index of Topics and Places